THE HOOD BATTALION

THE HOOD BATTALION

Royal Naval Division:
Antwerp, Gallipoli, France 1914-1918
by
LEONARD SELLERS

If I should die, think only this of me:
That there's some corner of a foreign field
That is forever England.

Rupert Brooke
Sub-Lieutenant, Royal Volunteer Reserve
of the Royal Naval Division's Hood Battalion

LEO COOPER
LONDON

First published in Great Britain in 1995 by
LEO COOPER
an imprint of
Pen & Sword Books Ltd, 47 Church Street, Barnsley, South Yorkshire S70 2AS

Copyright © Leonard Sellers, 1995

A CIP catalogue record for this book
is available from the British Library

ISBN 0 85053 386 9

Typeset by Chippendale Type Ltd, Pool in Wharfedale, West Yorkshire
Printed by Redwood Books Ltd., Trowbridge, Wilts.

This book is dedicated to my great-uncle, Albert John Walls,
and Joseph Murray of the Hood.

Contents

Part Three: The Hood on the Western Front

Appendix

Acknowledgements

I have had nothing but help and encouragement in researching and writing this account of the Hood Battalion. It started as a labour of love, and grew rapidly into an obsession as I became engrossed in my subject.

The sheer volume of support makes it impossible to write an outline of the help each person gave me, so I have simply listed their names on page 325. I can only add that I very much appreciate all the assistance I received, in whatever shape or form. Each person in the list knows their individual role, be it providing research facilities, papers, photographs, advice, permissions, critical reviews, or any other help.

I must particularly thank my wife, Elaine, and our two sons, Mark and Neil. All three suffered my research and the occasions on which I confined myself to the study with no word of complaint. Without their support I could not have completed the book.

It has not always been possible to trace the copyright holders of all the material I have quoted, and I would be pleased to hear from any such persons to whom this applies.

Leonard Sellers
Honeysuckle House

Maps

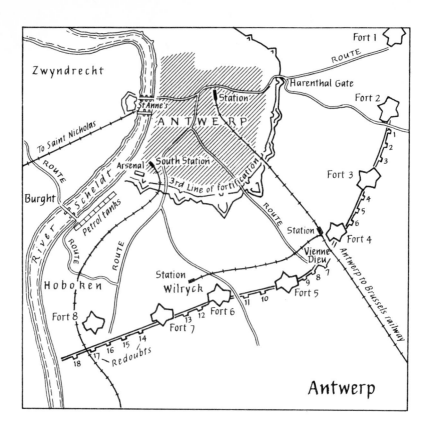

Antwerp

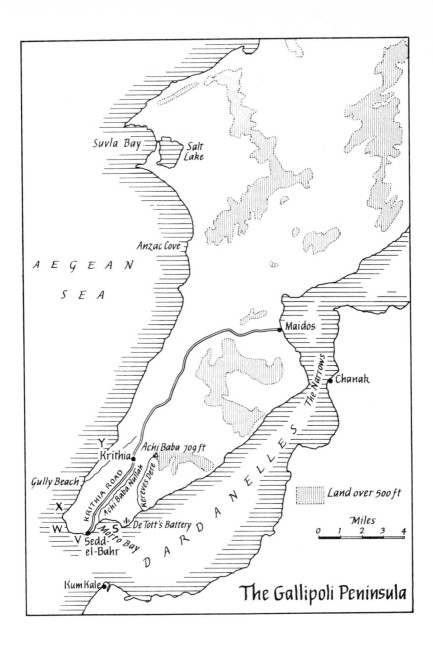

Suvla Bay

Salt Lake

Anzac Cove

A E G E A N

S E A

Maidos

The Narrows

Chanak

Y

Krithia

Achi Baba 709 ft

KRITHIA ROAD

Achi Baba Nullah

Kereves Dere

Gully Beach

X

W

D A R D A N E L L E S

Land over 500 ft

Miles

0 1 2 3 4

S

De Tott's Battery

Morto Bay

V Sedd-
el-Bahr

D

Kum Kale

The Gallipoli Peninsula

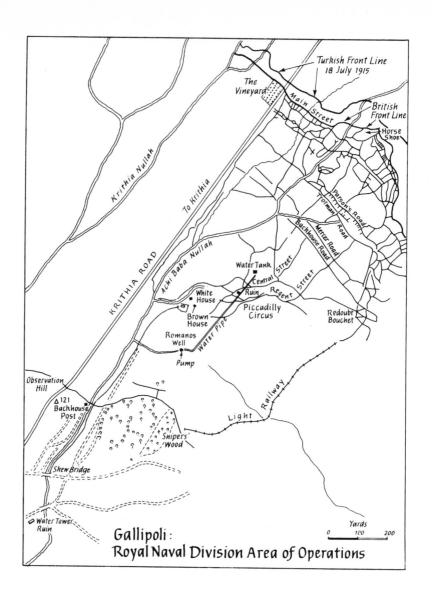

Gallipoli:
Royal Naval Division Area of Operations

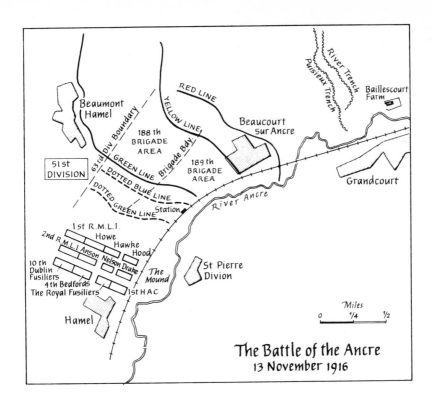

The Battle of the Ancre
13 November 1916

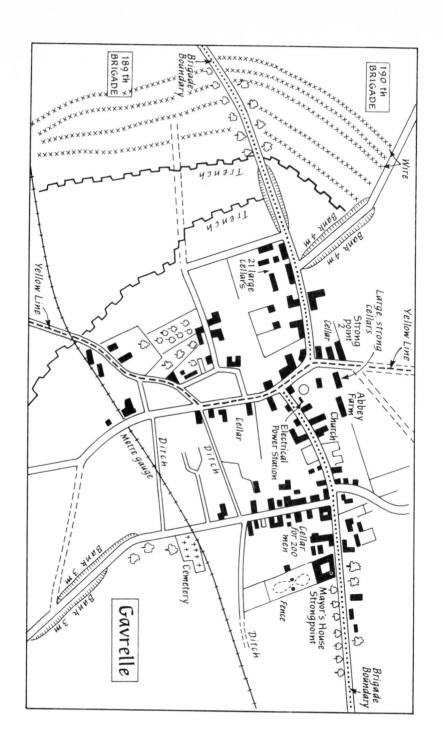

190th
BRIGADE

189th
BRIGADE

Brigade
Boundary

Wire

Trench

Trench

Bank 4m

Bank 4m

Yellow Line

Yellow Line

21 large
cellars

Large strong
cellars

Strong
Point
2

Cellar

Abbey
Farm

Church

Electrical
Power Station

Metre gauge

Ditch

Ditch

Cellar

Ditch

Bank 3m

Bank 3m

Cemetery

Cellar
for 200
men

Fence

Mayor's House
Strongpoint

Brigade
Boundary

Ditch

Gavrelle

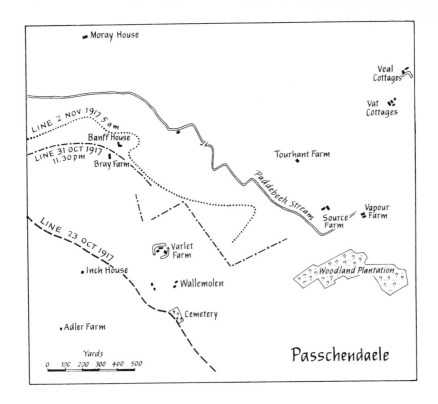

Moray House

Veal Cottages

Vat Cottages

LINE 2 NOV 1917 5 a m

Banff House

LINE 31 OCT 1917 11.30 pm

Bray Farm

Tourhant Farm

Paddebeek Stream

Source Farm

Vapour Farm

LINE 23 OCT 1917

Varlet Farm

Inch House

Wallemolen

Woodland Plantation

Cemetery

Adler Farm

Yards

0 100 200 300 400 500

Passchendaele

Introduction

It all started with a small gold locket on a simple base metal chain. This slightly dented piece of jewellery was given to my wife, Elaine, as a hand-me-down from my great-grandmother Caroline Walls. After her son's death Caroline had the locket engraved:

In Loving Memory of
Dear Bert
Killed in action at the
Dardanelles July 18th 1915

Inside was a photograph of my great-uncle, Albert John Walls, with one of my great-grandmother Caroline opposite. I wondered how he had met his fate in that distant land during the First World War, and my resulting researches led me on to what eventually became this history of the Hood Battalion of the Royal Naval Division throughout that war.

I found a story of colour and adventure, of frustrating failure and lost opportunities, terrible hardships, suffering and death, but balanced by determination and heroism, and later success in battle, orchestrated by great names of the age, including Churchill, Kitchener and Asquith.

My great-uncle Albert Walls was the eldest son of John Daniel Walls and Caroline Walls, née Duerr, of Commercial Road, Peckham London. He was born on 25 June, 1878, and should perhaps be considered fortunate to survive childhood: five of his brothers and sisters died before reaching the age of five.[1] Albert was initially a printer, in the general line of his father's work, but on 28 October, 1903, he joined the Royal Navy. He then saw service at Chatham naval base, on the armoured cruisers *Acheron*, *Leviathan* and *Bacchante*, and on the battleships *Illustrious* and *Agamemnon*, the last of which was, coincidentally, to play a leading role at Gallipoli.

Albert was discharged on 6 November, 1908, and transferred to the Royal Fleet Reserve on the following day with the rank of stoker first class and a character reference which described him as 'Very Good Throughout'. Thereafter he spent a week each year training on board navy vessels, until he was finally mobilized for war service on 2 August, 1914. He reported to HMS *Pembroke* at Chatham, and was transferred to HMS *Victory* at Crystal Palace for duty with the Royal Naval Division's Hood Battalion on 17 September.[2]

Formed at the beginning of the First World War, the division was made up of officers and men of the Royal Naval Volunteer Reserve, stokers of the Royal Fleet Reserve and seamen of the Royal Naval Reserve. The unit was Churchill's brainchild, earning from the Prime Minister, Asquith, the sobriquet of 'Winston's Little Army'.[3]

It was a division with a difference, not as other units, but soldier-sailors, which resulted in interesting combinations of officers and men. The men were mainly former naval reservists and new army recruits, a good proportion of whom came from the six recruiting areas of Bristol, Sussex, Clyde, Liverpool, Tyneside and London. Many Hood officers would in other circumstances have been future leaders of the nation, like Arthur 'Oc' Asquith, the Prime Minister's son, or William Denis Browne, one of England's best young musicians and critics, who was educated at Rugby and Cambridge and later studied under Busoni in Berlin.[4]

Another talented officer was Frederick Septimus 'Cleg' Kelly, an Australian composer and pianist educated at Eton and Balliol, who later studied music in Frankfurt and subsequently decided to settle in London. He combined music with outstanding athletic attainments: he stroked the Oxford eight and rowed in the Olympic Games; one of the greatest scullers of his age, he was three times the winner of the Diamond Sculls.[5] Bernard Freyberg already had a distinguished record in the armed forces of his native New Zealand; Patrick Shaw-Stewart had been a brilliant scholar at Eton and Balliol; Charles Lister, also of Balliol, was a diplomat and son of Lord Ribblesdale. Even Americans came to fight with the division, including the charming and good-looking young Johnny Bigelow Dodge.

But perhaps the best known of all was Sub-Lieutenant Rupert Brooke, the poet and symbol of the age, and, as it turned out, of the Gallipoli campaign. Destined to die of blood poisoning just before the first landings, his going seemed to be an omen of the outcome: so near and yet so far. His excitement and enthusiasm for the cause led only to his death, at the age of 27.

As the story unfolds we see the war gradually change from what were called the 'Tipperary days', when hopes were high, hearts were young, expectations soared, romantic ideals held sway, and blood flowed through youthful veins in the certain knowledge of early and righteous victory. Then came the reality of loss, numbness, mud, and just living from day to day. We see a generation swept away, and we see the Hood Battalion progress from Antwerp to the shores of the Gallipoli peninsula in the Dardanelles.

Steeped in history and romance, the setting for the sagas of Troy and Helen, the Dardanelles were known in ancient times as the Hellespont, leading to the Sea of Marmara and the prize of Constantinople. This is where Europe rubs shoulders with Asia, and centuries of bloody history and enmity had taught the Caucasian side to beware of the cruel demons across the water in Turkey. When the Turks allied themselves with Germany, Gallipoli offered a chance to change the course of the war, reduce its length, and in so doing save countless lives.

Many nations were present at Gallipoli: the British, the French with their Senegalese colonists, Australians, New Zealanders, Indians and Gurkhas all lined up on the Allied side, Turks and Germans on the other. The Allies very nearly succeeded, but delay, ineptitude, bad planning and the strangulation of supplies of men and munitions took their toll. Our story reveals a small fragment of this notorious campaign.

And then on to France and the Western Front, where the division poured its blood liberally into the fields of Ancre, Gavrelle and Passchendaele; but there was still a niggardly doubt in the minds of the army, who felt ill at ease with this manifestation of compromise and expedience. They may have been one of the best divisions available, but army men still had the feeling that these sons of Drake, Nelson and Hood would be better off on the ocean waves.

After the end of the First World War the experiment of having a naval division was not tried again. The experience and memory of the compromise required was too painful for all involved; so the ghosts of the Hood Battalion were left to roam the plain at Helles, looking forever to the unattainable heights of Achi Baba, or to wander among the blood-coloured poppies strewing the fields of France.

In writing this history I have tried to convey to the reader a sense of 'being there' by using first-hand accounts. It is not my story, but theirs. They experienced the fear and exhilaration of battle, the smell of death, the sound of oars in rowlocks, the expectation of voyage, and the glue of mud at the journey's end. None of us can go back; we can only look back and wonder at the suffering of those who went through this cataclysm and the changes they brought about.

Part One

THE EARLY DAYS

CHAPTER ONE

Formation and Training

Before the beginning of the First World War, plans for a naval land force were drawn up on the recommendation of the Committee for Imperial Defence: if war broke out a force of Royal Marines would be formed under the control of the Admiralty, to be known as the Advanced Base Force. When war was declared this project was put into operation, and a brigade of marines was established. However, there were large numbers of naval reservists available over and above those required for manning the fleet, so on 16 August, 1914, the Admiralty decided to add two further brigades to the existing marines.[1]

At that time the British army could only muster six divisions of infantry troops and two cavalry divisions. To meet this shortfall, troops were withdrawn from overseas postings and the Dominions to help where they could. New volunteer units were also formed and trained, such as the local 'Pals' battalions. But a division of naval reservists surplus to the fleet would undoubtedly be a great help; indeed, Lord Kitchener, in a speech to the House of Lords on Thursday 17 September, 1914, showed his keenness for the enterprise:

> Nor must I omit to refer to the assistance which we shall receive from the division of the gallant Royal Marines and Bluejackets now being organized by my Right Honourable Friend the First Lord of the Admiralty. Their presence in the field will be very welcome, for their fighting qualities are well known.[2]

The administration of the Naval Division was handled by an Admiralty standing committee presided over by Winston Churchill, the First Lord. They worked quickly to provide a base to house the first intake of men, to feed them, and to select their officers. In addition to the marine brigade, already partly formed, two naval brigades consisting of four battalions each of 880 men were to be organized in 16 double companies

7

of 220 men. This number was later changed, and each battalion was designed to be made up as follows:

Petty Officers (Royal Navy)	28
Petty Officers (Royal Fleet Reserve)	48
Petty Officers, Leading Seamen and Seamen (Royal Naval Volunteer Reserve)	424
Stokers (Royal Fleet Reserve)	250
Seamen under 30 years old (Royal Naval Reserve)	187
Total	937

A camping ground was found near Deal in Kent, and the War Office was asked to supply 700 tents to supplement the 170 marine tents already to hand. RNVR men were instructed to bring their own rifles, while arrangements were made to issue 4,000 rifles for the RNR and RFR. These were of the old Lee Enfield type, but orders were placed for the newer short type to be delivered at the earliest possible moment. Vickers received an order for 40 Maxim machine guns, to be ready in 10 days; four would be issued to each battalion, with four kept in reserve. Each company was to have a machine-gun section, and each of the three brigades was to form a field ambulance column. Orders were also placed for 4,000 military uniforms for the marines and 8,000 naval kits for the reservists, all to be in khaki.

At this early stage a decision was made which, as Douglas Jerrold states in his history of the Royal Naval Division, was a stroke of genius and had an incalculable influence in keeping alive some elements of naval tradition. The rudimentary first battalions were to be known by the names of famous admirals and naval bases:

1st Royal Naval Brigade – Commodore Wilfred Henderson, RN
   1st Battalion – Drake
   2nd Battalion – Hawke
   3rd Battalion – Benbow
   4th Battalion – Collingwood

2nd Royal Naval Brigade – Commodore Oliver Backhouse, RN
   5th Battalion – Nelson
   6th Battalion – Howe
   7th Battalion – Hood
   8th Battalion – Anson

3rd Royal Naval Brigade (Marines) – Brigadier-General Giles Trotman
   9th Battalion – Portsmouth
   10th Battalion – Plymouth
   11th Battalion – Chatham
   12th Battalion – Deal

Providing bands for the new brigades was a priority, although the quality was not important and it was thought likely that sufficient could be assembled from among pupils under instruction at the Naval School of Music.[3] In the event the 2nd Royal Naval Brigade acquired three bands: the headquarters Clyde Band of 24 men, the Anson Band of 28 men, and the Hood Battalion band, known as the Dundee Band, of 22 players.[4]

And so, with orders flying in all directions, the division was born in late August, 1914, and men and officers began to arrive. Many of the naval reservists were not happy with the prospect of becoming soldier-sailors and not going to sea, as John Bentham, an ordinary seaman later of the Hood, explains:

The commodore spoke to the men and informed us that all our hopes of going to sea were dead, as it had been found by the powers that be that the reserves of regular ratings were sufficient for the needs of the fleet and it had been decided to form a naval brigade such as was found in the Boer War. We were to go to Deal and company commanders were to attend a conference to work out details. This was a real blow and everyone was very depressed. We even held a solemn mock funeral in which our officers took part and a copy of the *Admiralty Seamanship Manual* was lowered into the Thames.

Gun drill was abandoned; everyone concentrated on rifle drill and we were served out with the old leather equipment as was used in the Boer War. Needless to say, it was in a shocking state, having been stored in the cellars of the barracks since the beginning of the century. It was hard as iron, mildewed and took hours of cleaning even to make it presentable. However, it is said that water will wear stone, and constant oiling, polishing, etc., did work wonders, but still we could not use the bandoliers to keep any ammunition . . .

The officers at Walmer had a great many problems whilst giving drill instructions. None of the officers had the slightest idea of army drill and it was quite a common sight to see company commanders reading out commands from the drill manual. It was the usual practice to march off on to the downs by companies and drill separately; but once clear of the camp and well out of sight, the usual order was fall out and carry on smoking, simply because the officers had not the faintest idea of what to do. The marine instructors used to despair of ever knocking us into shape and often said 'God help us if ever we are sent to the front', and that they would not be seen dead with us.[5]

The Hood Battalion was to be commanded by Lieutenant-Colonel John Arnold Cuthbert Quilter, a six-foot-tall former Guards officer, who had the unenviable task of turning this diverse collection of men into an efficient infantry battalion. His second-in-command for a period was Major the Viscount Bury of the Scots Guards; many of the commanding officers had served in the Guards.

Colonel Quilter was born in 1875 and educated at Eton and Trinity Hall, Cambridge. His military career began in the Leicestershire Militia, and he gained his commission in 1897 as a second lieutenant with the 2nd Battalion of the Grenadier Guards. He served with distinction throughout the South African campaign, sustaining a slight wound and being mentioned in despatches. At Biddulphsberg on 29 May, 1900, Quilter and a number of men showed great courage in entering an area of burning veldt grass of several years' growth and rescuing wounded comrades while under Boer fire. In 1914 he was appointed lieutenant-colonel commanding the St Helen's Battalion, Princess of Wales (South Lancashire) Regiment,[6] and later transferred to command the Hood. His background showed his undoubted qualities, and he soon gained a reputation for fine platoon and company training. He proved a good officer and was well liked.

Among the new officers was Bernard Cyril Freyberg, who was to become a Royal Naval Division legend. A New Zealander who had swum for his country at international level, Freyberg trained as a dentist. In 1911 he joined the 6 Haurali Regiment, a newly-formed territorial unit, and was gazetted as a second lieutenant; he later signed up as a special constable during a period of local strife involving strikers. Being a man of action, however, in March, 1914, he left New Zealand on board a Royal Mail steamer, ending up serving in the Mexican Civil War; then, hearing news of the outbreak of the First World War, he made his way to England.

Landing in London on Monday, 25 August, 1914, with the intention of finding a position in the armed forces, Freyberg was strolling across Horse Guards Parade one day when he encountered the First Lord of the Admiralty. Determinedly, Freyberg approached Churchill (in those far-off days without the benefit of bodyguards), and questioned him as to the advantages of applying for service with the RND. Churchill was initially reluctant to listen, but eventually encouraged the move. Acting on this advice, Freyberg contacted the New Zealand liaison officer to apply for a commission; he was in the right place at the right time, as many suitable candidates were only in their late teens or early twenties, whereas Freyberg was 25 and had held a territorial commission. He was made a temporary lieutenant (RNVR) in the Hood Battalion; shortly afterwards he was promoted and took over the command of A Company.[7]

On 2 September the Marine Brigade moved to Friedown camp, while the 2nd Brigade went to Lord Northbourne's park at Betteshanger in Kent. The Rev Henry Clapham Foster, a temporary chaplain with 2nd Brigade, described the park enthusiastically:

> Betteshanger and the surrounding country was admirably adapted for training purposes, and during the latter days of August, and throughout the month of September, numerous sham fights and night attacks were arranged. The men acquitted themselves exceedingly well both in the field and at the rifle ranges (with a large brick wall as their backdrop), which were now in full working order . . .
>
> Time passed quickly in camp, and the social side was by no means neglected. Two enormous YMCA marquees proved to be a godsend to the men, for here they could read, write letters, or hold an impromptu concert if they felt so inclined . . . The Rector of Betteshanger, the late Canon Bliss, and his two nieces did all that lay in their power to help both officers and men during their sojourn in their midst. The Rectory bathroom was at the disposal of all officers who were tempted to indulge in the luxury of a hot bath, and in their own grounds the Misses Lindsay worked most zealously night and day at a cosy canteen for the men, under the auspices of the Missions to Seamen.
>
> Lord Northbourne and his friends in the vicinity of the camp always took a kindly interest in the men's welfare, and he was frequently a spectator at the numerous boxing and football contests which were held in the camp. I remember very well a speech that he made at the conclusion of a vigorous boxing match between two rival battalions. He concluded by saying that the men had proved themselves excellent fighters with the gloves, and he had no doubt that when by and by they were called on to take part in a sterner fight they would acquit themselves equally as well . . .
>
> Many men availed themselves of the opportunity by coming at 5.30am to the picturesque and beautiful little church at Betteshanger . . . Parade service was a wonderful sight in those glorious grounds; the place selected was a gradually-sloping piece of ground close to the vicarage, and here, Sunday by Sunday, officers and men made their corporate act of prayer and praise. Lord Northbourne and his friends were present, as a rule, and some villagers would group themselves together just outside the railings close by.[8]

Unfortunately the needs of the fleet soon intervened, and many of the better-trained men were withdrawn. They were replaced by new RNVR recruits drawn from six areas: London, Bristol, Merseyside, Sussex, Tyneside and the Clyde. Winston Churchill was meanwhile making strenuous efforts to provide the division with its own artillery, including writing a letter to Kitchener at the War Office on 13 September, 1914:

> In these circumstances, is it not worth your while considering a bolder plan, viz. take the complete artillery of one of the least advanced territorial divisions; send it to India and bring home the regular artillery of a division? You could then count on the whole division being complete for service on 1 January. It is an awful pity to leave these splendid battalions keeping order among natives, when trained artillery is our bitterest need.
>
> I think myself that every regular battery in India, except mountain, ought to come home and be replaced by territorials.

On 19 September Kitchener replied that he had no artillery officers or batteries to spare, in view of the needs of the new army in training, and Churchill finally admitted defeat on 20 September:

> I think I had better give up the attempt to form the artillery of the Royal Naval Division. The task is too difficult and my resources too small.

However, Churchill still battled with Lord Kitchener on other fronts on behalf of his fledgling infantry, and Kitchener was forced to concede defeat on some points:

> As I have stated in the enclosed copy of the Admiralty letter, I think that it would be better for you to continue the present arrangements and obtain stores from the trade. It would not, in my opinion, be expedient if Admiralty orders took precedence over orders for the armies now being raised, although no-one can more thoroughly appreciate than myself the value of the Royal Naval Division.
>
> With regard to your proposal that a general officer should inspect the division, I shall be delighted to send a general officer down some time in December; I doubt whether an inspecting officer could at present moment form an opinion as to the fitness that the division is likely to reach for active service after 1 January.[9]

CHAPTER TWO

Antwerp

In September, 1914, the strategic Belgian fortress at Antwerp became at risk: Germany was advancing and bringing up its heavy howitzers for the attack. The Channel ports were threatened, and it was vitally important that these doors to Europe should remain open and secure.

Asquith, the Prime Minister, was very concerned; the Belgian government had concluded that they must leave Antwerp and withdraw in the direction of Ghent, but the British army was stretched by its shortage of infantry and unable to help. There was, however, the Royal Naval Division. Untrained, untested and undervalued they may be, but Winston's Little Army could come to the rescue.

On 3 October a meeting was convened between Lord Kitchener, Winston Churchill, Sir Edward Grey, Prince Louis of Battenburg (the First Sea Lord) and Sir William Tyrrell. They decided that Belgium should be urged to reconsider withdrawal, and the RND sent to stiffen their resolve and defend Antwerp.[1] The division would have no artillery support, so the campaign had little chance of success, but any delay in the German advance could protect the Channel ports and it was a case of using what one had. The recently-formed and infant force was to be blooded almost before it was born.

The RND 3rd (Marine) Brigade was already in France, guarding Dunkirk on Churchill's orders. General Aston, the overall commander of the Royal Naval Division, had left England on 19 September with a mixed force of 2,600 marines, the Queen's Own Oxfordshire Hussars, Commander Samson's aeroplanes, a number of armoured cars and 20 Royal Engineers. Their mission was to concentrate the enemy by giving the impression of being a considerably greater force, while using the armoured cars to cut railway lines.[2]

With the crisis in Antwerp, the Marine Brigade was moved to Belgium, with General Archibald Paris replacing Aston in command when Aston became ill. They arrived on 3 October and next morning took up position, in company with the 7th Belgium Regiment, on the left or western half of a semi-circular entrenched position facing the town of Lierre, with its wings resting on the right bank of the River Nethe above and below the town. The outer forts on this front had already fallen and trench bombardment was in progress, which increased in violence that night.

Early in the morning of 5 October the enemy crossed the river, which was not under fire from the trenches, and by midday the 7th Belgium Regiment was forced to retire. This exposed General Paris's right flank, but Colonel Tierchon of the 2nd Chasseurs made a gallant counter-attack, assisted by British aeroplanes, and restored the position by late afternoon. During the night of 5/6 October the Belgians tried to drive the Germans back across the river, but the attempt failed and resulted in the evacuation of practically all the Belgian trenches.

The few troops remaining tried to counter-attack, but were unable to make any impression as the bombardment was too violent. The exhausted Belgians holding the line consisted now of only 125 men of the 3rd Battalion Fortress Infantry, trying desperately to retain positions in trenches normally manned by 500 troops. Only 260 remained of the original 1,400 2nd Chasseurs, and just 280 Carabiniers. Three Belgian battalions had received no food or rest for 48 hours and it was evident that not much reliance could be placed on these troops. As the bombardment increased, the position of the British Marine Brigade was becoming untenable.[3]

A second line of defence had been hastily prepared, in the form of the RND 1st and 2nd Brigades, plus the army's 7th Division. The Rev Foster described the preparations:

The news that we were to leave immediately for France spread very quickly round the camp, and among the men there was a scene of boundless enthusiasm; loud cheers were raised as they hastily dressed and got their kits together. There was no time to lose. Breakfast was at 7am and at eight we were told the transport would be ready to convey our baggage to Dover.

The 2nd Royal Naval Brigade started on the march to the pier at about 9 a.m., amid scenes of great enthusiasm, two brass bands and a fife and drum band accompanying them . . . . The men selected some curious words for their own special 'marching songs', and these are, as a rule, set to familiar melodies. It would have astonished, not to say shocked, the Salvation Army had they heard the following words sung to a hymn tune when passing a public house:
    There's a man selling beer over there;
    There's a man selling beer over there:

Over there, over there, over there, over there!

There's a man selling beer over there.

Another favourite ditty with men on the march is a song with a somewhat unsavoury refrain:

Wash me in the water

Where you wash your dirty daughter,

And I shall be whiter than the whitewash on the wall.

Singing such ditties as these, we marched from Betteshanger to Dover. We were accorded a magnificent reception in the streets by crowds of people who cheered lustily and waved flags and handkerchiefs as we made our way to the pier . . . . At about 5pm our men commenced the somewhat dreary task of getting the baggage on board. We took with us, besides field kit, our base kit, and first-line-of-transport kit. At about 9.30 we were ready to sail, so well had the men worked . . . .

In a short time we were under way and slowly sailing out of Dover harbour. It was a strange, not to say uncanny, sensation to be leaving one's native land on active service for the first time . . . . Our escort, consisting of two destroyers, kept close to us during the whole of the night. The voyage, however, proved to be uneventful, and at about 4am on Monday, 5 October we anchored off Dunkirk.

For eight weary hours we lay off Dunkirk, awaiting orders, in a choppy sea. At last a French destroyer came alongside and a somewhat portly French naval officer shouted through a megaphone that we were to proceed into harbour and moor at the quay. It was just about noon when we entered.

Those were stirring days – the Tipperary days we might call them – and the war was but two months old. The cheers from troops and civilians on shore, re-echoed by a thousand throats on our transport, stirred the emotions, and will live in the memories of those who heard them to the end of life. But the most moving incident of all was when our brass band came up on deck and played the *Marseillaise*; nothing delighted the French more than this little compliment, and they cheered again and again as the ship moored at the quay.[4]

At Dover the 2nd Brigade had been given five days' rations and two million rounds of ammunition, all transported down from London. In Dunkirk Commodore Backhouse, the commanding officer, requisitioned more stores from a Royal Navy depot, collected maps and equipment from various departments, and met the British consul. He also visited General Sir Henry Rawlinson, who was to command the completed Antwerp relief force once the 7th Division arrived;

Rawlinson warned Backhouse it was on the cards that their trains would not get through to Antwerp.

The brigade began to leave at 10pm on 5 October, on what proved to be a slow but safe journey. At daylight on Tuesday, 6 October the trains were given a warm welcome as they passed through villages surrounding Antwerp, and the main station in the city was reached at 7.30am. On arrival they were marched by road to the suburb of Kiel and instructed to find billets. The marching men were greeted by great cheering; Belgian girls pinned little silk flags on their tunics and large jugs of light beer were brought out, from which the men filled anything that would hold liquid.[5]

However, shrapnel could be clearly seen bursting near the city and two captive balloons in the sky were helping to direct the German fire. Thousands of Belgians were engaged in constructing entrenchments, and a great number of fields had been flooded to check the advance. As the brigade continued on through the second line of defences they passed large bodies of retiring Belgian troops going in the opposite direction, utterly exhausted and very dispirited. Numerous ambulance wagons were bringing wounded out from the trenches in front of Lierre.[6]

The *Daily Mail* correspondent, J.M.N. Jeffries, described the scene:

As the hours advanced there were signs of breaking and disorder amid the troops. At some bifurcation or cross-point close to the front on the Lierre road (Kontich perhaps, or was it Lint?) there was great confusion, jamming of vehicles to and from the front, rearing of horses and shouts, ambulances involved with ammunition wagons, cars all honking and screaming at each other, with the prospect of enemy shells landing at any moment in the midst of the disorder; and no-one to direct, no-one to disentangle the jumble, which grew worse every minute.

No-one, that is to say, till a man jumped from a car and, hoisting himself to vantage upon some unseen pedestal or other, began to cry out at the mob in Anglo-French, and to point with vigorous, imperative gestures to this or that centre of the maelstrom. He was a remarkable and in that place an inexplicable figure, clad in a flowing dark blue cloak, clasped at the neck with silver lion-heads or something of that sort, after the fashion of the cloaks worn by prelates in Rome, and this cloak fell in great folds from this stretched oratorical arm. But there was purpose in his gestures, and power in his voice, and under his direction cars and carts were unlocked from each other, and the traffic gradually sorted into streams.

16

The car in which I was fell into its own channel and went past with the others, but as I looked back he was still at his post, poised like a statue, watching till the order he had created was installed with durable momentum. It was Mr Winston Churchill.

I did not fail to mention this characteristic and valuable little piece of work, for valuable it was, in my telegram that evening. But it was forbidden to be printed by the censors in London.[7]

Churchill was in the area inspecting the troops' current intermediate position, situated halfway between the original line and the second ring of forts round Antwerp. He found its flanks were in the air, and even if it could have been held the tired condition of the Belgian troops made this proposition most unlikely. A council of war was held, with the Belgian King presiding over his general staff. There were two courses of action: either to retire to the second line of forts or bring the 7th Division to Antwerp to recapture Lierre and the line of the River Nethe. This idea was dropped when it was made clear that the division could not remain permanently locked up in Antwerp after the line had been re-established, so the first option was favoured.[8]

The First Lord of the Admiralty had clearly become comfortable in his role of saviour of Antwerp. The Prime Minister wanted him back at the Admiralty as soon as possible, but on 5 October Churchill produced a shock of staggering proportions. He telegraphed Asquith and offered his resignation as First Lord in order to take command of both the relieving and garrison forces in the defence of Antwerp. As Churchill's friend Violet Asquith wrote, 'What amazed and shocked me was the sense of proportion (or lack of it) revealed by Winston's choice.'[9]

Churchill had got the taste for combat, and wanted more. If his request had been granted, men of the rank of major-general would have been commanded by a former lieutenant of Hussars, which would have ruffled too many feathers. But events decided the issue: there was no time left for Churchill to play the soldier.

Meanwhile, Commodore Backhouse and the 2nd Brigade had arrived at Wilrijk railway station to find the 1st Brigade already there, unloading stores. The men were given food, then advanced by road to move into prepared trenches: the Marine Brigade would be in the centre, with the 1st Brigade to their right between Boschhoek and Hove, and the 2nd Brigade to their left between Vrende and Boschhoek. The positions were about two miles from the German front line at Lierre. But on arrival the commanding officers were told about the change of orders resulting from the council of war: they were to go back and occupy trenches in line with the second ring of forts around Antwerp. As they moved, these orders were changed again, and the 2nd Brigade was eventually sent to billets at Vienne Dieu, where they were fed and turned in for the night.[10]

The chaplain, Henry Foster, writes:

A march of five miles brought us to the village of Vienne Dieu, a quaint spot on the confines of the city . . . . Here we halted and were to rest a short time before going up to the firing line . . . .

We were told that we were to be quartered for the night in an old château, standing in its own grounds and surrounded by trees. There was abundant evidence that the occupants had been wealthy people and that they had fled away in haste. There was a quantity of valuable furniture, and we found everything just as its late owner had left it.

We ascertained that one of the servants belonging to the house was still at her home in the village, and after a good deal of persuasion we succeeded in getting her to come and cook supper for us . . . . Those of us who are still alive will not readily forget the scene in that old room of the château. There we sat round the table, a light being supplied by a candle stuck securely in the neck of an empty bottle, eating like the gourmands who haunt Simpson's in the Strand and other famous eating-houses. Plates and forks were scarce, but pocket-knives came in exceedingly handy. The windows had been plastered up with brown paper so as not to let out a single streak of light.

There sat such well-known personages as Lieutenant-Colonel George Cornwallis West, Arthur Asquith, Denis Browne and Rupert Brooke, eating pieces of veal with their fingers and drinking coffee out of tumblers and milk jugs.[11]

Sleep was almost impossible, as the guns were firing on both sides, and at about 2.30am the next day (Wednesday, 7 October) orders arrived for the naval brigades to occupy the trenches between the forts in the second line of defence. The men were soon assembled and marched to their new positions.[12]

1st Brigade
Hawke Battalion between forts 2 and 3
Collingwood Battalion between forts 3 and 4
Drake Battalion between forts 4 and 5
Benbow Battalion in reserve

2nd Brigade
Howe Battalion between Lierre road and fort 5
Hood Battalion between forts 5 and 6

Anson Battalion between forts 6 and 7
Nelson Battalion in reserve at Château Elsdock, where the brigade
HQ was established.[13]

The infantry defences here were covered by strong barbed wire entanglements, but the trenches had no head cover or loopholes and,
being raised far above ground level, gave very little protection against
artillery fire. The men began digging shell-proof trenches in the rear
with entrenching tools borrowed from the Belgians. Backhouse acquired
other supplies for his men from the train still at Wilrijk railway station,
and a nearby depot in a linoleum factory, then busied himself visiting
all the trenches under his command and studying the plans he had
been given for retreat. The men were plentifully fed and quite con-
tented in the warm, dry weather.[14]

The 1st Brigade appeared to be not quite so well organized, nor in
such high spirits. Their battalions had reached position at about 5am,
and immediately set about trying to improve their situation with the
few available entrenching tools. But the men were tired and the lack
of water made itself felt; coupled with general ignorance of how to use
a pick and shovel, this resulted in little practical improvement. Four
buses loaded with supplies were received by the brigade, but, instead
of a self-contained bus-load for each battalion, all stores of one type
were loaded in one bus, so everything had to be sorted and reloaded
before they could be issued to the troops.[15]

The situation was now getting critical, as that morning the Germans
crossed the River Scheldt in force at Schoonaeroe above Termonde.
This move directly threatened the railway from Antwerp to Ghent,
and an urgent, hurried retreat from Antwerp was increasingly likely –
which would lead to the probable congestion and possible destruction of
the fragile pontoon bridges across the river in the city, and consequent
extensive losses of troops. Field-Marshal Sir John French, the British
commander-in-chief of Allied forces in Europe, sent Lieutenant-Colonel
Bridges from his staff in an aeroplane to give him daily reports on the
situation; and plans were put in hand to provide steamers and barges
to transport 7,000 men across the river in one go.[16]

At 3pm orders arrived to extend the 2nd Brigade's right flank to the
trenches between fort 7 and the number 16 redoubt, so Nelson Battalion
moved into this position. One company of Howe was relieved near to
fort number 4 by Drake Battalion, and went into reserve.

At 7pm the 2nd Brigade put up a furious fusillade. Backhouse
and Major Maxwell (the brigade major) went forward to discover
the problem, but found it was just a false alarm. There had been
continuous heavy fire all day from the forts and guns to the rear of
the RND, some of which fell short and endangered the men (one

Belgian redoubt was knocked out by fire from an adjoining fort), but German fire at this stage was mainly directed at the advanced villages. Very little was aimed at the forts and trenches, although there was casual shelling into the city itself.[17]

Bernard Freyberg had spent the day reconnoitring a possible withdrawal route for his company of the Hood. Whilst engaged on this he touched a section of electrified barbed wire: the current glued his right hand to the wire, and it was some time before the switch could be located and the current turned off. His palm and fingers were lacerated, the scars remaining for the rest of his life, but it was only the first of many injuries he would sustain before the war was over.[18]

During the night of 7/8 October German shells continued to fall on Antwerp with greater and greater intensity from 2am onwards. The water supply in the city had been cut, and soon some 100 houses were burning. Fortunately there was no wind, or the damage could have been far worse and the pontoon bridges destroyed. Backhouse was visiting General Paris at divisional HQ at 2am when a large shell burst only 10 yards from them, but their luck held and no-one was injured. Many shells burst around the commodore's car as he was returning to his position, while divisional HQ was moved back into Antwerp itself. 2nd Brigade HQ transferred to Wilrijk railway station, where shell-proof trenches were constructed in a nearby garden.[19]

As day broke on 8 October the shelling continued. Chaplain Foster writes:

> It was on this day that we first noticed any marked increase in the enemy's shellfire. His heavy batteries were very busy, Antwerp being the chief target, and by midday the town was literally deluged by a torrent of big shells, which burst with ear-splitting reports, terrifying both man and beast. The Rev Robert Primrose (the Presbyterian chaplain with the Hood Battalion) told me that he had taken a walk during the early hours of the day in the centre of the city, and had seen three or four houses blown down, with terrific force, as the wind blows down a house made with playing cards. The loss of life was considerable. Men, women, children, horses, dogs and cats were lying dead in the main streets.
>
> Some parts of the line held by the Naval Division suffered heavier bombardment than others, but so far, luckily for us, most of the shells were, as the men put it, 'Non-stop for Antwerp'. It is, perhaps, somewhat difficult for those who were not there to imagine the utter hopelessness and despair of the men who had been sent with the intention of defending Antwerp. Unknown to us, the fate of Antwerp was decided before we arrived.[20]

Before dawn on 8 October Paris received news from General Dossin, commanding the 2nd Belgian Division, that forts 1, 2 and 4 had fallen to the Germans. At 9am a conference was held to discuss the situation. It was agreed that, if the forts had indeed fallen, the entire line was untenable unless they could be retaken quickly; failing this, the whole line must be abandoned at nightfall and the defence withdrawn to the inner enceinte immediately round the city. For this purpose, however, the fortress troops in Antwerp were sufficient, so it was decided that the British naval forces and General Dossin's division should cross the Scheldt after dark and join the main Belgian field army to the west of the river.

The three forts had not in fact fallen to the Germans as reported, but later that afternoon their garrisons abandoned them and could not be induced to return, so the contingency plans were only a few hours premature. The condition of the Belgian troops was such that there was little hope of holding the line, but the Belgian CO, General de Guise, was determined to maintain the defence, step by step, to the very last. He chivalrously insisted that the British troops should be the first to cross the bridges, his final words being, 'Alors, c'est fini, mes hommes sont usés.'

Lord Kitchener was informed of the situation, and shortly afterwards orders were received that the British should withdraw across the river, that General Rawlinson had been instructed to assist in every way possible, and that trains had been arranged to be at the town of St Nicolas, to the west of Antwerp. General Paris had himself already decided that his Royal Naval Division would retire across the Scheldt after dark to Haesdonck, six miles west of Antwerp. The Belgian army was endeavouring to keep open communications with the city, but its men were too exhausted to dispute a serious enemy attack from the direction of Schoonaeroe, and were retiring behind the Ghent-Selzaete canal to try to re-form. A plan was put in motion to send two brigades of the 7th Division and two brigades of artillery by rail to Ghent to cover the flank of the RND retirement.

Bad news now came in that a German force of about a division, reinforced by 6,000 troops from Brussels, was attacking Lokeren and the railway between St Nicolas and Ghent. The only course open was to send the trains along the northern line from Selzaete to St Gillies Waes, a small town north of St Nicolas. Arrangements were made to protect the route, and one officer personally took seven trains down this line. Messengers were sent to General Paris to inform him of the change; as a safeguard, Commander Samson, RN, was sent in armoured cars with a duplicate set of instructions.

At 5.25pm General Paris held a conference with his senior officers and staff, and sent an order to the Royal Naval Division instructing them to retire on receipt of the order. The retreat began at about 7.30pm under very difficult conditions, with terrific confusion and congestion on the roads. Guards had been posted at the bridges, however, to keep the way clear for the RND.[21]

Commodore Backhouse described the retreat:

We had a conference of commandants at 4pm, but had no orders to give them for retirement. At 5.30pm Colonel Ollivant (on the RND divisional staff) arrived with orders for retirement at 10pm, followed a few minutes later by Captain Sketchley (also an RND divisional staff officer) with orders for immediate retirement. I sent Curzon, who was at Wilrijk with me, to collect his battalion and sent Maxwell to the Hood and Anson battalions, to evacuate and proceed to the pontoon bridge. I had a regrettable meeting with Belgian officers in charge of the reserves and who had brought in guns, in telling them of our departure.

The leading companies of Howe and Hood reached Wilrijk at 7pm, followed by the remainder of these battalions at 8.30pm, when we moved off to the pontoon bridge, the Anson and Nelson Battalions having gone separately. We had no difficulty in making our own way and had no shellfire. The road led close to the burning oil vats, but we did not have any difficulty in passing. We were received by General Paris on the bridge, who directed the 2nd Brigade to Zwyndrecht. Some shells burst in the burning oil vats soon after we had cleared the bridge, but the bridge was not shelled as we crossed. The arrangements of guides between Burcht and Zwyndrecht were very good. We had left behind two lorries with our stores besides the whole of our kit back at Wilrijk station.[22]

The Reverend Foster, who was with the Anson Battalion and came up just after the Hood and Howe, wrote about his experience:

Our men loathed the idea of a retreat, but the majority realized that every minute the position was becoming more critical and that immediate retreat was our only hope of escaping capture.

Almost all the Belgians had gone, except those in the forts, and in our covering fort only one Belgian gunner remained. One of our naval gun crews gallantly offered to remain and work the guns to cover our retreat, which they did up to the very last minute . . . .

In order to cross the Scheldt, we were forced to pass by the blazing petroleum tanks at Hoboken. The road was narrow, but it was the only road left. The fumes were overpowering and the intense heat proved too much for some of the men. The flames at

22

times blew right across the road, and large German shells were falling in amongst the tanks at the rate of four a minute. Sometimes a shell would burst with a terrific report in the boiling oil, and flames shot up to the height of two hundred feet.

As we approached the blazing tanks it was like entering the infernal regions. The burning oil had flooded a field on one side of the road and dead horses and cattle were frizzling in it. 'Now, boys,' shouted the officer, 'keep your heads and run through it!' And we did – but I don't know how we did it. Once we had got past the oil tanks we were in comparative safety for a hundred yards because the road was sheltered, but then for some thousand yards it was exposed again to the enemy's fire.

We were ordered to run at the double over this bit of road, and most of us were fortunate enough to reach the pontoon bridge over the river. A spy was caught by one of our battalions in the act of trying to blow up this bridge, but his designs were frustrated just in time, and a bayonet ended his career.

Sentries were posted at intervals while we went across, and shouted, 'Change your step!' every few yards. At last we were safely on the other side and breathed again. The relief felt by all ranks on getting across the river can hardly be imagined, and although even there we were by no means out of danger, yet we knew that a most important step had been taken.[23]

At 10pm the 2nd Brigade reached Zwyndrecht, then went on a further seven miles or so towards St Nicolas. After a long march they reached St Gillies Waes railway station at 7am the following morning, having covered some 20 miles from fort 5. Five special trains were waiting for them for the journey to Selzaete, close to the Dutch frontier, a route which would avoid German troops.

Describing the retreat, General Paris wrote:

The hopeless block on every road and through every village, caused by the movement of the Belgian army and the entire population with their cattle and goods, rendered intercommunication impossible. I myself was never able to reach the head of the column; in fact at least two trains had left St Gillies Waes before I arrived there.

These two trains had in fact left only partly filled, but it was easy for Paris to assume that they had both been full. He followed on by car once he was happy that the retreat was successful. However, confusion in communication and orders were to mean the loss of the majority of the 1st Brigade.

Commodore Henderson states that at 6.50pm Colonel Ollivant arrived from divisional HQ to inform him that instructions had already been issued for a general retirement, the intention being that the 1st Brigade should follow the 2nd. Henderson says this was shown to be impossible, and the two men agreed that the 2nd Brigade should not start their retirement until 10 p.m., thus covering the 1st Brigade's southern flank. Henderson issued orders for retirement at 8pm; Lieutenant Ingleby, on the 1st Brigade staff, took these orders to Drake Battalion but found that, unknown to brigade HQ, they had already left. It appears that divisional retreat orders were conveyed only to Drake, who withdrew without the knowledge of their commander. Henderson had also been wrongly informed that he should move via the Port de Malines, whereas Major Richardson at divisional HQ had planned for the 1st Brigade to proceed to St Anne's Bridge by the Harenthal Gate. Last but not least, Henderson was not told that the order required definite action.

As it happened, Henderson took the correct route, led by three officers who had carried out a reconnaissance earlier, but owing to the great fatigue of all battalions (including the 10th Battalion of Royal Marines Light Infantry, who had been in support of the 1st Brigade), the enemy shellfire, and the difficulties en route, they got considerably scattered. The majority of the marines and three remaining battalions reached Zwyndrecht by 4.30 a.m. the next day, and Henderson went off in his car in search of divisional HQ and supplies for his men, which he had been verbally informed would be there. But he could find no trace of either. By 8am the only food located was about four ounces of meat per man. Henderson did, however, get a report from the Belgian HQ that the enemy was likely to open fire on Zwyndrecht.

At 8.30am Belgian HQ came up with the information that billets and supplies were available at St Gillies Waes, and that the remainder of the RND were there; so, despite his men being without food or water, Henderson gave orders that battalions should move on to St Gillies Waes by 4pm. He went on himself to make contact with divisional HQ to arrange billets and supplies, but, arriving at 11am, it was the same story as in Zwyndrecht. He could find no trace of divisional HQ, nor any billets or supplies. All he found was one broken-down bus at the railway station, partly filled with biscuits. Further enquiries at the station elicited the information that about 5,000 British troops had left by train for Ostend earlier in the day! It seemed that divisional HQ had mistaken the arrival of Colonel Seely, commanding Drake Battalion, for the arrival of the whole brigade.

Meanwhile, the 10th Battalion RMLI, under Colonel Luard, arrived at St Nicolas by a different route and were told by the Belgian authorities that they would have a better chance of a train if they went to

Kemzeke, the next station after St Gillies Waes. They made their way there and got on a train, but at about 4pm it was attacked by German artillery at Moerbeke. The colonel, with some 150 men, managed to get away and escaped on foot to Selzaete; most of the rest, mixed up with refugees on the train, surrendered. The Germans did not stay at Moerbeke nor make any attempt to destroy the line, and the captured train was apparently taken on to Selzaete shortly afterwards, filled with refugees and a few soldiers, by a Belgian officer who was passing by and knew how to drive an engine. Another train with some 200 RND troops got through to Selzaete as late as 9pm

In the meantime, having heard from the traffic authorities at 6.15pm that the situation was critical and trains were returning because the Germans had cut the line, Henderson got a report that the enemy were advancing by train. Finding, as he thought, his last exit in the direction of Bruges had been closed, he says he reluctantly took the decision to cross the Dutch frontier. The Dutch were neutral, and going to them would mean internment, but this was nevertheless preferable to ignominious surrender to the Germans. Henderson felt that surrender was the only other alternative, as the men were in no condition to offer resistance thanks to lack of food, water, ammunition and entrenching tools. He and his troops were duly interned by the Dutch at Groningen.

Others did not agree that internment was the only option. Several groups of men made it to safety, among them a small party under Lieutenant Grant, RNVR, of Benbow Battalion, who had been sent to replace the Belgian garrison in fort 4 and had only received his orders to retire after midnight! He crossed the River Scheldt by steamer after the bridge had been blown up, and caught up with the rearguard of the battalions marching to Holland. Grant was ordered to cross the frontier with the others, but refused and was put under arrest. He broke out to make his way through to safety.[24]

Commodore Backhouse wrote in his diary:

Worrying day; clear that 1st Brigade is interned in Holland, but mystery how they got there. General Paris held a meeting of officers to justify his actions. Apparently the mistake he made was in failing to leave orders for Henderson at Gillies Waes. My luck was in getting away early.

The Hood Battalion had 10 men interned at Groningen, all of whom were seen on the march on the night of 8 October but were not on any trains. Most were seen on the outskirts of Antwerp, helping the sick along.

Major-General Paris made specific mention of a number of officers for good service during the operations, including Colonel Quilter (CO) and Sub-Lieutenant Hugh Cockburn Hedderwick of the Hood Battalion. The total casualties of 1st and 2nd Brigades in the Antwerp defence were:

Killed	5
Wounded	64
Missing	2,040.[25]

Field-Marshal Sir John French, commander-in-chief of the expeditionary force, sent a despatch to the Admiralty:

I have to state that, from a comprehensive review of all the circumstances, the force of Marines and Naval Brigades which assisted in the defence of Antwerp was handled by General Paris with great skill and boldness.

Although the results did not include the actual saving of the fortress, the action of the force under General Paris certainly delayed the enemy for a considerable time, and assisted the Belgian army to be withdrawn in a condition to enable it to reorganize and refit, and regain its value as a fighting force. The destruction of war material and ammunition – which, but for the intervention of this force, would have proved of great value to the enemy – was thus able to be carried out.

The assistance which the Belgian army has rendered throughout the subsequent course of the operations on the canal and the Yeser river has been a valuable asset to the Allied cause, and such help must be regarded as an outcome of the intervention of General Paris's force. I am further of opinion that the morale effect produced on the minds of the Belgian army by his necessarily desperate attempt to bring them succour, before it was too late, has been of great value to their use and efficiency as a fighting force.[26]

CHAPTER THREE

The Crystal Palace

In September, 1914, the RND established a depot at Crystal Palace to recruit and train the large intake of officers and men. After the three battalions created to replace those lost at Antwerp had been completed and despatched, everything beyond the most elementary instruction was moved to a training camp at Blandford in Dorset. But the Palace remained the location for initial instruction, lasting between four and eight weeks, and was also used for training officers and specialists on a longer-term basis.[1]

Captain Sir Richard Henry Williams-Bulkeley, Bart, the commodore at the Palace, issued orders outlining the daily routine on 12 September, 1914:

6.00am	Reveille
7.00am	Roll call
7.45am	Breakfast
8.30am	Sick to muster
9.00am	Parade
10.15am	Defaulters and requests
11.00am	Parade
12 noon	Cooks
12.30pm	Dinner
2.00pm	Parade
4.15pm	Cooks
4.45pm	Tea
6.30pm	Retreat and guard mounting
6.45pm	Cooks
7.00pm	Supper
9.00pm	First post
9.30pm	Last post and roll call
9.55pm	One 'G' warning bugle
10.00pm	Lights out

The North Terrace Gardens and Fairy Archipelago were placed firmly out of bounds, reinforced by warning notice boards, and any man found at these locations was dealt with under the heading of 'Breaking out of Camp'. However, on occasions there were problems, as shown by a divisional order from the commodore:

> It has been reported to me that considerable damage has been done to some of the boats on the river and other damage effected. Also that fruit trees in a garden adjoining the Palace grounds have been robbed and branches broken. Men are warned that a crime of this kind will be treated with the utmost severity. Further large pickets will be drawn from the men for duty to prevent such conduct, thus causing extra work and long hours. Sentries on certain pickets will be armed and ordered to fire on any man who does not immediately halt and reply to the sentry's challenge.

All officers were entitled to a personal servant taken from the ranks, and as far as possible from the battalion or company to which the officer was attached. Servants were excused from first parades and drills, but had to attend all the others. They received a payment of 10 shillings per month, at the officer's expense, in addition to their service pay.

A regular ceremonial was instituted in which the band fell in on the lower terrace at 7.50am, and at 8am played the 'Colours Up'. At this ceremony, and again at the 'Retreat' in the evening, all ranks had to stand at attention when colours were being hoisted or lowered, facing the flagstaff as the officers took the salute.[2] From the flagstaff flew the naval ensign and above it the commodore's flag: a red cross on a white background, with a round red spot in the top quartering with a triangular piece nicked out of the narrowing end. The flags flew on the quarter-deck of the ship *Crystal Palace*. Not a man was to proceed who failed to salute the flags in passing, and a sentry was placed to remind the defaulter of the respect due to the flags.

Upon joining the men had to be kitted up. They were marched to the issuing room in an orderly and uniform manner, and while waiting their turn were not allowed to smoke, but could stand easy and, as the instruction went, in an orderly formation.[3] By 3 December, 1914, the kitting-up procedure included issuing identity discs together with the necessary stamps. Each disc contains sufficient details to tell the original history of an RND man:

Royal Naval man
James Thomas Smith,
O.S. R.N.
255,789.
C.E.

Royal Navy Reserve man
James Thomas Smith,
O.S.
2569. A.R.N.R.
Pres.

Royal Fleet Reserve man
James Thomas Smith,
21678. R.F.R.
C.E.
Note that the RFR number is not necessary: the man's original (i.e. official) number is sufficient.

Royal Navy Volunteer Reserve man
James Thomas Smith,
O.S. R.N.V.R.
Bristol 6/4320.
R.C.
Enlisted before the war. The name of the division and the number of the company must be inserted.

James Thomas Smith,
O.S. R.N.V.R.
London Z/673.
C.E.
Enlisted since the start of the war. The name of the division is followed by a 'Z'.

James Thomas Smith,
O.S. R.N.V.R.
K.P./999.
C.E.
Army (Kitchener) recruit at Crystal Palace, transferred to RNVR.

James Thomas Smith,
O.S. R.N.V.R.
K.W./251.
Cong.
Army (Kitchener) recruit who joined original RND 1st Brigade and was transferred to RNVR.

James Thomas Smith,
O.S. R.N.V.R.
K.X./272.
Wes.
Army (Kitchener) recruit who joined original RND 2nd Brigade

The floor of the men's sleeping quarters was covered with a strong wooden framework of little pens in which hammocks were slung, usually three to a pen. During the day the hammocks were all neatly lashed in true navy fashion, looking like so many big white cocoons ringed with rope.[5] The deck planking, as it was called, was scrubbed daily and swabbed with disinfectant. Hygiene became a problem, though, when a number of men began to fall sick, and some even died. Spotted fever was diagnosed, and for two weeks 15 of Herbert Booth's vacuum machine inventions sucked up inches of dust from floors, pillars, walls and stairs around the building. Eventually some 26 tons of dust were removed and buried, which put paid to the epidemic. This did much to prove Pasteur's theory that the air around us could be germ-laden; everyone suddenly became hygiene-conscious and wanted a dust-sucking machine.[6]

All around the grounds and throughout the day there was drill and marching, marching and drill. Signals were flashed and bugles blew. There was a signals school at the Palace using heliographs: standing on the terrace one could see silver flashing in the green of the woods on the hillsides miles away. Instruction was given in wireless telegraphy, flag signalling and mast headlight flashing, in which winking windows talked in Morse code to each other. As a result of this specialist training, many men were despatched to the fleet for service at sea.

Little open-air schools could be found dotted around the grass whenever the weather was fair. Elementary musketry instruction was a common sight, the teacher seated upon the ground with a rifle across his knee, giving every detail of the proper rifle sequence to some 15 or 20 young men.

The Admiralty and commodore also gave thought to recreation for the men after their daily drills and classes. Throughout its long and varied life the Crystal Palace had been the home of fine arts and good music. For many years the Saturday classical concerts under Sir August Manns were renowned the world over, featuring the best artists from both home and abroad. As more concerts of a similar type were staged elsewhere in London the audiences at the Palace gradually declined. The Great Triennial Handel Festival, unique in the size of the orchestra, choir and audience combining to produce magnificent effects, started in 1857 but had to end in 1892 because of dwindling support.

Now, with hundreds of young men to keep entertained, Palace music took on a new lease of life. In 1914 the Palace could still provide a fine amateur orchestra and choir, who together gave a series of concerts. The YMCA took a strong lead in this, organizing music and entertainments each evening in which a constant succession of well-known vocal and instrumental artistes and entertainers generously gave their services. The men packed the concerts, and showed great appreciation for the different performers. The Crystal Palace band also played for several hours a day after drill; organ recitals were given in the afternoon by the musical director and organist, Walter Hedgcock; and chamber music and vocal concerts were arranged in the officers' wardroom.[7]

In the early days at the Palace the red triangle sign of the YMCA, known to the men as the YM, became familiar for more than just music as the organization worked for the well-being of all ranks in the RND. In the beginning only tents were used, but as things became more organized increased accommodation was made available. Firstly the Egyptian, Grecian and Roman Courts of the Central Transept were taken over for reading, writing and concerts. The Roman Court was devoted mainly to concerts, musical competitions, services and lectures, which were given nightly, plus three services on Sunday. Later the Moroccan and Alhambran Courts were also handed over, the latter of which held four billiard tables which were constantly in use during off-duty periods. Some 3,000 square yards in all were placed at the disposal of the YMCA – proof of the value of its work amongst the men.

The YMCA's motto was 'Loyalty and Service', and to fulfil this promise at Crystal Palace 84 voluntary workers ran a parcels counter, laundry receiving depot, post office, enquiry office, savings bank, refreshment department, fruit stall, and a library containing up to 2,000 books for reference and circulation. In the North End Gardens there was an open-air theatre where concerts and services were regularly given on a summer evening. Arrangements were frequently made for parties of men to visit places of interest and entertainment in the city. There was also a register of homes where free hot baths could be obtained, which were in constant use.

On Sunday morning church parades the men marched into the Central Transept to the strains of their band playing a quickstep, and formed up on the Great Orchestra. It was said that singing hymns here accompanied by the organ was a revelation, and an experience long remembered.

Physical training had a high priority, taught using the Royal Navy's Swedish system. Instructors were recruited from volunteers who had attained a high standard in earlier classes; keeping the programme operational was full-time work for one officer, one chief petty officer and 25 instructors. Sports such as boxing and wrestling were also encouraged, with medals and prizes awarded to contest winners. In the summer cricket, tennis and field-day sports were played; in winter there was football, basketball and running. A concession was obtained from Crystal Palace Football Club, so that all men in uniform could gain free admission to their football matches.[8]

31

Food was of the best quality, with catering by Joe Lyons. Ten thousand men could be seated for meals at the same time, and many recruits thought that the cooking was better than in their own homes:9

It is a man's fault if he does not get enough, for there is no stinting. I saw one of the men's messrooms laid for tea. A knife and fork tea, too. Every man's share of ham was separated from every other man's by greaseproof paper.

In May, 1917, Able Seaman H. V. Clark, a former schoolmaster, produced a small booklet entitled *Observations on the Life and Characters at the Crystal Palace*, and one of his poems gives a good insight into daily life there:

THE AVERAGE DAY AT THE CRYSTAL PALACE

The bugle's sounding
Its notes astounding
With joy awaking
Sweet couch forsaking.
Feet are pattering,
Teeth are chattering,
Boots are clattering –
Infernal row!

The lights are gleaming
Show faces beaming
(Some still dreaming)
Despite the row.
Strident hailings,
Despairing wailings,
Useless railings
From 'Starboard Bow'.

Kitbag key inserted,
Bag itself inverted,
Towel (badly dirtied)
Is extracted.
Soponaceous slab-O!
Hastily you grab-O!
Underarm you jab-O!

Scene III now enacted.

Begin ablutions:
Dirt contributions
In soap solutions.
(One light to guide)
Some are shaving,
Perils braving,
2d saving!
Safer side!

Upstairs dashing,
Colliding, crashing,
Hammock lashing
(Pull 'em taut).
Get a hustle
And a tussle,
Use a muscle,
Time is short.

Rush for cocoa,
Damaged boko,
What a joke-O!
Laugh like H . . . !
Liquid steaming
Down jumpers streaming,
Protestors screaming,
Fly Pell Mell!

The 'fall in' goes,
Sly POs
Cease to doze
And walk below.
Celtic gleemen,
Leading seamen,
Section B men
Complete the show.

The roll is taken:
'Lost', 'strayed', 'forsaken'.
What's left – For bacon!
(So rarely supplied.)
Adrifts are marked with 'A'
Special sicks put down as 'K',
Whom we must 'watch and spray'.

Cooks are selected,
Complaints are dissected,
Shirkers detected.
Then 'fall out the classes!'
For them is PTI –
Just watch the gravel fly!
Here's stuff for Printer's Pie!
Energy in masses.

The rest in gloom
Await their doom.
What duties loom?
'We are guard today,
Shall I be in, I wonder?
If so – a wretched blunder!
I'll protest, I will by thunder,
To Robert's Wray.'

Alas these whiners –
Forty-niners –
Tho' feeling sore
Are 'Elsey's Corps'.
How he rates 'em,
Endearing terms!
[censored]
How he squirms,
As he baits 'em!

Then Commander's Orders,
Prisoner's warders,
Daily routine,
No free canteen.
Then turn about,
Now breakfast's ready:
Steady, now steady.
Visions of salmon,
Or toothsome gammon,
Or lusty trout.

The animals fed,
Letters are read.
Boots are polished,
Beards abolished.
Now's for inspection:

Fall-in goes,
Ready in rows.
Striking a pose,
Foretop's perfection!

The flag is saluted,
The anthem toot-tooted,
The 'Carry-on' hooted,
Then march we to prayers.
Reads quaint little Chaplain,
A endearing young sapling,
With voice like a grappling-
Hook when it tears.

Then more PTI-ing –
Even POs are sighing –
Chiefs too are trying
To vigorous be.
Then to duties once more:
Some scrubbing the floor,
Some guarding a door,
Some retiring to snore
In placidity.

'Stand-easy' arrives:
Like bees in their hives
The 'shorts', the 'talls',
To the YMC stalls
Flock with their coppers.
Ladies both dark and fair
Smilingly serve us there.
Chic femininity
Claims our affinity –
Especially Foretoppers.

So passed away
The 'Average Day',
While the 'homebirds' pay
For our 'recreation'.
Each unit conflicting,
Coaxed, urged, or licked in
To shape (yes, or kicked in!)
For Britain's salvation.[10]

CHAPTER FOUR

Blandford

In late 1914 the main RND training centre was moved to a new camp
under construction at Blandford in Dorset, leaving Crystal Palace for
training officers, specialists and basic recruits. In early November, as
a temporary measure, the 2nd Brigade was sent from Betteshanger
to various barracks around the south of England: Nelson Battalion
went to Portsmouth, Anson to Chatham, Howe to Portland, and the
Hood to HMS *Vivid* at Plymouth.[1] But the Blandford camp was
nearing completion and received battalions of the 2nd Brigade from
27 November; the Hood arrived on 5 December, 1914.

The camp consisted of wooden huts in three main groups, numbered
A1 to A4, B1 to B4, and C1 to C4. Each group contained 16 outer
huts in two lines of eight, between which were five huts of different
sizes – mainly living units for 16, 14 or 12 men, plus ablutions and
storage. The camp was to be self-contained, and huts for the YMCA,
post office, Methodist Church, Church of England and medical area
were provided, in addition to canteens, and messes and wardrooms for
the petty officers and officers.[2]

The grassy areas apparent when the troops first arrived soon became
a quagmire of mud, so duck-boards were laid to help movement around
the camp.[3] Lieutenant Patrick Shaw-Stewart of the Hood wrote a letter
on 4 January, 1915, describing the work:

Road-making consists of walking up and down a wide slab of liquid
mud, between two rows of huts, waiting for one fatigue-party to bring
stones in buckets from one quarter of the compass, and another to
bring whins to put under them from the opposite quarter. The stones
and the whins between them form the road, as the term is understood
in our primitive circles. When the men bring them you graciously
indicate with your toe where they should go, and say, 'Smartly there'
and 'Double off, now.' That is road-making, and very chilly it is.[4]

Because of its exposed position Blandford camp was considered one of the healthiest training camps in the country, although the men had a different view. For bed and bedding they were issued with two trestles and three boards, two blankets, and a palliasse – hardly luxury. Each hut had a coke stove, but these were inefficient and let out fumes, which had an adverse effect on a number of men.

Training consisted of drill, marching, digging trenches, mock attacks and general battlefield situations. Joseph Murray of the Hood says they were instructed 'to lie down in the mud, mud up to your eyebrows, which was a whitish soil, but you had to be spick-and-span on parade the next day'.

Camp routine was run on navy lines. A ship's bell kept the watches: leaving camp was to go ashore, and being late in returning was being adrift. The RND refused to part with naval traditions: it was not subject to army jurisdiction, and its commanding general was responsible only to masters in Whitehall.

In December, 1914, all officers and men were issued with active service uniforms in khaki, instead of their former naval blues. The naval brigades retained a naval-style hat, but in khaki, with a tally around it showing the name of their battalion in gold at the front. Later pith helmets were issued, which looked naked without their puggaree: a long strip of muslin, about two inches wide, folded around the inside of the helmet. Overall discipline and efficiency improved as their greatly improved and distinctive appearance led to rivalry between the different battalions and brigades.[5]

A postcard on sale at the camp at this time parodied the sentiments of the troops:

What a happy place is Blandford

'What a happy place is Blandford' is a song that's rather new,
But I fancy that its topic should appeal to all of you,
For if anyone should ask you where your happiest mem'ries link,
You would answer in a chorus, 'Oh, in Blandford,' I don't think!
　Oh what a happy place is Blandford,
　Envied by all soldiers near and far,
　Oh my heart always inclines
　To the good old Al Lines,
　Oh what a merry lot they are.

We've a rather mixed collection in the Blandford RND,
For we've got 5,000 sailors who have never seen the sea,
And we've got a naval transport of 500 horse-marines,
The express design of Winston to supply the Turks with beans.

Oh what a happy place is Blandford,
Such a jolly place to war,
But if you've ever been to sea,
Gad, you'd love the RND,
Oh what a lucky lot you are.

Oh, they feed like lords at Blandford, on delicious bully beef.
They don't know what it died of, but suppose it died of grief,
For thinking of the men who've got to eat its tawny flesh,
But it's better than tinned salmon when the salmon isn't fresh.
Oh what a happy place is Blandford,
They love it more than any place by far,
But they think that eating rabbit
Is a rather nasty habit –
Oh how particular they are.

Now of all the many units in this variegated camp,
There is one that stands out clearly of a different sort of stamp.
For of all this khaki Navy in this wonderfull'st of shows,
There are none will stand comparing with the Blandford medicoes.
Oh what a happy place is Blandford,
There's no unit nearly on a par.
And we've got the best CO,
That this camp will only know,
Oh what a lucky lot we are.[6]

Many of the stokers, being men of the Royal Fleet Reserve and finding
themselves in what they considered to be more or less the army, were
not happy and were always grousing. Some got drunk in Blandford's
inns and public houses on the occasions when they could get ashore,
although regulations placed the town out of bounds after 8pm, and even
before then a pass was needed. Douglas Jerrold writes:

> The stokers of the Royal Fleet Reserve were the backbone of the
> battalions. Never smart men, they were to show great patience, en-
> durance and fighting quality which showed their depth of discipline
> and training. They knew the regulations and the suitable penalty.
> Newly-joined officers had to prove themselves to these men, and
> many can recall the experience of trying to exercise authority over
> the stokers with amusement but not much pride.[7]

Lieutenant Patrick Shaw-Stewart wrote of them in January, 1915:

> I have got the queerest command – imagine it – a platoon of Old
> Stokers! They are very queer fish to handle after the lamb-like Scots
> at the Crystal Palace. Their appearance is rather like the *Punch*

picture of the *Landsturm*, their language extremely fruity, and their cunning inexhaustible. But they have great 'character', and I dare say they may grow on me. But they have got a sort of standing grievance in the back of their evil old minds that they want to be back in their steel-walled pen, yelping delight and rolling in the waist, instead of forming fours under the orders of an insolent young landlubber.[8]

Thomas Mitchell of the Hood remembers one occasion when two men had committed a misdemeanour and were tried by a court martial. The court decided that the men should be drummed out of the RND, so the whole brigade was assembled on the parade ground in a square around the two men. The bugle major stood by and, on the word of an officer, stripped away every vestige of badge and identification mark from their uniforms, leaving only their trousers and jackets. The drummers then began the tattoo, and the miscreants were drummed out of the service and handed over to the civil authorities.[9]

The RND attracted officers of quality from the start, from the Naval Reserve and former Guards officers. The Hood Battalion was very fortunate at this time to recruit the services of many fine officers. Rupert Brooke got himself transferred from Anson Battalion after problems with another officer at Chatham; he joined A Company on the last day of November, 1914, under the command of Bernard Freyberg. The other four officers of his company were initially Arthur 'Oc' Asquith, who arrived on 10 November, 1914, Patrick Shaw-Stewart, who joined on 19 December, Denis Browne, and Johnny Dodge. Frederick 'Cleg' Kelly joined them on 23 February, 1915. This group was to be unsurpassed for its flair and intellect. Together with Charles Lister, the son of Lord Ribblesdale, they were to show the sacrifice of a generation – a type not to walk the earth again.

The officers at Blandford lived in wooden eight-man huts: Brooke's section was 15 feet long and just eight feet wide. He was able to decorate it to his taste, and furnished it with a table, a chest of drawers and a chair. In due course he acquired some scarlet curtains to hang at the window.[10] Brooke immediately showed himself to be concerned for the welfare of the men under his command – on 20 December he wrote to his mother:

About mince-pies and cakes – we're feeding half the company, about 120 men. Turkey, plum-pudding, etc. at midday; mince-pies, etc. for tea. Just as many as you can make. Will you wire how many teas you can get mince-pies and cakes for, to send me 10, 20, 50 or whatever it is. I'll get some more elsewhere.

Also please send me three bottles of my '87 port. We might as well drink it in the mess.[11]

39

His requests continued with a telegram to Katherine Cox:

> Send mince-pies for 60 men and a few cakes to me Blandford station immediately; get someone to help you.[12]

Brooke wrote later:

> I spend Christmas in looking after drunken stokers. One of them has been drunk since seven. He neither eats or drinks, but dances a complicated step up and down his hut, half-dressed, singing 'How happy I am! How happy I am!' A short fat inelegant man, in stocking feet. What wonders we are![13]

Having passed his holiday looking after his drunken stokers until they fell asleep, Brooke wrote on 1 January, 1915, to his uncle, the Reverend Alan Brooke, thanking him for some money:

> It was very good of you to send a pound for my men. I consulted them – they are reserve stokers, tamed painfully to military use – what would they like, the 50 of them, for a Christmas present. Believing in liberty I left them a free hand. But they didn't choose beer. They bought themselves halma, draughts (two lots), bezique and various games of throwing rings on to hooks and balls through holes. And they amuse themselves very happily with these, when the weather's too dreadful to go out – as it very often is.[14]

The Hood Battalion was given a week's leave of absence from 30 December, 1914, and dispersed to their homes. Sub-Lieutenant Rupert Brooke saw in the New Year at Rugby, went to Walmer Castle on 2 January, 1915, at the invitation of Violet Asquith, then on to London on 4 January for luncheon at the Admiralty with the Churchills and Mr Asquith. Brooke later said, 'I didn't get much out of Winston, but gathered we might be going out within six weeks or so.'[15]

My great-uncle Albert Walls's holiday was not nearly so grand: he went home, and during his leave visited his mother Caroline one evening. My father Marcel, then a small boy just four years old, still remembers this visit. Caroline asked Albert to give her a keepsake before he left for overseas, as she had the feeling that she would not see him again. All he had was his old service mug – not much to look at, as it had travelled many miles in his kitbag and was considerably battered, but he left it with her.[16]

Back in the harsh reality of service life, Rupert Brooke began arranging the purchase of a rifle with telescopic sights, costing eight guineas. All the officers were buying them for their platoons. On

15 January Major-General Sir Archibald Paris, the RND commanding officer, addressed all his officers at Blandford. He could only talk in general terms: the campaign was being prepared, but it would mean another six weeks' training.[17]

So training it was with a vengeance, Lieutenant Patrick Shaw-Stewart wrote in February:

> I have been marching literally 15 miles a day for all the last week bar two days, and once 20, and once 18, so I am, if possible, more in the pink of condition than ever, and very proud of the condition of my feet. The stokers on the other hand have very many blisters, poor souls, and complain bitterly that they aren't on the nice comfy sea.
>
> For the last week we have been on a 'billeting march' through the New Forest and thereabouts: Ringwood, Lyndhurst, Fordingbridge; about 15 and 18 miles a day. Then we were to have marched home on Friday, but we were stopped because some recruits from Crystal Palace had got spotted fever, so we marched back to Ringwood and stayed there till this morning and marched back today . . . . I think we should have stayed still longer, only we are to be inspected by Winston the day after tomorrow and must practise it tomorrow.[18]

On 17 February Winston Churchill duly arrived to inspect the Royal Naval Division at Blandford, in the pouring rain. Brooke described the events:

> What a day! A real Blandford day of the milder kind, mud, rain and a hurricane. First old Paris put the review off, because of the weather (but that was after we'd stood out like a battalion of Lears in the pitiless storm for half an hour). Then Winston turned up and demanded something. We were hurried out to an extemporized performance, plunging through rivers and morasses. It was like a dream. At one point I emerged from the mud, with my platoon, under the wheels of a car, in the midst of a waste. And in the car were what I thought were two children, jumping about clapping their hands, whistling and pointing. It was Eddie and Clemmie [Edward Marsh, Churchill's secretary, and Mrs Clementine Churchill] . . . . It is rumoured Winston was pleased, and impressed by our [2nd Brigade] superiority to the other brigades.[19]

Then on 20 February, 1915, Colonel Quilter addressed his officers of the Hood. The RND was to help force the Dardanelles and take Constantinople; it was expected that the fighting would last for anything from two to six weeks, so a short sharp campaign was planned. His words were electrifying to Brooke: 'It's too wonderful – the best

41

expedition of the war. Figure me celebrating the first Holy Mass in St Sophia since 1453.' Brooke was sure that it would be much more glorious and less dangerous than France, although a rumour doing the rounds held that the Hood was being considered as a spearhead for the landings, and 75 per cent casualties must be expected.[20] Brooke wrote to Violet Asquith:

Oh, Violet, it's too wonderful for belief. I had not imagined fate could be so benign. I almost suspect her . . . . But I am filled with confident and glorious hopes . . . . Shall we be a turning point in history? Oh God! . . . I've never been quite so happy; like a stream flowing entirely to one end. I suddenly realize that the ambition of my life has been – since I was two – to go on a military expedition against Constantinople.[21]

Much activity, kit inspection and general preparation followed Quilter's announcement, and the King was scheduled to inspect the troops on 25 February. A telegram arrived: could Clementine Churchill, Lady Gwendeline Churchill and Violet Asquith be given luncheon in the Hood mess? Colonel Quilter was of the opinion that the ladies should prepare for hardships.[22]

Inspection day dawned bright and clear. Violet Asquith described it as being a morning of brilliant sun sparkling on frost, with air like crystal. Before the main review Clemmie Churchill and Violet (later to become Lady Violet Bonham-Carter) cantered down the lines of men, drawn up in their battalions on the sweeping downland at a place called Three Mile Point, near the grounds of the present Blandford Camp. Then Winston Churchill and the Admiralty Board inspected the division.[23]

At 11.30am the King made his inspection, which was unusually detailed. He asked the 2nd Brigade three questions about marching, digging and rifles. The RND then marched passed the saluting base in columns of companies.[24] The Hood was preceded by its own silver band, and when Quilter roared 'Eyes right!' all their faces turned. Violet Asquith described Churchill as glowing with pride in his troops. The division returned past His Majesty again in double columns of fours, then gave the King three cheers and the bands played the national anthem.[25]

The following day was spent in kit inspection, and distributing ammunition and iron rations. Training was now complete, and the Rev Henry Foster wrote:

Our last day in camp was 27 February and in the afternoon of that day a large number of relations and friends assembled on the parade ground to bid us 'God speed'. The bands were playing national airs, the most popular being *For Auld Lang Syne*. How little did we realize then that many fathers and mothers were saying goodbye to their brave young sons for the last time. And yet we tried to 'keep smiling', and to look on the bright side, but it was difficult.[26]

At 7.15pm on 28 February the division (apart from the re-formed and untrained Collingwood, Benbow and Hawke Battalions) marched out of camp in pith helmets, with the rain pouring down. They marched 10 miles to Skillingstone railway station, now a private residence as the line has long since closed.[27] Foster continued:

Here was a long tedious wait, but our comfort had not been forgotten. Lady Baker, who lived close to Blandford, and who had on many occasions showed a kindly interest in the men's welfare, had arranged for a number of ladies to run a canteen in the vicinity of the station. Here a plentiful supply of hot coffee proved to be a Godsend to us all.

The only excitement was provided by some new mules, who lived up to their reputation for being the most frisky and unmanageable of all animals. I do not think any of us envied the transport officer or his assistants, who experienced the greatest difficulty in getting their charges safely deposited in the special train.

Our train left at 3.30am on Sunday 28 February, and we took off our equipment and boots and had a good sleep in the carriage. It was eight o'clock when we awoke in the morning, to find ourselves at Avonmouth Docks, Bristol.[28]

The adventure had just begun.

Part Two

THE HOOD AT GALLIPOLI

1. Royal Naval Division Recruiting Poster (*IWM*).

2. Able Seaman George Noble of the Hood Battalion. Note the tally of the newly-formed Royal Naval Division. These were worn in the early days prior to those of the individual battalions. (*Mrs L. Garrett*).

3. Albert John Walls. Showing the new khaki uniform and Hood tally (*Arthur J. Walls*).

4. Major-General Sir Archibald Paris, Commanding Officer of the Royal Naval Division (*IWM*).

5. Commanding Officer of the second R.N. Brigade, Commodore Oliver Backhouse.

CHAPTER FIVE

The Build-Up to Gallipoli

What kind of place was this peninsula set between the Aegean Sea and the Dardanelles, at the frontier of Europe and Asia? Nobody in England appeared to know! Plans, maps and general knowledge were woefully lacking. A spit of land some 53 miles long, with the town of Bulair at the northern end, it narrows south of Bulair to only three miles across. Near here were the fortified lines of Bulair, built by the English and French during the Crimean War. Moving south the land mass broadens out to about 12 miles at its widest point, narrowing again to less than five miles and extending downwards to the tip of the peninsula at Cape Helles. Roads were very poor, and the population merely eked out an existence by farming a few olive groves, vineyards and orchards, although very little land was under cultivation.[1]

The political situation in the Dardanelles was that Turkey, after much to-ing and fro-ing, had decided to side with Germany. Skilful diplomatic methods by a German military mission had paid dividends, and Britain was clearly outmanoeuvred. Russia, then hard-pressed in the Caucasus, asked for British assistance; in response, Winston Churchill and a few others planned a campaign to force the Dardanelles, secure a supply route to Russia, and create a second front in the soft underbelly of Germany and Austria-Hungary. Seeing the detailed plans, a Russian Grand Duke commented on 25 January, 1915, that the campaign had the Russian's entire goodwill, but they themselves could not help, as they were at present fully committed.

One of the ironies of the Gallipoli adventure is that by the middle of March the Russians had improved matters in the Caucasus and victory in the Dardanelles was not so pressing. The die had not then been cast, and the British could have withdrawn without harm or loss of face; but events had already gained their own momentum.

The original plan was that the Dardanelles would be forced by a naval operation only, using the fleet's older, more expendable ships.

On 19 February, 1915, naval attacks commenced against defensive Turkish forts and artillery: the ships were to overcome these in stages, until their final push through the narrows and out into the Sea of Marmara. This plan failed on 18 March, when an unknown and unsuspected line of mines sank three battleships. The navy was then withdrawn until the army had secured the heights above the ancient waterway, so enabling Turkish defensive positions to be dominated and allowing the fleet passage. A vital land feature was the hill of Achi Baba, possession of which would be a vital stage to enable direct naval fire to be controlled and directed, with some accuracy, upon the forts of the narrows. Heavy guns and howitzers, including the new 15 inch, could then be landed and brought into action.

On 16 February the British War Council met and made a number of decisions, including despatching the army's 29th Division from England to Lemnos rather than sending it to France. The politics and demands of both Western and Eastern Fronts thus came into conflict, and as early as the following day pressure was applied to Lord Kitchener to cancel the plan and send the division to France. Kitchener changed his mind regarding the 29th Division and postponed its departure, but other troops and stores were to continue. As a result the transports that were to carry the 29th were cancelled, without reference to the First Lord, and the fleet of 22 vessels assembled for the purpose was dispersed to other duties.

Upon finding that his orders for transports had been countermanded, Churchill overrode the instructions and renewed negotiations. He was too late to stop the fleet dispersal, however, and the earliest date that the transports could be reassembled was 16 March. By 10 March Lord Kitchener had swung back to the view that the 29th Division could be spared for the Eastern Front after all,[2] but the delay in resolve was to have a dramatic effect on the outcome of the campaign, as it gave the Turks time to prepare their defences.

Such lack of resolution and half-hearted support became a hallmark of the campaign: men, ammunition and shells were sent out on a somewhat piecemeal basis, while western and eastern policies constantly pulled in different directions. This lesser action was never wholeheartedly supported by many of the prime movers of policy. It is understandable that the first and main call on resources had to be France, but if Gallipoli was worth doing it was worth doing well, not grudgingly in a cheese-paring manner.

On 12 March Lord Kitchener told Sir Ian Hamilton that he was to command the Eastern Mediterranean Expeditionary Force. Aged 57 and a distinguished soldier, Hamilton had seen active service in the Boer War, later becoming chief of staff there. In 1904–5 he was on the staff in the Japanese War; then from 1905 to 1908 he was commander-in-chief in the eastern Mediterranean and inspector-general of overseas forces.[3]

Hamilton was despatched with very little information. In fact his aides had to visit second-hand book shops to obtain maps of the peninsula. Kitchener's instructions were clear on one point, however: nothing must be risked until the 29th Division had caught up and was available for the offensive, as this was to be the only regular division used in the campaign.

On 4 March the RND's Plymouth Battalion of marines had taken part in operations at Kum Kale on the Asian side of the Dardanelles, and also at Sedd-el-Bahr on the peninsula itself. At each location half a company landed to destroy enemy guns. On the Asian side there was some determined opposition and the British sustained about 40 casualties, mainly from heavy machine guns situated in windmills commanding the beach areas. The navy had to start a bombardment to cover the evacuation. On the peninsula there was little opposition, though, and the marines advanced some way inland, suffering very few casualties.

Sparrow and Ross's book *On Four Fronts with the Royal Naval Division* states:

> It is not generally known that even these were not the first landings in the Dardanelles. As early as February parties of Royal Marines, disembarked from ships, had marched through Krithia and reached Achi Baba with little or no opposition, while other detachments had gone ashore at Kum Kale in a like peaceful manner. In view of subsequent events, it seems strange that the ground could not have been permanently occupied then, instead of waiting until 25 April, by which time the Turks, now fully alive to our designs, had strongly fortified the positions.[4]

General Birdwood, who commanded the Australian and New Zealand forces, had been in the general area of the peninsula since early March and was keen to land before the Turkish defences gathered greater strength. Waiting for the 29th Division was equally unappealing to Sir Ian Hamilton, who was also eager to start:

> We might sup tomorrow night on Achi Baba. With luck we really might. Had I been here for 10 days instead of five, and had I had any time to draft out any sort of scheme, I might have had a dart.[5]

But orders were orders, and as the 29th Division journeyed slowly eastward the balance gradually tipped in favour of the defence. Time and tide waits for no man, but the expeditionary force had to wait for the 29th. When finally fully assembled, the Mediterranean Expeditionary Force comprised regular troops of the 29th Division; the Australian and New Zealand Corps; the Royal Naval Division; and a division of the French *Corps Expéditionnaire de l'Orient* (Senegalese and French territorial troops).

The Turks were meanwhile planning their defence. On 26 March a German officer, General Liman von Sa/nders, took over the role of commander-in-chief of the Dardanelles area and immediately set about improving Turkish defensive capabilities. Rather than a thin overall distribution of troops, he divided his forces into three fighting units. The 9th and 19th Divisions were to cover the southern tip of the peninsula; the 5th and 17th Divisions would remain near Bulair in the north; the 3rd and 11th Divisions would cover the Asian side of the Dardanelles. These units were to remain together as a group, leaving only a weak coastal defence. Flexibility and mobility were the watchwords: von Sanders could not cover all landing sites and eventualities, but rapid mobile response was tactically sound.

Von Sanders issued instructions that the Turks should be fit and ready to move at a moment's notice, so drill and route marches were the order of the day. Road construction began and barges were grouped for rapid transfer of troops from one side to another. Much of this work was done at night, invisible to inquisitive aeroplanes.[6]

So both sides made their plans and preparations – and both fretted that time was against them.

CHAPTER SIX

The Voyage

The Hood Battalion arrived at Avonmouth at 8am on 28 February to find the *Grantully Castle*, a twin-screw steamer of 7,612 tons, awaiting them. She had been built by Barclay, Curle and Company at Glasgow in 1910 for the Union Castle Line, under the supervision of Sir Donald Currie,[1] and requisitioned with 12 others to transport RND battalions as part of the Mediterranean Expeditionary Force. The RND troops numbered about 8,000 officers and men in total, so one ship was used for a naval air force unit, another for mule transport, and four for stores. The ships were to leave on 27 and 28 February, so stores were loaded at speed and the troops embarked rapidly, but extra time spent in packing the holds tidily with everything in its correct place would have saved considerable delay later.[2]

Once aboard, cabins were allocated to the officers, and both they and the men busied themselves organizing the baggage. On deck they found large piles of roped-down equipment and a considerable number of mules, plus 15 horses, nine bicycles, four two-wheeled vehicles, 32 four-wheeled vehicles, two water-carts and four travelling kitchens.[3] Orders were given for the men to stay on board and sentries were placed at the head of the gangway to ensure none went ashore. Later part of the Anson Battalion came aboard, as did members of 2nd Brigade HQ; with the new arrivals, conditions turned from reasonable to cramped.[4]

The ship sailed the same day, but as the mooring lines were cast, less than a dozen people were on the quayside to wave goodbye. One there was Violet Asquith, who had come down to see her brother off.

Sunday 28 February. I started at 7.30 for Avonmouth, driving through lovely sleepy Thomas Hardy country, stone villages over-grown with moss and lichen, narrow lanes with high, wild tangled hedges. Bristol by midday. Drove through and out the other side by the Severn winding between steep banks. Then a little town began, built round the docks. Showed my pass, a great door opened and let me through and I saw huge watery pens in which great ships were moored and alongside on the quays a confusion of soldiers' trunks, mules, packing-cases and gangways. I made my way past many ships before I reached the *Grantully Castle*. I watched and waited for a Hood cap and then asked for Oc. He was on board shaving . . . Denis Browne came and took charge of me and said he would go for Oc. Rupert appeared. He had 'failli', had to stay on board but had just managed to exchange his watch with Kelly and was free till four.

Oc joined us and we went off to an hotel recommended by Edwin Montagu, surrounded by sham rockeries. It was not quite all our fancy had pictured but not too bad for all that. They seemed quite happy about their food, which was the main thing. There was a long discussion about what their last drink should be and Burgundy was finally decided on. After luncheon Rupert's chief desire was, as usual, to get as warm as possible and we coiled ourselves almost in the fireplace till it was time to go and get a prescription made up for Patrick's throat – which was even more than usually poisoned that day. Being Sunday the chemist had to be knocked up with some difficulty. Rupert and I sat talking outside in the car while we waited and he showed me a lovely little new poem beginning 'When colour is gone home into the eyes'. He said in his usual, intensely quiet, modest-eyed way, 'I think the first line perfectly divine'.

We went back to the ship, dear Charles Lister passing us on the way and looking as mad as 20 hatters and as gay. Quilter in a taxi we easily outstripped. On arrival at the quay we found to our dismay that the ship had moved and was lying in the mouth of the harbour! We felt safe, however, with the CO behind us. I saw and spoke to him for a moment, also George Peel, then I went on board the transport with them. It was a not-bad Union Castle boat and they were only two in a cabin. I went in to see poor Patrick, who was lying in his bunk among cough mixtures and bandages looking as green as grass and very septic. I lingered on with Oc and Rupert with a terrible pre-operation feeling. The suspended knife seemed just above us all. Then the dull muffled siren booms began, charged with finality, and we knew that it was falling. Rupert walked with me along the narrow crowded decks, down the plank stairs. I said goodbye to him. I saw in his eyes that he felt sure we should never see each other again.

Oc took me over the gangway and we talked for a few moments feverishly. 'I shall come back,' he said. 'I may be wounded but I shall come back.' Another imperious hoot and he had to hurry back. The gangway was raised and the ship moved slowly out, the Hood trumpeters playing a salute on their silver trumpets as it passed the mouth of the harbour. The decks were densely crowded with young, splendid figures, happy, resolute and confident – and the thought of the Athenian expedition against Syracuse flashed irresistibly through my mind.[5]

The passengers were in the grip of excitement as to what lay ahead. This was a real crusade, a chance to make their mark that comes seldom to a man or generation. Not for them the frustration of France and static trench warfare bogged down in mud: they were going to fight the Turks. They felt that they were part of something larger than life. They were the chosen ones. As the ship moved away from the coast all eyes must have looked their last on England, wondering if and when they would return. The small fleet, escorted by five destroyers, cleared the Bristol Channel as the sun was setting, one of those glorious sunsets rarely seen but long remembered. The escorts bore away, and the journey had begun.[6]

A new experience for many was the feel of a moving ship beneath their feet, the wind and smell of the sea, with the sound of seagulls flying in their wake. The ship was to be their home for many weeks, and the young northern miners must have found it simultaneously both thrilling and threatening, but the routine of shipboard life soon became normal.

The men received a normal main meal of meat and potatoes, but as Joseph Murray, a seaman of the Hood, remembers:

The food was rotten, the tea was weak and we were only given one slice of bread with the tea for breakfast. But there was porridge. The problem was that the majority of the men took their plates down below, descending stairs without the benefit of a handrail. The resulting slopped porridge made the floor extremely slippery and hard to remain safely on both legs. On the deck there was a small cabin used as a canteen where during the day you could get biscuits, three of them and a portion of cheese for three pence.

Officers fared somewhat better: their food was good, and entirely different from that given to the men. Joseph Murray was Asquith's runner and says Asquith often sent him to Bernard Freyberg and Rupert Brooke's cabin with the request, 'With Mr Asquith's compliments and would they join him for supper,' or perhaps for tea.[7] The group of frighteningly brilliant young officers (Brooke, Asquith, Shaw-Stewart, Browne, Kelly, Dodge and later Lister) was renowned throughout the ship, and where they dined became known as the 'Latin Table'. Their gatherings were famous for their high spirits, wit and *joie de vivre*. Bernard Freyberg joined them. Although from a completely different background, he had the advantages of character and seniority in the

53

Hood. He was accepted and entered into a different world, from which time he never looked back.[8]

Sleeping arrangements for the men were very cramped: hammocks were provided, but it got so hot below decks that many took blankets and slept on deck. They had to get up early, though, as each morning the crew cleaned the decks with a hose and thought it a huge joke if they got the sleepers wet. Training continued, with company parades and semaphore instruction, but the groups found conditions very restricting and the sound of the neighbouring instructor's voice could be very off-putting.[9]

Recovering from his throat infection, Lieutenant Patrick Shaw-Stewart wrote:

> Also there is the constant difficulty of persuading the stokers to be (a) vaccinated; (b) inoculated. There was one party who absolutely refused, and as we can't compel, we had just peacefully to picket them, and give them statistics of the army in France, and reminiscences of South Africa. The only drawback was that I, the Coy. 2nd in Command, the Coy. Commander, the Commandant, and the Commodore all gave widely different statistics, mine being the most temperate and least effective.[10]

Recreation for the men consisted of cards, crown and anchor, and housey-housey. The latter was against regulations; if they noticed this evil officers tended to turn a blind eye, but on occasions the petty officers caught a group of men and hauled them away on a charge.[11] The lower deck had a melodeon (a kind of American reed organ like an accordion); the officers had a piano; and the musician Denis Browne, helped by Cleg Kelly as chorus-master, often attempted to induce grumbling stokers to sing folk songs.[12]

The ship steered west of the Scilly Isles to avoid submarines, and took a course 50 miles to the west of the usual navigational route. Entering the Mediterranean, they hugged the coastline of North Africa. In the distance could be seen dazzling buildings of white stone; and, further away still, mountains with snow-clad peaks. The ship passed the little island of Galite and, leaving Tunis behind, headed straight for Malta.[13]

The 2nd Brigade chaplain, Henry Foster, remembered this part of the voyage:

> In the evening, when all was still, there was one officer who was often to be seen pacing the deck alone. No-one ever thought of disturbing him, as we knew by instinct that he wished to be alone. It was Rupert Brooke. He gloried in those quiet nights in the Mediterranean, and remained drinking in the beauty long after

the others had turned in. Some of the unthinking ones, perhaps, scarcely understood this love of solitude, but they who knew the poet best could understand. 'It was so like him,' his mother wrote to me. 'However much he liked his companions, he always wanted some time to commune with his own soul.'[14]

They finally put into Valletta, Malta, on 8 March at about 3.30pm. It was a day of glorious sunshine, and they anchored off a fish quay. Some officers were given shore leave; the men were refused, greatly to their disgust. Brooke and Shaw-Stewart went ashore to the Union Club, where they met Charles Lister. Lister had been with Shaw-Stewart at Eton and Balliol, and was on the divisional staff on the strength of his knowledge of Turkish. At table he was talked into applying for a transfer to the Hood, after which they all went to enjoy *Tosca* at the opera house.[15]

The *Grantully Castle* weighed anchor at 11.30am the next day, but as they were leaving harbour a French ship slid in. Denis Browne hurriedly called his band out on deck, and they played the *Marseillaise*: as the British ship moved away into open water, the French could be heard cheering.[16]

On the evening of 11 March[17] the island of Lemnos was sighted, and they slipped into the harbour of Mudros Bay past the battleships *Queen Elizabeth*, *Agamemnon* and *Lord Nelson*. The harbour was a grand sight, with a great many ships riding at anchor, and the *Grantully Castle* found a position near to the battleships *Triumph* and *Swiftsure*. The following morning the old Russian cruiser *Askold* arrived with its five slim funnels. She became known to the British as 'the packet of Woodbines' or 'Willy Woodbine'. For a week the crew could go ashore and lie on the beach, interspersed with numerous naval landing exercises, which consisted of repeatedly rowing boats between the ship and shore.[18]

On 17 March the division was ordered to sail into Turkish waters the following day. All ranks were told that this was the big event, and that they were to land. Brooke wrote about the incident:

> The other day we – some of us – were told that we sailed next day to make a landing. A few thousand of us. Off we stole that night through the phosphorescent Aegean, scribbling farewell letters and snatching periods of dream-broken, excited sleep. At four we rose, buckled on our panoply, hung ourselves with glasses, compasses, periscopes, revolvers, food and the rest, and had a stealthy large breakfast. That was a mistake. It is ruinous to load up one's belly four or five hours before it expects it: it throws the machinery out of gear for a week. I felt extremely ill the rest of that day.
>
> We paraded in silence, under paling stars, along the sides of the

ship. The darkness on the sea was full of scattered flashing lights, hinting at our fellow-transports and the rest. Slowly the day became wan and green and the sea opal. Everyone's face looked drawn and ghastly. If we landed, my company was to be the first to land . . . . We made out that we were only a mile or two from a dim shore. I was seized with an agony of remorse that I hadn't taught my platoon a thousand things more energetically and competently. The light grew. The shore looked to be crammed with fate, and most ominously silent. One man thought he saw a camel through his glasses . . . . There were some hours of silence.

About seven someone said, 'We're going home.' We dismissed the stokers, who said, quietly, 'When's the next battle?' and disempanoplied, and had another breakfast.[19]

Nobody knew the reason for this demonstration, but it was in fact a planned feint to divert the attention of the Turks from what should have been the closing stages of the great naval attack to force the Dardanelles. Surprise mines sank three battleships and put paid to the matter, however, and the navy did not try again. The fleet sailed back to Lemnos, where rumours grew that the ship's freight was in need of reorganization. The general view was that if that was the case, it was a jolly good thing that they hadn't landed.[20]

On 24 March the anchor was once again weighed, and they made for Egypt and Port Said, disembarking on 28 March. The Hood, with the rest of the division, pitched their tents outside the dock area on a piece of dirty-looking ground about three minutes' walk from the Arab quarter of the town. Black sand was the chief hardship: it was on the move for most of the time, filling up the lines in their faces. They were near the salt lagoons of the delta and the Suez Canal: the officers and men would often swim in the canal, and have target practice nearby.[21]

Seaman Joseph Murray remembers:

The Arab quarter was out of bounds, but of course we went there. The Naval Division seemed to get on particularly well with the Australians. The Anzacs seemed to like the RND men with their khaki sailors' hats, a friendship seemed to grow up, and this remained throughout the campaign.[22]

At this time Lieutenant Charles Lister joined the Hood Battalion, after pulling as many strings to get away from HQ as most people pulled to get into it. He took over a platoon in Lieutenant-Commander Bernard Freyberg's company, and reports relate that all was very well at the camp. Lister wrote:

Everything you get in the town is excellent and we eat and drink like fighting cocks. We get delicious prawns for practically nothing . . . I am in a very good battalion, the Hood. It is great fun having a small executive command as I have.

He also wrote to his father, Lord Ribblesdale:

I have got a platoon and bellow out orders which I understand though darkly but which are carried out punctiliously by my men, who are mostly old hands, having been stokers.

Later Shaw-Stewart stated:

I missed the spectacle of Charles drilling stokers on Yeomanry lines – an entrancing one, I have been told. There is one story of how he marched a body of men on to the parade ground, before the eyes of the brigade, and in his resonant tone ordered them to halt in words suited to the evolutions of quadrupeds.[23]

Forty-eight hours' leave was given to officers in batches of three, and the first group picked for this short holiday were Rupert Brooke, Patrick Shaw-Stewart and Arthur Asquith. They caught the train to Cairo and stayed at Shepheard's Hotel. On 30 March they called on Lord and Lady Howard de Walden and Aubrey and Mary Herbert. This happy party motored to the Pyramids, viewed the Sphinx, and rode on camels. The heat was not excessive, but all three officers wore their pith helmets.[24] The next morning was spent in the bazaar. In the afternoon Brooke, having caught the flavour of Egypt, read Asquith a passage from *Antony and Cleopatra* describing her progress down the river.[25]

On 31 March there was a route march, in which Brooke did not take part as he was busy training his platoon in field firing exercises near the sea. He was seen running to and fro judging the marksmanship until sunset; it had been very hot, but Brooke had worn his helmet. Shaw-Stewart was taken ill with a touch of the sun, however.[26]

On 2 April the division was reviewed in the late afternoon by the commander-in-chief, Sir Ian Hamilton. The day was grillingly hot, the troops paraded early, and as a result had a long wait. Whilst drawn up for inspection, the only incident of note to relieve the boredom was that one officer's horse fell asleep and deposited his somewhat drowsy rider head first into the sand. It was fortunate that the embarrassed rider and his enraged CO had sorted matters out before the inspecting officer arrived.[27]

Brooke was not well and did not take part in the parade, as he had been sick twice during the night, had a bad headache, and was altogether out of sorts. He stayed on his camp bed, set up outside his tent under the shelter of a green canvas awning. The inspection went well, though, and the division was complimented on its appearance. The Hood Battalion band played and entertained.[28] Lister wrote:

> We marched passed with all the swagger of the rawest recruit, very self-conscious. My company has fine material, nearly all naval reserve men, hard nuts. I feel sort of a baby among them. There are many over 35. The sun was brilliant, and the bayonets flashed like magnesium when it is burnt. The men wear shorts now and step along very gaily.[29]

Joseph Murray recalls:

> We were told to cut our trousers off at the knees. We didn't have any scissors, so we had to use the jack-knife. Oh, dear me! Some of them had only bits of pants left when they had finished. It was funny. We got sunburn. I thought I was clever: I had a jar of vaseline and I rubbed it into my legs. I didn't know that the sun was so hot, and I nearly boiled. I could hardly walk.[30]

After the inspection Sir Ian Hamilton sat on the edge of Rupert Brooke's bed (it was rumoured that they talked about poetry) and offered him an appointment on the HQ staff aboard the *Queen Elizabeth*. Brooke would not hear of the transfer. He wanted to see matters through with his men. Sir Ian later spoke to Colonel Quilter, saying, 'Mind you take care of him. His loss would be a national loss.'[31] Brooke observed of his meeting with the general:

> He looked very worn and white-haired. I thought him a little fearful – not fearful, but less than cocksure about the job.[32]

Later Brooke began to sweat and his head became far worse, so he got up and obtained a cab to room 17 of the Casino Palace Hotel, where his colleague Patrick Shaw-Stewart was recovering from sunstroke. He took the bed opposite, and it was found that he had a temperature of 103°. A civilian doctor was called, who thought Brooke should be admitted to hospital. By the next morning he appeared to have improved, however, and the responsibility was passed over to the regimental MO. A diet of arrowroot, with nothing to eat or drink until this could be supplemented by some fish, was the prescribed cure, as both Brooke and Shaw-Stewart were suffering from an attack of dysentery.[33]

On 3 April the Reverend Henry Foster paid the sick a visit:

A large mosquito net of white muslin hung over his bed, and when I went into the room he pulled this to one side. Never had his face looked more beautiful than now. His eyes flashed with a brightness that was unearthly, and as he talked one read in his countenance that dazzling quality of mind which betrays itself so often in his poems.[34]

During this period Brooke wrote a ballad for Denis Browne, which he could set to music, showing that his mind was still on earthly matters:

> My first was in the night at one;
> At half past five, I had to run.
> At 8.15 I fairly flew;
> At noon a swift compulsion grew.
> I ran a dead-heat all the way;
> I lost by yards at ten to two.
> This is the seventh time today.
>
> Prince, did the brandy fail you too?
> You dreamt the arrowroot would stay?
> My opium fairly galloped through,
> This is the seventh time today.[35]

On the second day Brooke was worried by a small sore that suddenly developed on the left side of his upper lip. It throbbed and swelled for two days, then improved. It was not thought a serious matter by the MO, but subsequent events were to prove him wrong: Brooke's sunstroke and dysentery were acting as a blind for a more dangerous condition, of which the swelling was an early warning.

On 8 April Shaw-Stewart was much better, but Brooke was still thin, unsteady on his feet, and drawn in the face. Colonel Quilter visited the patient, suggesting that he should go to a military hospital, but Brooke was adamant that he would stay with the battalion.[36] He had written to Lascelles Abercrombie on 6 April:

I shall be all right in time for the fighting, I hope and believe . . . I know now . . . more certainly every day . . . what a campaign is. I had a suspicion from Antwerp. It is continual crossing from one place to another, and back, over dream-like seas: anchoring, or halting, in the oddest places, for nobody knows or quite cares how long; drifting on, at last, to some other, equally unexpected, equally out of the way, equally odd spot; for all the world like a bottle in some corner of the bay at a seaside resort. Somewhere, sometimes, there is fighting. Not for us. In the end, no doubt, our apparently aimless course will drift us through, or anchor us in, a blaze of war, quite suddenly; and as suddenly swirl us out again. Meanwhile . . . the laziest loitering lotus-day I idled away as a wanderer in the South Seas was a bustle of decision and purpose compared to a campaign.

One just hasn't, though, the time and detachment to write, I find. But I've been collecting a few words, detaching lines from the ambient air, collaring one or two golden phrases that a certain wind blows from Olympus, across these purple seas. In time, if I'm spared, they'll bloom into a sort of threnody.'37

About this time Brooke also despatched a number of letters to friends clearing up his affairs. This wind from Olympus, and his own premonition of early death, is shown in a short poem written early in April, 1915:

THE DANCE – A SONG

As the Wind, and as the Wind,
    In a corner of the way,
Goes stepping, stands twirling,
Invisibly, comes whirling,
Bows before, and skips behind,
    In a grave, an endless play—

So my Heart, and so my Heart,
    Following where your feet have gone,
Stirs dust of old dreams there;
He turns a toe; he gleams there,
Treading you a dance apart.
    But you see not. You pass on.38

On 10 April the *Grantully Castle* put to sea, with Brooke confined to his bed on sick leave. The Anson Battalion was no longer with them, having been ordered to Alexandria on 5 April, and shipboard conditions were greatly improved as a result. Major-General Paris wrote on the same day that during their stay at Port Said the division had behaved like lambs. There had been no crime and very little disease, and the inhabitants were loud in their praise. It was an unusual experience for him.39

But the men were happy to get underway again, as they were getting restless and had started to grouse. It had been necessary to stop the practice of sleeping out, as there was a danger that they could have been buried alive by drifting sand. Charles Lister also remembers seeing two fine specimens of fat, yellow locusts flitting in and out of his tent.[40]

The ship steamed very slowly, at about four knots, as it was towing a lighter to be used for disembarking troops of the 29th Division. Near the island of Kos the lighter broke loose in very rough weather, and a day was spent trying to locate it. Brooke stayed in his cabin for a number of days, but the general opinion was that he was improving. Denis Browne thought Brooke was noticeably thinner, although otherwise quite as usual and perfectly happy.[41]

On 14 April the ship arrived once more at Lemnos, only to find the anchorage of Mudros Bay was full. The RND transports were instructed to make for the harbour of Trebuki Bay, at the southern end of the island of Skyros. As the journey continued the men passed their time with semaphore practice, machine-gun drill and Swedish exercises. The battalion also held a fancy dress ball: Cleg Kelly and Denis Browne took it in turns to play the piano, and the men came up from below in a variety of costumes, from Zulus to Queen Elizabeth. They used all sorts of items to improvise their dress, such as the curtains from Browne's cabin and Huntley and Palmer's biscuit tins. A prize was presented for the best costume, in the form of a huge medal of an iron cross.[42]

Colonel Quilter addressed the battalion, saying, 'We intend to land at the toe of the peninsula or the lines of Bulair. We will give the Turks hell!'[43] Contemporary divisional notes on the character of the Turks stated that they did not like night attacks because they hated the dark, and invariably slept with a night-light. This led to endless fun and was parodied by Lister.[44]

On the evening of 17 April, with the *Franconia* (divisional HQ) leading the way, the fleet anchored in Trebuki Bay. Three hundred stokers (150 each from the Hood and Howe Battalions) were immediately sent back to Lemnos,[45] under the command of Hood Lieutenants Dodge, Gamage and Trimmer, to assist on board tugs and trawlers during the disembarkation of the main landing force.[46]

Brooke stayed on deck on 18 April, but many officers and men went ashore. A smell of flowering sage and thyme drifted across from the land, and the water of the harbour was so clear that one could peer fathoms deep to the seabed of different coloured marble. As evening drew in Lister and Shaw-Stewart were seen approaching in a boat, laden with cheese and a flapping tortoise. Next day exercises began, and Brooke went ashore. The hills shook with the sounds of gunfire as the stokers potted snakes. This was soon stopped by the officers, but, not discouraged, the men began arranging tortoise races.[47]

In April, 1915, Brooke wrote a poem about their idyllic voyage towards Gallipoli:

FRAGMENT

I strayed about the deck, an hour, to-night
Under a cloudy moonless sky; and peeped
In at the windows, watched my friends at table,
Or playing cards, or standing in the doorway,
Or coming out into the darkness. Still
No-one could see me.

                                    I would have thought of them
– Heedless, within a week of battle – in pity,
Pride in their strength and in the weight and firmness
And link'd beauty of bodies, and pity that
This gay machine of splendour 'ld soon be broken,
Thought little of, pashed, scattered . . .

                                    Only, always,
I could but see them – against the lamplight – pass
Like coloured shadows, thinner than filmy glass,
Slight bubbles, fainter than the wave's faint light,
That broke to phosphorous out in the night,
Perishing things and strange ghosts – soon to die
To other ghosts – this one, or that, or I.[48]

At dawn on Tuesday, 20 April the men were called to begin a divisional
field day. Brooke had been on watch for four hours the previous night,
and was tired at the start of the exercise. They were operating in a
dried-up river bed in a valley between the mountains of Pephko and
Komaro, overlooked by Mount Knokilas, the highest point on the
island. The afternoon was not excessively hot, but the valley was full
of sunlight; the stony ground made the going difficult, and reflected
the heat fiercely. About one mile up the valley, close to 2nd Brigade's
rendezvous point, was a small olive grove of about a dozen trees,
discovered by Browne, Shaw-Stewart, Lister and Brooke during a rest
break. All enjoyed the shade; Brooke commented to the others on the
strange peace and beauty of the spot.[49]

The exercise finished at 4pm, and Freyberg, Lister and Brooke
walked to the beach together.[50] It was suggested that they should
swim the mile back to the ship, but Brooke did not feel up to it, so
he followed in a fishing boat while the others took to the water. That
evening at dinner he seldom spoke; at 10pm he went to bed, saying that
his lip was swelling again, long before the rest of the party broke up.

Next morning Oc Asquith visited Brooke: his left upper lip was very
swollen, and he had pains in his head and back. Brooke thought he was

suffering from exhaustion after the field exercise of the preceding day. Then Denis Browne looked in on him, taking a cutting from *The Times* about a sermon of Dean Inge's, in which the last of his sonnets was quoted. Brooke told Browne that he was feeling very unwell, and that he was sorry Inge did not think his quote as good as Isaiah. The MO, William McCracken, found Brooke had a temperature of 101° and ordered a hot poultice for the swelling on his upper lip, but was not too greatly concerned about his patient's condition.

Shaw-Stewart went to see him at noon, to find an orderly still applying hot compresses. Brooke said that he felt damnably ill. When Shaw-Stewart visited him again later he felt somewhat better, so Shaw-Stewart outlined to him the general idea of a forthcoming feint attack which Quilter had described that afternoon in an address to the officers. Shaw-Stewart said Brooke needn't bother to leave the cabin for the attack, as he could alarm the enemy equally well by merely looking frightful through the porthole.

Browne also visited him again, although not thinking Brooke was seriously ill, but found him very drowsy, saying that he felt rotten and not to turn the light on. Browne called McCracken, who put his mind at rest: another officer of the Hood, Egerton, had recently had the same type of swelling on his lip, which had responded to treatment once poultices had been given time to work. However, that night Brooke's temperature reached 103°. McCracken became worried, thinking that if pneumonia developed his patient was in no condition to overcome the complication.[51]

The next day, 22 April, Brooke was in and out of a coma, and had pain in his chest and back. At 11am McCracken sent a wireless message requesting a second opinion; as a result, the divisional staff's second medical officer, Captain Casement, arrived, along with the fleet surgeon, Caskell, and the brigade medical officer, Doctor Schlesinger of Guy's Hospital. Brooke's sore was fomented and looked angry and swollen, and his temperature was now back to 101°. Opinions differed over the most suitable treatment, but there was general agreement that the swollen lip was, in the first instance, the result of a mosquito bite which had become infected. The original treatment for sunstroke had kept the illness dormant until he became run down and his resistance to infection was low. An incision was made in the swelling, and a swab taken for further investigation. Bacteriological examination of the pus by Doctor Henry Goodale, a junior medical officer on board the *Grantully Castle*, showed the presence of pneumonococci in large numbers. The patient's condition became rapidly worse: by 3pm his pulse was 190, his temperature 104°, and there was a large, spreading swelling across one whole side of his neck and face.

Very concerned, Schlesinger reported the details to his ADS, and they agreed that Brooke should be transferred to a hospital ship at the earliest opportunity.[52] McCracken noted that the only one in the vicinity was French:[53] the *Duguay Trouin*, built in 1878 and used as a naval school at Brest, then converted to its hospital function at the beginning of the war. Arrangements were quickly made, and at 4.30pm Brooke was transported across in a picket boat. When told of this, he took some persuading that it was the best plan. Denis Browne lifted Brooke out into the awaiting pinnace and Brooke appeared to recognize him, saying one word: 'Hallo'.[54]

There were no other patients on the hospital ship at the time, but a full complement of 12 surgeons. Brooke was given two adjacent cabins, standing by themselves on the upper sun deck, and was put in one of these. It was beautifully cool and airy. He received, in Denis Browne's words, every care and loving attention that the French could give him. He was even given an English-speaking nurse.[55]

General Sir Ian Hamilton was now very concerned, as can be seen from the letter he wrote to Edward Marsh on 23 April, 1915:

> This moment at 12.30pm, just as the mail is going, I have got a most alarming wireless from Naval Division telling me, for the first time, Rupert Brooke was ill and dangerously ill. The wording of the message terrifies me. Alas, what a misfortune! I have kept his ADCship open for him all the time and as soon as the Dardanelles affair was over he was, supposing us both alive, to have come on to my staff. But he was bound, he said, to see this first fight through with his own fellows. Whether it would have made any difference I can't say, but at least I could have told you something which I can't now. I have his last poems on my table: you know how deep was my admiration for his intellect, an admiration which lost nothing as so many admirations do by contact with his personality and appearance— Ah well – I pray fervently he may yet pull through.[56]

Word was now getting around that Brooke was in a serious condition:

Telegram from Major John Churchill to First Lord.
Rupert Brooke now on board French hospital ship *Duguay Trouin* has septicaemia. Condition very grave. Please inform parents and telegraph instructions if anything special.
Sent 1am 23/4/15. Received 5.40am Admiralty.[57]

On the morning of 23 April the surgeons found it necessary to give Brooke stimulants. They operated under anaesthetic to cauterize the infected area, and to establish a focal abscess in the thigh to try and draw off the bacteria concentrated in his neck. Asquith and Browne took it in turns to stay at his bedside. Brooke seemed once to regain consciousness, but nothing could be understood when he tried to speak. By 2pm his temperature was 106°; Chaplain Failes of the 1st Brigade was called and prayed at his bedside. At 4.46pm, when Browne was at the bedside, with the sun shining all round his cabin and the cool sea breeze blowing through the door and shaded windows, Brooke died, feeling no pain, according to the doctors. He was just 27 years old.[58]

Medical certificate number 24 gave the cause of death as *oedème malin et septicocomia foudroyante* (malignant oedema and rapid septicocomia)[59]. But there was now much to be done, as the *Grantully Castle* had received orders to sail for Gallipoli at 6am the next morning. Denis Browne recalled:

> We felt that he would hate to be buried at sea; he actually said in chance talk, some time ago, that he would like to be buried on a Greek island. A decision was therefore made to bury him on Skyros.[60]

To allow for this to be done in time, duties had to be shared out. At 7pm Browne, Freyberg and Lister set out to select a place for the grave and chose the spot in the olive grove where Brooke had rested just three days before during the field exercise. It was a most lovely place, about one mile up a valley from the sea above a watercourse, dry at that time but torrential in winter, and flanked by two mountains. At the feet of the olive trees the ground was carpeted with mauve flowering sage. An olive tree drooped over the grave site, leaning slightly forward and extending its upper branches over a small area clear of undergrowth. The officers broke the surface, then the men set to work digging the grave.[61]

While this was taking place, the Frenchmen aboard their vessel fetched small palm trees and placed them in a rectangle on the upper deck, in the middle of which was set the coffin under a British flag. There was no time to engrave a name plate, so Asquith asked a French orderly for a cauterizing iron and, by the light of a lamp, burnt deeply into the coffin the name and date. Rupert's pith helmet, holster and pistol were placed on the coffin, as he had no sword, and he was dressed in full uniform.[62]

A steam pinnace from the *Dartmouth* came alongside, carrying General Paris and some divisional staff; Colonel Quilter, Major Myburgh (second in command of the Hood) and a party of 12 officers of the battalion were in another boat. A third boat contained a French contingent. The coffin was lowered into Quilter's boat and the crew presented arms. Waiting them on shore were 12 bearers, all petty officers of the Hood, commanded by Shaw-Stewart, who formed a guard of honour drawn up on the quay. The journey to the grave began at 9.15pm As the moon was clouded over, men holding lamps were posted along the route to help the bearers over the rough ground. At 11pm Lister, by the grave, saw a lantern approaching. The leading man, called Saunders, was holding a large white-painted cross with the words 'Rupert Brooke' across the centre. He was followed by Lieutenant Shaw-Stewart with a drawn sword, leading the firing party. Then came the coffin, with General Paris and the officers behind.[63]

The grave was lined with sprigs of olive and flowering sage. Colonel Quilter threw in a wreath of olive, then Captain Failes read the Church of England burial service. Three volleys were fired into the air, and Shaw-Stewart presented arms. At the foot of the grave was a small white cross, presented by Brooke's platoon.[64] A Greek interpreter wrote in pencil on the rear of the larger cross, which had been placed at the head of the grave:

> Here lies the servant of God, Sub-Lieutenant in the English Navy, who died for the deliverance of Constantinople from the Turks.[65]

The service over, Asquith, Freyberg, Lister, Browne and Kelly stayed behind to gather lumps of pink and white marble, which they heaped into a cairn over the grave. As they stood there in a fitful breeze that made the trees rock gently, Denis Browne thought, as they all did, that he wouldn't wish a better grave, nor a different burial. Cleg Kelly wrote in his diary on 23 April:

> When the last of the five of us his friends had covered his grave with stones and took a last look in silence – then the scene of the tragedy gave place to a sense of passionless beauty engendered both by the poet and the place.[66]

The First Lord sent Major John Churchill a telegram at 11.50pm on 23 April, 1915:

> Personal from First Lord to Major John Churchill.
> Endeavour if your duties allow to attend Rupert Brooke's funeral on my behalf. We shall not see his like again.[67]

It had come too late, and John Churchill replied to Winston:

> I received your wire about poor Rupert Brooke but he was already buried. He had a most romantic funeral.

At dawn the *Grantully Castle* weighed anchor, heading for Gallipoli, and leaving behind the symbol of the generation. Brooke's sonnet, written in 1914, also became a symbol of the war:

THE SOLDIER

If I should die, think only this of me:
    That there's some corner of a foreign field
That is for ever England. There shall be
    In that rich earth a richer dust concealed;
A dust whom England bore, shaped, made aware,
    Gave, once, her flowers to love, her ways to roam,
A body of England's, breathing English air,
    Washed by the rivers, blest by suns of home.

And think, this heart, all evil shed away,
    A pulse in the eternal mind, no less
        Gives somewhere back the thoughts by England given;
Her sights and sounds; dreams happy as her day;
    And laughter, learnt of friends; and gentleness,
        In hearts at peace, under an English heaven.[68]

The suddenness of Rupert Brooke's death was deeply felt by all stations and conditions of men. Tributes were paid by many, and the 2nd Naval Brigade, Hood Battalion, sent a letter to Brooke's mother on 8 May, 1915:

> On behalf of NCOs and men of 4th Platoon, A Company, I send you their deepest sympathy in your sad bereavement in losing so grand an officer as your son was. He was loved by all the platoon, who feel his loss greatly.
> C. W. Sanders, PO
> J. R. Wells, PO
> T. Powell, LS
> F. W. Reyner, LS[69]

Sir Ian Hamilton was equally distraught, as shown by these extracts from his diary of 23 April, 1915:

> Rupert Brooke is dead. Straightaway he will be buried. The rest is silence.
>   Twice was the sight vouchsafed me in London when I told Eddie I would bespeak the boy's services at Port Said when I bespoke them.
>   Death on the eve of battle, death on a wedding day – nothing so tragic save that most black mishap, death in action after peace has been signed. Death grins at my elbow. I cannot get him out of my thoughts. He is fed up with the old and sick – nothing but the pick

of the basket will serve him now, for God has started a celestial spring-cleaning, and our star is to be scrubbed bright with the blood of our bravest and our best. Youth and Poetry are the links binding the children of the world to come to the grandsires of the world that was. War will smash, pulverize, sweep into the dustbins of eternity the whole fabric of the old world; therefore the firstborn in intellect must die. Is *that* the reading of the riddle?[70]

Winston Churchill paid tribute in *The Times* on 26 April:

Rupert Brooke is dead. A telegram from the Admiral at Lemnos tells us that his life has closed at the moment when it seemed to have reached its springtime. A voice had become audible, a note had been struck, more true, more thrilling, more able to do justice to the nobility of our youth in arms engaged in this present war, than any other – more able to express their thoughts of self-surrender, and with a power to carry comfort to these who watched them so intently from afar. The voice has been swiftly stilled. Only the echoes and the memory remain; but they will linger.[71]

Denis Browne wrote to Brooke's mother on 24 April:

No-one could have wished a quieter or calmer end than in that lovely bay, shielded by the mountains and fragrant with sage and thyme.[72]

CHAPTER SEVEN

The Gallipoli Landings

As the fleet moved out of Mudros harbour for the Gàllipoli invasion, each ship was sent on its way by spontaneous waves of cheering from the other ships yet to leave. All were going with great expectation and hope, if not a tinge of apprehension. A letter written by Patrick Shaw-Stewart on 15 April, 1915, makes it clear that fear of letting others down was a prime concern, along with wondering how one would stand up in comparison with others:

> As the war goes on I lose none of my old illogical aversion to being dead (though I constantly hum to myself *'ac velut anteacto nil tempore sensimus aegri . . .'* and then *'sic ubi non arimus . . .'* and all other unanswerable Lucretian arguments). I don't now think I shall run away, but I don't feel sure that I shan't do something catastrophically foolish from (a) lack of sense of direction; (b) lack of mechanical knowledge; (c) general lack of bushranging efficiency; or . . . who knows? (d) lack of a musical ear (from mistaking the Charge for the Retire).[1]

It was a moment of destiny which captivated the imagination of not only the participants, but also the public at home. Even schoolchildren in their playgrounds later took up the campaign in song:

> When the moon shines bright on Charlie Chaplin,
> His boots are cracking, for the want of blacking,
> And his little baggy trousers, they want mending,
> Before they send him to the Dardanelles.[2]

General Sir Ian Hamilton issued a special order on 21 April to fire the enthusiasm of the troops before the landings:

Soldiers of France and the King!

Before us lies an adventure unprecedented in modern war. Together with our comrades of the fleet we are about to force a landing upon an open beach in face of positions which have been vaunted by our enemies as impregnable.

The landings will be made good, by the help of God and the Navy; the positions will be stormed, and the war brought one step nearer to a glorious close.

'Remember,' said Lord Kitchener when bidding adieu to your Commander, 'remember once you set foot upon the Gallipoli peninsula, you must fight the thing through to a finish.'

The whole world will be watching our progress. Let us prove ourselves worthy of the great feat of arms entrusted to us.[3]

The initial landings took place on 25 April, and the planning was excellent, although it fell down on a lack of flexibility. The Turks were confronted by landings at no fewer than six locations, plus further diversionary operations by the French at Kum Kale on the Asiatic shore of the Dardanelles, and by the RND at the Gulf of Saros in the north. These multiple attacks ensured the defenders were thinly spread along the peninsula.

The Australians and New Zealanders were to land at Gaba Tepe, but after a navigational error they landed on a small beach (later known as Anzac Cove) some distance from their destination. The Turks were taken completely by surprise, as they hadn't expected a landing at this point, and rushed along the cliff-tops to defend their homeland. Much gallantry was shown by both sides that day. The Anzacs gained and held positions inland, controlling the high ground in places, but all attempts to advance further towards the narrows were repulsed.

Down south, in the Cape Helles sector, the 29th Division made six separate landings, supported by some RND units. At Camber, which was a small section of dead ground to the east of the fort of Sedd-el-Bahr, half a company of Dublin Fusiliers landed, but were soon withdrawn when they were unable to advance.

At 'V' beach the collier *River Clyde*, with landing ports cut into her side, steamed in towards the beach, heading for a narrow strip of sand near Sedd-el-Bahr. She was packed with troops: the Dublin and Munster Fusiliers, the Hampshires, the West Riding Field Company of engineers, and a platoon from Anson Battalion of the RND. The story of the *River Clyde* has been told many times, and it is not the task of this book to recount the dramatic events of this heroic action. Suffice it to say that very heavy losses were suffered; and that years later, on 11 November, 1960, Lord Freyberg said at the memorial service for Colonel Johnny Bigelow Dodge, DSO, DSC, MC:

During the actual landings Johnny and his platoon were detached from the Royal Naval Division and were put on board the *River Clyde*, the Trojan Horse surprise ship, and they were actually one of the first units to land at Cape Helles. When he saw that all was not going according to plan he led his platoon into the fighting, with the utmost gallantry, until he was badly wounded, and had to be sent home to recover. There is no doubt that during the landing operations in Gallipoli, and especially on the beaches, Johnny showed the greatest skill and courage, worthy of the highest praise.[4]

To the west of 'V' beach was landing area 'W', a strip of beach situated between Cape Tekke in the north and Cape Helles to the south. It was an obvious landing place, and had been suitably reinforced by machine guns, wires and trenches. Here the situation was no less dramatic than at 'V' beach: the British forced a bridgehead despite heavy losses; and the Lancashires were awarded six VCs in recognition of their gallantry in the action. The beach was later known as 'Lancashire Landing'.

To the north of Cape Tekke was 'X' beach, where the Royal Fusiliers and a small number of men from the RND's Anson Battalion were able to advance, in no small part due to the accurate broadsides of their covering ship, HMS *Implacable*. They later linked up with the Lancashire Fusiliers to the south at 'W' beach.

Further north still was 'Y' beach, west of the village of Krithia. The position was so hostile and inaccessible, with its high, steep cliffs, that the defenders had not considered the area a likely target for the invaders; but the King's Own Scottish Borderers and the RND's Plymouth Battalion of marines managed to scale the heights. Little or no opposition was encountered, and the two commanding officers walked around reviewing the situation. Some accounts even state that the troops got as far as entering Krithia. The capture of the village of Krithia and the high ground of Achi Baba was a real possibility at that point, and would have cut off the Turkish defensive force to the south. But the two officers, Colonels Koe and Matthews, were both of the opinion that they were in command. No order had been received on this point, and nothing was received or had been planned about exploiting their situation. As the men rested and brewed tea, the vital advantage of the day was slowly slipping away.

At about 7pm the flagship *Queen Elizabeth*, with Sir Ian Hamilton and his staff aboard, moved up the coast to 'Y' beach. They saw the cliffs crowded with troops, many inactive, brewing tea and resting, although some stores were being landed. Information was received that resistance had not been encountered. Commodore Roger Keyes, a staff officer on board the flagship, saw at once the significance of the situation. He pleaded with Hamilton to order the RND to steam south at all speed from the Gulf of Saros to reinforce this position, but Hamilton could not be convinced that he should commit his reserves.[5]

Commodore Keyes was then aged 43, and a man of vision and drive. He had entered the navy in 1885, serving at Vita, East Africa in 1890, and in China during 1900, at which time he was promoted to commander. He had held the post of naval attaché in Rome, Vienna, Athens and Constantinople, and since 1912 had been the commodore in charge of the submarine service.[6]

The flagship returned to 'V' beach, where it was found that the situation was now so serious that no new initiative could be undertaken until nightfall. A group of small British ships was heading inshore towards the beach, but Keyes ordered them to remain out of range and once more approached Hamilton. He put forward a second plan: these reinforcements should move around the tip of the peninsula to exploit the advantage which still existed at 'Y' beach. By this time the staff were convinced that Keyes's thinking was sound, but Hamilton would not interfere with the actions of the commander on the ground, Major-General Hunter-Weston. He did, however, despatch a message to the effect that he had a number of reinforcements available who could be landed at 'Y' beach if required.[7]

Hunter-Weston, who was viewing the events at 'W' beach, finally replied later in the day to say the reinforcements should land at 'W', which was what happened. So the advantage withered and died, as the Turks moved in to plug the gaps.

The situation could also have been exploited at 'S' beach at Morto Bay, near De Totts Battery in the Dardanelles itself. The 2nd South Wales Borderers and some members of the Anson Battalion took up a position that was not seriously threatened, remaining static until relieved on 27 April. If 'S' beach had been reinforced, the troops, by moving southwards, could have cut off the defenders at Sedd-el-Bahr.

But the commanders took a too narrow view of events. No campaign goes completely to plan; the unexpected always happens. Flexibility was required, but rigidity prevailed. A little known poem by Claude Burton describes the result:

THE ISTHMUS

The Isthmus of Gallipoli
Is Satan's own abode,
Where there isn't any water
And there isn't any road,
And the struggle for a living
Would disgust a British toad.

The cramped and narrow beaches
Are shelled by night and day,
The big cliffs swank above them
To bar the soldier's way.
But the British army got there,
And it's up to us to stay.

There's an endless panorama
Of unpleasant arid scenes.
And a range of rocky mountains,
Which are mostly big ravines.
And the men who fight among them,
They can tell you what it means.

We shall ever tell the story
How their glory brightly shone,
Who throughout a hell of carnage
Set their teeth and carried on.
But I wonder what they're thinking
Of the men who haven't gone.[8]

CHAPTER EIGHT

A Demonstration at the Gulf of Saros

While the main landings were taking place at the southern tip of the peninsula, the RND was busy making diversionary attacks in the north. On the evening of 24 April their transports steamed north for a rendezvous five miles south-west of Xeros Island, in the Gulf of Saros. Passing Mount Athos, the sky was lit up by the magnificent red glow of a glorious sunset.[1]

The transports were organized into three divisions:

1st Division
Escort: HMS *Canopus*, a battleship built in 1899 with a displacement of 12,950 tons; armed with four 12-inch guns and 12 six-inch guns; top speed of 18.5 knots.
Transports: *Franconia*
           Minnetonka
           Alnwick Castle
           Ayrshire

2nd Division
Escort: HMS *Dartmouth*, a light cruiser built in 1913 with a displacement of 5,250 tons; armed with eight six-inch guns; top speed of 24.5 knots.
Transports: *Royal George*
           Grantully Castle
           Inkonka

3rd Division
Escort: HMS *Doris*, a light cruiser built in 1897 with a displacement of 5,600 tons; armed with 11 six-inch guns; top speed of 18.5 knots.[2]

Transports: *Cawdor Castle*
             Gloucester Castle
             Cestrian
             Sonali

General Paris and his staff were in *Canopus*; the officers in charge of each of the two brigades, accompanied by their staff, were in *Dartmouth* and *Doris* respectively.

At dawn on 25 April *Dartmouth* and *Doris* began a bombardment of the north end of the Bulair lines, and, later, positions to the east. Meanwhile HMS *Jedd* and HMS *Kennet* (two 'E' class torpedo boat destroyers, constructed between 1904 and 1905, armed with four 12-pounders each and with a top speed of 26 knots) were reconnoitring likely landing places on the north shore of Xeros Bay. At one time *Kennet* stood too close into the coast and was fired upon, but sustained no casualties.

The next stage in the attack was a feint landing. On a signal from *Canopus* five of the transport ships each deployed a group of eight cutters towed by a trawler. Each cutter contained 20 men, who had been issued with life-jackets but no packs. The cutters from the *Franconia*, *Minnetonka* and *Alnwick Castle* made for a landing place on the eastern side of the bay; those from the *Royal George* and the *Grantully Castle* headed for the central beach. The transports remained ostentatiously in the background during the feint, ready to issue the general recall (a red, white and blue flag by day, one red light before the mast-head at night) when required.

After dark a small landing party from the Hood Battalion under Lieutenant-Commander Freyberg took to the water in a cutter. The plan was for the Hood platoon to land under cover of darkness, light flares on the beaches, fire machine guns and rifles, and generally make as much fuss as possible to create the impression of a much larger force and give the threatened invasion a hallmark of reality. However, some officers believed that, as the Turks had been forewarned of possible invasion by the ships' presence all day, the landing party would get a rough reception and many might not return. It was therefore decided that one man should attempt a landing alone and create a diversion with flares. Arthur Asquith wanted to go, but grave concern for the safety of the Prime Minister's son prevented this. The task fell to Freyberg, whose idea it was, and who was extremely keen to take part.[3]

Hood seaman Joseph Murray was part of the expedition, although not in Freyberg's boat:

In the early afternoon Leading Seaman Harris, my section leader, came and asked for volunteers who could swim. He had been ordered to get 30 men who were strong swimmers. I was the first of his section

75

he met, volunteer number one. The remaining 29 were soon lined up and taken below to the clothing store, where we were issued with a new pair of canvas shoes, like slippers, a cardigan and a woollen cap-comforter. We then went to the armoury for two bandoliers containing 50 rounds each.

Then came the briefing. We were going to be towed to within 800 yards of the shore. From there we were to row ourselves the rest of the way. We were the bait and were to attract the enemy's attention, so that they would be left in no doubt that this was the spot chosen for the landings. A fleet of transports had been in view all day, so we could be sure of a warm reception.

The Australian and New Zealand forces had already got ashore at Cape Tepe a little further down the coast, and the 29th Division had landed at Cape Helles at the toe of the peninsula. Our own little force would hopefully make the Turks hold troops in readiness here to contest a threatened landing. In the meantime, our troops already ashore would make their footholds. They could be reinforced as required.

At nine in the evening the suicide party, as we were called, were given steaming hot cocoa, as much as we could drink. A wit referred to it as the 'last supper'.

At 10pm we were ordered to man the ship's boat riding in the swell alongside. I led the way down Jacob's ladder. We had been warned that there must be no talking and absolute silence must be maintained. I nipped down fairly quickly, as I felt that if the chap following me stood on my fingers, I might forget the ban on talking. When all were aboard we were eased off, two to each oar, which were muffled with sandbags. So we were on our way. The oars cut the water as if they were handled by ghosts, not a sound, nor a single light anywhere. Away from the shelter of our transports we felt very cold, as we had left our tunics on board.

I was in the bow and Chief Petty Officer Milton was in the stern. I kept my eyes fixed straight ahead: it seemed a long way to shore. More than half an hour after we had left the *Grantully Castle* a brilliant flash followed by a deafening noise broke the silence and revealed our position. It was a salvo from a warship a mile or so away, but the flash lit up the whole coastline, now looking very close. I swung my rifle into the firing position, felt for my bandoliers and prepared to jump. I had seen the cliffs a moment before, but it was now darker than ever.

The bow struck something and swung to starboard. It was so dark that there were times when I could not even see the sea. Were we lost? If it was the intention to land, why didn't we? If we were to attract attention only, why not a few rounds of rapid fire? We had rifles and 50 rounds of ammunition each. If they were not to be used why on earth did we bring them with us?

It was early in the morning when we came back on board the *Grantully Castle*. How we found the old ship I shall never know, but I was certainly very pleased. We had been out in an open boat for many hours, and were so cold that it was difficult to climb up Jacob's ladder. At once we were served with that beautiful, piping hot cocoa, as much as we wanted.⁴

Murray was not aware of the change of plan, and that Freyberg was to land alone.⁵ Denis Browne was worried about his friend:

Freyberg has just gone off on a flare-lighting expedition, swimming. We are all anxious about him.

He has been wonderful the last few days. He loved and understood Rupert intuitively in spite of the differences in their temperaments; and last night when we were making the grave, he was as gentle as a woman, and as strong as a giant.⁶

But Freyberg returned safely at last, and submitted his report on 26 April:

Night Operation by Flare Party from A Company, Hood Battalion. At 9pm last night (25 April), as ordered, we left HM Transport *Grantully Castle* for the Western Landing Place to light flares; we were taken in tow by the steam pinnace of HMS *Dartmouth* and towed to within three miles of the shore, where we slipped and rowed in another mile. It now became evident that to proceed further without being seen from the shore would be impossible. At 12.40am this morning, I started swimming to cover the remaining distance, towing a waterproof canvas bag containing three oil flares and five calcium lights, a knife, signalling light and a revolver. After an hour and a quarter's hard swimming in bitterly cold water, I reached the shore and lighted my first flare, and again took to the water and swam towards the east, and landed about 300 yards away from my first flare where I lighted my second and hid among some bushes to await developments; nothing happened, so I crawled up a slope to where some trenches were located the morning before. I discovered they were only dummies, consisting of only a pile of earth about two feet high and 100 yards long, and looked to be quite newly made. I crawled in about 350 yards and listened for some time, but could discover nothing. I now went to the beach where I lighted my last flare and left on a bearing due south. After swimming for a considerable distance I was picked up by

77

Lieutenant Nelson in our cutter some time after 3am Our cutter, in company with the pinnace and the TBD *Kennet*, searched the shore with 12-pounders and Maxim fire, but could get no answer from the shore. It is my opinion that the shore was not occupied, but from the appearance and lights on the tops of the hills during the early hours of the morning, I feel certain that members of the enemy were there, but owing to the chance of being captured, and as I had cramp badly, I could not get further.[7]

Freyberg had been greased and painted black for his sortie; but when he began to swim out to sea on a compass bearing due south, his chances of being picked up were very slim, in view of the darkness of the night[8] and the fact that the boats could not show any lights. Luckily he was found about half a mile from shore, cramped, almost at the end of his endurance, and nearly dead from cold. For his gallant efforts he was later awarded the DSO, and his exploits were praised by his senior officers at the time. Lieutenant-Colonel Quilter sent in this report:

I have the honour to forward you herewith the attached report from Lieutenant-Commander Freyberg. I cannot speak too highly of the manner in which this officer carried out the difficult task assigned to him. He threw his whole energies into his preparations and carried the adventure through to a successful conclusion in an exceptional manner. As an example of resource, pluck, physical strength and endurance, his performance is worthy of the best traditions of both services. I would like to mention the assistance and support he received from Lieutenant Nelson: although his part was a secondary one, it was an important one, for a mistake on his part would probably have sacrificed the life of Lieutenant-Colonel Freyberg. He is an extremely cool and reliable officer and I selected him for the part for those reasons. The naval officers in the operation also carried out their parts in the most thorough and capable manner and the crews of the boats behaved in the manner one would expect in the navy.

Commodore Backhouse's report was equally complimentary:

I fully endorse the report of the OC Hood Battalion, of the resource-fulness and daring displayed by Lieutenant-Commander Freyberg. Lieutenant-Commander Freyberg is an officer of the greatest courage and determination, and has all the qualities required of an officer to rise to a high position in a military career.[9]

Joseph Murray recalls the other men all saying that they would have fol-lowed Freyberg anywhere; that was the type of man he was. Lieutenant

6. Naval Recruiting March in London. Men of the Royal Naval Division
marching through London to be reviewed by the Lord Mayor of London
who by virtue of his office was the Admiral of the Port of London.

7. The Lord Mayor of London inspecting men of the Royal Naval
Division outside the Guildhall (*IWM*).

8. Men of the Royal Naval Division at Vienne Dieu Fort, Antwerp, in October, 1914. Shortly afterwards it was blown to pieces by German howitzers (*IWM*).

9. Refugees passing through Vienne Dieu, Antwerp, 6 October, 1914. Note mattresses piled on the dog-cart (*IWM*).

Edward Nelson had been the biologist on Scott's Antarctic expedition before the war.[10]

As a result of all this effort by the RND and the navy, Liman von Sanders, the German commander of the Turkish forces on the ground, was told at 5am on 25 April that reports of landings had been received. Near his position in the upper Gulf of Saros numerous vessels of war and troop transports could be seen approaching the coast. He could himself distinctly hear a continuous roar of shellfire from that direction. Von Sanders stated:

> From the many pale faces among the officers reporting in the early morning it became apparent that, although a hostile landing had been expected, a landing at so many places surprised many and filled them with apprehension.

Von Sanders instructed his 7th Division, based at the town of Gallipoli, to march to Bulair. He himself rode to the heights of Bulair where he got a good view of about 20 ships, some of which were lying close in under the steep slopes of the coast, while others were further out. Broadside after broadside came towards the shore. The ridge on which von Sanders stood was covered with shell and shrapnel. It was an unforgettable picture, but nowhere could he see any troops disembarking from the ships.

Von Sanders decided to stay at Bulair because of the strategic importance of the area – this section of the peninsula had to be kept open at all costs – so he directed a Turkish general, Essed Pasha, to take command of the southern part of the peninsula. He witnessed the enemy repeatedly putting out boats and attempting to approach the coast, but always retreating under fire. Watching the action, von Sanders decided that the British were only making a demonstration attack. Their transports were not deep in the water, but vision was obscured as the ships were lined with dense rows of vertical branches, so he could not be sure whether large numbers of troops were aboard or not.

By the afternoon all the Turkish reports pointed to the conclusion that this was not to be a landing at all. However, von Sanders was still apprehensive in case the activity was a build-up to a night attack, so he remained on the heights of Bulair all night whilst the situation became critical elsewhere. By the morning the feint was revealed, but it had succeeded in diverting the defenders and holding forces away from the principal beaches.[11]

The plan at Bulair had been useful, and an officer of the Hood had shown that one brave and resourceful man could have some effect on the overall scheme of things.

79

CHAPTER NINE

The Hood Landings

After the successful diversion at Bulair, what did the RND do whilst the 29th Division were fighting desperately to drive the Turks from their strongholds in the south? Could they have been landed as reinforcements at 'Y' or 'S' beaches? The answer appears to be 'yes'.

Shaw-Stewart says they did nothing useful: 'We were simply hanging about.'[1] Murray has more detailed recollections:

> We steamed down the coast to Gaba Tepe. The Australian and New Zealand forces did not appear to have advanced inland: we could see fighting taking place on the slopes running down to the beaches. It was difficult to assess the position exactly. Anzac Cove was about 1,000 yards wide,[2] shaped like a bite from an apple. There were shells bursting on the hills and also on the beaches. We could see the troops quite clearly.[3]

Charles Lister wrote:

> The next day [Monday, 26 April] routine unrelieved was the order, and we did Swedish exercises in the sight of the enemy – rather sick at heart at the delays. We were then moved down to nearer the scene of action, and for three days watched our ships pound the hills and woods that crowned them. It was a wonderful spectacle: the shrapnel going up like white clouds and then bursting high up and sending down a spray of smoke like a firework, and the luddite green and yellow which could only be seen when the shell had actually burst on the ground.
>
> The row of one's own gun is deafening. The enemy shrapnel makes a shrill ghostlike scream as it goes through the air overhead. Occasionally little ant-like men could be seen making their way up the cliff face or creeping over the scrub-covered hillside. And once

or twice we saw Turks in retreat catching it from the ships' guns.[4]

Murray takes up the story:

> The *Grantully Castle* and the Royal Naval Division continued on to Cape Helles past 'Y', 'X' and 'W' beaches, and as we passed we could see flashing from the rifles. We saw the *River Clyde* beached at 'V' beach, and so on into the Dardanelles and Morto Bay. Bits of boats were floating about and some were full of bodies, a terrible sight.[5]

Denis Browne wrote in his diary:

> This battle is the most wonderful thing there ever was, as heroic by land as it is wonderful by sea. We watch with bated breath from the deck until our eyes drop out. The coast looks so peaceful and sunny, until suddenly a shell goes biff and up goes a high column of smoke.[6]

So the reserves carried on training while the opportunity to use them decisively by early reinforcement of key positions was lost. By the time they landed at 'W' beach, it was all too late. Thinking of their forthcoming landings, Lieutenant-Colonel Quilter wrote on 25 April, 1915:

> We are waiting to take our turn ashore in the great events that began this morning. We know little of how it's going, but are pining to throw our weight into the scale to turn success into something more brilliant, or to make a check into victory.
>
> I am confident of my lot, though it was a cruel blow having 150 stokers taken away without a second's warning [the stokers taken from Trebuki Bay to assist with boat duties in Lemnos]. They are really the backbone till the others have gained their experience.[7]

The Turks had planned two defensive positions south of Achi Baba: one line on the beaches, and a second four miles back. They were committed to a defensive campaign, which would give them time to muster their troops, spread thinly as a result of both von Sanders's tactics and the diversionary landings at Bulair and Kum Kale. It was good military strategy in an area ideally situated to defence and harassment, and would give them the advantage once the first thrust of sudden attack had petered out. They fell back from the beaches to their second line of defence, so on 27 April the British were able to advance two miles across an undefended open plain.

Sir Ian Hamilton issued a special order on 28 April to bolster the morale of his troops after the excitement of the initial landings:

I rely on all officers and men to stand firm and steadfast to resist the attempts of the enemy to drive us back from our present position, which has been gallantly won.

The enemy is evidently trying to obtain a local success before reinforcements can reach us, but the first portion of these will arrive tomorrow and be followed shortly by a fresh division from Egypt.

It behoves us all, French and British, to stand fast, hold what we have gained, wear down the enemy and thus prepare for a decisive victory.

Our comrades in Flanders have had the same experience of fatigue after hard-won fights. We shall, I know, emulate their steadfastness and achieve a result which will confer added laurels to French and British arms.[8]

On 28 April the RND was temporarily broken up as the Marine Brigade and 1st Naval Brigade were ordered to land and assist at Anzac Cove. The Plymouth Battalion of marines and Drake Battalion were to be attached to the 29th Division. By 3pm on 29 April the Anzac landings were complete, and the fleet moved down the coast to support the hard-pressed 29th, who had suffered extensive losses in the Cape Helles sector. Hood and Howe Battalions and the divisional and 2nd Brigade HQs were landed on 'W' beach, where they would be in reserve under Commodore Backhouse, reporting to General Hunter-Weston. The Plymouth Battalion was given beach duties.[9]

Joseph Murray recalls:

The Hood landed about 10pm on Thursday, 29 April. They got aboard lighters and then transferred to a barge and waded ashore. The landings had taken some time, some men going ashore earlier. When I got into the water it was only about one foot deep, and we walked over stones as there was little sand under the water. There was extensive barbed wire in the water, but I had no trouble as the barge we were in had crushed it. On the barbed wire were bits of uniform, equipment and guns.[10] Men had been seen in the daylight still down in the clear water, having been killed by the weight of their heavy packs.

The scene on 'W' beach was like Dante's Inferno; a terrible sight. Wounded were calling out for help, and there were several heaps of bodies, about 20 or 30 in each heap. We lined up on the beach, but the Turks started shelling and we were troubled by shrapnel, so we made our way to a position on the slope above the beach.[11]

'W' beach, where the Hood landed, is now closed and part of a military camp. Rusting remains of lighters and piers rot in the sand and sea. On each side of the beach, cliffs dominate the sandy crescent; in between, the land extends upwards in a gentle slope to the fields above, where the Hood dug in on their first night ashore. Charles Lister wrote:

We passed a chilly time on the windswept, plateau-like field, with the flare of smoking towns on the skyline as red as red dawn.

The next day, 30 April, the Hood went forward over the ridge and took up positions in support of the 29th Division, digging funk-holes in the long grass behind the firing line. There was much work to be done in landing stores, and occasionally Turkish shells would fall in the water near where they were working. They were also troubled by snipers. Some of the battalion probed the scrub and surrounding small clump of trees to flush out the snipers, but without much success, and they continued to find targets.

After dark, Lister relates that they dug themselves little nests in the heather and drank rum. Occasional shells passed over their heads. One or two fell just short of his position. At about midnight the dug-in troops were woken by a tremendous volume of rifle and machine-gun fire, which seemed to Lister to be at their very doors. It lasted for about an hour, and then the Hood was ordered to advance through a marshy ravine overgrown with water weeds and olives.[12] Murray remembers:

We went forward to assist the French on our right. We were in extended line – we just didn't have enough troops. Later it appeared as if the Turks were going to get through on the left flank. There was no front line as such, just groups of men holding an area. In the advance I never saw any Turks clearly, only dead ones as we advanced. You saw a single figure ahead, or dark shapes like groups of men, and I kept firing my gun; but in the dark you couldn't tell if you had hit anyone.[13]

In fact Anson Battalion was on the extreme right next to the French, and the Hood was in the middle, across the Achi Baba nullah. The nullah was to become the RND's sector for many months, nicknamed Frenchman's Gully by the men in honour of the first troops in there. Not as deep and dramatic as some other watercourses in the area, it descended on the east side of the Krithia road from the brooding, dominating hill of Achi Baba itself. The division's position was slightly right of centre and linked up with the French, who were holding the area around the deeper Kereves Dere waterway. These streams were mainly dry in spring and summer, and provided good lines of communication. The Howe was on the left, alongside the 29th Division. Commodore Backhouse was meanwhile setting up his brigade HQ in the area, known throughout the campaign as the Backhouse Post.[14]

The whole brigade was supporting French and Senegalese troops; the latter were unsteady, firing their rifles off in the dark in all directions. Murray wrote of them:

The Senegalese troops seemed afraid of the dark – they put up rapid fire in all directions and then decided to retire. We seem to have the permanent job of retaking the trenches that the Senegalese vacate, yet whilst they are with us they are excellent fighters. Their broad everlasting grins soon captivate even the most dour of us.[15]

In daylight the Hood advanced past many Turkish dead. According to Lister:

One officer advanced up a certain gully and counted hundreds of dead. They must have lost enormously. The Turks were retreating and all the British reserves had been drawn into the line apart from Cox's Indian Brigade, which had just landed. The British position on the peninsula was very thinly held.[16]

At 10am on Sunday, 2 May they were ordered to advance again. It was a beautiful morning, with the sound of birds singing merrily. The Hood marched up the gully and moved out to the left, bayonets fixed. But, as Joseph Murray relates:

The Turkish firing squad was waiting. We thought that, after the punishment we had given them during the night of 30 April/1 May, they had moved out. We were wrong. Shrapnel and machine-gun fire made the men spread out. We advanced about 400 yards from our old position in some short rushes, until the hail of bullets made a further advance impossible. An order came to dig in.[17]

With the advance held up, reinforcements were sent in the form of the 2nd Hampshires, a regular unit of the 29th Division. Seeing them moving forward the Turks increased their shrapnel fire, but the Hampshires came on in perfect formation. The scene made a lasting impression on Murray and other naval troops watching:

They came up just like puppets on a string. They would advance 20 yards and get down as one. Up together, advance, then down together, all the time getting less and less. Their advance under such terrible fire was an object lesson to we civilian soldiers, and the value of training was brought home to us during those glorious minutes.[18]

The fire became so intense that, on the evening of 2 May, Lieutenant-Colonel Quilter had no alternative but to order the Hood to retire with the Hampshires. Lieutenant Lister's company was the last to retreat, and as they went a shrapnel burst about 30 yards behind Lister; he was struck in the buttock and was soon bleeding profusely. Despite this, he wrote of the event that his men had done well, considering the trying circumstances and their relative rawness.[19] Total Hood casualties in the short-lived advance were five officers and 75 men killed or wounded.

On Tuesday, 4 May, just before dawn, firing broke out on the extreme left, and soon the whole line was taking part. The activity died down shortly after daybreak and things became comparatively quiet, with only the warships shelling on occasions. The men of the Hood could see the shells bursting on the slopes of Achi Baba.

At 6pm that day the battalion took over the trenches running across Achi Baba Nullah and around the area of Backhouse Post from the French. The line consisted of a series of funk-holes about two feet deep, with concertina wire running across the gully.[20] The French had stuck bayonets into the ground and tied a number of old jam tins filled with stones to wire stretched between them, but it was not very effective as an early warning system.[21] Joseph Murray remembers the deceptive peacefulness:

The sector was quiet, so we sat under the stunted trees and among the bushes and brewed tea. The Turks were miles away, or so it seemed, although the snipers were active. It was a strange feeling to be sitting at ease in the front line without a care.

After dark that night the French, on the right, started firing rapidly and wildly, according to Murray:

They must have fired in all directions again, as two of us were wounded by their large copper bullets. The firing spread along the front.[22]

On Wednesday 5 May the Turks could be seen reverting to the defensive again, strengthening their lines. Sniping became a constant nuisance, although it was thought to be German-trained rather than Turkish.

Several Turks were caught inside the RND lines, where they had hidden in holes with plentiful supplies of food and ammunition. the naval troops regarded them as very brave men.

Some enemy units were saying they wanted to surrender in large numbers; but, as Major-General Paris discovered, this was not always to be taken at face value:

> Only yesterday, 4 May, 1915, a considerable number approached our trenches with arms slung. When they were within 80 yards one of my officers went out. Two or three Turks immediately laid down and fired, wounding him in two places. You can imagine!

The breaking-up of the RND on 28 April had left General Paris temporarily without executive responsibilities, which caused further dissent amongst those in command. Paris criticized the overall strategy in a letter of 5 May, 1915:

> It is a grievous error landing the Australians so far away from the 29th Division. They are quite out of touch, and can only hold on, being besieged all the time.[23]

CHAPTER TEN

The Second Battle of Krithia

The hill of Achi Baba dominated the Dardanelles, and with it the thoughts and vision of the attacking forces. Although only 706 feet high, from its slopes the defending Turks could get a good view of British and French activity. Their dramatic panorama also included the awe-inspiring sight of British and French warships anchored in a crescent all the way round from the straits to the Aegean Sea. The fleet was a symbol of power and when it launched broadside after broadside on to the Turkish positions nothing could move above ground. But these broadsides could only be generally aimed and randomly effective, because the exact siting of the Turkish defences was unknown.

The Turks and their German officers had done their work well: trenches and machine-gun positions were well hidden by design and placement, and camouflaged by plants, undergrowth, scrub and clumps of trees. Advancing British troops did not know where the next burst of machine-gun fire would come from, mowing down a line of men. It was difficult to get to grips with the enemy, and they could fight for days without seeing a single Turk. The only signs of the enemy's presence were bullets and shells finding their targets and leaving gaps in the line.

The Turks also made good use of gullies running down from the hill towards the sea: Gully Ravine, Krithia Nullah and the Achi Baba Nullah (also called Kanli Dere) were on the British front; while the French had to contend with the Kereves Dere, running down to the Dardanelles. These gullies could be used both for defence and for transporting men and equipment out of sight of prying eyes.

In short, the Turks had a fine defensive position, so the invaders decided that a major offensive should be mounted to gain the vital heights of Achi Baba. They had to capture the village of Krithia, and Achi Baba itself. Nothing less would do, but there was disagreement as to how the objective should be achieved. Sir Ian Hamilton wanted a night attack, or at the very least a dawn advance, but General Hunter-Weston, the CO on the ground, would have none of it. He was concerned about his lack of regular officers and units, so he ordered the attack to start at 11am after a preliminary bombardment. His logic seems hard to understand, as the men would advance in full sunlight, allowing defensive fire to be aimed at them at will. What is more, British supplies of shells were woefully lacking: there was little high explosive, so the artillery mainly had shrapnel.

However, the advance duly began at 11am on 6 May, with the 29th Division on the left flank, the French on the right, and the Composite Naval Brigade under General Paris and the 2nd Brigade under the French General d'Amade in the centre. The 2nd Brigade (Hood and Anson Battalions with A Company of the Howe) was initially intended merely to support the French, but their orders were changed shortly before the start of the advance: they were to move forward to the left of the French, with the Hood leading the way.

The Hood moved off up the Achi Baba Nullah in Indian file until they reached open country, where they spread out and continued in short rushes. A Turkish machine gun was known to be guarding a well (called Romano's Well by the RND, after a well-known Edwardian eating place) and to avoid this they were ordered to move left. This led them to a swampy area under heavy Turkish fire, and a number of men were lost crossing the marsh. The enemy machine guns could not be seen, but they were perfectly sited. Fewer men rose after each rush, but the Hood still moved forward blindly, repeatedly changing directions.[1] Joseph Murray remembered it vividly:

The fire appeared to be coming from all directions, yet we could not see a single Turk nor any sign of a trench. I saw that we were making for a place called the 'White House', near another 'Brown House'. They were without roofs, more like shacks than houses. We rushed through a vineyard to capture it. As we got there I saw that Lieutenant-Commander Freyberg and another man named Chalmers were in the White House with a captured machine gun. I think they were trying to get it working.

We then took up a position along a small ridge just beyond the house, where we were joined by several small groups. There were about 50 of us. We waited as we were counted and then were ordered to alter direction, swinging round, thereby allowing us to take up a position behind another small ridge at right angles to the first. There was an opening about 20 yards to our right which looked like the entrance to the vineyard; the intention was to go through it and spread out behind. There must have been a machine gun trained on the opening. We had to climb over dead and injured, and then I ran about 30 yards before falling down in a patch of prickly scrub.

After a little while I heard a man called Townsend calling to me, and without raising my head I crawled up towards him. Houghton and Yates were somewhere behind, and crawled up later. There was no-one else moving. We were the only ones to get through that opening. We decided that there appeared to be better cover in the thicker scrub about 10 yards ahead of us. We ran forward and, as we reached it, Yates was hit in the abdomen. He bent to his knees, rolled over, and then got to his feet again, turning round and round. He rushed forward, but fell groaning after a few yards.

The three of us crawled forward towards him. Houghton reached him first, but while trying to comfort him he was shot through the head. The same bullet, spent though it was, took a piece out of my knuckle. Poor Houghton died crying for his mother. He said he was 17, but if he was 16 he would be lucky. Totally unsuited for this rough life, he never once complained. Always willing and eager to help, he himself was now beyond help. There was nothing Townsend or I could do for him or Yates.

No-one else came forward. The bullets were hitting the sandy soil all around us, with the dust getting in our eyes. How soon would it be before they hit us? Townsend suggested that we should move forward. It took courage to rise, but nowhere could be worse than there. Together we ran forward, with the bullets singing in the air and pitting the ground. Ten to 15 yards we ran, then buried our heads in that prickly, beastly-smelling scrub, but there was no respite.

It must have been two hours since we began our advance. There was not a soul in sight, friend or foe, nor had we seen one single trench. If only we knew where everybody was. We kept moving carefully, but with no particular object in view save trying to avoid the hail of lead that seemed to be following us. Obviously our movements were being watched by the Turks, but where the devil were they?

There was a small mound some distance to the right: after many short rushes we reached it, and for the first time since we started we felt comparatively safe. We took stock of our position. We had not fired a single shot. If we could only get a glimpse of a Turk we would have some idea of the direction we should take. We rested for a while, and came to the conclusion that we had advanced too far and that our best course of action would be to dig ourselves in and wait. Townsend sat up and with his entrenching tool began to dig. This movement brought even more lead towards us. We lay flat again, with the bullets coming in all directions. Townsend said he thought that we were surrounded. I had thought so long ago!

Over to the right about 100 yards away we could see what appeared to be a ditch. We could not stay where we were much longer, so with a dash of about 30 yards to begin with we set off in that direction. A few shorter rushes brought us close enough to crawl the last 10 or so yards into the ditch, which was barely 18 inches deep. We felt much safer now. We had only guessed its existence because of the long green grass. There was a little water here and there – rather stagnant, of course, but it quenched our thirst. We chewed the grass, which reminded me of my father saying that we should all have to eat grass before the war was over.

What a stroke of luck to find this tiny oasis! It was easy to dig here, and the rain of lead seemed to be high overhead now. We recommenced digging and soon had quite a small but comfortable hole. A little water trickled in, but water anywhere or of any sort was an asset out here. Now that we had a fort, we arranged for one of us to rest while the other kept a lookout. Sitting in the water I fell asleep, for I don't know how long. Donald [Townsend] awakened me, saying he thought he could see someone moving on the left, close to a solitary tree which we had been near a little while ago. For a second I saw three moving figures, but they were gone. We agreed that, if our sense of direction was correct, they should be our men. True, we had been fired on from that angle most of the afternoon, but then we had been fired on from all angles. We decided to keep a sharp eye out for them in any case.

We were conscious of the fact that our faces were burnt almost black, and that we had not washed for a week. Our sun helmets had been discarded days ago: the pith helmet was all right for sentry duty, and the extended back was good for protecting the neck whilst we were standing, but when we lay down to fire they would fall off. We were wearing woollen cap-comforters, and could easily be taken for Turks, whose headgear was similar. At that moment this was not so good.

If the figures behind that tree would only move again we would be pleased, but war is most unobliging sometimes. I promised Don that I would keep my eye on the tree if he rested awhile, and he was soon asleep. I kept my eyes glued in that direction for quite a while, but on glancing round to look at Don I saw the French Senegalese coming up, a long way behind and on our right, but coming in our direction. I gave Don a gentle kick. In a flash he was levelling his rifle at them, but pulled himself together and apologized. 'I thought it was Johnnie,' he said. 'What about the other side? They must be Turks after all.'

For the first time we began to appreciate our position – and what a lousy position it was! We were between the advancing French and the Turks, right bang in the middle, and both sides were firing in our direction. To make matters worse, it was getting dark. We hoped that these big black fellows would reach us before it was really dark, as it would confuse matters if they didn't.

We were keeping low and discussing how we could attract their attention when Don spotted at least a dozen Turks beside that tree and opened fire. We were having a bit of our own back now. It was like shooting rabbits – waiting for them to run, then bang! We had been the rabbits all day, now we were the gamekeepers, and about time too.

A few moments ago we had been wondering how to attract attention, but now our firing solved the problem. The Senegalese began to pay us far too much attention for our liking. It was bad for our health. Of course, they were not to know that we were on their side, and that hours ago we had captured the ground they were now trying to gain. Where the devil had they been all this time, anyway? However, this was not the time or place to argue; and, judging by their fire, they were in no mood for argument.

The light was fading, but we could see them quite plainly. We stuck our woollen caps on our bayonets and waved cautiously, but this made things worse. We were definitely in a bit of a jam. It looked certain that we should be shot if we stood up, but if we laid low until they reached us they would stick us like pigs, and I didn't much care for their very long, three-cornered bayonets. They, like us, had suffered much from snipers, so we couldn't expect any mercy. We would have to sort this lot out, and sharply, as they were less than 50 yards away. One more rush and they would be upon us.

As we had good cover we agreed to lie low until they were almost upon us, then jump up and hope that it worked. Mercifully for Don and me they just kept firing, taking no aim whatsoever but simply letting off their rifles. We jumped up, but our timing was a fraction too soon and we had to parry their thrusts, calling out 'Ingleesh Johnnie! Ingleesh!' I could have run my man through quite easily, but instead I swung my butt round, catching him square on the jaw with such force that he sank to the ground. I tried to pick him up at once, but another six-footer rushed towards me. I met him with a parry, but he came with such force that neither of us could rectify our moves. We collided so violently that we were both partially winded, and each of us lost our rifles. We were having a real rough-house when my monster was wounded in the leg, and thank goodness for that. He could not get up, and I kept repeating, 'Ingleesh! Ingleesh Johnnie.'

What a relief when I saw that infectious grin on his ebony face. Don was having a rare go with three burly fellows. He had one on the ground when my former opponent cried out something I did not understand. It gave Don a breather, but they kept him covered. They could shoot him now, but Don didn't seem to realize this. He just stood laughing, and when he made a move towards me one of his opponents fired, but missed. My wounded chap called out again sharply, and broad grins spread all round. We were accepted as brothers.[2]

This was just one small fragment of the day's events in the Hood sector. It is clear that Murray had in fact been left behind; the rest of the Hood and Anson had bypassed the position after heavy resistance at that point. The Hood reported that by 12.30pm they had advanced far past the Turkish forward trenches by the White House. For several hours Denis Browne, Patrick Shaw-Stewart and eight other men found themselves in the foremost position of the whole brigade front, and had to shelter behind a little bean-shaped hill. Some 80 men dashed across exposed ground in twos and threes to join them and hold the position, but eventually the fire became so heavy that they were all obliged to retire.[3]

Commodore Backhouse wrote in his diary for this day:

Hood started advance at 11am Could see no signs of French troops moving into position in front of us, and at 11am, when the time fixed for the advance had arrived, decided to send on Hood in order to fill up the gap between British right and French left.

Hood Battalion started advancing at 11am and received no opposition for the first 300 yards, then came under rifle fire from the ridge of hill 300 yards on our right and sustained casualties. They advanced and occupied White House, 1,000 yards forward, from where they got some cover. A company or more with Myburgh advanced still further, 300 or 400 yards, and received full fire from the enemy. Poor Quilter was hit quite early in the advance, and was shot in the chest and killed almost instantly. Could see signs of French forward movement and, knowing them to be concentrating on Hill 300, sent our Anson to support Hood, who were becoming isolated.[4]

On the extreme left of the line little progress was made, and the French advance was also disappointing. In their first serious engagement, the Hood, Anson and Hove Battalions achieved the most substantial advance of the day, but by 3pm no sector had got anywhere near the main Turkish positions, and at 3.30pm General D'Amade ordered the Hood and Anson not to advance any further, as the rest of the force could make no progress. At 4.30pm the whole line received orders to halt. A gap in the line had been created by the 2nd Naval Brigade's extensive advance, spearheaded by the Hood, so Drake Battalion was sent forward to dig in on a line joining the Hood's left with the 29th Division.[5]

But the advance had cost the naval battalions dearly in dead and wounded. My great-uncle Albert Walls was wounded in the battle by a bullet in the thigh. On 9 May he was sent to the 2nd Field Ambulance, and later the same day transferred to a clearing hospital. He was out of action until 19 June, when he returned to the peninsula aboard the *Seang Bee*.[6]

Commodore Backhouse summed up the position in his diary:

Sustained many casualties, especially in the Hood and Anson Battalions, and the effective strength of the battalions at midnight was:
Hood   10 officers and 343 men
Howe   15 officers and 456 men
Anson   11 officers and 352 men.[7]

As Backhouse had seen, the Hood Battalion CO, Lieutenant-Colonel Quilter, was killed leading his men into battle carrying an oversize walking stick. He was buried near Backhouse Post in a gully close behind the trenches at position 169 L3.[8] The Rev Henry Foster conducted the burial service and wrote later:

This brave officer was laid to rest at about eight o'clock in the morning, in the presence of Commodore Backhouse and the staff of the 2nd Naval Brigade. A firing party from his battalion fired three volleys over the grave as their last token of respect, and the buglers sounded the Last Post; this being the only occasion, as far as I know, on which an officer in Gallipoli was buried with full military honours . . . . Shortly after, I buried Lieutenant Walker of the Howe Battalion, in the same place. Both funerals took place in a dangerous spot, under a hail of shrapnel, but we managed to get through without a casualty.[9]

Quilter was one of the most popular officers in the whole RND, and a member of the Hood wrote this poem shortly afterwards:

93

IN MEMORY OF COLONEL QUILTER

You've heard of the Hood Battalion
Of the 2nd Naval Brigade.
We reckon we've done our duty,
And a little history we've made.

We honoured our gallant Colonel –
Quilter by name was he.
The deeds of the Hood Battalion,
Alas he lived not to see.

The day we went into action,
He led us like a man,
And faced the bullets bravely,
And never flinched a span.

His presence was a tonic
In the midst of danger and strife.
But in the hour of victory
A bullet took his life.

All honour to Colonel Quilter,
The Battalion mourns his loss.
The only things we could give him,
Were a grave and a wooden cross.[10]

The advance went on again on 7 May, starting at the left of the line, but appeared to be failing by 3pm. A general attack was ordered, with a brigade of New Zealanders from the composite division sent across to assist. The 2nd Naval Brigade under General d'Amade and the Composite Naval Brigade under General Paris were each given the same tasks as the previous day: to ensure that they kept in touch with each other and with the troops on the flanks. The Hood was in reserve to Howe and Anson, but no substantial advances were made.

At dawn on 8 May another advance was attempted, but the French on the left of the line were unable to move forward. During the attack the courageous Anzac troops lost one third of their 3,000 men. But at 6pm the French surged forward along the Kereves Spur, having some success until the Turks started bombarding them with high-explosive shells. They tried once more, and captured a strongpoint later known as the Bouchet Redoubt. Hood and Howe Battalions advanced behind the French in support until 7pm, when all units on the front were ordered to dig in.[11] The second battle of Krithia had been fought to a standstill.

Patrick Shaw-Stewart wrote in a letter on 8 May:

I suppose everyone feels much as I do after a week or so of war: it is very exciting, and a thing a man should not have missed; but now I've seen it and been there and done the dashing, I begin to wonder whether this is any place for a civilized man, and to remember about hot baths and strawberries and my morning *Times*. We have been a good bit in the trenches (I am lying in a reserve one now, just in case the enemy's shrapnel should be wider of the mark than usual), and twice in action. The second day was exciting enough for anyone: my next-door neighbour hit four times, and me finding myself to my great surprise in a position so much in front of the army that I had to pretend to be a daisy, and crawl away with a few men at dusk. Since then I have been hit at three yards' range with an accidental shot plumb on the right heart, where the bullet lodged in my trusty Asprey steel mirror – almost as good an advertisement for that firm as Oc's wound for the government.

Looking back on the last fortnight (from which we are now resting), I see really nothing much except one day's advance – and then I never saw a live Turk that I could swear to. Today I am much more interested in nature – the most divine poppies and vetches making the whole place red and blue, and a quite black cypress grove full of French artillerymen, down which I took 100 stokers this morning to bathe sumptuously in the actual Dardanelles themselves! And the great and startling beauty of blue jays and cranes, the latter as large and frequent as aeroplanes.[12]

Brigadier-General Woodward, deputy adjutant-general of the Mediterranean Expeditionary Force, issued another special order on 9 May to boost morale:

Sir Ian Hamilton wishes the troops of the Mediterranean Expeditionary Force to be informed that in all his past experiences, which include the hard struggles of the Russo-Japanese campaign, he has never seen more devoted gallantry displayed than that which has characterized their efforts during the past three days. He has informed Lord Kitchener by cable of the bravery and endurance displayed by all ranks here and has asked that the necessary reinforcements be forthwith despatched. Meanwhile the remainder of the East Lancashire Division is disembarking and will henceforth be available to help us to make good and improve upon the positions we have so hardly won.[13]

The dead lay in heaps and lines where they had been hit by machine-gun fire, and the survivors were in a terrible condition. 9 May was spent evacuating the wounded, burying the dead and replenishing supplies, but the Turks never ceased their continual harassment from concealed machine guns, shelling and sniping, even though there was no continuous Turkish position for 500 yards.[14]

The Turkish snipers were very skilled: there were tales of soldiers shot in the head through small observation holes. The British carried out frequent sniper drives to try to rid themselves of the menace, and often found snipers behind their own lines. Commodore Backhouse recorded in his diary on Sunday, 11 May that several snipers had been found and shot in British lines that evening.[15]

On 10 May the Turks attacked vigorously against the French and the 2nd Naval Brigade on their left. At one point they seemed about to break through, and only a timely counter-attack saved the line. The same day, 2nd Naval Brigade was transferred back to General Paris's command; on 12 May they were withdrawn to a rest camp south-west of Achi Baba Nullah (where they were joined on 13 May by the battalions which had been sent to support the Anzacs). General d'Amade was sorry to see them go, visiting the brigade in their rest camp to read them a letter he had sent to Sir Ian Hamilton:

> In accordance with your orders I am returning the 2nd Naval Brigade to the Composite Division. It is my pleasant duty to place on record how much I have appreciated the brilliant military qualities, the devotion to duty, the courage and the intrepidity of the three valiant battalions – Anson, Howe and Hood – of which it is composed. It is a great honour and a great satisfaction to me to have during 6, 7, 8 and 9 May the devoted, active and ever-ready collaboration of Commodore Backhouse, an officer who has inspired his troops with those noble qualities to which every French soldier who has seen them at work renders homage.[16]

The Hood Battalion presented the general with the machine gun they had captured at the White House on 6 May.

On 18, 23, 24 and 27 May further advances were made, extending the line by nearly half a mile at the cost of only 50 casualties. These RND losses were very small in comparison to those suffered during the second battle of Krithia, yet the gain in ground was approximately the same. The first stage of the campaign had now reached a conclusion, but none of the objectives had been achieved (and none ever were to be). It was all too late. The naval battalions had been reduced to an average of 500 officers and men each, having started the campaign with a complement of over 900 in each battalion.

On 28 and 29 May they were reinforced by the arrival of the three battalions which had been left behind in England for training, and the RND was reorganized according to its original plan: Hawke and Benbow joined Drake and Nelson to form the 1st Brigade; Collingwood joined Howe, Hood and Anson in the 2nd Brigade; Plymouth, Portsmouth and Chatham formed the Marine Brigade. But in the battles of April and May the division's effective strength of 10,500 men had been reduced by half (excluding the new arrivals). The blooding of the older battalions had been terrible.

The campaign now changed in character: from a fluid pattern it developed into trench warfare. The French remained on the right of the peninsula, adjacent to the Dardanelles. Next to them was the RND, spread across Achi Baba Nullah and to the right of Krithia Nullah. On its left was the 42nd Division, then the 29th Division, and finally Cox's Indian Brigade positioned across the gully to the sea.

An order from Major-General Braithwaite, chief of general staff, on 25 May explained the position:

Now that a clear month has passed since the Mediterranean Expeditionary Force began its night-and-day fighting with the enemy, the General Commanding desires to explain to officers, non-commissioned officers and men the real significance of the calls made upon them to risk their lives apparently for nothing better than to gain a few yards of uncultivated land.

A comparatively small body of the finest troops in the world, French and British, have effected a lodgement close to the heart of a great continental empire, still formidable even in its decadence. Here they stand firm, or slowly advance, and in the efforts made by successive Turkish armies to dislodge them the rotten Government at Constantinople is gradually wearing itself out. The facts and figures upon which this conclusion is based have been checked and verified from a variety of sources. Agents of neutral powers possessing good sources of information have placed both the numbers and the losses of the enemy much higher than they are set forth here, but the General Commanding prefers to be on the safe side and to give his troops a strictly conservative estimate.

Before operations began the strength of the defenders of the Dardanelles was:

Gallipoli Peninsula   31,000 and about 100 guns
Asiatic side of Straits   41,000

All the troops on the Gallipoli Peninsula and 50 per cent of the troops on the Asiatic side were Nizam; that is to say, regular first line troops. They were transferable, and were actually transferred to the side upon which the invaders disembarked. Our expeditionary force effected its landing, it will be seen, in the face of an enemy superior not only to the covering parties which got ashore the first day, but superior actually to the total strength at our disposal. By 12 May the Turkish army of occupation had been defeated in several engagements, and would have been at the end of their resources had they not meanwhile received reinforcements of 20,000 infantry and 21 batteries of field artillery.

Still the expeditionary force held its own, and more than held its own, inflicting fresh bloody defeat upon the newcomers; and again the Turks must certainly have given way had not a second reinforcement reached the peninsula from Constantinople and Smyrna, amounting at the lowest estimate to 24,000 men.

From what I have said it will be understood that the Mediterranean Expeditionary Force, supported by its gallant comrades of the fleet, but with constantly diminishing effectives, has held in check or wrested ground from some 120,000 Turkish troops elaborately entrenched and supported by a powerful artillery.

The enemy now has few more Nizam troops at his disposal and not many Redif, or second class, troops. Up to date his casualties are 55,000 and again, in giving this figure, the General Commanding has preferred to err on the side of low estimates.

Daily we make progress, and whenever the reinforcements close to hand begin to put in an appearance, the Mediterranean Expeditionary Force will press forward with a fresh impulse to accomplish the greatest imperial task ever entrusted to an army.[17]

Propaganda came from the other side, too; towards the end of May Turkish aeroplanes flew over the RND lines and dropped leaflets:

Proclamation to the Anglo-French Expeditionary Forces

Protected by a heavy fire from a powerful fleet, you have been able to land on the Gallipoli Peninsula on and since 25 April. Backed up by those same men-of-war you could establish yourselves at two points on the peninsula. All your endeavours to advance into the inner parts of the peninsula have come to failure under your heavy losses, although your ships have done their utmost to assist you by a tremendous cannonade implying an enormous waste of ammunition.

Two fine British battleships, *Triumph* and *Majestic*, have been sunk before your own eyes by submarine boats, all protective means against them being found utterly insufficient. Since those severe losses to the British Navy your men-of-war had to take refuge and have abandoned you to your fate. Your ships cannot possibly be of any help to you in future, since a great number of submarines are prepared to suppress them.

Your forces have to rely on sea transport for reinforcement and supply of food, water, and ever kind of war materials. Already submarines did sink several steamers carrying supplies for your destination. Soon all supplies will be entirely cut off from your landed forces. You are exposed to certain perdition by starvation and thirst.

Even desperate attacks will not avert that fate from you. You could only escape useless sacrifice by surrendering. We are assured that you have not taken arms against us by hatred. Greedy England made you fight under a contract. You may confide in us for excellent treatment. Our country disposes of ample provisions; there is enough for you to feed you well and make you feel quite at your comfort. Don't further hesitate! Come and surrender.

On all fronts of this war, your own people and your allies' situation is as hopeless as on this peninsula. All news spread among you concerning the German and Austrian armies are mere lies. There stands neither one Englishman, nor one Frenchman, nor one Russian on German soil. On the contrary, the German troops are keeping a strong hold on the whole of Belgium and on conspicuous parts of France, since many a month.

A considerable part of Russian Poland is also in the hands of the Germans, who advance there every day. Early in May strong German and Austrian forces have broken through the Russian centre in Galicia. Przemysl has fallen back into their hands lately. They are not in the least way handicapped by Italy's joining your coalition, but are successfully engaged in driving the Russians out of Galicia.

These Russian troops, whose co-operation one made you look forward to, are surrendering by hundreds and thousands. Do as they do! Your honour is safe!! Further fighting is mere stupid bloodshed![18]

The Hood reaction to this material is shown in a piece of doggerel current at the time:

THE HOOD ALPHABET

A is for Asquith, Arthur or 'Oc',
Who's winged by a bullet just now and a crock.
B is for Burnett, a scout bred and born;
Both bullets and snipers he treats with mere scorn.
C stands for Chalmers, who grouses all day,
But works like a Trojan, as all of us say.
D denotes Daglish, who's positive quite,
That one's view's either wrong, or else perfectly right.

Egerton's E, and my very good friend,
Who has read through this trash and helped me no end.
F is for Fergie, and Freyberg as well;
Both jolly good fellows, but different as h**l.
Graham is G, or adjutant really:
His arm's in a sling and he's doing but queerly.
H is for Hedderwick, Hood and the rest
Who've been into action and well stood the test.
I's for ideas that we all of us hold,
That to get through the straits would be better than gold.
J stands for Johnny, unselfish and kind;
He's hit in both arms, but pretends he don't mind.
K stands for Kelly, that oarsman of fame,
Who's now lending a hand at a different game.
L is the line of the trenches we hold:
Hot and dusty all day – at night terribly cold.
M stands for Maxim, with Martin and crew;
Without their stout help, I don't know what we'd do.
Nobb knows the drill-book from first page to last,
While Nelson at scouting cannot be surpassed.
O is the orders that must be obeyed,
Though one's dying for sleep and one's nerves are all frayed.
P is for Parsons, as calm as can be,
Though I fancy he'd rather be fighting at sea.
Q is for Quilter – he's now laid to rest:
A leader of men, he was one of the best.
R for recruits who have stuck it A1,
And are proving a thorn in the flesh of the Hun.
Shaw-Stewart and Shadbolt both start with an S;
One excels at finance, and the other at chess.
T is for Trimmer, who's hit in the head;
He's now convalescent, but ought to be dead.
U is unselfishness shown by our Doc;
He's one in a million and stands like a rock.
V is for these verses – they're awful, it's true;
But I'm not a born poet – that's evident, too!
Waller is W, small but replete
With good stories and jests from his head to his feet.
For X, Y and Z there are no words I know
That fit into this rhyme, so I'll just let them go.[19]

CHAPTER ELEVEN

June, 1915

June came in with General Sir Ian Hamilton planning for the next major attack, which was to be on 4 June. The fresh battalions had somewhat filled the RND's deficiency in numbers, though these replacements were not battle-hardened like the old hands. But there was a plus: this was the first time since Antwerp that the whole division had been together under its commander.

Like the second battle of Krithia, the next push was to be a direct frontal attack along the whole Turkish line. The difference was that the British front line was now up against its Turkish counterpart; the static stalemate of trench warfare had set in, and the location of the Turkish lines was known. The objectives were less grandiose, too, and the first attacking waves were not given the summit of Achi Baba as their prime target.

Against these advantages, the Turkish army had been extensively reinforced. The Kereves Dere ridge ran along their left flank, opposite the French, and was immune to attack beyond a dangerous advance along the line of the ridge. It formed the major question mark over the outcome of the battle, in that the ridge ran diagonally across towards the RND's front line. The French had valiantly fought their way forward another 200 to 300 yards in an earlier battle, but unless they could move the deeply-entrenched Turks any gains made by the RND would be jeopardized, as the defenders could enfilade the British at will from the high ground. The RND's success or failure hung on the performance of the French, and any deficiency on their part could prejudice the final result along the whole British line.

The RND front was the smallest sector in the line, being somewhat less than 1,000 yards long. The division had to supply two brigades for the corps general reserve. The Marine Brigade and 1st Brigade, less one battalion, were chosen for this task, leaving 2nd Brigade, under Commodore Backhouse, for the main advance. The experienced Hood,

Howe and Anson troops would attack the first two Turkish trenches, and a redoubt situated on the right near the brigade's boundary with the French. Anson would be on the right, next to the French Senegalese, Hood would again take the centre, and Howe would be on the left, next to the 42nd Division's Manchester Brigade. Collingwood's A and B Companies (less one platoon) and D Company (also less one platoon) would support them. Collingwood's C Company, plus one platoon from B and one from D, were to act as reserves, with picks and shovels if necessary.[1]

Backhouse had a total of 2,140 troops at his disposal, organized in four groups:

Garrison	400 – Howe, Hood and Anson
First Line	930 – Howe, Hood and Anson
Second Line	500 – Collingwood
Consolidating party	310 – Collingwood.[2]

At 2.30am on 4 June the 2nd Naval Brigade moved forward from their rest camps across the broken ground and into Achi Baba Nullah – past Backhouse Post and the grave of Colonel Quilter, past croaking frogs whose orchestration cut through the silence of a pitch-black night. Once they were in position, the reserves moved forward to their allotted areas: Drake went to Backhouse Post, and Hawke to the rest camps.

Unfortunately, General Hunter-Weston had learned no lessons from the events of 6 May, and the attack was timed for noon. A bombardment of sorts began at 8am, and the rate of fire increased somewhat at 10.30. At 11.20 the artillery ceased and the infantry were instructed to cheer, showing fixed bayonets above the parapets and opening controlled fire from the trenches. This was designed to draw the Turkish reserve troops up to the front line, so that when the bombardment resumed at 11.30 they would be caught in the heavy artillery fire. But as soon as the troops started this feint the Turks swept the British lines with machine-gun and rapid rifle fire. The simple fact was that the British didn't have enough shells, and their bombardment had been derisory. The men faced the prospect of advancing in full sun towards an enemy in good defensive positions whose capacity to inflict heavy losses had not been substantially reduced by artillery.

Joseph Murray remembers the preparations for the attack:

I was Asquith's runner, so all the officers knew me by name. Commander Parsons called to me, 'Murray, here. Take six men down to Backhouse Post and bring up some ammunition.' I picked the first men I could find, and we brought up one lot. When we got back Parsons said, 'I would like another load; can you manage another load?' So I took the six back and collected some more. On the way up, when we had almost got to the firing line, we sat down for a rest about 50 yards from the line. Commodore Backhouse came along, and said, 'Hallo, hallo, what's the idea?' I was next to him, and in the navy you had to ask permission to speak to an officer, so I said, 'Permission to speak, sir?' 'Yes,' said Backhouse. 'Permission granted.' 'This is our second journey, sir.' The officer replied, 'Not too bad, not too bad at all. Don't take too long.' He then moved on.

The ammunition detail made their way back to the front line and reported to Commander Parsons, who was to lead the advance in that section. He told Murray and his party to garrison the trench, but Murray was worried in case anything happened to Parsons and it was thought they were dodging the column rather than obeying direct orders to stay in the trench. He went off in search of his platoon to tell them of his new posting, scrambling along a couple of trench bays past a dozen or so men on his way. When he got to his sector he found three men had already been killed on the firing step and parapet. Another officer was approaching, asking around, 'I am looking for Murray: does anyone know where he is?' As he walked towards Murray, calling, 'I'm Petty Officer . . . ' he was shot dead, and Murray never found out what he wanted. In this one small part of the line alone, four men had been killed before the advance even began.

Commander Parsons was standing on a short ladder in the five-foot-deep trench, just below the parapet, checking his watch and counting down the time for the advance, with a reassuring smile on his face. All watches had been synchronized at 8.15am as part of divisional orders, so Parsons counted each minute. The time seemed like an age: each man was lost in thought, wondering if a view of a dusty trench, bodies and blood would be his last sight of the world.

'Are you ready?' asked Parsons. 'Come on, then, follow me.' He went up the ladder over the parapet into a hail of machine-gun fire, and was killed before he could even draw breath. Many of those following him just fell back into the trench, or forward across the parapet. The Turks inflicted horrendous casualties: only half the troops got forward the 50 yards to the dead ground immediately in front of the Hood trench. They had been ordered to rush without firing straight into the enemy's trenches, but the Turkish front line at this point lay between 200 and 400 yards from the RND. However, after a short breather another mad charge took the survivors up to the Turkish trenches, where they jumped down eight feet into cover. The British artillery had made little impact on the defences, but the position was unoccupied beyond enemy dead and wounded.

As he arrived at the first trench Joseph Murray felt a blow on his chest. He fell head first into the trench, on top of a dead Turk, and lapsed into unconsciousness. When he came to he found one of his eyes refused to open, but it turned out to be simply glued up with congealed blood from the dead Turk. Murray had been struck in the chest by a burst of machine-gun fire, but his belt and ammunition pouch seemed to have acted as protection from the bullets. He had trouble getting to his feet, though, as he was still partly stunned. He found his rifle, but the trench was too deep for him to climb out, so he made his way along it for about 50 yards until he came to a shell hole where he could scramble up. At the top he found his platoon officer, a small man called Lieutenant Leonard Cockey, sitting on the parapet making a sketch of the Turkish defensive positions.

The Collingwood Battalion was ordered to attack at 12.15pm; looking back as he lay in the protection of some scrub, Murray could see them advancing between the British and Turkish front lines. The Turks were still in command of the Kereves Dere ridge, ensconced in three tiers of trenches banked one above the other up the slope, and they could find targets for their machine guns with ease. Only 300 of the Collingwood even reached the advanced British trenches, and very few ever got to the Turkish defences: Murray saw not a single Collingwood man reach the first Turkish trench in his area, and he had an extensive view from his position. The British could only have got across by crawling, but Murray saw none.

A few remaining Hood got as far as the third Turkish trench, which was just a ditch, but the situation was impossible. The Howe had made little progress on the left wing, the French had not advanced along the Kereves Dere, and Turks could be seen advancing on the flanks. The Hood was ordered to retire, and for the forward troops the order came only just in time.[3]

Lieutenant Denis Browne had been on the left of the Hood line, leading about 250 men across a front of 200 yards. Their objective was the further of two enemy trenches about 350 yards ahead. On reaching the first trench, Browne jumped in and bayoneted a Turk, but was almost immediately shot in the left shoulder. Turning to one side, he bayoneted another Turk, then another bullet drove the iron buckle of his belt into his body. A British petty officer came to his rescue and bound up his wounds. Browne fainted, but recovered quickly and offered his rescuer his watch and some money. They were refused, but the petty officer did accept Browne's pocket-book before he was obliged to retreat in haste. The ground was retaken by the enemy immediately, and Browne was only reported missing a week later. His body was never recovered. The petty officer later gave Browne's pocket-book to Patrick Shaw-Stewart, who found inside it a message for Edward Marsh, Churchill's secretary:

104

I've gone now, too. Not too badly, I hope. I'm luckier than Rupert, because I've fought. But there's no-one to bury me as I buried him, so perhaps he's best off in the long run.[4]

Returning to the front line, the surviving troops found a horrific scene. Many had died before they got out of the trench, falling back into it; others had been wounded and crawled back to die. In places the floor was three or four deep in bodies. Men were still hanging over the parapets, others were slumped on the firestep. Some of the remaining troops had no option but to stand on their dead comrades, while the bodies on the parapet provided extra cover for the living.

The failure of the French to advance along the Kereves Dere ridge had a domino effect on British efforts. The RND advance became a carnage, which led in turn to difficulties for the 42nd Division on the left: they had captured and were holding three lines of Turkish trenches, but now had to withdraw down their flank back to the Turkish front line. In his book *Gallipoli Memories*, Compton Mackenzie writes:

> They thought that the French had let them down completely on the right. Patrick Shaw-Stewart was seen running along waving his cane and shouting, '*Avancez! Avancez!*' The Senegalese came out of their trenches, advanced 17 yards, and then bolted back into them like so many gigantic rabbits, after which nothing would persuade them to show themselves again.[5]

In his report of 5 June Commodore Backhouse wrote that the French did not advance more than 20 yards, and not more than 12 men left their trench. Lieutenant Jones, the senior unwounded officer in Anson, reported that his party captured the redoubt but that he saw no French.

General Paris was now concerned that the Turks might counterattack, so Drake was ordered up to the front line. The British planned to advance at 2.15 p.m. with French artillery support, so extreme efforts were made to get the French to assist with the renewed attack; but the French commander would not help, and all endeavours to get him to change his mind failed. But consolidation of the line was now a priority, and at 2.30pm Benbow Battalion was moved up into the gully from the corps reserve. Paris then ordered the battered Hood, Howe and Collingwood Battalions to be relieved by Nelson and Hawke.

The whole battle had been a disaster: some 1,900 men and 70 officers of the 2nd Brigade had advanced at noon on 4 June, and the following day Commodore Backhouse reported that casualties totalled 1,319 men and 61 officers.[6]

The newly-arrived Collingwood Battalion suffered terribly, losing 25 officers and around 600 other ranks. By the end of the day only three officers were left alive: Sub-Lieutenant John Watts of A Company, 4th Platoon; Sub-Lieutenant Kenneth Oldridge of A Company, 3rd Platoon; and Sub-Lieutenant Robert Ritson of the machine gun section. Deprived of their officers, many of the remnants of the battalion were shepherded out of the battle by Chief Petty Officer Carnell, who was awarded the DSM for his service that day.[7] He was later promoted to be an RNVR sub-lieutenant and posted to Hood. The surviving men, meanwhile, had lived through horror, and many were in such a state that they could no longer be relied upon.

The Hood lost 12 officers and approximately 300 other ranks; they also lost a second CO. Lieutenant-Colonel Charles Kennedy-Crawford-Stuart, who had replaced Colonel Quilter after the latter was killed on 6 May, was in his turn killed by a bullet in the jaw on 4 June.[8] The scale of the Hood losses can be judged by the fact that, since the battalion landed at Gallipoli on the night of 29 April, in Joseph Murray's section (one petty officer, one leading seaman and 12 men) eight had been killed: Petty Officer Warren, and Able Seamen Packwood, Kelly, Mutch, Buckley, Yates, Houghton and Aston.[9]

The remains of Hood, Howe and Collingwood Battalions now had to be reorganized. Paris's solution was to disband the newly-arrived Benbow and Collingwood Battalions completely and transfer their officers and men to Hood, Howe and Anson. As a result, the two Naval Brigades ended up having only three battalions apiece.

The battle on 4 June had a profound effect on both the RND and the expeditionary force's commander-in-chief, Sir Ian Hamilton. Hamilton had watched the attack from close quarters, not isolated from events this time, and his emotions had swung from hope to deep disappointment. Compton Mackenzie, who was on Hamilton's staff at that time, wrote:

> A black depression fell. I stood for Sir Ian Hamilton to pass back along the trench. Then with one glance over my shoulder at that accursed hill of Achi Baba, which stood with hunched, defiant shoulders between us and Constantinople, I followed the single file procession down the trench. Nobody spoke a word.[10]

After 4 June the Helles campaign was limited to minor operations, while efforts to strike a decisive blow were made on other fronts. The morale of the men was suffering: Murray saw a colleague deliberately put his thumb over the muzzle of his rifle and pull the trigger to avoid going back into the line. Murray had to cut away the hanging flesh so the wound could be bandaged to stop the extensive bleeding. The man, in a state of panic, told Murray he couldn't stand it any more and begged him not to give him away; Murray, after much soul-searching, concurred with the request.[11]

On 18 June Paris arranged for the 2nd Brigade to go to a rest camp on the nearby island of Imbros. Two-thirds of the Hood left Gallipoli, followed the next day by the remainder. While enjoying this leave Commodore Backhouse became ill with dysentery. On 26 June he was petitioned by 63 Hood stokers, who wanted to go to sea. Perhaps affected by his illness, influenced by the peace of Imbros, or simply aware of the deep dissatisfaction of many of the troops, Backhouse wired Major-General Paris to ask leave to discharge the stokers to the fleet.

The immediate result of the communication was that Backhouse was recalled at once. Back in Gallipoli, he wrote in his diary on Monday, 28 June that after breakfast he had a long argument with Paris regarding the break-up of the 2nd Brigade, to which Backhouse was strongly opposed. Backhouse was taken to see General Hunter-Weston, and spoke about the possibility of applying for the naval artillery. Backhouse ended his diary entry by stating: 'I am convinced that the Royal Naval Division is in a dying condition.'[12]

On 29 June Major-General Paris wrote of the incident:

My army has been giving me some trouble, particularly the 2nd Brigade (Commodore Backhouse). After our fight on 4 June it was really reduced down to 1,100 and with little prospect of speedy reinforcements. However there was a . . . battalion, the Benbow, which I broke up for drafts, and with the remains of the Collingwood Battalion brought the 2nd up to the respectable total of 2,500. I then got them sent to Imbros for a rest and to reorganize. The holiday was a failure. After a few days Backhouse reported grave discontent, and that the new officers and men wouldn't mix with the veterans, and recommended breaking up the brigade and that he should go to sea!

My reply was simple: return here at once. And then I had a heart-to-heart talk with the officers; explained the difference between peace and war, and how my powers of dealing with disloyal officers could be carried on. My friends received it with a little astonishment when I explained there was no such thing as resignation and their only way of leaving the peninsula was on a stretcher or as a prisoner.

Backhouse put in for sick leave, which I sent him on. A few hours later he sent me a letter withdrawing it. I told him what I expected, and hope things will now smooth out.[13]

In many ways it is not surprising that there was trouble among the men of the amalgamated battalions, as of the only three Collingwood officers left, two were on sick leave and the other was away having dental treatment. There was nobody to guide the men of their former battalion. However, Joseph Murray (who, being a miner in civilian life, had been attached to the RND engineers for sapping and well-digging duties, and didn't go to Imbros) has a different view:

> I don't remember any trouble there. I know they came back after about a week. I didn't go myself. But, mind you, I don't disagree with it because we got such a bashing on 4 June. Anything would be better than Gallipoli.[14]

Some time after this Paris visited Hunter-Weston at his HQ, and Compton Mackenzie remembers a conversation between the two men. Hunter-Weston spoke enthusiastically of a successful action on one portion of the front:

> 'Many casualties?' asked General Paris, in a voice that could not hide the bitterness he felt on behalf of his own splendid division. And as I think of General Hunter-Weston's reply, I fancy I saw a falcon strike angrily at some grizzled, trusty old dog.
> 'Casualties?' he cried, eyes flashing, aquiline nose quivering. 'What do I care for casualties?'
> The other rose from the chair. 'I must be getting back,' he growled. 'You'll stay for tea?' 'No thanks.'

There was obviously a huge difference in character between Hunter-Weston and the burly, florid Paris; perhaps, indeed, as wide as the chasm in nature between a dog and a falcon.[15] The difference is pointed up by a remark made by Paris in a letter describing the terrible casualties:

> A dreadful feeling of having caused unnecessary losses by doing something which might have been done better some other way must be like a doctor who makes a fatal mistake. I can only say I've honestly done my best, but the feelings remain.[16]

Years later a poem was found in Patrick Shaw-Stewart's handwriting:

> I saw a man this morning
> Who did not wish to die:
> I ask, and cannot answer,
> If otherwise wish I.
>
> Fair broke the day this morning
> Against the Dardanelles;
> The breeze blew soft, the morn's cheeks
> Were cold as cold sea-shells.

But other shells are waiting
Across the Aegean Sea;
Shrapnel and high explosive,
Shells and hells for me.

O, hell of ships and cities,
Hell of men like me;
Fatal second Helen,
Why must I follow thee?

Achilles came to Troyland
And I to Chersonese:
He turned from wrath to battle,
And I from three days' peace.

Was it so hard, Achilles,
So very hard to die?
Thou knowest and I know not –
So much the happier I.

I will go back this morning,
From Imbros over the sea;
Stand in the trench, Achilles,
Flame-capped, and shout for me.[17]

Hood Battalion, Royal Naval Division
List of officers as at 12 July, 1915

Name	Rank	Date of Appointment
Myburgh, A.	Major	25.2.15
Freyberg, B.C.	Lieutenant-Commander	1.9.14
Nelson, E.W.	Lieutenant-Commander	20.10.14
Asquith, A.M.	Lieutenant-Commander	10.11.14
Gillard, H.	Paymaster	19.12.14
Shaw-Stewart, P.H.	Lieutenant	19.12.14
Buckland, L.	Lieutenant	20.10.14
Paine, C.W.S.	Lieutenant	10.6.15
Molesworth, E.M.	Surgeon	10.6.15
Kelly, E.D.F.	Sub-Lieutenant	23.2.15
Egerton, W.H.	Sub-Lieutenant	23.10.14
Heald, I.	Sub-Lieutenant	10.6.15
Webb, W.F.	Sub-Lieutenant	10.6.15
Carnall, W.	Sub-Lieutenant	12.6.15
Barclay, W.E.	Sub-Lieutenant	10.6.15
Ritson, R.	Sub-Lieutenant	9.6.15
Lister, the Hon C.A.	Lieutenant, RM	30.3.15

The following are sick:

Chalmers, A.G.N.	Lieutenant (attached RE for mining)
Oldridge, K.	Sub-Lieutenant
Watts, J.C.	Sub-Lieutenant

The following are wounded:

Burnett, S.O.	Lieutenant-Commander
Nobbs, E.	Lieutenant
McCracken, W.J.	Surgeon
Gamage, E.M.	Sub-Lieutenant
Cockey, L.H.	Sub-Lieutenant

Taken from the Backhouse Papers, Imperial War Museum, reference 86/31/1. There is also a note that Major Myburgh and Sub-Lieutenant Ritson were at Imbros for dental treatment.

10. Rupert Brooke.

11. Lieutenant-Commander Bernard Freyberg at Blandford Camp in February, 1915 (*Lord Freyberg*).

12. Patrick Shaw-Stewart.

13. The Hon Charles Lister.

14. Lieut Johnny Bigelow Dodge (*Lord Freyberg*).

16. Lieut Frederick Septimus 'Cleg' Kelly, killed in action 13 November, 1916 (*Illustrated London News, 9 December, 1916*).

15. Lieut William Denis Browne (*Professor Jon Stallworthy*).

17. Arthur Asquith (*Hon Mrs Rous*).

LIEUT. F. S. KELLY,
R.N.V.R. The famous Eton and Oxford oarsman, who won the Diamond Sculls three times. Awarded D.S.C.

18. Rupert Brooke outside his hut at Blandford Camp, Dorset. (*Professor Jon Stallworthy*).

19. The Hood Battalion Officers at Blandford Camp in February, 1915.

From left to right, back row —

Lt Arthur ('Oc') Asquith, Lt Jacobs (battalion interpreter), Lt Edmond Waller, Lt Shadbolt.

From left to right, middle row —

Lt Edward William Nelson, Lt Rupert Brooke, Lt W.M. Egerton, Lt John Bigelow Dodge, Lt William Denis Browne, Unknown, Lt Charles Martin, Lt Eric Gamage, Lt Douglas Cassey, Lt Ernest Nobbs (Quartermaster).

From left to right, front row —

J.C. Gilliard (Paymaster), Lt John Ferguson, Lt Commander Bernard Freyberg, Lt Commander Raymond S. Parsons, Lt Commander Alexander Graham (Adjutant), Lt Colonel John Quilter, Lt Commander W.F. Burnett, Lt Commander J. Daglish, Lt A. Hughes, Lt The Hon Maurice Hood, Lt Commander H.C. Hedderwick (*IWM*).

CHAPTER TWELVE

July, 1915

The period after the battle of 4 June was one of reorganization and rest, interspersed with routine supply duties and fatigues. By 10 June, swelled by some 225 men and three officers transferred from the disbanded Collingwood Battalion, the Hood could muster 14 officers and 705 men. These separate parts had to be welded into another effective fighting force, but this would not be easy. Having returned to the battalion after injury, Lieutenant Charles Lister described the task ahead in letters written between 23 June and 1 July:

> I shan't find my battalion much in the swing of it yet awhile; we are, I fancy, too reduced, and now getting ourselves together again under our ex-second in command, Major Myburgh . . . .
>
> The battalion is a mixed lot now, filled up with odds and ends from new formations, etc. . . . I am now a second-in-command of a company under a real type, Chalmers by name, whom I am very fond of, but this will not last for long when more of our wounded return. I am the baby of the Hood. We have been subjected to pi-jaws on the subject of a brigade reorganization, which has been necessary in our case and accompanied by some friction, as it involved the break-up of two young battalions to make us up to strength . . . .
>
> Soldiers, of course, have much practice at stump oratory, as the most junior platoon officer is supposed to lecture his men. I have studiously avoided doing so.

As the calendar moved on to July, the Hood and the 2nd Naval Brigade were still not in a front line position. Further extracts from Lister's letter of early July give an indication of the conditions:

> My dug-out is now fairly well organized, though I had two wet nights owing to holes in my waterproof sheets, which treacherously let the

water-pool there find its way to the apertures and pour down on my devoted head. Shells come down from time to time. Yesterday three burst on our lines, without doing any damage bar riddling poor Patrick's best khaki tunic (luckily he was not in it, but it was hanging on a tree) and covering his sleeping bag with soot. One fell in the lines next to us, killing two and wounding ten men. So it is purely a matter of chance . . . .

At night our camp looks lovely, with little lights in the dug-outs shining through the sacking and waterproof sheets, and the olive-trees in relief against the night sky and silvery in the moonlight. The darkness, moreover, hides the grassless state of our lines . . . .

The men in the trenches seem most cheerful and pretty comfort-able, though they don't get much sleep, as heat and flies stop their getting it by day and rifle-fire and watches stop them at night. I am rather annoyed at this continual state of inactivity, as we can't really get to know our men or train them if we are always doing fatigues and living under the eye of the Turkish gunners. Our new men want a lot of shaking down. We have not enough officers . . . .

I did some sniping at a Turkish loophole, and had two shots hitting the iron round of the loophole quite neatly. The men love sniping . . . .

The beaches are the most extraordinary places, full of dug-outs, and just like London, for no-one knows who his next-door neighbour is, and to find any one is practically an impossibility. The beach take themselves very seriously, and one would think that no-one else on the peninsula is in any danger whatsoever.[1]

At the foot of the cliff on 'W' beach, a swarthy, square-faced Greek set up a canteen. When word got around that he had opened up shop, queues of up to 100 men would form to buy his strings of fly-laden figs and, on occasion, tins of condensed milk. The figs were no doubt a prime source of dysentery, but the temptation was real for men fed on hard biscuits. Joseph Murray remembers:

I used to have an awful row with him because I wanted some milk and all he had was those figs. He wanted the condensed milk kept for the officers.[2]

The Greek was a successful entrepreneur, and prices on the beach were high. He was also not averse to dabbling in other fields, as Able Seaman Thomas Mitchell-Fox of the Hood noted:

Somebody spotted that he was using a lamp and signalling to a Turkish boat somewhere or other. He was court-martialled and shot.[3]

But the ageless versatility of the British serviceman easily overcame this trade embargo, using an old sailors' stunt. The men engaged in unloading lighters alongside the pier had a dual function: to carry a box from the lighter, then return with a lump of rock to throw into the sea to reinforce the pier against the ravages of the waves. Boxes would often get broken in transit, and it was not unknown for a partly-broken box of condensed milk to fall into the water. According to an unwritten law, the man carrying the broken container would also 'accidentally' fall into the sea, and was then entitled to first claim on the salvage. The others would quickly show their prowess as underwater swimmers, and on most occasions all the conspirators would find plenty to satisfy them. Murray says that the condensed milk kept him alive. But this state of affairs only operated between the lighters and the beach: rations transported from the quartermaster's stores to the front were never touched, as this would have been sacrilege in the eyes of the men.[4]

As one made one's way from the beaches towards the RND front line one passed four large water-towers; now no more than ruins, at the time they were between 50 and 80 feet high. On his first visit to the sector Compton Mackenzie saw what looked like factory chimneys emerging from groves of trees on the eastern side of the peninsula – apparently the remains of a Roman aqueduct.[5] Today no stone can be found to show these piles of masonry ever existed, and research indicates that they were most unlikely to be sections of an ancient aqueduct, so their true function is unknown. After the water-towers came Skew bridge: simply wooden planks set at an angle over the watercourse.

A quarter of a mile beyond Skew bridge towards Achi Baba, Backhouse Post was set to the east of Observation Hill. Established shortly after the landings as 2nd Brigade's HQ, the post was also adopted as the divisional supply dump, as it was the last point which could be reached by wheeled vehicles. Although not free from enemy observation and shellfire, it had the advantage of some shady trees and a small stream close by. It was signposted by a tin notice, roughly triangular in shape, with the words 'Backhouse Post' painted in black on all three sides. (This sign was removed from the Peninsula by Major Bruce Allen of the 7th Royal Scots, and now rests, protected by a sealed triangular box, in the Royal Scots' regimental museum in Edinburgh Castle.)[6]

Continuing north-east, Sauchiehall Street trench ran parallel to Achi Baba Nullah up to the White House and Brown House positions captured in the Hood advance on 6 May. Beyond these shack-like buildings, an extensive system of interlaced trenches led forward towards the goal of Achi Baba. One main junction was called Piccadilly Circus, and near it the military maps marked a ruin: Joseph Murray remembers seeing the ruins of a mosque with a domed roof at this spot. The trenches extended all the way to the most advanced front line positions, just forward of a vineyard on the far side of the Krithia road, and about one mile from the village of Krithia itself.

At the front line a policy was adopted of sapping by day, and digging in the open and wiring at night. Occasionally they were able to swim in the sea, which was an experience of sheer joy for the troops, plunging naked into the warm water to clean off the dust, dirt and lice of the land. Lister commented:

> The bathing here is very pleasant, though care has to be exercised in avoiding dead horses. Once out of their reach the water is deliciously cool and clear.[7]

On 5 July the monotony was broken by a small Turkish attack directed towards the French and Anson Battalion, who were then temporarily attached to the 1st Naval Brigade. Two extremely smart German officers were seen urging their Turkish troops to advance, but the troops seemed reluctant and the main attack never developed. About 20 of the most adventurous assailants forced their way into the Anson front line trench, but Anson's commander, Major Bridges, organized a counter-attack and the invaders were quickly driven out. Just then the Anson officer in charge of the front line came out of his dug-out after finishing his breakfast, completely unaware that the Turks had paid them a visit.[8] This episode amused other members of the RND for months; lads of the Hood would enquire of a member of the Anson, 'Have you had any breakfast?'[9]

On 6 July the RND was relieved at the front by the newly-arrived 52nd Division. A renewed offensive south of Achi Baba was also planned, although opinions were divided: the senior officers at the front still wanted a low profile approach of defence and minor operations, so that rest and reorganization could be effective; the general staff felt that another attack was the more urgent need. A compromise was reached: the attack would be carried out by the 52nd, the only fresh division available. They would advance in the centre on 12 and 13 July, to bring the British front line level with the gains made on the right and left flanks.

Hunter-Weston, still showing his lack of forethought and overall knowledge of the condition of his troops, had originally planned for the RND to lead the attack. Only when numerous medical reports were sent to his HQ did he reluctantly accept that the division was on the verge of exhaustion and, after two months of fighting, had long passed the limits of human endurance. Robert Rhodes James, in his book *Gallipoli*, wrote:

The fact that this proposal had ever been made dramatically illuminates the ignorance of the conditions of individual units which reigned at Corps Headquarters; in so narrow a front, this was inexcusable.[10]

The 52nd Division's attack was the bloodiest engagement to date in proportion to the numbers involved in an offensive. Known as the Action of the Achi Baba Nullah, it started at 7.35am on 12 July, one of the hottest days yet endured at Gallipoli that summer. The Turkish trenches on the right, along the Kereves Dere ridge, had been taken by trench troops on 21 June, so the major problem of Turkish enfilade fire suffered by the RND advance on 4 June was lessened. To ensure the problem did not recur, the 52nd Division was to attack firstly on the right, advancing on the left when this flank had achieved its objective.

By the evening the situation was somewhat confused: the troops on the right and left flanks had both pushed forward and gained ground, but in the centre they had not got beyond the Turkish trench lines. The fighting had been so fierce that all the 52nd Division's reserves had been drawn in, so the RND Chatham, Portsmouth, Plymouth and Drake Battalions were advanced to the 52nd's divisional reserve. Hood, Howe, Nelson and Hawke Battalions were under orders to move at 10 minutes' notice.

That night the general position remained unchanged, but by the morning of 13 July the communication trench between the 52nd's forward troops (157th Brigade, in advance trenches near Achi Baba Nullah) and other divisional units was threatened. The maps on which the operation was planned were incorrect, showing a third-line trench which did not exist. RND Battalions were ordered to attack at 4.30pm to rectify the situation, but congestion in the trenches meant that orders to some units were late in arriving. Many RND men were lost, especially from the Marine Brigade and Nelson Battalion. Douglas Jerrold commented:

> Only those who actually witnessed it can imagine the unbelievable confusion of the battle, the sickness of the troops, intensified a hundredfold by local conditions and the tenacity of the Turkish resistance . . . . As night came on the conditions were well-nigh unendurable. Some of the worst scenes ever experienced on the battlefields of France or Mesopotamia were crowded into this narrow front of half a mile, over which fighting had been continuous for nearly 48 hours, where many hundreds of men lay dead and dying, where a burning sun had turned the bodies of the slain to a premature corruption, where there was no resting place free from physical contamination, where the air, the surface of the ground, and the soil beneath the surface were alike poisonous, foetid, corrupt.[11]

Major-General Paris wrote on 21 July:

> The other day we had to capture some trenches which the 52nd Division (Terriers) had taken and lost. The most awful confusion; 15 battalions, mostly in a state of panic, filling up all the trenches and communications which were only built for four battalions. No orders or reports could be sent or received. The captured Turkish trenches beggar description.[12]

The line gained at the end of the battle was short of the objective, but was, in General Paris's opinion, the best the division had yet held from a military point of view, the task now one of consolidation, defence and reorganization. The 52nd Division was withdrawn from the front line and the RND took over the whole sector. Douglas Jerrold continued:

> Here for 10 days hardly less anxious and no less unpleasant than the actual days of battle, the division laboured on the essential tasks of burying the dead, reconstructing the trenches and pushing forward barricades along the trenches communicating between our own lines and those of the enemy. The strain on the troops must have been almost unprecedented in the annals of defensive warfare but the work proceeded, battalions worked at high pressure for short spells in the front line, and within less than a fortnight conditions reverted to normal.[13]

My great-uncle, Albert Walls, was killed at this point in the campaign, and I have pieced together some of the details of his death from contemporary papers, maps and letters. Studying the war diary of the RND Signals Company for Sunday, 18 July and comparing it with a trench map drawn on the same day (marked 'Secret – Not to be Taken into Action'), one finds point P is in the possession of the British:

> Have reached 100 yards east of P towards S and men still moving along. Nothing much to report in the relief of the line except relief of 5th Highland Light Infantry by 6th East Lancashires. The company in Horseshoe trench E12B will be relieved later, after dark. Only patrols pushed towards S from P. The enemy in E12 as far and beyond junction of E12 and PS unoccupied. Very shallow and broken and filled with dead. Untenable for the enemy.[14]

Commodore Backhouse went up to the front line that day and wrote in his diary:

> Walked to point P and along new trench cut by Deal overnight, thence along the line to Horseshoe. Did a lot of crawling to arrange

new works. Visited East Lancashires in Plymouth section and Hood and Howe in line. Arranged new works. Terribly hot in trenches, flies and stench awful.[15]

Lieutenant Charles Lister wrote a letter on 18 July which tends to support the family belief that Albert was killed by a sniper:

We are in the trenches. We went in about three days ago. They are old Turkish trenches, with one or two admirably protected dug-outs, which we suspect the Turks have been made to hollow out for the German officers. It is fairly whiffy, and there are quite a number of dead in the neighbourhood, and the tell-tale stocking or end of boot is now and then seen protruding from the trench wall. We get our share of sniping, even in the support trench, which I have seen most of. One has to drop nimbly past certain critical corners. But there is no need for anyone to get hit if they keep down. The Turks are sniping from a long way off and fire by chance. The communications trenches are rather ticklish by day, though safe enough by night. There are occasional dead bodies where people have been killed, and it is an awful job getting our men past them: they have a sort of supernatural fear of trampling on their own dead – this kind of feeling of awe is felt also by the men in the case of Turkish dead.[16]

Albert Walls, service number Chatham B 5397, stoker first class, aged 36, didn't keep his head down. A Turkish sniper found his mark and Albert was killed in the general area 500 yards east of the Krithia road and slightly in advance of the Vineyard position. His body joined the other corpses nearby. Like so many at Gallipoli, he has no known grave and his remains lie hidden and lost. For him the battle had ceased to rage, the rotten flesh ceased to smell, and the hunger and danger ceased to gnaw. Albert's son was made fatherless by this solitary, well-directed Turkish bullet, and spent his childhood being passed from grandparent to grandparent; he later emigrated to start a new life in Australia. Every bullet, shell and bayonet-thrust which takes a life has far-reaching implications for those left behind. Things are never the same for the bereaved.

But Albert died not primarily by the hand of that Turkish sniper, who was only defending his homeland, but because of the delays brought about by the ineptitude and lack of resolve shown by many of the army leaders and politicians. If they had acted with decisiveness and spirit in the early stages, they could or would have saved Albert's life and many thousands of others. The campaign would have been won, and there is no telling the implications of such a success on the outcome of the First World War.

Albert served under Rupert Brooke, who in 1914 had written this poem:

THE DEAD

Blow out, you bugles, over the rich Dead!
  There's none of these so lonely and poor of old,
  But, dying, has made us rarer gifts than gold.
These laid the world away; poured out the red
Sweet wine of youth; gave up the years to be
  Of work and joy, and that unhoped serene,
  That men call age; and those who would have been,
Their sons, they gave, their immortality.

Blow, bugles, blow! They brought us, for our death,
  Holiness, lacked so long, and Love, and Pain.
Honour has come back, as a king, to earth,
  And paid his subjects with a royal wage;
And Nobleness walks in our ways again;
  And we have come into our heritage.

These hearts were woven of human joys and cares,
  Washed marvellously with sorrow, swift to mirth.
The years had given them kindness. Dawn was theirs,
  And sunset, and the colours of the earth.
These had seen movement, and heard music; known
  Slumber and waking; loved; gone profoundly friended;
Felt the quick stir of wonder; sat alone;
  Touched flowers and furs and cheeks. All this is ended.

There are waters blown by changing winds to laughter
And lit by the rich skies, all day. And after,
  Frost, with a gesture, stays the waves that dance
And wandering loveliness. He leaves a white
  Unbroken glory, a gathered radiance,
A width, a shining peace, under the night.[17]

On 20 July the French artillery fired for half an hour from 5.30am, at which time Freyberg sent men under the command of Lieutenant Lister and Sub-Lieutenant William Egerton forward along a Turkish communication trench as far as a redoubt. This was found to be filled with Turkish dead, so they erected three barricades and returned. The operation would have been an entire success but for a shell, probably French, bursting in the British trench and wounding

Lister. Freyberg, who had just taken over command from the sick Major Myburgh, was hit in the stomach;[18] six other men were injured, including Able Seamen W. Bunting, W. Knox, John Cameron and Jos Rooney. As a result of this incident Lieutenant-Commander Edward Nelson was left in charge of the Hood and Lieutenant-Commander Arthur Asquith in charge of the firing line.[19]

On 1 August the RND was moved out of the firing line and replaced by the 42nd Division, but their rest period had been too long in coming and they were a shadow of their former selves. After the battle on 4 June the division had stood at 208 officers and 7,141 men; by 1 August it had been reduced to 129 officers and 5,038 men. Douglas Jerrold states:

> The strain of the July battles and the subsequent fortnight in the line had definitely broken not the fighting spirit but the physical health of the men. Even of the five thousand officers and men remaining at the beginning of August, not 10 per cent would have been considered fit in France for duty in the quietest part of the line. In Gallipoli at this time all officers and men who could actually walk to the trenches were reckoned fit. On any other classification the campaign must have been abandoned.[20]

Commodore Backhouse was transferred to naval artillery on 1 August, in response to the commodore's request in June. Before leaving, he addressed the men of Hood and Howe and wished them well. The division was shortly to receive another blow: 300 fleet reserve stokers were ordered to leave Gallipoli, as the fleet needed them urgently and this call had priority over their present commitment. The RND thus lost its backbone of battle-hardened, trained men, and, with the heavy losses sustained by Hood, Anson, Howe, Nelson and Drake, now had no reserve men left.

Sir Ian Hamilton wrote to the First Lord, Winston Churchill:

> The Naval Division has done really superbly. They have suffered proportionately heavy losses. The particular brigade I spoke of [2nd Brigade] will, if it receives reinforcements within a fairly short time, be second to none as a fighting machine in the service. If on the other hand, I am forced by circumstances to shove it into another severe fight before reinforcements come, then it will be so pulled down in strength that there will not be enough of the old soldiers remaining to leaven the new drafts.[21]

This weaker, changed RND was too reduced as a unit to be thrust into any major new engagement. Not many of the excited young men from the *Grantully Castle* were left, having shed their blood to buy a few yards here and a few yards there as the campaign south of Achi Baba became stalemate. Another reorganization was thus implemented: two marine battalions were formed out of the previous four, joining Anson and Howe to form a new 2nd Brigade. Lieutenant-Commander Freyberg was promoted to the rank of commander, in overall command of the Hood.

CHAPTER THIRTEEN

The Slow Drift to Evacuation

August, 1915, opens with an account by John Forster of the Hood:

> From August onwards the campaign continued in trench warfare,
> with the usual spells of duty in the firing line, time spent in the
> reserve trenches and rest on the beaches or base camp. The periodic
> raids on each other's front line, and night wiring parties in no man's
> land, went on until the evacuation in January, 1915.
>
> The highlight events were those in which we could enjoy bathing
> from the beaches, particularly Morto Bay, where there was a fine
> stretch of golden sand; but many times we were scared off and had
> to scuttle for our lives when 'Asiatic Annie', a big Turkish gun,
> and 'Hasty Richard' or 'Quick Dick', another menace in the way
> of artillery, would open up on us without warning.
>
> Every soldier and sailor who served at the Dardanelles would
> know of these two famous guns, both mounted on the mainland
> of Asia. Annie was a real lady, though, for she gave the troops
> ample warning of her mighty shots. A flash and a puff of smoke
> would be seen, then a bugle alarm would be given by one of our
> sentries on duty. The time lapse of half a minute or so was a good
> bonus for those on the peninsula to take whatever cover they could
> find. Quick Dick, on the other hand, had no sooner fired than its
> shell took no time in bursting on Gallipoli.
>
> At this time sickness became the chief enemy, not the Turk, as a
> cause of casualties to the British. Dysentery was the main plague.
> Considering the conditions of the battlefield in those hot summer
> months, this was almost impossible to avoid. The swarms of flies
> feasting on the corpses, the poor latrines, and the general lack of
> clean fresh water, made an epidemic a certainty.[1]

The clinical symptoms of the various forms of dysentery were very similar: gripping pains and the desire to go to the toilet, followed by difficulty in passing water. A high fever at the outset usually subsided, but the cheeks would become flushed and the face anxious and pinched; slight delirium and mental confusion could result. Considerable thirst was another symptom, accompanied by a white or yellow-coated tongue. Side-effects of some forms of the disease were arthritis and liver abscesses.

Thomas Mitchell-Fox of the Hood explains:

The treatment for dysentery was, on Gallipoli, chlorodyne, and almost every man-jack on the peninsula had dysentery in some shape or form. Some were hardly able to stand up. The other treatment given, at the sick-bay or first aid station, was chocolate.

If you had a choice I'd rather go to France than Gallipoli, because the conditions on the peninsula were simply deplorable. You see nothing was arranged, neither camp, hut, nor anything. You simply burrowed like rabbits.[2]

Foster continued:

At this time fresh water was in very short supply, and I had the experience of trying to shave and then wash in red wine. This was in fairly good supply from the French troops.

During the slow advance of the British on the peninsula the few water wells we came across had either been destroyed or poisoned by the retreating Turks. All the drinking water issued to our troops was highly chlorinated, and after filling one's water bottle it was recommended and well advised to pop in an extra one or two pellets.[3]

HQ's plans did take account of the problems of infection and sanitation. A small booklet issued by General Sir Ian Hamilton, concerning lines of communication and areas of concentration, covered such aspects as the incineration of infected matter and camp refuse to avoid creating breeding places for flies. It also mentioned constructing urinals to prevent soiling the ground in camps, bivouacs, outposts, and during halts on marches. The best general disinfectant was said to be 1.5 ounces of liquor *cressoli saponatus* in a gallon of water. Regimental sanitary detachments were to be employed, using only non-commissioned officers and men trained in sanitary duties; these units were to be changed as seldom as possible.[4]

A quarter of a mile from Backhouse Post was a small tributary branching away towards the Dardanelles. Romano's Well lay up this branch, and by 18 July, 1915, RND engineers had constructed a pipe to pump water from this well towards the front line and reduce the water shortages. The pipeline ended in a tank situated in a trench near to the start of the main communications trench. This latter was called Central Street, and lay between two others known as Oxford Street and Regent Street.[5]

On 1 September the RND's fleet surgeon, Arthur Gaskell, in a report to the division's commanding officer, stated that the majority of diarrhoea cases were caused by water-borne poison. Carelessness was not uncommon among even the best-trained water duty men, so a sanitary medical officer was employed in each division to supervise the water duty men. The RND's sanitation area was later divided into three sub-areas: area 1 ran along the left flank of the French line from the front back to the first of the so-called water towers; area 2 covered the rest of the front line held by the division; area 3 incorporated the rear lines, divisional HQ and the 1st and 2nd Brigades' HQ.[6]

The food was uninteresting, with little or no variation. Main meals were tins of bully beef, which immediately attracted swarms of flies when opened. Field kitchens supplied a corned beef stew, but there were never any vegetables. The cheese was greasy and often inedible. Fried bacon was provided in the mornings, but it was so salty that white deposits could be clearly seen on the surface of the meat. There was also hard tack (square biscuits in Huntley and Palmer's tins), and a never-ending supply of apricot jam which the flies enjoyed more than the men.

A. Boothway of the Hood remembers:

We only got one pint of water a day, and very salt bacon with lots of fat. When I got the opportunity to make a complaint to General Paris about the salt in the bacon, I did. But it didn't get me anywhere.[7]

Another attack was now planned, to take place on 6 August, and General Hamilton sent his usual special order to hearten the troops in preparation:

Soldiers of the old army and the new,
  Some of you have already won imperishable renown at our first landing or have since built up our foothold upon the peninsula, yard by yard, with deeds of heroism and endurance. Others have arrived just in time to take part in our next great fight against Germany and Turkey, the would-be oppressors of the rest of the human race.
  You veterans are about to add fresh lustre to your arms. Happen what may, so much at least is certain.
  As to you, soldiers of the new formations, you are privileged indeed to have the chance vouchsafed you of playing a decisive part in events

123

which may herald the birth of a new and happier world. You stand for the great cause of freedom. In the hour of trial remember this, and the faith that is in you will bring you victoriously through.[8]

The attack took the form of a landing on the Suvla beaches, with much supporting activity at both Anzac Cove and Helles. The Helles attack involved the 29th and 42nd Divisions, with the RND 1st Brigade forming the corps reserve on 6 and 7 August and, in General Paris's words, ready to turn out. This was the long-awaited attempt at a major breakthrough, but the same problems of muddle, mismanagement and lost opportunities took the field. It was the last straw. Reputations were ruined, and drift and depression became the masters.

As August progressed the RND was in and out of the front line: on 16 August the 2nd Brigade and the Hood relieved the 88th Brigade, then were in turn relieved by the Nelson on 19 August.[9] Conditions in the firing lines were still very bad, and the stench was very trying. It was difficult to get rid of the trench soil and this became a heavy fatigue. Reinforcements for the division arrived during the month, as Paris reported on 25 August:

We had some welcome reinforcements the other day. I was rather horrified when I saw them. Twenty were young, 40 more were war babies. I am sending home again the 14-, 15- and 16-year-olds. One was found crying in the trenches! Poor little devil. A useful man to send here! However, many are good stuff.[10]

On 23 August Charles Lister was injured for the third time, yet again by shellfire. He wrote to his father from a hospital ship on 26 August:

Just think, I have been wounded once more, the third time. We were in a trench, observing the Turkish trenches. I went along to see what had happened, got my people back into a bit of a trench they had to leave, then went down to the trench, thinking that the show was over, and then got it, being stuck in the pelvis and my bladder being deranged, and slight injuries in the leg and calves.

I have been operated on, but am sketchy as to what has been done. I am on a hospital ship, comfy enough, but feeling the motion of it a good deal, and I have to be in bed and cannot change my position. The hours go by slowly, as one does not feel very much up to reading. However, I got to sleep all right.

I feel this will be a longish job, and I don't know where I shall do my cure – perhaps Alexandria. My doctor is quite happy at the way things are doing. The shell that hit me killed one man and wounded the others.

Forgive this scrawl, but it's not easy to write.[11]

But this was the last time Lord Ribblesdale heard from his son. Charles Lister died from his wounds on 28 August, 1915, and was buried in the East Mudros military cemetery on the island of Lemnos. Patrick Shaw-Stewart wrote of him:

> The men, both stokers and recruits adored him. They always called him 'Lord Lister' . . . He was constantly doing the most reckless things, walking between the lines with his arms waving under a hot fire from both sides; but his last wound, like his others, was from a shell in a trench, and no blame could attach.[12]

The RND took over a new area from the 29th Division, between Gully Ravine and the Krithia Nullah. Sniping was still a problem, as General Paris reported on 28 August:

> The enemy have generally limited their efforts to sniping and a little bombing, in both of which we have gained a decided superiority, though in the southern barricade there is one Turk who has hitherto defeated all attempts to dislodge him. He has broken many periscopes and periscopic rifles, and bombs have no effect.[13]

The wooden periscopic rifles were often too conspicuous, and as a result were frequently hit. But the persistent sniper opposite the Worcester barricade was knocked out by 12 October, and on 24 October it was reported that some success had been obtained with telescopic rifle fire at a range of 1,200 yards when three Turks were hit coming out of Krithia.[14]

On 31 August the RND pushed a barricade 50 yards down an old Turkish trench and found many bodies, most stripped of their clothing. During the following months sickness continued to be a problem, but much work was done in the trench lines. General Paris said on 4 September:

> I do not consider that the increase [in sickness] is in any way due to the amount of work the division is called upon to do. My rule is that for corps and divisional work not more than one half of the effective strength, omitting Nelson Battalion, is to be employed on any day, night work to count double.[15]

Enterprising RND engineers had meanwhile been busy constructing an offensive weapon in the form of a large catapult. Two of these devices, with crews, were loaned on 13 August to the 52nd Division, which was so impressed that on 14 August they asked for more. But only one more catapult was available, and this was needed for officers' instruction classes during the following week. Unfortunately, on 21 August the first accident involving a catapult occurred: the pull failed to operate while a lighted bomb was in the bag and one man was killed. By 10 October, with many more catapults in use, there had been no less than five other accidents, all due to failure in throwing the bomb clear. Fortunately there were no additional casualties, but the catapult was damaged each time. Eventually a 'cricket ball' bomb was found to be the answer to the problem.

In the middle of October enemy activity increased somewhat, and as a result the RND's expenditure of 3.7 inch mortars began to exceed their weekly allowance. The mortars were all the more necessary as they had no trench areas with a good field of vision to use as hand bombing stations. Failing sufficient shells, large quantities of *cheval de frise* wire were laid in front of the British trenches.[16] The division's machine guns were particularly active at this time, as Paris reported:

> The machine guns have done excellent work. We now have four guns on the Turkish trenches J and G, enfilading many, and the observation is so good that bullets can be dropped into almost any trench. I am convinced these guns cause a good few casualties and so far their positions have not been discovered.

At the end of October additional drafts were brought in to reinforce the RND, totalling 42 officers and 1,037 other ranks. Paris was reasonably happy with them:

> The marines were most satisfactory: a good sprinkling of older men, and the new officers were not too young and have some previous experience.
>
> As regards the RNVR drafts: a very fair average on the whole, but the standard is not high. Some young boys – the average age would probably work out to about 23 or 24. Physique good, and the men seem keen. Average training five months, and with some trench work will soon be a useful addition to the division.[17]

In October the RND rest camp was moved to the left of the peninsula, behind their front lines. The new camp consisted of rows of oblong dug-outs, five feet deep at the back and six feet deep at the front, draining into seven feet deep communicating trenches. Work on the camp continued until the end of November, after which the troops experienced better conditions than they had known since they landed in April. Then, on the night of 26/27 November, the weather broke. John Forster remembered:

One of the worst times was the severe rain, snowstorms and extreme cold which came down on us so suddenly in November. I was in the front line at the time and just could not keep warm. A northerly gale blew and the hard frost lasted for three days, with a temperature of 18° Fahrenheit. The effect of this bitterly cold spell on men who were still suffering from the effects of a tropical summer was definitely bad. Most of us were in the open with only blankets, inadequate to such an emergency. Many died of cold, and others were evacuated sick. There were many cases of frostbite among the troops, too. I was fortunate in only having chilblains.[18]

Joseph Murray shared the experience:

It was not too bad when it was raining, before the snow, or when it stopped and froze, but we suffered with the cold. After three or four days there was brilliant sunshine and the snow melted, making large water flows. All the men were despondent and had to get on the tops of the trenches, Turks and British alike. Water came down like a tidal wave, carrying bits of flotsam and jetsam which made dams of the wood, bodies, etc. These would then give way, creating a sudden rush of water.[19]

After this period conditions improved, however, because the cold and frost had killed the summer sickness. But in mid-December the RND was ordered to take over and relieve part of the French line on the right, together with their rest camp on the cliffs above Morto Bay. Forster relates:

With some dismay, thinking that the French sector would be more primitive and less well organized than our own, we set off to the new position. And nothing could have been further from the truth. The ground was rocky and more hilly, and the trenches and dug-outs much deeper than those we had been used to. They were built round with stone, and were weatherproof. Corrugated iron was used for all roofing.

It was striking to us to come across such quantities of strong corrugated-iron sheets, and this was the basic material for building of dug-outs. It was almost splinter-proof, being a good ¼ inch thick with the magic words 'Made in England' stamped on each sheet.

The officers' quarters were really comfortable, with tables and chairs and even wooden floors, doors and windows, but no glass. The whole camp had been built as if to withstand a siege for a long time.[20]

CHAPTER FOURTEEN

Ending the Campaign

On 11 October Lord Kitchener sent a telegraph to Sir Ian Hamilton:

> What is your estimate of the probable loss which would be entailed to our forces if the evacuation of the Gallipoli Peninsula was decided upon and carried out in the most careful manner? No decision has been arrived at yet on this question of evacuation, but I feel I ought to have your views. In your reply you need not consider the possible future danger to the Empire which might be thus caused.[1]

Hamilton replied on 12 October to the effect that such a step could well mean the loss of not less than half the total forces, plus heavy losses of stores and guns. He concluded by commenting that, with luck, the loss could be considerably less than he estimated.

Within two days, on 14 October, it was decided to recall Hamilton from Gallipoli. One of his last actions as commander of the Mediterranean Expeditionary Force was to inspect the RND trenches, where he was met by General Paris. He paid particular attention to Hood and Hawke Battalions, speaking to Bernard Freyberg and Cleg Kelly.

Hamilton's replacement was General Monro, a firm believer in the idea that the only way to win the war was to kill Germans on the Western Front, and that anything ancillary to this goal was a sideline. He was an officer of some experience, having commanded an army in France. Monro arrived at the Dardanelles on 28 October, landed on 30 October and briefly reviewed the situation with the local commanding officers, but never ventured beyond the beach areas. He formed the opinion that the evacuation should take place.

After much discussion Lord Kitchener decided to visit the battlefields himself, landing on 9 November. His inspection led him to conclude that the troops could maintain a defensive position for an extensive length of time unless very heavy Turkish reinforcements were moved against them. Nevertheless, and after much changing of minds, the evacuation was ordered.

Operations began at Suvla and Anzac Cove, where 20,000 troops were taken off on the nights of 18/19 and 19/20 December. The withdrawal was a complete success, and the Turks and Germans had no idea that it was happening: the British High Command's planning was excellent, in that onlookers saw no detectable change to the Allied position. At 4am on 20 December the last boat pulled away from the shore, leaving behind them a very perplexed army of defenders.

Guns and men began to be transferred southwards, now the Turks had only one front to worry about. But lightning would not strike twice on the same peninsula, and it would be difficult for the British and French to have equal success in evacuating Helles. Turkish and German observation would be extra keen, to spot the slightest change and ensure the prey did not escape again.

On 7 January, at around midday, the Turks put up an awe-inspiring bombardment in the area of Gully Spur: the first stage in a major attack to test the British line and see if it was still strongly held. The subsequent Turkish advance was vigorously repulsed, so von Sanders was convinced that no evacuation was under way. Little did he know that plans were at an advanced stage.

The depth of the planning can be seen in an RND evacuation order issued on 30 December, 1915. Official records and correspondence were to be sent off from each brigade on 31 December in the hands of responsible people. All sick and weakly men, and all superfluous material, transport stores, supplies and ammunition were to be removed, leaving only sufficient to maintain a minimum garrison for the last week. Concealment was all-important, so care must be taken to continue burning all regular fires, incinerators, and so forth. The appearance of dug-outs and horse lines must not be altered. All waterproof sheets, tarpaulins and other coverings must be left in position until the last night. Dumps of supplies and other stores that were visible to aircraft must, when empty, look as if they covered the same area of ground as they had when they were full; empty boxes and cases must be laid out to replace full ones. On no account were useless articles to be destroyed by bonfires. Similarly, action against the enemy must be maintained at a constant level. Everything must appear as normal as possible, whether viewed from the land or the air, until the last night.

Most of the RND was to be evacuated on the nights of 6/7 and 7/8 January, 1916, leaving on the final night only 4,000 infantry, 150 divisional engineers, 220 men in a medical unit and 75 in a signals unit, plus divisional and brigade HQs. The RND Marine Brigade's 2nd Battalion was to garrison and hold the line from 'V' beach (where the stranded *River Clyde* would be used as a keep) to Hunter-Weston

Hill on the cliffs above with 400 men and three machine guns. The 29th Division would supply a garrison for the defences from 'W' beach to Hunter-Weston Hill. The RND would retain six machine guns: four in the front line, and one in each of two rear defensive lines (the *ligne de repli* and the Eski lines). Each front line brigade would carry out the main evacuation at 8pm, leaving one gun in position until 10pm. The 150 men in the *ligne de repli* and the 230 men garrisoning the Eski lines would evacuate at the same time as the remaining front line troops, and a boat was scheduled for 10.30pm to collect them from the shore.

Parties and individuals left behind to block communications were not forgotten: if they became detached from their main group they were to head for 'V' beach by the shortest route, joining any other groups they may meet on the way. A dressing station would be established on 'V' beach, marked by a Red Cross lamp. After the last evacuation trip a trawler would patrol the *River Clyde* area of 'V' beach to pick up beach demolition parties and stragglers.

On the last night the remaining troops had to travel as light as possible. Their packs, blankets and waterproof sheets were sent off on the previous night, leaving them with only greatcoats and equipment. All ranks were to wear a narrow white band on their right arms, put on after dark on the last night. Troops in the front line would have to muffle their feet by tying folded sandbags round their boots.

To evacuate, RND men must pass through the wire fence at a gateway on the Sedd-el-Bahr road, about 200 yards from the ruined fort, where they would be met by members of the embarkation staff. The officer commanding each party had to hand over a parade state showing the exact numbers of all ranks in his group; these details would be telephoned through to the embarkation officer on the beach. Each party would then be guided to the RND mustering point, marked by lights with the letter A, and the embarkation officer would confirm when lighters or boats would be available. Guides would conduct each party to the embarkation point, where troops were to file on board as quickly as possible. Strict discipline and absolute silence were essential.[2]

On the day of the evacuation, Patrick Shaw-Stewart wrote:

> I and the French artillery commander (the only representative of his race now remaining) are passing the afternoon walking up and down with a great appearance of calm, looking at our watches, sniffing the air for the least suspicion of wind that might get up and be a nuisance, and from time to time lighting a new little bonfire and destroying a few more maps and papers . . . .
>
> Well, I have certainly seen the campaign of the Dardanelles – the beginning, the end, and all the middle. I am lucky to be walking off it, but I mustn't speak too soon, as they are shelling the beach from

the region of Troy, and I have got to get to the *River Clyde* somehow in an hour or two. Meanwhile, I am hanging on to the telephone, which my signallers are itching to dismantle . . . .

I am waiting on shore and it is as quiet as the grave, except when the batteries from Asia send us an occasional shot. If they had any idea of what we are up to they would simply make hay of the beaches, and it's rather satisfactory to feel we are cheating them, and they will wake up in the morning and find us gone.

But on the whole it's nothing to be proud of, for the British army or the French either – nine months here, and pretty heavy losses, and now for nothing but to clear out.

I wonder what next?[3]

Joseph Murray also remembers the evacuation:

When the French left the peninsula and the Royal Naval Division took over the French lines you then never met a soul. Whilst nobody said anything about evacuation, we knew that there was something, but we didn't know at that period that Anzac and Suvla had been evacuated. When we needed ammunition or food we had to go right down to the beach; normally we went to a dump halfway between. There was nobody except us in the firing line.

I was then near to the large gully on the left of the line, as I was still with the miners – part of the RND engineers, having been loaned from the Hood Battalion towards the end of June. There were eight of us, and at about eight or nine o'clock, when it was dark, we were told that we were all to leave. We had to tie down our water bottles so they wouldn't rattle. We put sandbags round our feet, and anything which jingled had to be left behind. The rifle had to be empty, so I put mine on the parapet and fired a shot – not to kill anybody, but just to empty it. We each had a white band around our arm.

We went along the firing line until we came to the gully. We couldn't get across it, so we walked to a place called the Zigzag. We then got up the cliff on to the other side. Every time we stopped we fell asleep. We were so tired – we hadn't been to sleep for three days. Because of this I kept my hand on the bloke in front, as the others did also.

Alongside the Krithia road there was a very wide mule trench, called something like Eastern or Western. We followed this trench, and were now a long way from the firing line. When we left the Krithia road we got out of the trench. There was a breeze blowing. Funny, I then remembered all the men who had started and now were all dead. I could see them in my mind.

When we were just beyond the Eski lines we had a rise up the cliffs at 'V' beach; from the firing line it had been downhill. Two shells dropped very, very close. I don't know where they went – I didn't bother to look. We kept on walking and walking.

There were shells which looked like they were from Asiatic Annie. They didn't have the proper range; they couldn't get over the cliffs at 'V' beach. We were walking towards the shells. I thought, 'This is tragic, we are walking into them,' as we knew that they were aimed at 'V' beach. I saw a big flash in front of us, and there was a noise like a train coming in the distance. I hoped Annie didn't get the range. We were climbing the hill, and when we were about 100 yards from the cliff there were another two shells. They must have dropped on the beach. We counted up, and reckoned that once we saw the flash we had 28 seconds until the damned thing arrived.

We stopped and all sat down, as we were so tired. In addition to the eight of us we had picked up some more people on the way. No more shells came, so we got on to the cliffs at 'V' beach. We had to walk along the top of the cliffs to the *River Clyde*. I remember thinking, 'Damn it all! We are telling everyone else to keep off the skyline, and here we are.' But it was the only way to get there.

We found our way down, and as soon as we got to the beach another blinking shell came over. It dropped in the sea, short of us, and as it did so we hid against the cliffs. We eventually got to the *River Clyde*. We stayed on board for probably a quarter of an hour, then went down the gangplank into barges. There were tarpaulins on the barges to deaden the sound. I think they were specially made to carry water, and they had an entrance at the bows and at the stern. It was so full there was only just enough room to squeeze in. The bloke in front of me was as sick as a dog.

We pulled out, and I think two or three shells fell between the *River Clyde* and the trawler that we were making for. Then we boarded a destroyer: there are no railings on a destroyer, only a rope along the side. I remember lying down in full kit. When we left the ship to transfer to a picket boat, I saw several rifles and packs had been left lying on the deck. Whether the men had left them, or they themselves had been lost on the way out, I do not know.

Later, when on shore, I was lying on the beach, and a French Canadian nurse from the hospital came along. She said, 'You are all right now, all right, sonny. You are quite safe, you are at Lemnos.' She kept saying this. Then she asked, 'Where are all the others?' I said, 'I don't know; there won't be many more to come.' She then kissed me, and tears came into her eyes. She thought I was the only one left of a thousand. I think in fact only about 200 of the Hood survived, having served through the Gallipoli campaign. She went away, saying that she would be back and was going to get some help. She kept repeating, 'You are quite safe.' She returned with two men and an armchair, and they carried me back on it. I was laid on a table and they took my boots off! I said, 'That's a relief – I haven't had my boots off for a couple of months.'[4]

On 14 January, 1916, Sub-Lieutenant Ivan Heald of the Hood wrote a letter describing his part in the evacuation:

The great evacuation was the simplest thing. We just took our rifles off the parapet, marched down to the beach, and sailed away.

I wonder if you would have slept soundly if you had known that I and a few Tyneside boys were all there were to hold the Empire's line across the whole battalion sector the last three hours of that tense night! A wide front, and never did man listen to sound so anxiously as I did, sitting alone in the old French dug-out in the red glow of a charcoal brazier. I was fearful that any moment there might come clamouring in my ears the furious babbling splutter of 'rapid fire', which would mean an attack.

But hours wore on in a healthy sequence of occasional bombs and steady sniping, and half an hour before midnight I made a tour to the end of my line, where my commander, Freyberg, with Asquith and six men, were holding the chaos of mine craters and trenches which the French named *La Ravine de la Mort*. You will have heard of Freyberg, who swam ashore to light flares among the Turks at Enos. They both decided there was time to finish some biscuits they had left in a dug-out, and after this I got the word to go.

A touch on the back of the last man and he climbed down from the firing step and touched the next man farther along, and quietly we filed out of the long firing line, and, as we stole away, I could hear the Turks coughing and talking in their trench 20 yards away. Two or three times, to hide the shuffle of the men's gear against the side of the trench, I jumped on the firing step and let my Webley-Scott bark at Achi Baba, and somewhere on the left someone fired a farewell Very light, which lit up the sandbags until the blackness came welling up out of the trench again as the rocket died away.

So we shuffled past the telephone station at the top of the communication trench, and there we left Freyberg, Asquith and Lieutenant Kelly, the Diamond sculler and musician. They were all the garrison of that part.

Now we were fairly on our path for the three-mile march to the beach, and oh! but it was cheery as I filed down that trench at the rear of my men to hear the Turks still sniping at the dug-out.

133

We came to other telephone stations, reported ourselves, and passed on to where the road starts over the open across by Backhouse Post, White House, Clapham Junction and the Zigzag! How much in later days will those Gallipoli names mean to men who knew them once as well as their own village street.

The Turk's own moon was in the sky, a perfect crescent with a star, and a wind rising dangerously from the north. Now and again a wistful sigh of a spent bullet, and ever wheeling behind us the shaft of the great Chanak searchlight. Down at Cape Helles the hospital ship lay, her lights one wonderful bar of green and red and gold. Night after night for eight long months the Turkish sentries have seen that ship of stars as they peered over their parapets, and tomorrow they will see it no more.

Now we are on the macadam road to Sedd-el-Bahr. The men talked little among themselves, and I think we were all awed by the bigness of the thing, and saddened by the thoughts of the little crosses we were leaving behind us – the little wooden crosses that were creeping higher every day to meet the crescents on that great sullen hill. There must have been a dead man of ours to pave every yard of that last march. And we were leaving them, lads of our platoon, gallant officers who were merry at mess, who died to win trenches we had left behind us. Trudging past the sombre-brooding cypress trees we remembered our dead and the pity and tragic waste of it all, and tried to hope that some day a British service bugle would once again ring out over those little graves in that lost land of ours.

We toiled on to other parties coming through the roofless village of Sedd-el-Bahr, all anxious now with the knowledge that a Turkish telephone message would stir Asiatic Annie to pound us with shells. Sure enough one came as we waited on the beach. We saw the great flash blotted out by the night, the warning 'G' on a bugle sounded, and, full of foreboding, we began to count the 27 seconds which Annie gives one to think about one's sins before she drops her shell on the beach. This one squabbed miserably in the sea, and none followed.

The beach was awesome with the throbbing of motor-launches and the shouts of naval officers making perilous berths alongside the sunken steamers which make the pier. The big *River Clyde* lay under the old castle, where the Dublins and Munsters poured out of her sides to fringe the sands with death eight months before, and I thought of the night in May I landed, when the smell of the East came strangely out of the soft white dust, and the myriad noises of war were fresh and fearful in my ears.

There is a curving yellow cliff here, and the foot of it was one long black line where the battalions were moving slowly on to the pier.

The whole place reeked of paraffin, and we guessed that dawn would see the beach ablaze. Over the listed sunken ship we clambered, and a jolly naval petty officer chased us along a gangway to the deck of a pitching black silhouette of a destroyer.

Seven hundred and fifty war-weary men covered the deck of that destroyer before she slid out into the night, and I think most of us were asleep before we had lost the shore lights. Dawn found us far away, tossing in half a gale, and next day we learned that we had missed the great sight of the night, for after we had left the engineers blew up the few stores that could not be taken, and our last sacrifice to Mars went up in great sheets of flame.

EVACUATION

So quietly we left our trench
That night, yet this I know –
As we stole down to Sedd-el-Bahr
Our dead mates heard us go.

As I came down the Boyau Nord
A dead hand touched my sleeve,
A dead hand from the parapet
Reached out and plucked my sleeve.

'Oh, what is toward, O mate o' mine,
That ye pass with muffled tread,
And there comes no guard for the firing trench,
The trench won by your dead?'

The dawn was springing on the hills,
'Twas time to put to sea,
But all along the Boyau Nord
A dead voice followed me:

'Oh, little I thought,' a voice did say,
'That ever a lad of Tyne
Would leave me lone in the cold trench side,
And him a mate of mine.'

We sailed away from Sedd-el-Bahr,
We are sailing home on leave.
But this I know – through all the years
Dead hands will pluck my sleeve.[5]

Eric Wettern, of the RND engineers, translated a German history of the period:

Anzac and Suvla had been evacuated in December, 1915. Our 8th Corps continued to hold Helles, and the Turkish commander-in-chief was speculating on his opponent's intentions. Was England going to make Helles into a second Gibraltar? Liman von Sanders reckoned that without command of Achi Baba this was not tactically feasible. He therefore concluded that Helles was definitely going to be evacuated.

How much more satisfactory would the withdrawal on 20 December have been if, in addition to the strategic and moral attainments, we had been successful in achieving a great tactical result: the capture of a large part of the enemy army and all its artillery! General Liman von Sanders now resolved to make every effort to achieve this at Helles. There the enemy would not be allowed to escape unscathed.

All possible measures were taken to grapple with the first signs of a withdrawal. Strong forces – eight divisions – were held ready behind the four divisions holding the front line so that artillery could be quickly moved forward to deal with the enemy trenches and obstacles. The best timing for the attack would be if the evacuation was already in hand and a portion of the troops and materials already withdrawn, so that the remainder could no longer reckon on support other than by their fleet. The difficulty, however, was to decide on the correct timing.

In order to pin the enemy down, General Liman von Sanders ordered increased artillery activity, for which a number of the batteries from the Suvla and Anzac fronts had already started to move south on 20 December. A field artillery detachment under German command was allocated for the night hours to the extreme point of Kum Kale so as to bombard the enemy beach at Sedd-el-Bahr. Also the other batteries on the Asiatic side which had just received the first consignments of ammunition from Germany were given orders not to economize ammunition. The German ammunition, with its remarkable explosive effect, was, on his own admission, causing the enemy heavy losses.

On 7 January the commander-in-chief ordered a sectional attack against the enemy's left flank, in order to force a decision as to whether the enemy's front lines were still strongly held. After two hours' intensive barrage – the first that the Fifth Army had been able to deliver (which gave the enemy a foretaste of what was coming to him if he held on much longer) – the infantry attack was launched, but was immediately held up under strong English fire. The object was, however, achieved, viz to ascertain that the enemy apparently still held the south front in strength.

8 January passed in relative quiet. Observation from Achi Baba and from the Asiatic side showed nothing out of the ordinary. The evening reports from the front were quite normal. Behind the front-line trenches one heard the usual noises, and their gradual subsidence as the night wore on. Towards midnight, as usual, fire died completely down on both sides. A strong wind arose, an ally of the Turks, causing difficulties for shipping on the open beaches facing south. Hour-long quiet and silence. From the narrow no-man's-land there came no messages from the patrols stationed there. The night service of the telephone had nothing to do.

Towards 4am numerous explosions were heard in the far distance. Then the dark sky reddened from the reflection of large fires on the coast. Immediately the Turkish trench garrison sprang into life. Red rockets were sent up, followed immediately by very heavy artillery fire against the beaches. The advance of the infantry was, however, hindered by the numerous deep trenches, between which all gaps had been closed with crinolines and blocked with mines and booby traps. In spite of every endeavour, the infantry only reached the beaches when the last English transports were already long since in safety.

With the evacuation of Sedd-el-Bahr in the night of 8/9 January, the last act of the drama closed. The Gallipoli campaign was ended. The German history continues:

This account would, however, be incomplete without reviewing the reasons for this outstanding outcome: an evacuation without losses. The difficulties of such an operation were quite stupendous – the entire English front, some five miles long, was opposed by a watchful enemy in positions which were in places within speaking distance, and nowhere more than 300 yards distant. (At one point the distance between the opposing posts was three yards as the bomb flies!) The entire occupied area, and in particular the beaches, was under observation from dominating Turkish positions and, without exception, lay within range of the Turkish artillery. From beneath these watchful eyes, tens of thousands of troops and a vast amount of material had to be evacuated – a task which the available shipping could only tackle in batches.

Moreover, the whole operation was dependent on factors of weather, wind and sea. With south and south-westerly gales, frequent at that time of year, embarkation at the southern point was impossible; a storm would make the coast inaccessible. It had to be reckoned that, after a large part of the troops had already been shipped, a storm might interrupt the continuation of the evacuation. If the Turks attacked under these conditions, a great loss of troops and material would be inevitable.

The fact that the evacuation proceeded smoothly and without loss (an outcome which the English themselves had not expected) lay to some extent in a series of fortunate circumstances. Chance and luck, which play so great a part in war, are never more essential than in the difficult operation of withdrawing from tactically unfavourable positions in the face of an enemy at point-blank range. And, as the English readily admitted, they had quite astonishing good fortune. During the 10 days of the evacuation from Anzac and Suvla a light wind blew offshore, so the sea was as smooth as a mirror, and the embarkation from Helles went equally well. A south wind gathered force during the last and decisive evacuation night of 8/9 January, but by the time it grew to storm force the beach had been cleared. If the raging gale had come a few hours earlier, the English would not have escaped so lightly!

But all these were passive circumstances: the British High Command must be credited with appraising and mastering the overall problem in a quite outstanding fashion. They succeeded in deceiving and surprising the Turks completely; the superbly skilful evacuation plan, thought out in the minutest detail, renders them full honour.

No observable change in the ordinary pattern of trench life could be allowed up until the last moment: lights in the trenches, camp fires, to and fro movements of small columns, occupation of battery positions even if with only one gun, and spoof disembarkations were amongst the many small details which contributed to fooling the Turks. A particularly successful feature was that, from as early as the beginning of December, the British would slacken fire gradually towards midnight. The Turks found nothing unnatural or suspicious in the quiet night hours during the evacuation, as previously forward probes had always found the trenches strongly held.

The embarkation sequence was arranged so that on the last day only the full garrison of the front line and a little artillery remained ashore – just sufficient force to repel a moderately strong infantry attack. On the evening of 8 January there were still 17,000 troops at Helles: the strength of the Allied forward line had been noted by the Turks in their probing attack on 7 January, and they had no idea that nothing remained behind this line.

The most difficult moment of the whole operation, the final withdrawal from the front line trenches, was brilliantly handled. To disengage the entire garrison unobserved was a task of appalling difficulty, silently carried out in successive waves after dark, while final detachments continued to make their presence known in the usual ways. When the trench noise subsided at around midnight it raised no suspicion among the Turks. The very last parties withdrew along detailed routes marked so as to be identifiable in the dark, setting minefields and closing gaps with previously-prepared wire obstacles as they left. On reaching the beach they set fire to any remaining material on shore, ignited the mines and were taken on board waiting vessels. But by the time the fires and explosions were seen the last ships were already at sea.

It remains a question whether or not the Turks should have spotted the withdrawal, at least of the final troops, despite the superb planning and execution of the evacuation. The Turkish front lines were only alerted by heavy mine explosions and fires on the southern point at 4am, two or three hours after the trenches had been cleared.

The next day dawned bright and clear: the snow-crowned heights rose radiant and proud above a deep blue sea. Waves lapped softly on the shore, and far out at sea masts proclaimed the continued presence of the British fleet, still watching the straits. A hotly-disputed labyrinth of Turkish trenches snaked across the slopes of Achi Baba, facing an equal network of empty British trenches. All around an unending expanse of wire entanglements glittered in the sunlight, sending back the reflections of myriad tiny stars, as if to commemorate the equal numbers of warriors buried in the ground below.[6]

During the nine months of fighting the RND suffered enormous casualties:

	Officers	Other ranks
Killed	102	1,551
Died of wounds	26	576
Died	5	233
Wounded	199	4,838
Prisoners	–	2
Total	332	7,198[7]

In researching this book I interviewed one of the few survivors of the Hood, who fought through Gallipoli and later France: Joseph Murray, then aged 93. He was blind and partly deaf, but despite this he remained cheerful and quick-witted, looking back into his mind to see pictures, and to remember times and friends of long ago. As he sat there, with a small green beret on the side of his head, he became determined to sing me a song of Gallipoli; he tried his best to remember it. As he sang he was not just a bent, old man, but the embodiment of the

British fighting man. He could have been singing the song of Agincourt, Crecy, Blenheim, Waterloo or Trafalgar. No matter what hardship he might encounter, somehow his spirit pulled him through.

(To the tune of *The Mountains of Mourne Come Down to the Sea*.)

The old Gal-li-poli is a terrible place,
Where the boys in the trenches the Turks had to face.
But they never murmured, and smiled through it all,
Very soon they expected Achi Baba to fall.
At least, when I asked them, that's what they told me,
And in Constantinople we would have a fine spree.
But if the war lasts till doomsday it's there we would be,
Where the old Gal-li-poli sweeps down to the sea.

The morning we landed I'll never forget,
As we stood on the beach with our clothes wringing wet.
Although we were soaked right through to the skin,
We didn't have time to dig ourselves in.
As we rushed over the brow we came under fire,
And lots of our chums got caught on the wire,
But those that were free went forward doggedly
Where the old Gal-li-poli sweeps down to the sea.

We took several trenches before we could stop,
For we had old Johnny Turk right on the hop.
When he saw the caps and the tallies we wore,
He just turned round and fled without asking for more.
He cried, 'Allah, Allah', but that was no use,
For we were determined to take no excuse,
So we gave him the bayonet, which meant RIP,
Where the old Gal-li-poli sweeps down to the sea.

We don't grow potatoes or barley or wheat,
So we're aye on the look-out for something to eat.
We're fed up with dry biscuits, greasy bully and ham,
And we're sick of the sight of that apricot jam.
We like steak and onions, fried ham and eggs,
Or a nice big, fat chicken with five or six legs,
And a drop of that stuff that begins with a B,
Where the old Gal-li-poli sweeps down to the sea.

While up in the trenches wild rumours we hear –
It's enough to make any man go on the beer.

140

They say that we are all going home very soon,
But I'd sooner believe there's a man on the moon.
They say that in Blighty they are waiting for us
And when we arrive there will be such a fuss;
But we didn't believe them, for we would still be
Where the old Gal-li-poli sweeps down to the sea.[8]

It is winter still. It seems as if nature itself is sunk in reverence over the graves of tens of thousands of Turks and British; as if the ground, soaked in blood and torn with iron, has at last fallen into a long-overdue sleep. And yet already this sunny land is stirring with renewed life. In the timeless sequence of growth and decay, forces are already at work to heal the wounds of a stricken land. In the colourful splendour of an eastern evening by land and sea comes a mood of dreaming. The fight for the Dardanelles is over. Will it be the last fight on this road which links and divides the peoples of half the world?[9]

GALLIPOLI

Upon the margin of a rugged shore
There is a spot, now barren, desolate,
A place of graves, sodden with human sore,
That time will hallow, Memory consecrate.
There lie the ashes of the mighty dead,
The youth who lit with flame obscurity,
Fought true for freedom, won thro' rain of lead
Undying fame, their immortality.
The stranger wand'ring when the war is over,
The ploughman there driving his coulter deep,
The husbandman who golden harvests reap
From hill and ravine, from each plain and cover,
Will hear a shout, see phantoms on the marge,
See men again making a deathless charge.[10]

20. The *Grantully Castle* in Mudros, March, 1915. (*Professor Jon Stallworthy*).

21. The three officers at the Sphinx, left Arthur Asquith, middle officer Rupert Brooke, on the right Patrick Shaw-Stewart. (*Professor Jon Stallworthy*).

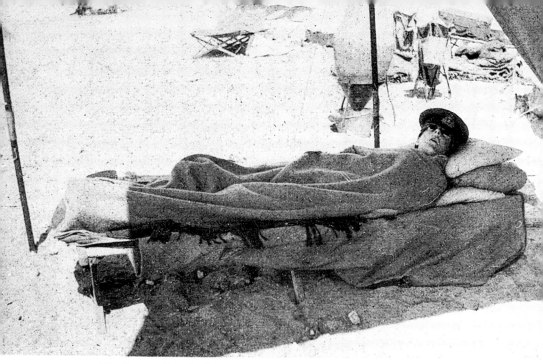

22. Rupert Brooke ill under the green canvas awning on 2 April, 1915. This photograph was taken by Denis Browne and mentioned in his letter to Edward Marsh of 25 April, 1915. Brooke himself called it "On a couch of pain" in his own letter to Marsh. (*Professor Jon Stallworthy*).

23. View from the fo'c'sle of SS *Grantully Castle* showing the French Hospital Ship. Taken by Lieut Commander Hedderwick of the Hood Battalion on 23 April, 1915. At this time Rupert Brooke was dying on board (*IWM*).

24. Rupert Brooke's grave (*IWM*).

25. HMS *Canopus*, 1900 (*Public Records Office*).

26. Hood Battalion Officers on the boat deck of *Grantully Castle* March, 1915. Asquith is sitting on the right, with Johnnie Dodge standing on the extreme right. Kelly and Brown in the middle (*Lord Freyberg*).

27. Photograph taken on the *Grantully Castle* by Lieut-Commander Hedderwick of the Hood Battalion. It shows Lieut-Commander Freyberg at the rangefinder on the gunwhale. Also shown are officers Parsons and Hood (*IWM*).

28. Men of the Hood Battalion on board SS *Grantully Castle* watching the landing of troops at Gallipoli. British battleship off starboard bow, SS *Royal George* off port side. Taken on 27/28 April, 1915, by Lieut-Commander Hedderwick (*IWM*).

Part Three

THE HOOD ON
THE WESTERN FRONT

CHAPTER FIFTEEN

The Future in the Balance

The Hood Battalion – and the Royal Naval Division – returned to Lemnos to lick their wounds, much changed from nine months before, when the thrill of the unknown had so excited the adventurers. They had fought, and fought well, but had been beaten by a valiant foe and circumstances outside their control. Not only did the troops mourn their dead colleagues but, back home, families had to begin to pick themselves up and start again.

My great-grandmother, Caroline, not only had the locket engraved in Albert's memory, but also had a small memorial stone made to commemorate his death. This was placed, for reasons best known to Caroline, on the unmarked grave of an old family retainer called Mrs Bond, who used to do the washing. She had died in 1910, at the then remarkable age of 100 years and six months, and was buried in the old borough cemetery in Forest Hill, London. My father, Marcel, remembers that for many years he had to walk 2½ miles each way with his family to tend the grave and supply fresh flowers in memory of Albert – a trying task for a boy of only six or so. Caroline was by then on crutches,[1] and as the years passed the grave became neglected. When I visited it in 1989 (plot 21839-52), I found that the whole area had been cleared. Mrs Bond's last resting place had been a pauper's grave, and no sign of Albert's memorial could be found.

On the Gallipoli peninsula the peace of centuries returned, and nature began slowly removing the scars of battle. The Commonwealth War Graves Commission maintains six cemeteries in the Helles area; there is also a New Zealand memorial, in Twelve Tree Copse Cemetery. At the south-western tip of the peninsula stands the Helles Memorial, which commemorates some 20,763 men for whom there are no known graves: 18,985 from the United Kingdom, 248 from Australia, and 1,530 from undivided India.[2]

Meanwhile, the future of the RND hung in the balance. 'A critical

145

moment has come in its history,' wrote the Second Sea Lord to the First Lord in a report on 13 January, 1916, discussing Admiralty policy on the RND:

> It was agreed on all hands that it should be (to all intents and purposes) an integral part of the army so long as the operations at Gallipoli were in progress. These operations have now come to an end, and the duties of the Royal Naval Division, so far as we can at present see, are confined to garrisoning Lemnos and the adjacent islands. In these circumstances we must not rashly embark upon new capital expenditure in connection with this branch of the service.
>
> There seem to be three policies open to us.
>
> 1. We may hand the division bodily over to the army making full reservations of the rights of individuals.
>
> 2. We may keep the division as it is, with a total strength somewhere about 36,000 men.
>
> 3. We may retain the Naval Division, but gradually reduce its numbers.
>
> There is much to be said in theory for the first of these courses; but on the whole I am inclined to think that it would be a pity to destroy a corps which now has a distinguished history behind it or to plunge ourselves into all the difficulties of detail which a change from sailors to soldiers will necessarily involve.[3]

There had always been friction between the Admiralty and the War Office over the use of naval brigades. On 23 August, 1914, when the RND was first formed, Vice-Admiral Slade submitted a report to his seniors outlining the historical background of such forces. Admiralty policy had always been to avoid employing naval brigades except for operations near the coast, and to use them as a rule only when command of the sea was practically assured. When events had necessitated the withdrawal of the men owing to a threatened disturbance of naval communications, the army had always complained that it had been weakened and its safety jeopardized. Indeed, Slade cited numerous instances of the evil results of the misuse of naval forces on land:

> There is no precedent for them being used in purely continental operations. The tendency has rather been to withdraw the brigade when it shows inclination to be drawn into such operations . . . .

Egypt, 1801

A leading case of the difficulties likely to arise by naval brigades engaging too far in land operations whilst the enemy have a fleet in being was in Egypt.

After the successful landing at Aboukir, Abercromby found he could not advance on Alexandria without retaining seamen and marines to maintain the flow of supplies and to hold the lines of communications. While they were thus deeply engaged news came that the Brest Squadron had entered the Mediterranean to interrupt the operations. Lord Keith then wished to recall his men and to move off Alexandria to meet the enemy's squadron.

Abercromby protested it would affect all his operations and a dangerous state of friction was set up between the two commanders-in-chief. The general expressed himself very strongly. 'As far as I can see at present,' he wrote to the admiral, 'I shall consider your withdrawing as a dereliction of public service. I cannot indeed conceive that you can see it in any other light. Linked together as the two services are, they cannot be separated except on the absolute certainty that no measures have been taken at home to prevent the interference of the Brest Squadron.' Keith replied that owing to the chances of the sea nothing could be done which would make such interference impossible; but he gave way and allowed his men to remain at great risk rather than bring about a breach between the two services.

Port Arthur, 1904

Here the fleet crews and guns were temporarily lent to the army to defend the land front, but when the ships were repaired it was found it was practically impossible to withdraw them. When the naval staff asked for them in order that the squadron might put to sea the army openly and with much bitterness accused the navy of wanting to run away and desert them. A very bad feeling was engendered between the services and it is said that the taunts of the army were one of the main causes of the squadron's continued inactivity . . . .

In principle and practice naval brigades are intended for combined operations only. If used as a purely military unit while the enemy's fleet is still potent, experience shows that at a time of crisis the effect is likely to be a serious disturbance of either the military or the naval plans and possibly of both.[4]

On 6 January, 1916, a telegram was sent to the Admiralty saying that the RND general had been placed under army orders, and that General Birdwood (commander of the Anzacs) had given directions for the division, of about 6,000 rifles, to garrison the nearby islands. It was thought that a few guns would be required at Mudros and Tenedos; so, after the highly successful evacuation of Gallipoli, Vice-Admiral Sir John de Robeck (who commanded the fleet in the east Mediterranean) had ordered the RND carry out these duties. Major-General Sir Archibald Paris, the RND commander-in-chief, was to be based at Mudros with the bulk of the division; and temporary military governorships were vested in Brigadier-General David Mercer (commanding officer of the RND 1st Brigade), who was to take over Imbros with two battalions, and Bernard Freyberg, who was to occupy Tenedos with the greater part of the Hood Battalion.[5]

The division arrived on the islands as winter was having a last fling. It rained heavily for days, and fierce winds brought hail, sleet and snow. There was a terrific storm at Mudros, where some four inches of rain fell in 36 hours and most of the tents came down. But the troops remained in excellent spirits, and their health was good. Apart from dysentery and paratyphoid fever, there was little to complain about.[6]

Sub-Lieutenant Ivan Heald wrote from Mudros on 14 January, 1916:

> We are all safe in camp here after many dangerous days. I have not been able to send letters, as none were sent away.
>
> It is pleasant here, and we bathe in the sunshine. We may get leave or we may stay here and garrison this island for some months. I have had no letters for three or four weeks, but there is a big mail on the beach here. It is great to be walking on the top of the ground after all the dug-outs and trenches.[7]

New uniforms were issued to the Hood Battalion on 17 January, and they were inspected by Major-General Paris. Much to the disgust of the old hands, the rank and file were offered 10 days' leave on Malta.[8] The men had expected English leave, and an eye witness account of the parade makes it clear that there was some ill feeling:[9]

> General Paris was justly proud of his division, and whether it was his intention to visit all battalions in turn in order to express his appreciation, I know not. Suffice it to say that the 'Hoods' were paraded for the general's inspection; and after saying some nice things, he announced his intention of giving the officers leave to England and the men, if they cared, leave for Malta.
>
> His speech was listened to in silence, but when the acting commander called for three cheers for the general the gallant Hoods gave him the raspberry. The general went pink and in a fit of choler cancelled all leave for the battalion and confined all ranks to camp for seven days.[10]

After taking their punishment, one batch of the Hood finally left for their 10 days' leave on Malta: men of the old Collingwood and Benbow Battalions absorbed into the Hood after the terrible battle of 4 June, 1915. It was to their advantage to accept the offered leave, but the old hands refused it. The Hood Battalion disintegrated: some men were sent to garrison Tenedos, and C Company was divided. The 1st and 2nd Platoons went to guard stores in East Mudros, whilst the 3rd and 4th Platoons took over the village of Kosta.[11]

On Friday, 25 February HMT *Olympic* docked in the harbour at Mudros with about 10,000 reinforcements for the Royal Naval Division. The ship left again two days later with, among others, 38 officers and men of the Hood going for leave in England. On 26 February Major-General Paris wrote home:

> The Admiralty are a long time making up their minds what to do with their *enfant terrible*, the RND. They are better to hand it over to the army, which is the only sensible solution, and it doesn't help having strained relations.
>
> One little (true) story as an example. When the army evacuated Imbros they wished to receive two anti-aircraft guns. Navy objected. Army ordered their removal. Vice-Admiral refused to supply transport. Sir A. Murray wired personally to de Robeck – 'Am I to understand you refuse to allow anti-aircraft guns which I ordered to be removed from Imbros, to be embarked?' De Robeck replied, 'Your assumption is correct!', and the guns are still there. I think I said something before about the cordial co-operation of the two services. It helps such a lot!
>
> I am sending 550 ranks home on leave in the *Olympic* – lucky beggars. I wish I could come too, but it's impossible until the future policy is settled. Then I may find myself out of employment.
>
> For the first time in history the RND are over strength, and it does seem an incredible waste leaving us to garrison islands which require only a few police. Meanwhile, unknown to general headquarters in Alexandria, I have managed to send a brigade to help at Salonica. As likely as not when they hear about it, it will have to come back. I am now trying to get the whole division sent there.[12]

By late March the division was enjoying beautiful, warm weather. Sub-Lieutenant Bentham had been an AB with the Collingwood during the Antwerp defence. He had escaped from internment in Holland, obtained a commission on his return to England and was sent out to join the Hood. He writes:

> A job I had was officer in charge of the pickets at Kastro, and my duty was to prevent the smuggling of spirits out of the town to the troops scattered all over the island. I had a house on the front, a horse, and a motor boat complete with crew from HMS *Nelson*. All liquor confiscated by my outposts was brought to me to be destroyed. On one occasion I had five gallons of brandy which

was all poured away. I had a real good time, and was entertained by the inhabitants. The band came over and played in the square when Lieutenant-Commander Asquith visited me. A very nice Greek schoolmistress made me a suit of pyjamas and Asquith always pulled my leg about these. They were brown with pink roses on them. Close by were the old thermal baths nestling at the foot of Mount Therma and which were built by the Trojans. Cleopatra is recorded to have visited them during her visit to the Greek islands. They were baths carved out of solid rock and from the mountain a steady stream of water nearly boiling poured into it. Clouds of steam always surrounded the place and it was an ideal volcanic steam. The Greeks used it and families, mother, father, sons and daughters, all got in together. I noticed that officers and Canadian nurses from a hospital ship followed that excellent custom. Of course, I refrained from sheer modesty!

However, all good times come to an end: Commander Freyberg returned from leave and thought we had gone soft, and so started some strenuous training. During his leave, he had seen the Prime Minister, Mr Asquith, and had got a tentative promise that we should go to France.[13]

On 27 March parts of C Company of the Hood were recalled to Mudros for the consecration of the British cemetery at Portianos on Lemnos. The ritual was performed by a bishop who had been staying with Paris, and a typed hymn-sheet was produced for the troops, showing hymns 399 and 608. Paris wrote:

We had a most picturesque ceremony, at the conclusion of which the mayor and inhabitants made political speeches and the school children cheered. Quite a unique affair, but everyone was pleased.[14]

Wednesday, 29 March found the Hood again on parade in the late afternoon. All the men of the original Hood Battalion who had landed on the peninsula in April, 1915, were ordered to take two paces forward. Joseph Murray obeyed, one of only 15 to step forward out of the 900 men present. They were told off for English leave, but no date was mentioned.[15]

Vice-Admiral de Robeck was now making strenuous efforts to keep the division as an effective fighting force. He despatched a telegram to the First Lord at the Admiralty on 13 March, 1916, marked private and personal:

Have seen General Paris regarding red/action [urgent] RN Division. Sincerely trust that question of reduction may be reconsidered. It

150

would be national misfortune. The men who have fought magnificently have great *esprit de corps* and the units are up to war strength. Whole force can be fully utilized with advantage here when training now in progress is complete.

The admiral followed this up with another telegram on 17 March:

I consider it would be far better and in the public interest to keep RND as at present constituted. It is now an efficient force with officers and men in best of spirits and with great courage. Decision is having most demoralising effect on units whom it is proposed to disband and all hope decision may be reconsidered.

The Admiralty replied to de Robeck by telegram on 20 March:

The Admiralty orders have been thoroughly considered and cannot be modified. At the same time the Admiralty fully recognize the magnificent services rendered by the division and very much regret the necessity for the order. It must be realized that the situation demands the most careful husbanding of resources and no sentimental reasons can be allowed to interfere with this object. The division is definitely allocated to the garrisoning of the three islands and no operations are to be undertaken outside them without very definite orders or permission from the Admiralty.[16]

In a letter of 30 March Paris wrote:

The much-feared blow has fallen and this unfortunate division will soon cease to exist as such . . . . The breaking-up of units has been a very distressing business; the not least trying part of it is saying goodbye and a few words. I'm not good at that sort of thing and dislike it intensely.

Even the Naval Division sometimes get into trouble – witness a row of malefactors now tied to stakes outside my window doing what is known as field punishment number one. A very unpleasant way of spending a couple of hours when the day's work is done. Quite like the old days of the pillory![17]

Up to 500 men with previous sea experience were despatched for service with the navy. Discontent grew among those left behind on the islands, and as a result petty officers and men sent signed petitions to the Admiralty, written on such items as YMCA leaflets, requesting service in the fleet. On occasion this somewhat unusual form of application appears to have worked, as the Admiralty sometimes relented and allowed the transfer.

On Sunday, 2 April, Paris once again inspected the Hood Battalion. Joseph Murray remembers the parade:

> We marched passed Sir Archibald Paris and Vice-Admiral de Robeck. In a short speech, Paris told us that the division would soon be disbanded through no fault of our own. The admiral's inspection was taken to mean that the navy were about to hand us over to the ship-breakers. Where did we go from here? We were fully-trained soldiers masquerading as sailors in name only, with plenty of fighting experience behind us.[18]

But matters were proceeding at some speed between the War Office and the Admiralty: a clue can be found in the RND's divisional HQ war diary. A Colonel Stroud began a lecture tour around the islands talking about military law, and on 16 April the RND was placed under the Army Act. The information was relayed to the division by de Robeck, with the news that they were being transferred to the army. All arrangements for English leave were cancelled and the battalions began to reassemble. On 1 May orders were received to form a new battalion, the 2nd Hood Battalion, under Lieutenant-Commander Asquith.[19]

Despite this inter-service activity, the islands remained peaceful. The only break was when an enemy aeroplane was seen over Lemnos on 4 May. It was fired on by British ships, but did not come within range of the island's anti-aircraft guns.

Back in England, the War Office notified the commander-in-chief of the British army in France that the Lords Commissioner of the Admiralty had decided to transfer the RND. Its reserves would be in England, and its records would go to the War Office. The division was to assemble in France as soon as the necessary arrangements for sea transport from the Mediterranean could be made and the War Office would assume entire responsibility for the division's administration from the date they landed in France. However, a complete transfer was impossible, due to the legal status of officers and men from enlistment, and the fact that the Admiralty would still be the paymasters.

Details of the present composition of the division in the Mediterranean were sent to France, plus details showing the units required to complete the division to war establishment and the source from which each was to be obtained:

Present composition of RND

Approximate numbers

	Officers	Other Ranks
Divisional HQ and HQs of 1st and 2nd Brigades	15	84
6 RNVR battalions	207	7,333
2 Royal Marine battalions	59	2,537
Part of divisional RE HQ, and 3 field companies of RE	14	542
Divisional Signal Company	4	216
Divisional Cyclists Company	3	117
Divisional train	35	558
2 field ambulances	25	764
Ordnance details	–	–

Proposed composition showing source from which deficiencies are to be supplied

Divisional HQ

1st Naval Brigade
1st Hood Battalion
2nd Hood Battalion (to be formed at Mudros)
1st Drake Battalion
2nd Drake Battalion (to be formed at Blandford depot)
Brigade machine-gun company (to be formed at Mudros)

2nd Naval Brigade
Howe Battalion
Nelson Battalion
1st Hawke Battalion
2nd Hawke Battalion (to be formed at Blandford)
Brigade machine-gun company (to be formed at Blandford)

3rd Marine Brigade
1st Anson Battalion
2nd Anson Battalion (to be formed at Blandford)
1st Royal Marine Battalion
2nd Royal Marine Battalion
Brigade machine-gun company (to be formed at Blandford)

Divisional Artillery
To be provided from a TF division at home.

Divisional RE
HQ
3 field companies (personnel required to raise to Pt VII to be provided from Blandford)

Divisional Signal Company
1 Divisional Squadron (to be found by War Office if required)
1 Divisional Cyclist Company (additional personnel to be provided from Blandford)
3 field ambulances
1 sanitary section
1 mobile veterinary section (to be found by War Office)
Divisional supply column (to be found by War Office)
Field butchery (to be found by War Office)
Field bakery (to be found by War Office)
5 depot supply units (to be found by War Office)
Casualty clearing station (to be found by War Office)
Ammunition sub-park (to be found by War Office).[20]

In the meantime General Paris had left the islands for a holiday in Italy and was blissfully unaware of these changes. He visited the Italian front, then made his way to Paris. On 6 May he wrote:

> I left Mudros last month – services no longer required as the poor RND was to be broken up and all arrangements to this end had been made . . . . In Paris I found an urgent wire, five days old! It informed me that the War Office had taken over the RND, which was to be completed to a full division to organize and train in France at once . . . .
> Rather startling and pleasing, but it means much work.[21]

On 7 May Greek elections were held on the islands, and as a result all officers and men were confined within a restricted area. At 6.40pm that day the 1st Royal Marine Battalion and three companies of the Howe Battalion embarked on SS *Briton* for Marseilles.[22] HMT *Minnewaska* arrived at Lemnos on the afternoon of 13 May and disembarked relieving troops: the 8th Garrison Battalion King's (Liverpool) Regiment and one field company of the West Lancashires (Territorial) Royal Engineers. An advance guard of two officers and 62 men from the Hood then embarked on the *Minnewaska* and sailed for France on 15 May. The remaining 26 officers and 873 men of the battalion followed in the *Ionian* on 16 May; other RND units sailed on the *Arragon*.[23]

A new chapter had been opened. The romance of the voyage to Gallipoli had gone, as had the vast majority of the Hood officers and men who had sailed away on that crusade of hope back in early 1915. The tide of war had changed. The illusion of noble sacrifice had tarnished and hardened into the growing realism of the times. Now the Royal Naval Division would have to sail the continent of Europe as soldiers, under the white ensign.

CHAPTER SIXTEEN

A Division Reborn

The Hood arrived at Marseilles at 8pm on 21 May and disembarked from the *Ionian* at 4pm the following day.[1] The battalion paraded on the quayside with their band playing, then marched to the railway station. Murray remembers:

> The people of Marseilles made an awful fuss of us, and I thought to myself 'Thank the Lord somebody knows we're here.' We said, 'All right, mate, the Naval Division is here, you can stop worrying,' and all that type of nonsense. Because we stole away from Devonport, Blandford and the Dardanelles we never had a send-off, and it was never recognized, but here in Marseilles they made a fuss of us. Lasses were running along the lines kissing the fellers. We began to think we were humans now; we had been animals for the last 12 months.
>
> We got to Lyons, where the French Red Cross people also made a proper fuss of us. They kept insisting we should drink tea and so on.[2]

However, Thomas MacMillan, who had sailed on the *Minnewaska* and was shortly to become a clerk at the 189th Brigade HQ, engaged in typing numerous orders for the Hood, wrote of his entry into Lyons:

> The shouting set up on approaching this city brought a considerable number of natives to the station, but to our dismay they could not enthuse. Try as we might, we could not even extract a smile from them. I had heard a good deal about 'Gay Paree' and the vivacious French, but this crowd looked as if they had come from the city of Despair and we are bound for the city of Destruction.
>
> 'Surely all of them cannot be mourning the loss of relations or friends,' I thought, as I observed the preponderance of black

garments. No! We had struck France when her spirits were very low, and when she was despairing of a successful termination to the war. *Tipperary* no longer brought free drinks, nor did *Pack up your troubles in your old kitbag* make them smile.[3]

Eventually the battalion arrived at Abbeville at 5am on Saturday, 17 June, where they boarded a train for a five-hour journey to Bruay. A march of 11 miles found them in the village of Dieval, where the Hood was billeted in barns.[4]

The nominal roll of Hood officers on 10 June shows the formation of both the 1st and 2nd Hood Battalions:

Temporary Rank Appointment	*Name*	*Regiment*
1st Hood Battalion		
Commander, RNVR Commanding Officer (substantive rank: Captain)	B. Freyberg	Royal West Surrey
Lieutenant-Commander Adjutant	W. M. le C. Egerton	RNVR
Lieutenant	L. H. Cockey	RNVR
Lieutenant	I. Heald	RNVR
Lieutenant	E. A. Edmondson	RNVR
Sub-Lieutenant	C. F. Wright	RNVR
Sub-Lieutenant	G. H. Tamplin	RNVR
Sub-Lieutenant	L. F. Callingham	RNVR
Sub-Lieutenant	F. A. Cole	RNVR
Sub-Lieutenant	F. C. Hill	RNVR
Sub-Lieutenant	T. Barrow Green	RNVR
Sub-Lieutenant	P. H. Bolus	RNVR
Sub-Lieutenant	B. H. Oldridge	RNVR
Sub-Lieutenant	R. J. Hall	RNVR
Sub-Lieutenant	H. Gealer	RNVR
Sub-Lieutenant	J. D. Baird	RNVR
Sub-Lieutenant	G. T. Davidson	RNVR
Sub-Lieutenant	H. Donaldson	RNVR

Lieutenant-Commander Acting Commanding Officer	A. M. Asquith	RNVR
Lieutenant Second in Command	F. S. Kelly	RNVR
Lieutenant Adjutant	J. C. Hilton	RNVR
Lieutenant	S. H. Fish	RNVR
Lieutenant	R. J. Apthorp	RNVR
Acting Lieutenant	J. W. Morrison	RNVR
Sub-Lieutenant	C. A. Markey	RNVR
Sub-Lieutenant	J. L. Holland	RNVR
Sub-Lieutenant	J. C. Forster	RNVR
Sub-Lieutenant	J. H. Bentham	RNVR
Sub-Lieutenant	D. F. Bailey	RNVR
Sub-Lieutenant	R. V. Chapman	RNVR[5]

On 22 June General Paris wrote a letter from RND HQ:

I wonder if there will ever come a time when this division will run on ball-bearings . . . .

We were to have had volunteers from the army as the Admiralty won't enlist any more. The only hitch there is that there are no volunteers! Then the Admiralty has stolen men by the hundred. All who go on leave never return, and some thousands are hidden in ships. It doesn't make it easy! Here the army say we are fighting the navy as well as the Hun! Of course it was the greatest mistake forming the division, but it would be a worse one to break it up now. We've survived a few storms, and I've hopes of getting through this . . . .

The villages and country in the neighbourhood of this front line are a sad sight. The strange thing is that even now some inhabitants remain, and you see children playing in the streets. In the fields one only sees old men, women and children doing all the work . . . .

I am comfortably housed: a nice château on the top of a hill, with a billiard room as my private office. I should prefer it if the owners were not here. Count, countess, sister and two squalling infants – they never seem to go out, and all shake hands every time we meet! My French isn't equal to conversational small talk. It's quite a nice square house, no water and of course no bathroom . . . .

We are very fortunate in our mess. A capital staff, all good men, and we get on well together. Further, we have now quite a good cook, and it makes a difference. When compulsion was introduced several cooks sought new places, including one from the Junior Carlton Club. We pay him five shillings a week – not quite his usual wage![6]

The number of men found available for service in the Royal Naval Division had proved less than expected, and an appeal for volunteers from the army to transfer for enrolment in the RNVR had not been successful. None of the officers asked to volunteer for service with the RND had consented. It was therefore proposed that the divisional infantry should consist of the original two Royal Marines battalions and the six RNVR battalions formed into two brigades, and that the third brigade should be formed from four army battalions, paid and administered by the Army Council. The short-lived 2nd Hood Battalion was to be reabsorbed into the 1st Hood, and any surplus personnel sent home to Blandford.

The division was to be known as the 63rd (RN) Division, with the original RND battalions in the 188th and 189th Brigades:

188th Brigade – Brigadier-General Robert Prentice
Howe Battalion
Anson Battalion
1st RMLI Battalion
2nd RMLI Battalion

189th Brigade – Brigadier-General Lewis Philips
Hood Battalion
Hawke Battalion
Drake Battalion
Nelson Battalion

190th Brigade – Brigadier-General Giles Trotman
1st Battalion Honourable Artillery Company
4th Bedford Battalion
7th Royal Fusiliers
10th Dublin Fusiliers[7]

The Naval Division was now to be trained in army ways, and arrived at training camp to discover that the 29th Division and New Zealanders who had been with them at Gallipoli had preceded them. Joseph Murray remembers the reorganization:

We were told, 'Look, you are in the army now.' For some reason or other the division got the number of the 63rd. I can't remember anybody ever telling me we belonged to the 63rd. It was never made public, as far as we were concerned.

159

We were treated as raw recruits, forming fours, right turn, shoulder arms and slope arms. Then we had to poke at sacks hung between two posts with the bayonet.[8] The instructor said, 'That's all wrong.' We had to alter the RND style of bayonet fighting – up until then the navy stance had been used and considered very efficient. Now, instead of bending the knees in a sitting stance, we must bend the left knee only. The right leg must be rigid and the body leaned forward with the weight on the left leg. The point of the bayonet will be a foot nearer the enemy than it was with the old naval style – provided, of course, that he is coming towards you, and you are waiting for him to oblige.[9]

Route marches, night training and gas exercises followed, as Murray recalls:

You had to have a fear of gas, so they shoved you through what they called a mild dose, but it was all guesswork. We were coughing and spitting and blowing our noses; our eyes were watering for days. Then we had to go through wearing gas masks. With a gas mask you had to cover your mouth and you had nippers on your nose. If you didn't you got all steamed up and couldn't see anything. It was a damned nuisance.[10]

This training continued for three weeks. Sub-Lieutenant Bentham writes:

The war still seemed a long way off, and Lieutenant Kelly, Sub-Lieutenant Chapman and myself with 12 petty officers and leading seamen were sent to Rouen for a bombing course. There was a stir when we arrived at the camp, which contained 5,000 to 6,000 men, and nobody knew who or what we were. We still maintained our naval ranks and Kelly had a full moustache and beard [the army was not permitted to wear a beard]. Kelly stipulated that the navy took precedence on parade, much to the army's annoyance, and we lined up behind the band and led the parade off the parade ground.

What a time I had in Rouen: the fortnight went very quickly. It was whilst we were there that I first heard Kelly play the piano. He was a master, and had given recitals at Queen's Hall before the war. He had also won the Diamond Sculls two years running. But he was very eccentric: he washed his teeth at least 12 times a day, and loathed getting his hands dirty, so he was never without gloves.[11]

On Thursday 29 June the Hood moved to Villers-au-Bois in the Vimy Ridge section of the front. The following day the battalion received its baptism of fire on the Western Front, under a heavy artillery bombardment. A cable trench was being dug on the ridge about 100 yards behind the front line and the Hood was troubled by shrapnel. Murray found trench life on the Western Front was entirely unlike anything he had experienced at Gallipoli.

It was a different war altogether, honestly we were astounded . . . .

When we went out with the 17th Division, we had to go out wiring at night. They were making such a terrible row. I thought to myself, 'Cor blimey, where the hell are the Germans? Oh! There, a mile away!' In the Dardanelles you had to sneak out, crawl out . . . . Anyway, on the Western Front we went out wiring. It seemed alarming that we were able to walk around in no-man's-land as if you were on a football field. Never saw a German. From my personal point of view 90 per cent of the men who went to France never saw a German.

When the war began there wasn't so much artillery on either side. That was the standard for us in the Dardanelles. We never had more than the British army had in 1914. We didn't have ammunition, we didn't have the guns. To make the comparison, at the Dardanelles the front line was always fully manned. All the men we had were in the front line, and the cooks, etc., were in the second line, 50 to 100 yards behind. After another 50 yards was the support line. All fully manned. But with the increase in artillery that situation couldn't be tolerated in France. The front line there was only held by a couple of men with a machine gun, and the reserve trench was only held by a few, in case there was an attack. The main position was a quarter of a mile behind. So they could afford to retreat half a mile without any loss at all. But in the Dardanelles you would have been in the sea. That was the whole difference.

At the Dardanelles, when the trenches were only 10 to 15 yards apart, you were on the look-out all the time. You had to keep awake and keep your eyes open, day and night. In France you didn't have to look out at all. You knew you had a machine gun in the front line, and of course as soon as he saw anything happen he used to set off, brrrrr, half a magazine.

With the guns of the artillery barrage jammed together wheel to wheel in France, in five minutes the whole of the front line section would be decimated. So it was useless to man the first three lines; they were held by patrols. But we couldn't get used to that. You have no idea: we tried to knock a nail in without making a noise. It was silly, really.[12]

161

The ex-schoolmaster, H. V. Clark of the RND wrote a poem about
the constant artillery barrage:

THE GUNS

Hear the rattle of the guns!
Maxim guns!
How incessant is their prattle
As they shoot towards the Huns!
How they crackle, crackle, crackle,
Through the hanging clouds of smoke,
While the rifles seem to crackle,
'We, too, desire to tackle these
Kultur-ridden folk.'
Saying, 'Ping, ping, ping.
'Tis the song of death we sing,
To the ravishers of Belgium and
The slayers of her sons.'
Hear the guns, guns, guns, guns,
Guns, guns, guns!
The cracking and the clacking
Of the guns!

Hear the bombing of the guns!
Three-inch guns!
How voluminous the sound, as from
Twenty thousand drums!
Hurling cylinders of hate, whose
Bursting seals the fate
Of many gallant warriors 'over there'.
Limb-rending chunks of steel,
Making wounds that never heal
On bodies fair.
And the men behind the breach,
Who reload amid the screech
Of 'iron-ware',
And who, loading, loading, loading,
In an automatic way,
Scarcely feel a slight foreboding
In their awful Stygian play.
Oh, the guns, guns, guns, guns,
Guns, guns, guns!
The banging and the clanging
Of the guns!

162

Hear the crashing of the guns!
Twelve-inch guns!
How the earth seems to recoil
From these devastating ones!
How they clang, and crash and roar,
As their flaming, belching throats,
Towards the foe!
For every shell titanic,
Bursts with a force volcanic,
Hurling tons
Of earth and iron pieces all aglow;
And the mass of stone concreted –
Tower of strength! – is now deleted.
Refuge vain!
That, but yesterday so proudly
Reared its head, and 'spoke' so loudly
O'er the slain.
Oh, these guns, guns, guns, guns,
Guns, guns, guns!
These fortress-breaking,
Crater-making guns![13]

The Battle of the Somme started on 1 July, and the division was used as a reserve, as front line cover, or for working parties at various locations. Their time as an attacking force was yet to come. They then moved to the Souchez sector by night: it was impossible to move formed bodies of men forward in daylight, as the whole area was overlooked from Vimy Ridge, and by numerous observation balloons behind the enemy lines. The battalions marched in at night, platoons 100 yards apart, each with a guide from its outgoing opposite number to lead them directly to their own particular defensive position.

Bernard Freyberg wrote about trench life at this stage of the war:

Before taking over a sector of the defence, the battalion commander of the incoming troops visited the line; he got a map from the present tenant showing how it was held, and then altered the method of defence according to the idiosyncrasies of his general. He found out danger spots and any other points of interest, arranged for guides, found what part of the relief could be carried out in daylight, and struck as hard a bargain about filled tins of water to be handed over in the front line as the good nature of his *vis-à-vis* allowed.
  The company commander visited his opposite number before the men started to arrive, and they made a tour of the company zone

of responsibility. He saw that all the sentries and Lewis guns were properly posted, and that all the remainder of his men stood to arms at their definite fire positions; he questioned all the platoon commanders to see they understood their orders in case of hostile attack, and checked all anti-gas and SOS arrangements. While the company commander was taking over the defence, the two sergeant-majors checked the stores at company headquarters, and the incoming sergeant-major took over all the ammunition, tins of water, iron rations, lights and other trench stores in the company dump.

When all arrangements in the trenches were to his satisfaction, the incoming company commander took over command and allowed the outgoing troops to file away down the communication trenches. The relieving troops were now left to their own devices. A message was sent to the battalion headquarters by telephone, to the effect that the company relief was complete. The order to stand down was given, when the posted sentries remained at their posts while all the rest of the men stood down and prepared for their night's labours. The next sentry reliefs usually turned in to sleep, while all who remained were detailed to the various jobs taken over with the sector, such as emptying sand bags from the mine shaft, helping the engineers to make deep dugouts, putting out barbed wire entanglements, drainage, digging latrines, carrying trench mortar ammunition and so on, without touching the questions of fresh work or trench maintenance.

Work in the front went on until one hour before dawn, when the order to 'Stand to arms' was given. All men in the sector ceased their labours or their sleep, put on their complete battle kit, patrols came back to their trenches, and everything was made ready to receive and repel a hostile attack. When day broke the order to 'Stand down' was given, when a reduced number of sentries kept a vigilance during the hours of daylight. Those not on sentry duty were warned that the platoon commander's inspection was due to commence in half an hour. To prepare for this, they had to clean and oil their rifles, take every one of their 150 rounds of ammunition out of their equipment, brush, oil, and place them in neat heaps on a folded waterproof sheet, along with their iron rations; their box respirators were inspected at the alert position. When the officers had inspected all the arms and equipment of their men, they then inspected the men's feet, and to avoid having all the men with their boots off at one time, it was carried out in relays, the even numbers taking off their boots while the odd numbers rubbed their feet, and vice versa. Even in very wet trenches, the men were made to sit in deep mud to do this, so vital was it to stimulate the circulation to prevent trench feet. In many cases whale oil was used for rubbing the feet and legs to render the skin waterproof. When the inspections were finished the men shaved (they used the mirrors out of the trench periscopes and water from shell holes) and by the time they had finished, breakfast had arrived.

In such a tedious and hard life, meals were great events. Sleep, the only other factor besides work, was dependent to a great extent upon shellfire, and the climate conditions of the cubby-hole in which they slept.

Breakfast was cooked in the reserve line, as the smoke from any fires further forward drew shelling on to the infantry. The meal usually consisted of fried bacon, tea, bread, jam and the rum ration, which had been kept over from the night before. The rum was kept because, if given at night, it might have sent the sentries to sleep, whilst with the food at breakfast it heated their cold wet bodies, and enabled them to snatch a few hours' painful sleep.

Most of the men slept until dinner, which was at noon, and consisted of cold fresh or preserved meat, pickles, bread and butter; the tea and sugar ration did not run to three times a day.

After dinner they worked on jobs that were not under enemy observation, such as drainage and sorting out and cleaning bombs and ammunition. Tea was at four, and just before dusk the whole trench garrison again 'Stood to arms' for an hour, and then carried on with the nightly routine.

Night was a time when all manner of people prowled about. Colonels or ratings, it was all the same in the dark when going from post to post, or out on patrol. The sentries standing in the shadow allowed each to come, so that the point of the bayonet was at their throat before stopping them with a sharp, but very low, 'Halt!' Then a pause to see if they obeyed, followed with the time-honoured 'Who goes there?' Great friendships were made whilst going the rounds at night. A colonel got to know the voices and minds of his men before he could match a face to them, and there's many a young subaltern or recruit who, during a surprise bombardment, lay on his belly in the same wet shellhole as his colonel, and when a chance shell might have made them companions for all eternity, it's little wonder that during life these friendships have remained.

This life in the front line usually lasted three days, when an inter-company relief took the company back into the support or reserve line for a similar period. On the sixth night the battalion moved to reserve, into a back area, where a number of men were required to dig on back lines trenches, but this work could be done by day, and the men got their rest at night.[14]

Sub-Lieutenant Bentham describes some incidents in the trenches:

Lieutenant Kelly was very eccentric, and intensely keen on cats. We never had less than four or five cats in the line with us, and when we went out to rest each platoon officer had to take one in a sandbag. His constant calling to his batman for fresh water to clean his teeth got on everyone's nerves.

Shortly after we took over the line, Kelly came to me one evening and told me to collect a petty officer and a bomber and to follow him, as he was going to explore the ground in no-man's-land. We crawled out on hands and knees and, looking round to see if the bomber was behind me, I found that he was crawling on all fours with a Mills grenade in one hand and the pin in his mouth. If he had slipped, I should not be writing this now. I hastily made him put the pin back. Presently Kelly whispered that his boots were making too much noise, and told me to carry on and left me alone. I did the job, although very scared, and got back to our lines feeling a very brave fellow and well out of it.

I went down to our dug-out and told the others where I had been. Knowing my turn for watch would not be for another two hours, I took several large swigs of neat whisky, as the water bottles were empty, and turned in. Just as I was dozing off, I heard Freyberg's voice calling me. I jumped up and climbed to see him outside the dug-out. He said that Kelly had reported my having been out alone, and he wanted me to take him out and show him where I had been. The whisky had begun to take effect and I was full of Dutch courage, so I climbed over the parapet and walked straight over no-man's-land, kicking empty bully tins and tearing my clothes on old wire and swearing each time, exhibiting as little care as though walking through a field at home.

After we had been out some time, stopping dead when star shells went up, Freyberg whispered, 'Where are we?' As if I knew! I was quite happy! There in front of us was the German parapet – we heard them talking. Cautioning me to be quiet, Freyberg indicated we should start to return to our lines. Just at that moment shrapnel burst overhead and we heard bullets whizzing all round us, but we threw ourselves flat and in doing so I cut my hand. Needless to say, we arrived back at a different place to where we left and one of the sentries challenged us. Not hearing our reply, he started to fire at us, thinking that we were an enemy patrol. Luckily for us he missed, and we gave a loud shout to cease fire. In we scrambled and dropped down into the trench. Freyberg immediately scolded the sentry for not being a better marksman! When we walked back to our part of the line, Hall, Bailey and Edmonson were waiting

166

there with Kelly, thinking that Freyberg would hand me over to Kelly to be put under arrest. Instead of which he said, 'This intrepid young officer nearly walked into the enemy trench.' He then said goodnight to me and walked off . . . .

One day we received a message that we must try to identify the German regiment in front of us, and whoever succeeded was promised seven days' leave in England. At the end of a little sap which ran out from our trenches, we could get within speaking distance of a sap which came out from the German lines. We thought the Hun was inclined to be friendly, and extra care was taken not to frighten him.

We started singing and he joined in, especially when Kelly sang extracts from *Siegfried*, and he would always carry on where Kelly left off. We did our best to entice him over without success, so five of us crept out one evening and found him alone. We hastily put him to sleep, secured his papers, cap and badge, and returned.

We sent in our prizes and awaited the promised reward, but all we heard was that our neighbours had been over the previous night and supplied all the information required.[15]

Joseph Murray was sent to the orderly room and told that he was to attend a course at a Lewis gun school in Paris-Plage:

It was like being a schoolboy. The instructors were very smart, buttons shining like little suns, creases of their trousers so sharp that you had to be careful you didn't lacerate your bum rubbing up against them.

The instructor took the gun to bits in only a minute, then explained everything to us and reassembled it. 'Now you want to know how to fire, don't you? Well you pull back the cocking handle that winds the spring up . . . . ' 'What spring?' 'The spring is in here, 29 lb of tension. And along the barrel, about four inches from the end, is an aperture. When the shot is fired, gas follows the explosion. It travels that four inches, goes down that little vent, hits the piston, and drives it back. That winds it up for the next one, and that's the automation.' I found it most interesting, and the guns were lively little buggers.

Murray did well on his course, largely thanks to reading instruction manuals constantly in an effort to help another student (an old Gallipoli hand from a different division, whom Murray immediately befriended), and was called in to see Freyberg about a week after he got back to the battalion. 'I've got a letter here from the Lewis gun school: they think very well of you. How would you like to be an instructor?' Murray agreed, provided that he could remain as an instructor with the Hood rather than going to teach at the gun school. 'I think I had better stay here, because I know the men. We're different from them. We are a different class of people, we in the firing line. I'm not complaining about them; they are most kind and helpful, but we are a different crowd.' So Murray was given the task of instructing the Hood Battalion in the ways of the Lewis gun. He picked his own section from C Company as the first trainees; instead of going on a working party they found themselves in a local barn under the instruction of Able Seaman Joseph Murray.

In September, 1916, Murray went on leave, the only leave he'd had since joining the RND back in 1914. He went to company HQ to get his instructions and papers: the battalion had been sleeping in huts in a wood when they were not in the front line, and the band were playing as Murray passed by:

The Hood Battalion had a lovely band, and just behind the huts Kelly, a classical scholar and a wonderful musician, was conducting the band, playing Tchaikovsky's *1812 Overture*. It was originally composed for the opening of a cathedral in St Petersburg; but at the last moment they thought that the guns firing would affect the stained glass and might break it. But we heard it as Tchaikovsky had wanted to hear it: all the guns were firing like hell.[16]

Kelly had planned this performance of the *1812 Overture* for some time, and finally achieved it in a wood full of gun batteries.[17]

On Thursday, 5 October the Hood got their first sight of a tank. Murray, who had returned from leave, describes the excitement:

We had a new interest: we had heard of a new weapon, the tank, but, apart from a glimpse of them at a railhead at Acheux, we were in the dark as much as everyone else as to the precise nature of this wonderful new weapon that would make our job as infantrymen a piece of cake. These monsters would flatten the maze of barbed wire and overrun machine-gun posts and trenches alike. All we had to do now was to follow in their wakes and mop up. They could, and would, demolish everything in their path, and rifle fire was useless against their armour plating. They could span any known trench, climb down and out of any crater. They could win the war on their own. Here they were, about a dozen of them, huge clumsy brutes, squatting on the hard unshelled ground, stationary and silent. My first thought was to wonder if they were capable of any movement, as they looked so clumsy and so heavy.

At this moment we are prepared to believe in anything that might end the present stalemate of trench warfare.[18]

A German newspaper published a description of the tank, written by a war correspondent on the Western Front:

When the German outposts crept out of their dugouts in the mist of the morning of 16 September and stretched their necks to look for the English, their blood was chilled in their veins. Two mysterious monsters were crawling towards them over the craters. Stunned as if an earthquake had burst around them, they all rubbed their eyes, which were fascinated by the fabulous creature.

Their imaginations were still excited by the efforts of the bombardment. It was no wonder, then, that imagination got the better of these sorely-tried men, who knew well enough that the enemy would use every means to destroy our steel wall of fragile human bodies. These men no longer know what fear is. But here was some devilry which the brain of man had invented, with powerful mechanical forces, a mystery which rooted one to the ground because the intelligence could not grasp it, a fate before which one felt helpless.

One stared and stared as if one had lost the power of one's limbs. The monsters approached slowly, hobbling, rolling and rocking, but they approached. Nothing impeded them; a supernatural force seemed to impel them on. Someone in the trenches said: 'The devil is coming,' and the word was passed along the line like wildfire.

Suddenly tongues of flame leaped out of the armoured sides of the iron caterpillar. Shells whistled over our heads and the sound of machine guns filled the air. The mysterious creature had yielded its secret, and the men came back to their senses; their vigour and tenacity returned when the English infantry rolled up in waves behind the 'devil's coaches'.[19]

Trench life held no great fascination for Lieutenant Ivan Heald, who found things very dull and volunteered for the Royal Flying Corps as an observer. He duly left the Hood – only to be shot down and killed with his pilot on 4 December, 1916, whilst flying over the German lines. He was aged 33 when he died.[20]

On 16 October the Hood was told that Major-General Paris had been wounded near the village of Mailly-Mailly, where he had gone with Major Sketchley to visit the 190th Brigade holding the left flank of the divisional sector. Joseph Murray recalls the battalion's reaction to the news:

Some say he was wounded on 12 October and others 14 October, but the actual date did not matter. The loss of the general did. Everyone spoke well of him; he had been in command of the division since 1914, and was the bulwark between us and the army. We were navy personnel and fought under orders from the Admiralty whilst he commanded. Now he had gone, what would happen to us?[21]

The War Office now had the opportunity to standardize this ill-bred outfit and ensure compliance to army ways in the 63rd (RN) Division. Winston Churchill explained the quandary in his introduction to Douglas Jerrold's history of the RND:

When the division went to France in the spring of 1916 a new set of difficulties began to assail it and even to menace its existence. It was a naval division. It had different rates of pay, different ranks, different customs, different methods, different traditions, from those of the British Expeditionary Army. Its officers and men used consistently the naval parlance on every occasion. To leave their camps, in which the white ensign flew and bells recorded the passage of time, men requested 'leave to go ashore'; when they returned they 'came aboard', and when they did not they were reported as 'adrift'. Men were 'rated' and 'disrated', and for sergeants and lance-corporals they had petty officers and leading seamen. Anchors were stencilled on their limbers and emblazoned on their company flags, and their regimental badges were in the form of the crests of the admirals whose names their battalions bore. When ill or wounded they attended 'sick bay'; field kitchens were the 'galley'; the King's health was drunk sitting in the 'wardroom' – where officers wanting salt are even reported to have been heard asking their neighbours to 'give it a fair wind'; all Wrights were 'Shiner', and all Clarks were 'Nobby'. Many of the men and some of the officers requested 'leave to grow', and paraded creditable beards in the faces of a clean-chinned army.

It need scarcely be said that these manifestations inspired in a certain type of military mind feelings of the liveliest alarm. To this type of mind anything which diverged in the slightest degree from absolute uniformity according to the sealed pattern was inexpressibly painful. Yet these very peculiarities of the Royal Naval Division, this consciousness they had of partnership with the great traditions of the Royal Navy, these odd forms and ceremonies, this special nomenclature, which were cherished and preserved so punctiliously by officers and men, few of whom had ever been to sea, were in fact the mainspring of their exceptional prowess. It is strange how men deprived of everything that makes for happiness and pleasure in human life, confronted with the cruellest trials and under the constant menace amounting almost to certainty of death, find comfort and revivifying strength in little things which to others, freed from these circumstances, living in an easy and exalted sphere, only appear trivial and perhaps, absurd.[22]

Leadership of this motley crew was handed over to Major-General Cameron Deane Shute, who had seen service with the Welsh Regiment and the Rifle Brigade.[23] Perhaps he was told that the army hadn't wanted the RND in the first place; that they were the result of a compromise with the Admiralty, and a cuckoo in the nest. Perhaps his brief included specific instructions to bring the rogue elephant into line. Whatever the truth of the case, he soon set about changing things with gusto and energy. Antipathy grew between the divisional rank and file and their general, as Bentham reports:

> It was now the end of October, and an order came through from General Shute to say how grieved he was to see how careless the RND were in leaving their belongings strewn about the trenches; in future discipline was to be tightened up and we were to salvage everything possible. Company commanders vied with one another as to the amount of salvage they could collect, and we all knew that General Shute was out to catch us: he had not time for us then, and rather thought he had command of a rabble.
>
> One day Hall's orderly left his rifle propped up outside the entrance to Hall's dugout, plastered in mud, as it was literally impossible to keep anything clean in our part of the line. We were below having a meal when there was much commotion outside and we were called up. We found Colonel Freyberg, our CO, with General Shute, and a white-faced anxious-looking Kelly hovering in the background. General Shute had the dirty rifle in his hand. Who did it belong to? Disgraceful! Just what I thought! Etcetera, etcetera. Before the poor wretched batman could claim it, Hall stepped forward with a gleam of triumph in his eye, and said that it had been salvaged from the mill the previous night and he was sending it down to the salvage dump. Kelly nearly had a fit and our CO grinned, well knowing or guessing the real truth. The result was General Shute congratulated Hall and said what a pity there were not more like him.[24]

A poem was written by the RND officer A. P. Herbert, and sung with glee by the men to the tune of *Wrap me up in my Tarpaulin Jacket*:

> The general inspecting the trenches
> Exclaimed with a horrified shout,
> 'I refuse to command a division
> Which leaves its excreta about.'

171

But nobody took any notice,
No-one was prepared to refute,
That the presence of shit was congenial
Compared with the presence of Shute.

And certain responsible critics
Made haste to reply to his words,
Observing that his staff advisers
Consisted entirely of turds.

For shit may be shot at odd corners
And paper supplied there to suit,
But a shit would be shot without mourners
If somebody shot that shit Shute.[25]

On Wednesday 18 October the Hood took over a position on the firing line with their right flank on the bank of the overflowing River Ancre, immediately in front of the village of Hamel. There was a small island in the middle of the river, in front lay Beaucourt-sur-Ancre, and on the high ground on the other side of the river they could see the Schwaben Redoubt and Thiepval Wood, or what was left of it. C Company's right flank was the road that wound its way along the flooded valley towards Beaucourt, a little more than a mile to the north-east. Joseph Murray was unimpressed:

Good God, what an awful place! Will the rain ever cease? It is impossible to even try to do any reconstruction, and there is certainly much hard work to be done; everywhere is flooded. Jerry is out in front and must be much better off, as he is holding the higher ground: the Beaumont-Hamel to Beaucourt-sur-Ancre ridge. He has held the ridge for years and has resisted all attempts to dislodge him, and there have been many since the Somme offensive opened on 1 July.[26]

After the rain cleared Sub-Lieutenant Bentham wrote:

Every night there were wiring parties, covering patrols, etc., and very little rest. Our casualties were larger, as we were constantly being sniped. The main discomfort was the water in the trenches. Alternative nights we had to occupy the island. It was just large enough to contain an old water-mill, but one had to be very cautious as one or two parties had been found at dawn with their throats cut by Huns, who used to come down in a boat with muffled oars and overpower the sentries.

My first experience was a little terrifying. Having crept out through the marshes and water at low tide, I got my party all safe and intact and posted the sentries. I then crept up to the mill in pitch dark and saw two green eyes glaring at me. I switched on my torch and pointed my revolver at the creature, which turned out to be an enormous cat; it had gone quite wild, having remained in the mill since it was first evacuated. The night passed quickly and dawn found me ready to leave, for the island was full of evil associations, and was very eerie.[27]

Having left the front again, on 2 November the division was paraded for inspection by Major-General Shute. They stood out in lines for three hours in the pouring rain awaiting his arrival; then the inspection was postponed until the following day. The Hood went into barns and lit fires in an attempt to dry out.[28]

On 3 November Joseph Murray found himself on parade only a few feet from where the general stood to address his men, so he could hear clearly all that was said. Shute started by praising the division, stating what wonderful men we had on Gallipoli and here in France. He went on:

> The place you are going to attack now is one of the most formidable parts of the firing line on the whole Western Front. The Germans have been there umpteen months, and it's covered with dug-outs. We have made five different attempts, as you know, but we must get that ridge. If we don't take it the whole advance on the Somme and further down towards Bapaume will be in danger of being encircled, like a pincer movement. We must have that ridge at all costs.
>
> I am going to tell you this much. You know what you have to do. The more prisoners you take the less food you will get, because we have to feed them out of your rations.[29]

With these direct instructions straight from the horse's mouth, Murray and his colleagues felt they knew just where they stood. After the inspection the Hood Battalion was presented with cap badges, although not by the general. Murray remarked:

> Now we are somebody's children, and we have cap-badges to prove it. Hitherto we have felt somewhat naked without some sort of label, but now we are fully dressed.[30]

CHAPTER SEVENTEEN

The Battle of the Ancre

Since 1 July, the first day of the battle of the Somme, progress had been slow. By October the high ground of Thiepval Ridge was in British hands, but the Germans still remained rock-solid on both sides of the River Ancre at Grandcourt and across the river at Beaucourt. Extending northwards, they were still entrenched at Beaumont Hamel and Serre, resulting as a clearly defined salient. Offensives in this northern sector had failed to dislodge them, unlike progress in the south.

The 63rd (RN) Division was to fight in the area north of the Ancre, a tributary of the Somme. By October the area was the responsibility of General Gough's Fifth Army. Sir Douglas Haig wanted another offensive there, as he was being pressured by the French to support their efforts at Verdun, which had now turned for the better. The big question mark was the weather. Would it improve sufficiently for an attack before winter set in? Gough was given a free hand by Haig; it would be his decision.

The new offensive was planned to start on 13 November, using 12 divisions: the 2nd, 3rd, 18th, 19th, 31st, 32nd, 37th, 39th, 48th, 51st, 63rd (RN) and 4th Canadian.[1]

As the RND had no previous experience of a large offensive operation in France, General Shute held two conferences for brigadiers, brigade staffs and all commanding officers. At the first of these he explained the outline plan, and covered all the points he wished to be explained to his troops and practised if time permitted. At the second he went through the complete orders one by one, to ensure both the spirit and the letter were thoroughly understood. He also spoke to two of the brigades on parade when they were out of the front line.[2]

The existing trenches on the divisional front were unsuitable for forming up an assault. Three lines of assembly trenches had to be completed before 13 November, when the offensive was due to start. This was very tiring for the troops, but Shute's order was proved

29. Men of the Hood Battalion (Machine Gun Section) R.N. Division standing in a shell hole made by 'Asiatic Annie' in the middle of their rest camp. Taken on 4 May, 1915, by Lieut-Commander Hedderwick. The man on the extreme right is the author's great uncle, Albert John Walls (*IWM*).

30. The Backhouse Post. The well-known base of the Royal Naval Division. Situated near the Achi Baba Nullah and Observation Hill. Commodore Backhouse can be seen standing in the foreground (*IWM*).

31. White House, a position captured by the Hood Battalion, on 6 May, 1915. Lieut Ferguson (with hand to mouth) was killed on 4 June. Photograph taken by Lieut-Commander Hedderwick (*IWM*).

32. British and French troops in a position known as Brown House. Taken on 6 May, 1915, by Lieut-Commander Hedderwick. This position was used as a field-dressing station from 7 May, having moved forward from its former position which had been a small hill close by Backhouse Post (*IWM*).

33. Lieut-Commander Hedderwick having his hair cut. On his right are machine-gun belts drying. Taken on 29 May, 1915 (*IWM*).

34. Lieut-Commander Hedderwick with his men in a front line trench. Taken 29 May, 1915 (*IWM*).

35. Lieut Cockey washing in a stream. This stream was used for all purposes, being the only water near. Photograph by Lieut-Commander Hedderwick (*IWM*).

36. Lieut-Commander
Raymond S. Parsons, Hood
Battalion, Royal Naval
Division. *Illustrated London
News* 10 July, 1915.

37. SS *River Clyde*, photograph taken by Lieut-Commander
Hedderwick from Sedd-el-Bahr (*IWM*).

sensible in the circumstances. Bernard Freyberg, commanding officer of the Hood, wrote:

> The divisional commander, General Shute, decided to dig the whole assembly trenches on our brigade front, in one night; he detailed a party of 1,000 to finish the job: 500 to work from 7pm till midnight, and 500 from midnight till 5am. In this way he hoped to avoid casualties in the diggers, as once any fresh trenches were discovered they drew heavy enemy shellfire for some days.
>
> A military operation of this class, which involved large bodies of men working close to the enemy, required considerable care and forethought. The most difficult part was getting the men out quickly, quietly and with no confusion: as they arrived in a constant stream, only a hundred yards from the enemy machinery, a system of guides had to be prearranged to prevent any congestion occurring.
>
> The zone of activity of the working party had to be isolated from German patrols; to ensure this, a strong covering party from the garrison of the sector of defence, who knew the local geography of the ground, were posted under a separate commander. This was a most necessary step, as to lose mastery of no-man's-land was to risk discovery, and consequent failure. The strength of the covering party we used was a Lewis gun and four men with bombs and rifles, every hundred yards. After the party had been posted, the working party was led in small numbers by conducting officers to their part of the task.
>
> The bulk of the men came from reserve battalions, and had to march from their rest billets four miles along a road, and then face a long, slow, tedious tramp in the dark, 2,000 or 3,000 yards up muddy and narrow communication trenches, where every forward step had to be felt for, while a hand shielded the face and neck from being caught on the telephone wires which crossed and recrossed the trenches everywhere.
>
> The arrangements for the working party had been very badly carried out. The men came from all units in the brigade, and it was obvious when they arrived at my headquarters in Hamel village that something would have to be done; so they were formed up and placed under Commander Asquith, who took them forward. Half-way up the communication trenches the head of the party was badly shelled, and was forced to come back to wait until the shelling had ceased. The rear half of the party came back too far, and an hour was wasted before they could all be collected together again.
>
> They started forward a second time, and got as far as a trench called Peche Street, 600 yards behind our front line, when the enemy artillery put down a very heavy shoot on it, killing six men and

wounding many. During this bombardment, Commander Asquith and a subaltern named Fox (who were leading the party) were buried: they were both badly shaken, and Asquith's ear-drums were broken by the concussion of a shell. They carried on in spite of their troubles, trying to get the party together again, but the men, who were now badly rattled and under-officered, got completely out of hand and retired to Hamel in spite of all their efforts, in most cases after having thrown away their picks and shovels in the panic. By this time it was 11 o'clock, and so far not a shovelful of earth had been turned.

The second relief was due to arrive in half an hour, so we decided to send the first party back to camp and concentrate all our efforts upon the second. We told this party before starting what they were in for, and that in the event of machine-gun fire or shelling there was no question of their coming back; they were to lie down where they were and take their chances. We managed, after some casualties, and a great amount of difficulty, to get the second party on to their task by one in the morning, after six hours very hard work; and, once to their task, they set about digging as only Tyneside miners can. Coming away presented no difficulties, and they disappeared quicker than it takes to tell.[3]

On 22 October Lieutenant-Colonel Freyberg (known affectionately as 'Khaki Jack' or 'Tiny')[4] issued a Hood Battalion order for forthcoming attack, listing officers who were to go to Heuauville for instructions:

A Company
Lieutenant Cyril Edmondson
Sub-Lieutenant Arthur Bright-Smith
Sub-Lieutenant Frederick Cole
Sub-Lieutenant James Watson

B Company
Lieutenant James Hilton
Sub-Lieutenant Donald Bailey
Sub-Lieutenant Dunn
Sub-Lieutenant Collins

C Company
Lieutenant James Morrison
Sub-Lieutenant Trevor Jacobs
Sub-Lieutenant Arthur Skipper
Sub-Lieutenant Thomas Cresswell

D Company
Sub-Lieutenant William Carnell
Sub-Lieutenant John Baird
Sub-Lieutenant Joseph Clark

2nd Echelon
Sub-Lieutenant Reginald Carder
Sub-Lieutenant Bassett

3rd Echelon
Sub-Lieutenant Robert Barclay-Brown
Sub-Lieutenant Reginald Cleves
Sub-Lieutenant Cook

To HQ
Captain Lionel Montagu
Sub-Lieutenant Frederick Hill
Sub-Lieutenant William Arblaster
Sub-Lieutenant Harry Gealer[5]

The following day the battalion moved to Mesnil and all surplus gear was stacked at HQ. Lieutenant Edmondson was given the additional task of supervising its removal, whilst Sub-Lieutenant Skipper arranged billets at this new location. The Hood officers were chosen for the attack:

Headquarters
Lieutenant-Colonel Bernard Freyberg
Lieutenant Cyril Edmondson
Sub-Lieutenant William Arblaster
Sub-Lieutenant Frederick Hill (Lewis Gun Officer)
Sub-Lieutenant Harry Gealer (Signals Officer)

Four companies were to take up position from the extreme right to the left flank in the listed order:

B Company
Lieutenant Frederick Kelly
Sub-Lieutenant John Bentham
Sub-Lieutenant Robert Hall
Sub-Lieutenant Thomas Cresswell

D Company
Captain the Hon Lionel Montagu
Sub-Lieutenant William Carnell

177

Sub-Lieutenant Philip Bolus
Sub-Lieutenant Ralph Chapman

C Company
Lieutenant Sidney Fish
Sub-Lieutenant Herbert Donaldson
Sub-Lieutenant Raymond Apthorp
Sub-Lieutenant Arthur Hart

A Company
Sub-Lieutenant Lawrence Callingham
Sub-Lieutenant Samuel Wood
Sub-Lieutenant Frederick Cole
Sub-Lieutenant John Forster

Ordinary ranks amounted to about 535.[6]

Freyberg wrote about the choice of officers:

> We had, when we marched into the Somme battle area, some 52
> officers of unequal quality, and we knew that when we marched out
> in a few weeks' time, only a third would remain. It was important
> that the battalion should be officered by good men both after as well
> as during the battle; and as the complement of officers we were
> allowed to take into each assault was 20, we decided to take our
> 12 best and our eight worst. The worst were all told why they were
> picked, and that they would have good men in front and behind to
> keep an eye on them; often these officers, spurred on by the thought
> that they were undergoing a careful examination, excelled. They were
> then given unstinted praise and recognition, and having once done
> well they seldom looked back.[7]

A preliminary operational order outlined the Hood's objectives. The
battalion was to make an assault on enemy trench systems to the left
of the River Ancre. The 188th Brigade would have a frontage of 600
yards: the Hood on the right and the Hawke on the left were to
assault and clean up the first three lines of enemy trenches. Then
Drake on the right, with Nelson on the left, were to advance through
Hood and Hawke and assault the German fifth line limits, shown as a
dotted blue line on their maps.

These waves were to be assembled so that the first wave was about
200 yards from the railway line. The second wave would be some
40 yards to the rear, with the third and fourth waves each a further 40 yards apart, marked by white tape.[8] As soon as the troops

had formed up at their assembly areas, brigadiers were to inform divisional HQ with code words:

188th Infantry Brigade – Margate
189th Infantry Brigade – Southend
190th Infantry Brigade – Clacton[9]

The first and second waves were to be fighting waves and should push ahead as close to each other as possible, entering the German front line at 10 yards distance. They were to push forward after the barrage to the Hood's first objective, the enemy's third line, killing and generally terrorizing any enemy who remained, and to clear up this third line.

The third wave was to push forward with all speed and clean up the enemy's second line and nearby shell-holes below and between the second and third lines. The fourth wave was to follow the third as closely as possible to the German first line and clean it up, plus the shell-holes as far as the second line. It was hoped that the mopping up would be done as quickly and thoroughly as possible, after which the third and fourth waves were to push forward and occupy the enemy's third line so the battalion could be reorganized in preparation for the next advance.

In the reorganization, the crest of the trench was to be given to every second man; they were to get out and lie in front of it, where they would be joined by half the surviving officers and NCOs. The rest still in the trench were to form the new second wave. The disposition had to be completed as quickly as possible, as the barrage timetable would not wait for any stragglers.[10]

Every sixth man was to carry a sandbag, marked with a green 'B', containing 12 bombs. Each man was issued with the new phosphorous bombs, known as P-bombs, which looked like large jam tins. They were too big to fit in pockets, so a wire holder was devised to attach the bombs to the belt. In addition the men received two Mills bombs (the first time these had been issued to the RND apart from training); and each man was supplied with either one packet of 'Roman candles' or one Very light, on a 50/50 basis, to be carried in the tunic pocket. There were two bandoliers per man, each containing 50 rounds.[11]

The third and fourth waves were to carry picks and shovels in equal proportions, tied to their packs with the head of the pick fore and aft over the shoulder and resting on four sandbags tied above and across the pack.[12] All men with wire-cutters wore a yellow armband on the left arm and carried wiring gloves in their belts. Fifty-six runners were selected, identified by blue and white armlets.

Trench feet were becoming a problem, so prior to the battle orders were given to ensure that all ranks rubbed whale oil on to their feet, up to the thighs. This was considered most important, and added greatly to the men's comfort. Officers were instructed to inform all ranks that trophy hunting was absolutely forbidden: offenders were to be shot on sight.[13]

Douglas Jerrold, adjutant of Hawke Battalion, describes the scene and conditions before the attack:

The rain turned into snow and then into frozen mud and mist. It was only on 9 November that the sun shone for one fitful morning, and all the staffs from all the headquarters in echelon, stretching back to St Omer, came out to inspect the wicket and decided that it would be fit for play in four days time. We were only a mile behind the line at Hebuterne, in tents floating in a sea of mud and slush, across which those gifted with a sense of balance could slide but never walk. And we, too, got up on 9 November and looked at the sun and knew what was going to be said behind, where there were waterproofs and clean sheets and green grass. For it was a perfect morning. It was obviously far too good for regimental officers to be alive.

So we got our orders, and on 10 November we marched back to Mesnil, where we were to stay the night before moving up the line on 11 November. The attack was to begin at 6am on Friday 13 November.

The roads just behind the line were, of course, almost impassable, and it had become bitterly cold. Snow was still lying in places, though the rain held off. On this point the staffs had guessed right, and now, at last, the die was cast. The preliminary bombardment had already begun and the preliminary retaliation. Three hundred yards outside Mesnil the road was blocked with the debris of two transport wagons and their horses, victims of this preparatory zeal. It was not, in the circumstances, an enchanting spectacle, and my horse refused so absolutely to pass it by that I dismounted and walked the rest of the way. I have never been on a horse since.

Mesnil was cold – it always was. It was the only place we ever struck in all our wanderings where any kind of comfort was utterly impossible. There was nowhere to sleep, nowhere to sit, nowhere to look and nowhere to walk. The abject discomfort of our battalion, reduced by casualties and sickness to barely 400 men in six short weeks, was a grimly humorous commentary on the efforts of the powers that were to ensure that we went into fighting fit and at full strength. It wasn't, of course, anyone's fault in particular. It was just the last end of the year's campaigning, and we were the last piece.

We ourselves had a few expectations. General Paris (late commanding officer of the 63rd RN Division) had told his battalion commanders before he was wounded that man for man and officer for officer the Naval Division was incomparably better, in his judgment (and he had never praised the division before), than nine-tenths of the divisions in France; and that it was here, in the Ancre valley, that we should show it. His successor's very different opinion irritated but did not wholly convince us.

Officers left out of the attack bombarded me with bitter complaints, and one at least came up the line and led his company, in direct defiance of orders.

The most difficult hours, from my own point of view, were those from dusk on 12 November till dawn, when the attack began, for we were holding the line and were therefore responsible for superintending the assembly of the four battalions who had massed, mostly in the open, on our battalion frontage, in front of and immediately behind the front line, in battle order. If the Germans had spotted any movement, a major disaster involving far more lives than anything that could ever have happened on the last night of the Gallipoli campaign was inevitable. Everything passed off well, and by midnight we had synchronized watches. The bar was open and our company commanders came in for drinks.

It is probably a good thing that the work of preparing for battle under trench warfare conditions is so extremely disagreeable. It is, of course, pleasanter to step out on to the battlefield from a ballroom, and pleasanter still to step off a battlefield, as we had done 10 months before, on to a well-appointed ship, where you only had to ring the bell to get a whisky and soda. But after three days such as we had gone through, during which no-one could have had more than a couple of hours' sleep, there was undoubtedly, as we remarked over our drinks, 'a great deal to be said for being dead'. If we had had orders, as we half-expected, cancelling the attack, I really believe that our discipline, never our strong point, would have broken down.

And yet we knew, as a matter of certainty, that most of us (all of us, as it turned out) would be dead or wounded in 24 hours.

We were in the front wave of the attack, with Freyberg's Hood Battalion on our right, attacking up the valley. Next to us was Ramsey Fairfax's Howe Battalion. Behind us, to pass through us to the second objective, was Burge's Nelson Battalion. All of them our friends.[14]

Asquith's brother Raymond had been killed earlier in the autumn of 1916, and Lord Haig was apparently of the opinion that he could not allow the additional strain of Arthur's possible death to be put on the shoulders of the Prime Minister. He was therefore posted from his command and placed in a more secure staff job – a bitter blow to both him and the battalion.[15] But his departure was a bonus to Captain the Hon Lionel Montagu:

For weeks we had been preparing the thing; our CO gave us most clear and detailed orders, which we had explained to the NCOs and

men. Originally I was not to go, being second in command of the
company, but I persuaded the CO to take me as assistant adjutant.
Then, when Asquith was taken away, I am glad to say that I was
given command of D company.[16]

Thomas MacMillan was by now a clerk with 189th Brigade HQ:

Battalion commanders were coming and going. In the absence of
Commander Freyberg, Lieutenant-Commander Asquith put in an
appearance. He had just left the mess one day when I entered
and caught the tail-end of a discussion between the general and
the major concerning him. The general expressed his appreciation of Asquith as a soldier. The major agreed, but added, 'Why
keep him; you never can tell when some woman in London will
have him removed to the rear?'
I gathered that Commander Asquith had been summoned to the
brigade office and instructed to proceed to some job on the corps
staff in order to be out of danger, but he so hotly resented the
interference from London as to require compelling to get him to
comply. The general had been considering how the order could
be countermanded as I entered.
I was dismissed, and could only conclude that no further action
was taken, since the commander left for corps HQ.[17]

Montagu continues:

After being ready on three occasions, it was always postponed on
account of the terrible weather. You have no idea what a lot of
arranging and issuing of stores has to be organized. There is a lot
of work for the company commander; he has to arrange how the
bombs, P-grenades, picks, shovels, spare ammunition, wire-cutters,
wire gloves, Very lights and Roman candles, and last but not least
the rum, are to be carried and used. He has to decide whom to leave
out, and during the bad weather when everyone is soaked through
for days he has to try to prevent the men from going sick. I must
say they were all splendid, and gave a good foretaste of what they
were going to do. The only time I had any trouble with an NCO or
a man was when I had to leave one out of the 'push'.
At last the day was fixed for 13 November; we had had it fixed
so often before that we were sceptical, but I believed that it would
come off this time, though I remember saying that the 13th was an
unlucky day, and so it was – for the Germans.
All our plans had of course been fixed; the Hood Battalion was
to advance helped by a company of the HAC, with the railway and
the River Ancre on our right. We were to move off first and take the

three first lines of trenches, and reorganize in the third trench. The Drake Battalion was then to go through us and take a line just above a road, called Station Road, running down to the railway station and river. We were then to go through the Drake and take a line called the Yellow Line just this side of Beaucourt; and then another brigade was to come through us and take Beaucourt.

On the night of 12 November we got into our assembly positions and spent one night there. It was of course very cold. We arranged our companies in waves in depth, by platoons about 10 yards apart. Everyone had a definite job; the first two waves were to go straight ahead as close to our barrage as possible and take the third line of enemy trenches. The third and fourth waves were to clear up the second and third lines respectively, and then rejoin on the third line. I decided to go with the third wave, as being most likely to give me control of my company.[18]

Joseph Murray takes up the story:

When it was quite dark we moved forward over the open ground following a white tape to our firing line; then, without any aid, a considerable distance into no-man's-land before reaching our assembly trenches in alignment with our left flank. The Hood formed up in four distinct waves, roughly a man every two yards. Behind were the other two battalions, the Drake and the 1st HAC (Honourable Artillery Company), assembled in the same formation. On that reckoning, on our particular patch of no-man's-land there were 12 lines of men lying in the open. We who were to lead the attack were roughly 200–250 yards from the enemy. My company, C, with B on our right, were in position at seven o'clock.

It is extremely dark. I cannot see the hands of my watch, but I can feel the dampness of the mist on my face and assume it is about midnight. I may be hopelessly in error, but it doesn't really matter, for nothing matters any more. Each and every hour is the same. I fancy I can see a figure approaching on my left; maybe it's a ghost. I can not hear any footsteps and there is no reason for anyone to be wandering about; we are all supposed to be sleeping. After what seems to be an eternity, I realize it is no ghost; it is my colonel, Colonel Freyberg, who is having a quiet chat with the chap in the next hole to me. I sit up with much difficulty. He apparently recognized an 'old hand', maybe because I had been Asquith's runner whilst we were in England as well as on the *Grantully Castle* during our voyage east and when we landed on the Gallipoli peninsula. As such, I had with the usual preface, 'With Mr Asquith's compliments, sir,' delivered messages to him.

'You, too, are still with us! So pleased to see you. Make yourself as comfortable as you can and good luck. Do try to get some sleep.' With those parting words he disappeared into the darkness.[19]

Freyberg gives his account:

At midnight I went round our battalion and had to step over men as I walked. It was unnaturally quiet; the men all seemed asleep, but closer inspection showed them awake, lying there with their heads on their arms, peering out into the night. One or two spoke, but the bulk seemed to be in another world. I asked some of them next night, as we lay out in the shell-holes in front of Beaucourt, what they were thinking about; they all said their thoughts were of the future; none thought of the past.

There had been some shelling, but not on our sector; otherwise the night had passed in complete silence. At 5.15am there was a slight stir all along the line, the ghost-like sound of thousands of invisible men sitting up and taking off their greatcoats; and in spite of all the warnings, there came the slight mellow note of the wooden entrenching tool handle against the bayonet scabbard. Then came the unmistakable smell of tea, and we knew that for many it would be their last meal.

At 5.30am, with 15 minutes to go, I went across quickly to see that everything was in order. The patrol in front was in trouble, some bombs were thrown, and it retaliated as it withdrew. On the extreme right I stopped to talk to Kelly, who commanded B Company. We had been daily companions for the last two years, and he, Asquith, Egerton and I were the sole survivors of the battalion who left Avonmouth for Gallipoli in February, 1915. I wanted to take both his hands and wish him 'God speed', but somehow it seemed too theatrical; instead we talked rather awkwardly, and synchronized our watches. I walked back along our sector, speaking to the men I recognized. The old hands, whom I called by name, answered with a 'Yes sir, I'm here again,' which recalled similar meetings on dark nights, and made me wonder which of them would answer the call at the next attack?

At 5.40am all the assaulting troops fixed bayonets; they muffled the bayonet catch and ring, and the rifle muzzle, with their great-coats, to strangle the metallic click as the two engaged. Everything was now ready, save the opening and closing of the bolt as they stood up, transferring a cartridge from the charge magazine to the chamber.

The officers stood counting the minutes to zero, looking at their luminous watches, and at 5.45am to the second the whole sky

184

in the rear was suddenly lit up by hundreds of flashes, and the guns had fired. The sound reached us some seconds later, and about seven seconds after the sound thousands of shells passed a few feet over our heads and burst in an impenetrable wall 150 yards beyond. Our 12 waves were now running hard to get clear of the enemy counter-barrage . . . .

Some of our guns were shooting short of the barrage into our assembled infantry. They seemed to be dropping very short on our right, and we were afraid for B Company. Everywhere was confusion; we were nearly choked with the acid stink of cordite; while in the luminous mist all we could see were lines of phantom figures, the top half of their bodies bent forward, their arms in an unnatural position rigidly holding their rifles at the high port, while their hurrying legs gave them the appearance of diving into the whirlpool ahead.

As we advanced it became lighter; there was considerable enemy fire, especially from our left flank, which made all our men unconsciously turn half left, and but for our compasses would have drawn us to it.

Owing to the mist the fire was unaimed, and we passed by Whaleback Redoubt in safety, leaving a lot of our dead and wounded in our wake. There were a few enemy dead, and prisoners had started to be brought in.

I saw one of our men having difficulty with four prisoners he was taking back; he started by marching behind them, but had to reverse the order to prevent them from being shot as they emerged from the mist into view of each successive wave. Our men had taken them for enemy combatants and were heard to say, 'Some bloody Boches', accompanying their remarks with indiscriminate shooting. The last I saw of the party was our man walking in front, followed by the prisoners who clung to him while he waved his arms, calling out in a frightened voice to those in front, 'For Christ's sake, don't shoot.'[20]

Bentham was in the Hood's first wave:

Directly the barrage lifted we in the first wave got up and walked slowly forward, as one had to be careful not to walk into our barrage. In spite of the intensity of the barrage, machine guns began taking a toll of those of us advancing. Where there had been hundreds on either side of me, I seemed to be alone with my runners and bodyguard; everything was smoke and hell let loose.

The first group of Germans we came to had their hands up, except one who I shot through the stomach. We threw phosphorous bombs down the dug-outs, which forced the inmates to come up, and some of my men bayoneted them as they did so. It was not that they were that way inclined, but that they had lost all semblance to a civilized being. The inferno was enough to send any sane man absolutely berserk. Prisoners were sent to the rear after being disarmed and, not being able to spare any man to go with them, a lot were shot on sight by the waves coming behind.

Suddenly a shell burst among us, and when the smoke had cleared I found my two runners killed. I was wounded myself through the thigh, and nearly all the remainder were maimed. I gave my map and instructions to an NCO and told him to carry on. He was killed just as he left me. This was at exactly 6.15 a.m. We had certainly had a hectic half hour and now it was all over.

One of my lads was wounded in the lung and was coughing up bright red blood, and it wasn't long before he died. The remainder took what shelter we could in a crater, as the enemy were plastering us with shells. Wave after wave of reinforcements passed us, shouting, 'Got a blighty, lucky devil', etc. Then we got our first aid packages and bandaged our wounds as best we could; my leg was pumping out blood. At about 10am our battalion medical officer, McCracken, came along and dressed our wounds. He poured iodine into my wound and told me that would stop me laughing in church! He had to go on with the battalion, but said some stretcher-bearers would be along later.

Lying with our backs to the front, we could see reinforcements coming over the brow of a hill at the rear; not far away hidden in an isolated pocket was a German machine gun, which took a terrible toll of those men as they showed against the skyline. I tried to crawl and ascertain where this devil could be, but it was too far away, so I shouted until someone came along and told him, and sure enough shortly afterwards the gun was stopped. I had given my morphine tablets to the more seriously wounded to deaden the pain, but soon the effects wore off and they started moaning with the pain. It was now afternoon and no-one had come along. We opened our iron rations and had something to eat, those of us who could do so, but one poor lad with a shattered arm and smashed shoulder blade was praying to die and begged us to put him out of his misery. The afternoon dragged on and I realized that stretcher-bearers would not find us in the dusk which came down. German shells were still dropping all around, and we wondered if one would find us and finish us off.[21]

The Hood cleared up the enemy's first line system thoroughly, despite the difficulty of locating the dug-outs in the dark. In the first wave the battalion lost a number of officers. Lieutenant Cyril Edmondson and Sub-Lieutenant Harry Gealer were both killed by a sniper at about

6.30am; Sub-Lieutenant Arthur Hart was also killed; Lieutenant Fish and Sub-Lieutenants Chapman, Forster, Wood, Cole, Callingham, Hall, Bentham and Creswell were all wounded.

Lieutenant Sidney Fish, having received a wound to his foot, continued to advance and with another officer organized mopping-up parties in the railway cutting, beyond which the Hood's first wave had passed. Two hundred Germans were captured, and nine officers who refused to surrender were killed. Fish then pushed forward again until ordered to the rear for treatment; he was awarded the Military Cross for his efforts.

Strong positions on the right flank, previously noted by divisional intelligence, had been very effectively dealt with by heavy trench mortars during the previous week. However, in attacking a bombing post in the enemy's third line, Lieutenant Cleg Kelly was killed – another gone from that unique group assembled on the *Grantully Castle*. Back in his Gallipoli days, whilst at Cape Helles, he had composed an elegy for strings in memory of his great friend Rupert Brooke. This work tried to introduce the atmosphere of Greek temples and the movement of leaves in the olive trees. No-one would produce an elegy to him: the influences of mud, mist and cold would not have been fitting.[22]

Montagu continues his story:

I speedily found myself, with about 60 men and two platoons of the Drake Battalion, too far ahead, having gone over the three lines without seeing them, though we had bombed some dug-outs. We were right in our own barrage and suffered a few casualties from it. I felt rather lost, but fortunately recognized the station and Station Road, of which I had previously made a mental note when we had gone across to the other side of the river (Schwaben Redoubt) to study the ground on this side over which we had to advance. This stood us in good stead now. I knew that I had got too far ahead, but did not like to bring the men back as nothing could be more demoralizing. I brought them back two moves of 20 yards to get more behind our barrage. My servant, Wright, was hit here in the leg by our own artillery, just by me. I wrote to my CO saying where I was, and that I would wait till he came up. I saw him soon afterwards on the line, above Station Road, and it began at last to grow lighter. After this all was plain sailing, as he immediately took charge of everybody and ran the whole show. He is a magnificent person.

He immediately reorganized us, giving me the right, and, watch in hand, waited for our barrage to move. At the exact moment we moved on again about 20 to 30 yards above our barrage, Freyberg in front with Arblaster, Hill and myself in close attendance. We had lots of talks in the pauses of the barrage. We then got to our next objective, the line just this side of Beaucourt. Here we captured a German mail and ration dump. We opened their parcels and smoked their cigars, and found lots of good things to eat, including sausages and cakes, as well as socks, etc. From the letters we discovered that it was the 2nd Guards Reserve Regiment against us.

Here Freyberg told us to dig two lines of trenches. Picks and shovels were scarce, but the men dug splendidly with their entrenching tools. Our doctor joined us here, having dressed and evacuated nearly all our wounded under heavy fire. We got news here also that Kelly, Edmondson and Gealer had been killed; also that one of our clearing parties had captured a major, five other officers and about 600 men.

According to plan Freyberg then organized us for the attack on Beaucourt. I was to remain in charge of the two trenches. We could not understand why the barrage did not move on. This barrage was very good except for a heavy howitzer, which kept dropping short among our men about 30 yards behind us. It was a beastly sensation and very bad for our men. Freyberg had been hit twice slightly by our barrage, but it did not seem to affect him at all.

We had got into touch with the troops of the Cambridgeshire Regiment on the other side of the river. Our left was, however, in the air, and we could see German SOS lights going up on our left rear, which was rather alarming. We then got a message to say that the barrage would not move on, but would remain in front of us till the situation on our left had become clear. In the meantime, the German snipers and subsequently their machine guns had become very active from the edge of Beaucourt. I had taken over a small wiring party in front of our firing line. I soon had one man killed and another wounded from snipers, and I reported to the CO that wiring there in daylight had become impossible. He agreed and we gave it up till night. We continued improving our trenches all the afternoon; thank goodness, we had got them pretty well dug before the snipers and machine guns started.

Freyberg put us in charge of the second trench, about 20 yards in the rear of the first. We sent many reports and maps back to the brigade, but the runners had to run the gauntlet of the enemy snipers. The officers with the Hood at this time were Freyberg, Arblaster, Hill, Carnell, Bolus, Donaldson, Apthorp, [the doctor] and myself; all that were left out of 21; and with the Drake Battalion, Bennett, Fox and Hank and their Doctor, Pocock. The Drake CO and second in command had been killed.[23]

The reason for the delay stemmed from the beginning of the attack. All the brigades reached their forming-up place punctually and without loss; but the trenches on the left were heavily shelled after assembly was completed, and some 70 casualties were incurred before the operation began.

The dense mist meant that once daylight arrived it was impossible to see even 50 yards ahead. Troops disappeared into the fog, and runners lost their way. Many casualties no doubt occurred through mistaking British troops for the enemy, and it was impossible to use aeroplanes or visual signalling. But the mist was a two-edged sword, and also gave the division important advantages. Not only were the enemy completely surprised by the attack, but their artillery could find no definite targets for fear of killing their own men.

The RND found an enemy strongpoint near the centre of the divisional front, and considerable casualties were caused by its machine-gun fire. Drake's CO was mortally wounded and other officers killed by fire from this direction. On the right centre, the Hawke and Nelson came under fire from the same machine gun; Hawke's CO and three of its company commanders were casualties, and the battalion lost so heavily that only a few odd parties reached the third line. The Nelson lost nearly all its officers, and as a result remained far behind the barrage.

On the left and left centre the 1st Royal Marines and Howe Battalion, with the 2nd Royal Marines and Anson behind them, were also held up by machine-gun fire, both from this same point on the right and from the direction of 'Y' ravine. Here the attack, with the exception of small groups, did not succeed in penetrating beyond the German second line for a considerable time, and in some places did not penetrate beyond the first line. A large proportion of company commanders was killed or wounded. Owing to this, and to the fog, the chain of communication completely broke down, so beyond knowing that all was not going according to plan, HQ were for some time in overall ignorance of the actual situation on their left flank.

It now became clear to General Shute that he could not hope for the attack on the Red Line to be carried out simultaneously, all along his front, at the time ordered in the barrage's timetable. He accordingly instructed his divisional artillery to maintain the barrage just 1,500 yards in front of the Yellow Line until further orders.

Meanwhile, HQ was aware that all continued to go well on the right flank; at 9.36am news was received that the Hood with parts of the Drake under Freyberg had reached the Yellow Line at 8.30am, with a total of 400 men and 11 Lewis guns. Freyberg was preparing to assault the Red Line with only 200 men and eight Lewis guns as soon as the barrage lifted, intending to leave the remaining 200 men and three Lewis guns to consolidate the Yellow Line. But as the division's left was still being held up, and despite Freyberg's anxiety to attack Beaucourt village at once, Shute decided not to allow him to make the attempt with such a small force until troops were also well established on the Yellow Line to his left. It subsequently transpired that elements of the 188th Brigade had actually reached the Yellow Line between Station Alley and Railway Alley, and had found it unoccupied by Germans, but, finding no-one on their right or left and being without officers, they had retired again to the Green Line.

By noon it was clear that the Germans' third line was still held in strength, so Shute ordered the artillery to rebombard it for five minutes at 12.20 p.m. At the conclusion of the bombardment all available infantry in the front and second lines assaulted, but the attack was unsuccessful.

As soon as Shute heard the assault had failed he asked permission from corps HQ to use six tanks which should have been at Auchonvillers, but was told they had been ordered back to Beaussart the night before. He was able to arrange for three of them to be brought back as soon as possible. This was not a simple task, and took so long that the tanks could only be sent into action against the strongpoint at daybreak the following day. The 188th Brigade was ordered to detail an officer to reconnoitre a route, and be available to guide the tanks to it.

Information now came in that the Hood was suffering many casualties from snipers in Beaucourt and on the south-east side of the Ancre. As a result the 190th Brigade were instructed to push forward the HAC. Requests for more bombs and ammunition were met by sending supplies via the bridge across the Ancre at the mill, so the Hood received some 500 more grenades.

The situation at 5pm was that on the extreme right the Hood Battalion with elements of Drake, Nelson and Hawke, plus some HAC, were holding the Yellow Line from the Ancre to Railway Alley. Parts of the 7th Royal Fusiliers and HAC were in the Green Line immediately behind them. The centre and left of the Green Line were held by some of the 188th Brigade, and the Dublin Fusiliers and Bedfordshire Regiment of the 190th Brigade. The balance of the 188th Brigade was in the German front line system, where the enemy still held a large part of their third line and portions of their second line. At 6.41pm General Shute received orders to consolidate the positions already gained, and to prepare to attack early on 14 November.[24]

At 10.11pm a message was received from V Corps HQ:

The Corps Commander congratulates commanders and troops including the heavy and field artillery on their magnificent and successful efforts today under trying conditions.

The Commander-in-Chief has unofficially expressed his satisfaction. Stick it.[25]

CHAPTER EIGHTEEN

The Second and Third Days

Captain Montagu resumes:

During the night we got up more picks and shovels, water and rations, though we had been living pretty well on the German rations. The sniping and machine-gun fire continued all night, and I was told to go back and report the situation to the brigade; I need not come back. On my explaining to the CO, however, that I was not in need of rest and that I would sooner go back with the battalion, he agreed to let me stop. Some spare officers joined us here: Morrison, Jacobs, Baird and Watson.

We stopped out all night, and it was even colder than the night before. We had caught a stray prisoner and, as I know a little German, the CO sent for me in the night to question him. He was 20 years old and of the 62nd Regiment; he had got lost and seemed glad to be a prisoner. He had on him enough rations to stock an officers' mess for a week; two water bottles, one containing cold coffee (delicious) and the other a liqueur (which was rather sweet), a camera and an electric torch. He said he thought the Germans would win the war, but I don't think he was very sure about it. His rations and drink were very welcome.[1]

One of the relief officers, Sub-Lieutenant Trevor Jacobs, takes up the story:

The push started at somewhere near six in the morning, and I was sent to reinforce an hour or two later. Getting up there was a devil of a job, being enfiladed from either side and most of it being done in the open. Three of us going to another brigade were blown up by a shell, and another suffered the effects of a machine gun. I walked over very nonchalantly and did not even bother to double, just to show how cool I felt (I don't think). The real reason was to preserve my strength for later on. I did occasionally, when it became rather warm, flop into a shell-hole for a short respite. We eventually arrived at our destination. Of course we passed very many dead, and any number of stretchers.

HQ was a shell-hole, and the officer in charge at once gave me a job: to construct a trench on our left flank, which was in the air. I was given 'carte blanche', and had to find the men, plan the trench and get it done before the next day. The only implements we had were entrenching tools, the picks and shovels having been lost during the push. And wonderful to relate, we got the job done and got down about three. Of course I made the best use of existing shell-holes. We did it under shell, rifle and machine-gun fire, and standing up of course we had casualties. An officer who came up told me later that he expected to see me drop at any moment, but as you see the expected did not happen.[2]

The 6am attack had been well prepared. The objective of the division's left was the Yellow Line, with the 51st Division simultaneously attacking Munich Trench between the original divisional boundaries. The target for the advanced troops on the division's right was Beaucourt village. The artillery shelled both locations throughout the night, and became intense at 6am on the left, lifting off at 6.12 for the assault by two battalions of the loaned 111th Brigade, supported by the 188th Infantry Brigade in the Green Line. With this advance on the left the troops under Lieutenant Colonel Freyberg, who were already in the Yellow Line, were ordered to assault and capture Beaucourt. This attack was to be supported by the advance of troops of the 192nd Brigade, holding the right of the Green Line, who were later to replace Freyberg's men.

The attack on the left began punctually, but the troops of the 111th Brigade were held up immediately by machine-gun fire from the Yellow Line and from their left. They lost direction, and were attracted eastwards towards Beaucourt village itself. The result was that the Yellow Line from the left of the divisional boundary up to half-way between Station Alley and Redoubt Alley was not captured, though the 111th Brigade succeeded in reaching it from the latter point to their junction with Freyberg's force.

Meanwhile the three tanks arranged by Shute had approached the British lines during the night, and arrived at the rendezvous an hour before dawn. They were met by Lieutenant Allan Campbell, RNVR, who had been detailed by the 188th Brigade to reconnoitre the route and guide the tanks to the strongpoint which had taken such a heavy toll the day before. He got on to the leading tank, which he himself steered towards the enemy's line.[3] Just before they started out a hostile

5.9 shell fell, knocking out one of the tanks and making a hole in it. It was still dark at the time and thick mist hung about, so almost certainly it was merely a chance shot.[4]

The two remaining tanks crossed into no-man's-land successfully, but found the ground very muddy, so they turned southwards along no-man's-land in the hope of finding a better place for crossing the enemy's front line trench. One tank then crossed half-way between the German's first and second lines, where it got stuck. The other tank also stuck on the British side of the German line. Both tanks went into action with their six-pounders, and the Germans immediately raised the white flag. As there was some delay in the Germans coming out to surrender, however, the tank crews got out with their Hotchkiss guns and advanced along the trench towards the enemy. The Germans surrendered at once, and two officers and some 400 men were taken prisoners.

The prisoners were troops from the 55th, 22nd and 32nd Infantry Regiments, the 2nd Guards Reserve Division, 11th Reserve Division and the 103rd Division. The German officers were very disheartened, saying all their men were done in and tired out, and that their third line trench consisted only of weak companies with machine guns who were also done in and would be glad to surrender. This appeared to be true, as Lieutenant Campbell then saw a white flag in the German third line. To make sure, Commander Fairfax proposed to his HQ that he should send a party under a German-speaking officer up to this third line to tell them that if they did not surrender within half an hour an intense barrage would be put down on them. Approval was given, on the understanding that surrender had to be unconditional.[5],[6]

In the meantime Freyberg's force had taken Beaucourt and a very large number of prisoners. Reports came in that prisoners were pouring through Hamel. The Hood's Captain Montagu takes up the tale:

In the morning of 14 November we got orders that at 5am a brigade would attack and try to get level on our left and that at 7.45 the 190th Brigade RND and the troops under Colonel Freyberg were to attack Beaucourt. Freyberg soon had the thing organized. I was to lead the second wave in support of him from the second trench. The prospects seemed to me very doubtful. The snipers and enemy machine guns were so active that it was dangerous to show your head even for an instant, and we were due to attack at 7.45.

By this time the trench of which I had command had become packed tight by people (HAC and so on) jumping in and taking cover, so I passed down word for everyone to clear his rifle and be ready to start at 7.45. I had always heard that it was impossible to advance against hostile machine guns unless our artillery had just knocked them out. But these ones and the snipers were quite unaffected by our barrage, which seemed feeble. Such were my doubts that I sent a message to Freyberg by one of my runners (Tucker) at 7.15 to ask him if he intended to attack. He never got the message as Tucker was killed, but he told me that he had exactly the same doubts and nearly called it off. I simply remained watching him from my trench.

At 7.45 our barrage became a little more intense, but nothing like enough to stop the snipers and machine guns. I saw Freyberg jump out of the trench and wave the men on. Three men followed from my trench, then I got out with my runner, with the bullets raining past us – one through my sleeve. The first wave stopped three times. Freyberg was knocked clean over by a bullet which hit his helmet, but he got up again. I and my runner dived into a shell-hole and waited about half a minute. I said I would go back to get some more men out of the trench, and crawled about 10 yards back to do so. Then about a dozen men came out, and I got up and waved the rest on, and they all followed.

We soon got into Beaucourt (absolute ruins, of course) and found that the Germans would not face our men and were surrendering in hundreds. It was an amazing sight. They came out of their holes, tearing off their equipment. I myself rounded up at least 50, waving my revolver and making them run back past me, shouting at them, 'Schnell'. They offered us food and souvenirs, and were only too anxious to propitiate us. Our doctor and others soon had them employed carrying back our wounded.

I caught up with Freyberg about half-way through the village, and asked him if I was still to make a trench on the near side of the village as originally intended. He told me 'no', but that I was to bring up all the troops I could to the far side, and especially Lewis guns. I found four Lewis guns taking up positions overlooking the swamp and river, where nobody could possibly have crossed, much less attacked. I soon had them out of that, and sent them forward. I also found a captain and company of the Royal Fusiliers making a trench which faced right on to a steep bank. After explaining things to him he took his men out and forward.

I then went with Arblaster, our scout officer, and sited a trench on the high ground on our left front and set some pioneers on to digging it. By this time the beastly snipers had started at us again in the village, and had caused a lot of casualties. They fired in the roads, and you could not tell from which direction they were coming. It was also rather tricky wandering through the ruin of this village among the surrendering Germans, as one never knew if some more stout-hearted Hun would not have a shot or throw a bomb at you. Some did. There was one sight I shall never forget: a very nice

194

German spaniel sitting in the mouth of a dug-out surrounded by dead – all his friends gone and us strangers coming in. The snipers were the worst part, however. Major Norris (who used to instruct me at the Crystal Palace and was second in command of the Hawke) was next to me, making in Freyberg's direction, when I suddenly heard him call and down he went. I felt sure he was dead. Arblaster and I took cover from the snipers then for 10 minutes, and then went and found Freyberg at about 9am.

I found he had again taken charge of everyone, arranged for the consolidation of the village and made disposition of the troops. He sent Arblaster off to do a reconnaissance of the line. The sniping went on vigorously while we made a sort of battalion HQ. For the first time we got the phone up, and also sent off a message. I'd many talks with Freyberg during the previous day – how sorry he was about Kelly and Edmondson, etc. We had a long talk here – how proud he was of the Hood, how splendidly the battalion had done in attacking and carrying the three objectives in two days, including the strong village of Beaucourt, consolidating two lines and taking over 1,000 prisoners besides machine guns and a vast quantity of stores. He told me he had always dreamed of taking Beaucourt. I told him that if I got out of it all right I would call a racehorse Beaucourt. All the time he was sending messages and explaining our disposition to brigade. Colonel Harrison arrived as I had just taken out my ration of pâté de foie gras to eat.

Suddenly it started – heavy shelling such as I had never experienced. Not in ones and twos, but in dozens, and all big 5.9 howitzers. The house telephone, SOS rockets, and so on were blown to blazes. Our runners and Harrison's party scattered. Freyberg said, 'They are ranging on this house,' and he and I took cover in a shallow trench alongside some HAC. Here we lay for about half an hour, initially on our stomachs. I don't want to exaggerate, but I was sure that 30 of these big shells fell within 20 yards of us. During the shelling we discussed the situation and agreed that it probably meant a Boche counter-attack. I know I expected to see them on top of us at any moment. We passed the word to the HAC to look to their rifles. I remember Freyberg commenting on the fact that few of the shells were duds; we feared gas shells and took out gas helmets, which we did not put on but continued to sniff. There was something comforting in what I usually thought was an unpleasant smell.

Two or three times we were half buried by bits of houses and earth and stones. One in particular I remember hit the bricks and smothered us with a bright pink dust; but it could not last. We were placed with an HAC man at the end of the trench; then Freyberg; then myself; then a wounded HAC who had struggled into the trench and lay on my legs and gave me cramp; then other HAC men. One shell fell a bit closer than the others. I felt something hit me in the small of the back, but it did not seem to hurt at all.

Then I heard Freyberg say, 'Goodbye, Montagu', and then, 'Steady, Hood', and I saw he was hit and going a very bad colour. He asked me if I had any morphia and I said 'no'. He then produced a tube and asked me to give him some. I have him a $\frac{1}{4}$ grain and labelled him to say that I had done so. I then dressed his wound with my field dressing (he had none) as best I could. There was a hole in his neck which was bleeding rather profusely. We lay there for about 10 minutes and I thought he was going to die; I told him I would go and get two or three men to carry him down, but he told me on no account to move. It was just as well because the chances of getting men to carry him down during that heavy shelling were slight and he weighed about 16 stone. He kept giving me orders about informing the senior officers of the HAC and the troops on our flank. I can here say that the shell that wounded him and me killed the HAC man next to him, wounded again the man who had lain on my legs and killed the man next to him. It also made a hole right through the edge of my shrapnel helmet, just touching my ear and making it bleed.

Suddenly he said, much to my surprise, 'Do you think I could walk to the dressing station?' I told him it was quite safe (which it was not, owing to the heavy shelling which still went on), but the going was very rough. We got up with less difficulty than I expected, and walked down with him leaning heavily on my arm.

I shall never forget that walk down; it is curious how instinctively one chooses the best going for oneself, and I had to make an effort to find a patch for his feet round the shell-holes. The heavy shelling still continued, but the worst part was passing the badly wounded men who prayed me to help them. He faltered badly once, but I told him he had *got* to go another 30 yards. I did not know exactly where the dressing station was, but found people to whom I shouted for directions. The whole distance was about 300 yards. The regimental aid post was down a very steep bank, and here I found most of the remnants of the Hood and Drake. There were naturally plenty of people to take over Freyberg, and he immediately had a good dressing from our splendid regimental doctor. He handed over the battalion to me, telling me to carry on and giving orders all the time.

I think I must tell you here what a splendid person Freyberg is; not only had he behaved with marvellous courage and heroism throughout, but he showed real military genius. We all absolutely leant on him. I believe that the great successes won by the battalion and by the army were due to him and him alone. If he is spared, the whole world will be talking of him soon. You can imagine what a gap he left when he was wounded.[7]

Sub-Lieutenant Trevor Jacobs continues his account of the day's events:

The next morning, at dawn, we took Beaucourt. I fired about 40 rounds with a rifle. It was extraordinary to see the Boches rushing up to surrender with hands up, any number of them. I commanded some to attend to the wounded, and was pleased to see one of their own machine guns hit a German. The Boches gave us a period of rest for about two hours, during which I bandaged a few wounded men; not a very nice job, especially when you are a novice, but they were very plucky.

Then the Boche artillery started, and they turned an enormous amount of their heavies on to us. It was absolute hell. Luckily I had insisted just previously upon my men digging hard, which gave us little more depth and cover, though we had to continue with entrenching tools. I saw one man blown up 50 to 70 yards high and come down without any clothing on, and I saw the lower half of another man blown up quite near me. I had put my groundsheet and field-glasses down in order to dig better, and a few minutes afterwards they were both blown up.

I had received news that all my company officers were wounded and I had to be ready to take command of my company, which was also mixed up with other men I had commandeered. In fact I was really quite prepared to carry on – providing I was spared. Our CO was badly wounded in the neck, but I hear he is getting on well . . . .

When night fell the bombardment grew less, though of course we kept digging. Then we were told the relief would arrive shortly, but it did not do so until 2am the following morning, so we carried on digging. During one moment at night, while I was looking for wire, I momentarily lost my bearings; it was very dark, and I nearly got to the German line. Luckily I found out in time and about-turned. By the by, I have just received some papers that were picked up on the battlefield and among them is one from the staff, who require me for the Intelligence department. I shall see our CO, Lieutenant-Commander Egerton, tomorrow. I know he does not want to lose me, as he told my OC, and I like him very much, also my company and I have every admiration for my men, whom I think get on well with me. I lost my orderly, who has gone back wounded, so I asked another boy if he would like to take it on. He said, 'I would follow you with the platoon

197

anywhere, sir. But I would rather remain with the boys than become an orderly.' I felt quite complimented.

To resume, we were eventually relieved and marched back for about one hour's rest to the German strongpoint, taken that morning by a tank and which surrendered with 300 prisoners. Had I seen that strongpoint and the surrendering earlier in the day I would have shot at least 10 Germans, even if they did much to surrender to us. I never saw anything so tragic. It was a shambles, any amount of our brave fellows being all around in shell-holes. Terrible wounds, some of them with half a head blown off, others without legs or arms, others with numerous bullet wounds. I bound up some pretty horrible wounds myself.

I rested from 7am to 8am in a German dug-out, sitting up. The smell was appalling: after investigation I found that my head had been resting practically against a dead German officer, who was in a fearful state. The tunic I wore has a great deal of blood on it.

Poor Hart's last words were, 'I'm wounded; carry on.' It was a machine gun that did it . . . . I am marching along as the second in command of my company, but I suppose my steel helmet and unshaven appearance will make me hard to recognize. All the commanding officers of the brigade have been killed. A fine set of men they were yesterday. We marched 12 miles to Douleein and today further on to Fieuvillers, where we may have to submit to a GOC inspection. When the GOC, General Shute, met us at Eugelbeiuer he said, 'You Hoods are wonderful; the men are magnificent and the officers are marvellous. Two army corps have already tried to take the position and failed. You have accomplished it.'

My company went in 150 strong and came out with 85. They were lucky.[8]

Meanwhile the wounded Sub-Lieutenant Bentham and his men were still in their shellhole:

My wound by now had set hard and, numbed with the cold, I did all I could to cheer up the others. The night passed, seeming a lifetime, and we began to despair of being found at all, as there was no sign of life whatsoever. Dawn came and turned into day, and then an officer I knew to be one of the reserves came along. He looked white and scared, and asked me where the front line was. I told him it must be a long way now, but he would jolly well soon recognize it when he got there. Off he went and I never saw him again, but that same officer was later shot for cowardice. He had deserted his support troops who, without an officer, never arrived in the front line. John Bull, however, without knowing the true facts, made a great fuss about it; placards were headed 'Shot at Dawn' and 'Tragedy of a Young Boy Officer'.

Another badly-wounded boy died that morning, and others were of the opinion that we should perish there. It was now over 24 hours since we were knocked out. Thank God it wasn't raining. Our iron rations were finished when at 2 p.m., exactly 36 hours after being hit, a party of German prisoners under a guard came along with stretchers. I saw every man depart and wished them luck, and at last it was my turn. Off I went on a stretcher and was taken to the advanced dressing station, which was under shellfire. I saw many of my brother officers, some so mutilated that it was only a question of hours before they died.[9]

Captain Montagu wrote:

There are just one or two things I would like to record before I leave Beaucourt – one is that I lost my stick, a Malacca cane given me at Monte Carlo, and which I had with me all the time at Gallipoli as well as on many a racecourse. I lost it under the brick wall at the same time as the pâté de foie gras when the heavy shelling started.

Another is that Pocock, the Drake doctor, came up to look for Major Norris, and I told him I thought he was dead. He said if I thought he was dead it was no use looking for him. Fortunately I said he was not dead when I left him, though pretty bad, and then I showed him the shell-hole where he lay. He got carried down in a waterproof sheet by four German prisoners, and I saw him in hospital doing well two days ago with a bullet-hole through his lung.

Another thing is that, when we were lying in the trench expecting a counter-attack, we got the greatest confidence from our aeroplanes (we had seen none on 13 November), which went up and down quite low over the German lines signalling to us and peppering them with a machine gun. It seemed to be master of the whole situation, and a strong link with the Higher Command. We had not seen a staff officer, except one who left hurriedly. After I had taken over the battalion, I found that they had all taken shelter and were packed under this bank from the heavy shelling. There was no real protection, but thanks to providence the Huns never really dropped a shell into the place, though I know several of us expected it every moment. It would have caused a terrible tragedy.

We got into communication with brigade and were informed that we would probably be relieved that night. As a matter of fact we were relieved at about 1am, and went back to the strongpoint which had held up our left the day before. I reported the battalion (about 200 strong) to the brigadier on the way, and he congratulated us on our success: the brigade held a record for France for the ground and the number of prisoners taken; and the Hood had done particularly well.

We spent the night at the strongpoint. It had obviously been the scene of desperate fighting and was full of gruesome sights. It was one of those underground warrens of which you have read, and held about 300 men. There were some wounded still in it. It had evidently been taken largely by the aid of two tanks, which were still there. Fortunately one of the officers turned up with the rations, and the ever-welcome rum! It was our third night in the open in mid-November, the last two spent without overcoats or blankets. Most of us went down into the dug-out, and I and the doctor got three hours' sound sleep, though there was a dead German officer in the bunk above. We found plenty of food, including soda water, in the dugout. There is no doubt that the Germans do themselves *much* better than we do, and are better supplied with everything.

The next morning we left a party to help collect wounded and moved back. I formed up the battalion properly and marched them in. The divisional general met us and thanked us again, saying we had done simply splendidly. He repeated this at a review two days later, and said that Freyberg had been recommended for the VC. Sir Douglas Haig came and spoke to us the same afternoon, shook hands with most of us and was very complimentary. The brigadier told him I had been wounded and he asked lots of questions. As a matter of fact, I got my wound dressed on the morning of 18 November. The doctor said that if he had seen it on the field he would have sent me back, but it did not worry me at all. It was only a little septic, but the doctor has been amusing himself keeping it clean twice daily now.

I am awfully glad the Hood has done so well. I always thought that it was a magnificent division with splendid officers and men. Edward Beddington brought me to dine, and the army general asked to hear my story. He told me that no division had done better, and that it was one of the best divisions he had under him. Our losses were fairly heavy, particularly among officers – 22 out of 23 who first went up, and five who came up the second night, and about 250 other ranks. The losses are not heavy considering the successes gained. I am glad to say that owing to luck there happened to be no more casualties after I took over the battalion and brought them back. It was of course pure luck, and had nothing to do with me personally. The men and officers of the Hood have admittedly done the best of the division. I hope they now get their fair share of honour and leave.

Thanks largely to the efforts of the RND, Haig was able to attend the Chantilly Conference with the French with the benefit of a British success at this battle of the Ancre. And much of the RND's success was due to the officers and men of the Hood. As Montagu says:

> Units got hopelessly mixed up, and the Hood under Colonel Freyberg, with various odd units of other battalions, took all three of the divisional objectives, including the village of Beaucourt.[10]

Sub-Lieutenant Bentham described his recovery in England:

> An officer comes on the train and allocates each case to hospitals where there was a vacancy. I was advised to say that I would like to go to a private hospital this time, as the last time I was wounded I went to a general hospital. I said all this, and the chief medical officer asked me where I went last time, so I said Millbank. He said, 'OK, I'll send you to Park Lane for a change.' I was taken to number 26, the home of Mrs Freddie Guest, and it was like entering a palace. I was placed in the pink ward on the ground floor, and this meant pink silk pyjamas, eiderdowns, etc.; together with a bevy of pretty nurses, mostly VADs recruited in Mayfair. I soon settled down to enjoy myself despite my wounds, and the officer in the next bed told me to have a box of chocolates on my bedside table as the nurses liked to come and have a chat. My particular nurse was named Bunty, a very pretty girl, and when I was well enough to go upstairs to the bathroom, she said she was going to bath me. 'Not on your life,' I said, for I feared I might disgrace myself.
>
> When Colonel Freyberg heard that there was an RND officer downstairs, despite the fact he was extremely badly wounded he tried to come down to see me, but as I was so much better I went up to him and congratulated him on winning the VC. He then told me that he would like to give every officer an MC, but he decided to give them as far as possible to those who had lost a limb, as it might help them in civvy street. One afternoon Commander Asquith also came to see me, before going up to see Freyberg.[11]

CHAPTER NINETEEN

Reorganization

On 27 December, 1916, the War Office wrote to the Admiralty:

The military efficiency of the 63rd Royal Naval Division has suffered seriously owing to the following difficulties arising from the fact that the naval units of the Divisions are administered partly on a naval, and partly on a military, basis.

(a) Failure in the supply of Royal Naval Volunteer reserve recruits. At the present rate of recruiting there is no prospect of completing the naval brigades of this division to war establishment, and maintaining them. The Army Council have no power to allot to the Royal Naval Volunteer Reserve recruits called up under the Military Service Act, and the reserves have to be maintained by volunteers, which are not forthcoming in sufficient numbers.

(b) Want of a wider field of selection for officers. As promotion in the naval battalions is carried out within the battalions, officers are never brought in from other battalions; consequently these battalions cannot maintain the standard of efficiency attained by other battalions, which are frequently reinforced by selected officers from outside.

(c) The lack of experienced non-commissioned officers. Non-commissioned officers of experience are practically non-existent in the naval battalions, with the exception of a few Royal Marines, and these are too old and far below the high standard of pre-war marines.

Proposals for transfer of naval and marine personnel of the 63rd (Royal Naval) Division from the navy to the army

(1) Officers to be asked to transfer to the army. Any necessary expenditure incurred by officers consequent on transfer to be refunded. It is not proposed to reckon service in the Royal Naval Division towards the army gratuity under Article 497 of the Pay

Warrant. Officers who are unwilling to transfer to be placed at the disposal of the Admiralty.

(2) Royal Naval Volunteer personnel other than officers to be offered a bounty on transfer to the army. This bounty to be based on difference for six months between the pay and separation allowance of a Royal Naval Volunteer and that of a soldier of the equivalent rank in the same arm. For each man who loses by transfer, any men unwilling to transfer to be placed at the disposal of the Admiralty.

(3) All naval titles such as 'Temporary Lieutenant-Commander', 'Acting Sub-Lieutenant', 'Petty Officer', 'Leading Seaman' etc. to be replaced by military titles.

(4) In order to maintain the esprit de corps, the present designation of the battalions to be retained as part of the new military title.

This letter caused a certain amount of irritation at the Admiralty, as can be seen by the note on the side of the relevant file:

Unless there is some strange prejudice at work, I cannot help feeling that the War Office staff are acting in pure impatience. I should have thought that before writing this letter the Army Council would have sent over some officer to discuss details. Possibly the controversy as to the naval medical officers may have caused irritations. I think even now our letter should rather invite a conference before the Army Council decide, rather than afterwards. The late First Lord deliberately decided that the division should be retained as a fighting unit, and there will be political agitation to be prepared for if a radical change is made.

As regards the main difficulty, recruiting, it was felt that unless there were someone to watch over its results such as this might be expected and a mediator offered his services (if the Admiralty and War Office agreed) to superintend such work.

The Admiralty replied to the War Office on 10 January, 1917:

My Lords concur fully in the desirability of maintaining unbroken the valuable fighting traditions of the division and it was in order to prevent the virtual disappearance of a corps with a distinguished war record behind it that the previous transfer of the division to the control of the War Office was made. They are of opinion, however, that from this point of view the solution proposed in the letter will not prove satisfactory, and after careful consideration they have regretfully come to the conclusion that the only alternatives are to permit the present arrangements to stand, or to agree to changes so drastic that they must practically break up the division, even though some proportion of the personnel may be left and the names of some of the battalions.

The main objects to the present system appear to be the difficulty of maintaining the supply of Royal Naval Volunteer Reserve recruits and the complications involved in the administrative details of the division.

As regards the first, whilst my Lords are aware that reinforcements for the Royal Volunteer Reserve Battalions cannot be supplied by compulsion, it is a matter of considerable surprise to them to learn that the requisite volunteers cannot be obtained. The rate of pay offered both to ordinary seamen, RNVR, and to privates, RMLI, is higher than the corresponding army rates, and it may be noted that in the table of Royal Naval Volunteer Reserve pay forwarded with your letter, no account has been taken of the field allowance of 3/6d per week payable to petty officers and men, nor of the good conduct pay which many men are now receiving. Further, although the pay is higher, the men enrolled for these battalions will be employed only on the same services, for which men in other divisions of the Army are liable. There are therefore obvious advantages to joining the Royal Naval Volunteer Reserve, and if these facts are clearly explained, when volunteers are being called for, it seems unlikely that much persuasion will be required to obtain recruits in sufficient numbers.

As regards administration it is recognized that the present constitution of the division must involve many inconveniences and anomalies, but this has long been the case and has not been found to prevent the maintenance of an efficient fighting force, whose value in the field has been proved on many occasions.

The decision of this question must of course rest with the Army Council, but it appears to their Lordships that the difficulties involved in a continuance of the present arrangement, although real, are not insuperable, and that from the point of view of the most effective use of men for the conduct of the war, the best interests of the country would not be served by altering the status of the division at the present time.

Should, however, the Army Council be convinced that a radical reconstruction of the division must be carried out, it is considered that the personnel should be disposed of along the following lines.

Royal Naval Volunteer Reserve Battalions
All men who belonged to the Royal Navy, Royal Fleet Reserve, Royal Naval Reserve and Royal Naval Volunteer Reserve before the war should return to the naval service without exception.

The remaining Royal Naval Volunteer Reserve officers and men should be given the choice of transferring to the army or of reverting to the navy.

Royal Marine Battalions

My Lords are unable to agree to the transfer of these battalions to the army and it would be necessary therefore for them to cease to form part of the 63rd Division. The officers and men composing them may be divided into three classes.

(a) Long service officers and men who should revert without exception to the Admiralty service, in which they are at present much required.

(b) Short service officers and men raised by the Admiralty who should be given the option of transferring to the army or reverting to the Admiralty.

(c) Officers and men raised by the War Office for these battalions who should be transferred to the army.

The engineers have already been transferred to the army. Similar arrangements should be made for the divisional train and medical units, with the exception of the naval medical officers and any long service Royal Marines, who should revert to the naval service.

It has been assumed that in the case of officers and men transferred to the army financial compensation will be made on the lines indicated in your letter. The actual transfer of accounts etc., will involve considerable clerical labour, and will take some time to effect.

It will be necessary that in cases where officers or men are given a choice, the conditions upon which they will transfer to the army or will be accepted for naval service should be fully explained and understood by them beforehand.

In view of the opinion expressed in the latter part of paragraph two, my Lords would suggest that some further consideration is necessary before a decision upon the main question is reached and that a conference should be held between representatives of the Admiralty and the War Office to discuss details.

As a result of this correspondence arrangements were made to hold a conference on Thursday, 5 February in the House of Commons. The Admiralty was represented by the Right Hon Sir Edward Carson, First Lord; Rear-Admiral Michael Culme-Seymour, director of the mobilization division; Major-General David Mercer, adjutant-general of the Royal Marines; Sir Alfred Eyles, accountant-general of the Royal Navy; and T. D. James, assistant accountant-general. They also produced a handout to give their viewpoint:

205

Royal Naval Division

Formed in September, 1914. Consisted of three brigades viz. two RN and one RMLI.

RN Brigades

Originally consisted of officers and men of the RNVR, RFR and RNR. At the time Kitchener's army was formed approximately 2,400 men for whom army could not find accommodation were transferred to the RN Division.

Afterwards numbers were augmented by entry of temporary officers and men (RNVR) who were recruited to the Admiralty under the direction of Commodore Sir Richard Williams-Bulkeley. These officers and men were trained at the Crystal Palace and at Blandford.

RM Brigade

At first were formed entirely of active service ratings supplemented by pensioners and RF reservists. Six hundred men of Kitchener's army were transferred in September, 1914, and then temporary officers and short service men were entered as Royal Marines for the period of the war. Have always been maintained and paid as a definite RM unit.

The RNVR men were entered for service in the Royal Naval Division but there is no doubt, both from the posters issued and the methods of recruiting, a large majority were under the impression they would serve with the fleet. Many of the old RNVR officers and men who had entered previous to the war very much resented being employed on land operations and were anxious to serve afloat as they had joined and been trained in the RNVR for that purpose. This applies specially to many RNR stokers who were drafted to the division.

Admiralty have borne all expenses of pay, training, family and separation allowances and disability pensions. They also built the camp at Blandford and clothed and equipped the whole force up to the time they were lent to the War Office for the Dardanelles operations, when they drew their clothing and equipment from army sources.

The army took over the recruiting, clothing and equipment, but not the pay, in May, 1916, since when the division has been serving in France.

There is considerable difference between the status of the RNVR and the RM battalions. The latter consist largely of permanent officers, NC officers and men of the Royal Marines and form an integral part of the naval forces and, therefore, with the exception of the temporary officers and men, could in no case be transferred to the army. They are all receiving Royal Marines rates of pay with field allowance and afloat allowance, which is considerably higher than army rates.

On the other hand, the large majority of the RNVR ranks are temporary only and it would be disbanded at the conclusion of the war.

The bonus offered would probably benefit the married petty officers

38. Men of the Royal Naval Division coming back to a rest camp in Gully Ravine (*IWM*).

39. Able Seaman George Noble wearing the Hood Battalion's cap badge and over the top of it the Royal Naval Division's brass shoulder title. (*Mrs L. Garrett*).

40. Fred King of the Hood Battalion, wearing the Division's brass shoulder title and battalion badge (*the Joseph Murray collection from Dr M.E. Occleshaw*).

41. The Hood Battalion Band. The Commanding Officer, Bernard Freyberg, is in the middle (*IWM*).

42. Battle of the Ancre. German Trench Howitzer captured at Beaucourt-sur-Ancre (*IWM*).

43. Battle of the Ancre. The Mill at Beaucourt-sur-Ancre. Captured by the 63rd Naval Division on 14 November, 1916 (*IWM*).

44. *Illustrated London News*, 20 January, 1917. Edmondson was killed in action, 13 November, 1916.

45. *Illustrated London News*, 3 February, 1917. Hart was killed in action 13 November, 1916.

LIEUT. CYRIL ARTHUR EDMONDSON,
Hood Battalion, Royal Naval Division.
Mentioned in despatches.

SUB-LIEUT. A. REGINALD HART,
Hood Battalion, R.N. Division,
Officially reported killed.

46. Joseph Murray at Longlet, 1917, after his injury at Gavrelle (*Joseph Murray papers*).

47. Surgeon William McCracken of the Hood Battalion (*IWM*).

48. Battle of Albert. Wounded of the Royal Naval Division in their jumping-off position near Warlencourt for the attack of 25-28 August, 1918, waiting to be taken back (*IWM*).

and men, but the single men would lose. Probably the accountant-general's representative would have worked this out in detail.

After settling down, the officers' prospects would possibly be better as they would have a greater scope and their promotion need not be confined to units of the RND. The men's prospects would not be seriously affected once the change was made, provided this was done voluntarily.

To sum up, the following are points of importance:

(1) Both officers and men undoubtedly have a grievance at the back of their heads by reason of not being employed afloat. They consider they have been 'messed about' by the army.

(2) If transfer takes place it should be laid down:

(a) That it is voluntary on the part of officers and men.

(b) That officers should retain their rank and seniority.

(c) That officers should reckon their service towards army gratuity from the date of their entry in RND (War Office propose not to count this).

(3) Officers and men resent officers from army units being brought in to command, or as second in command, over the heads of officers who served for long periods in the RN Division.

In Hood Battalion recently a lieutenant was promoted from the ranks of a Highland regiment and brought in as CO with rank of lieutenant-colonel over the heads of many officers who had served through the Gallipoli campaign with distinction.

A major was similarly brought in to one of the RM battalions over the heads of several senior captains.

(4) Finally, the want of tact and sympathy displayed by the present GOC (Major-General Shute) which has been very much felt by all ranks. His harsh and unsympathetic treatment both before and after the fighting on the Ancre, where the division did so well, has undoubtedly lowered the general spirit and morale of the division and created a feeling of unrest.

(5) The principal complaint of the army authorities is that the RN battalions lack trained and capable petty officers and this is undoubtedly correct.

Any changes such as proposed by the War Office would, under existing conditions, probably entail the break up of the division as a whole, and in any case if officers and men are given the option of transfer, only a small percentage would turn over.

As regards the marines, ample use could be found for them and the navy could also utilize a good proportion of the RNVR ratings, and some might also be transferred to the Royal Marines for garrisoning the Greek islands.

Whether, in view of the efforts now being made by the War Office to obtain men from every quarter, it is to their advantage to risk breaking up the division of trained and seasoned men, appears to be very doubtful.

Lord Derby, in the chair, explained the difficulties of maintaining the division from the War Office standpoint: the chief problems were difference of pay, lack of NCOs, and a dearth of recruits. Sir Edward Carson replied, giving figures, and suggested there were only two courses open: to let things remain as at present, with the War Office taking steps to get recruits, or to abolish the division.

The adjutant-general disputed army figures, but pointed out that they included men sick, at base and at Blandford, as well as those at the front. Sir Edward Carson then highlighted two grievances: loss of seniority on transfer, and cutting out officers' rights to gratuity. Lord Derby replied that any officers transferred from the RND to the army should retain their seniority – that it should be the date of their rank in the RND – and they should similarly be eligible to count time for gratuity.

Sir Edward Carson further remarked on the lack of sympathy of the GOC, and the fact that officers had been brought in over the heads of seniors in both the naval battalions and the RM. General Bird stated that it was impossible to part with RM battalions. Lord Derby agreed, and said that in any case no man could be spared for at least four months. He proposed a gradual reduction. Sir Edward thought the War Office proposals should be put on paper.

It was not until 7 March that the War Office wrote to the Secretary to the Admiralty:

> As the proposal to recognize the 63rd (Royal Naval) Division on a military basis has, for the present at least, been abandoned, and as the personnel of that division continue to be paid from Navy Votes, there appears to be no advantage in transferring their numbers to Army Vote A. I am accordingly to express the hope that their Lordships will concur in the view that Navy Vote A should continue to bear them.

Once more the RND had survived, but it had been a hard fight which was to prove to be only a battle won, not the war. One matter of grievance was overcome, though, when Major-General Shute was succeeded on 19 February by Major-General C. E. Lawrie, only 11 days after the conference. The division still had some political clout and friends in high places, and in the traditions of the navy was not going to sink without a struggle.[1]

CHAPTER TWENTY

The Action of the Puisieux and River Trenches

After being injured by a shell splinter in the abdomen in the battle of the Ancre, Joseph Murray was taken to a hospital in the rear for treatment. The wound was comparatively minor, however, and he journeyed back to find his battalion on 29 November, 1916. He had some difficulty locating the Royal Naval Division, as nobody knew where it was:

> I thought to myself, this looks crackers; here I am in khaki uniform making enquiries about the navy. We always got that. 'Navy! What the hell are you doing here?' It didn't matter who we asked – they couldn't understand the idea of a naval division.

After a period of rest at the seaside, the battalion did some light training and were then ordered back to the line at speed. A few days on the move took the division to an area well known to them, at Mesnil, near to the River Ancre. They moved up towards the front line where Murray, who had been promoted to the rank of leading seaman, was called with other NCOs to the company office – simply a hole in the trench with a large tarpaulin drawn across it. They were told that an attack was going to take place, led by the Hood with the Hawke on their left. It would take eight minutes to complete.

Lieutenant Jacobs produced some very dull aerial photographs, which looked just like negatives, and pointed out machine-gun posts, but it was not very clear. The object was to advance and take two trenches called Puisieux and River, which were perched on the crest of the Beaucourt ridge and dominated the position, but had been much damaged by shellfire. When these had been taken, an NCO had to raid Baillescourt Farm to get information. Leading Seaman Jacky Charlton, the senior Lewis gunner, volunteered for the job; Murray would act as his bodyguard with his Lewis gun team.[1]

Lieutenant Colonel D.C.M. Munro, who had taken over command of the Hood from the injured Freyberg, issued an operational order outlining the plan of attack. Hood would advance on the right with Hawke on the left, Nelson in support, and Drake in reserve. The dividing line between the Hood and Hawke was Miraumont Alley.

A Company was to attack the system of trenches south of the Beaucourt-Miraumont road in three waves. The first wave would be two platoons, followed at a distance of 20 paces by the second wave of one platoon, and a third wave of one platoon 60 paces behind them. C Company was to extend the attacking line northward in two waves at a distance of 20 paces; each wave would comprise two platoons. D Company would attack in a similar formation on the left of C Company, with their left on a line running through and along Miraumont Alley. Each company was to push out a battle patrol of one Lewis gun, one bombing section and one rifle section. The leading waves were to move straight through to the final objective. B Company would be in support, prepared to move forward to assist in consolidating the front line.

Greatcoats were to be worn over the men's equipment in the attacking companies, but were to be left behind for the advance. Runners would wear a red badge on the left forearm. Each man was supplied with 120 rounds of ammunition per man, except bombers, Lewis gunners, scouts, signallers and carrying parties, who got only 60 rounds apiece. Every other man carried a P-bomb or a flare.

All other ranks carried considerable additional equipment:

Four sandbags	Passed through belt
One iron ration	In mess tin
Two days' preserved ration	In haversack
One box respirator	Slung
One Very light cartridge	In entrenching tool case
One pair of socks	In haversack
Two No 5 grenades	In pockets

The battalion was to be in position at 15 minutes before zero on 3 February, 1917, forming up on a line of luminous discs situated about 100 yards in front of the outpost line. As the barrage lifted at zero plus six minutes they were to rush forward to Puisieux Trench and get to grips with the enemy. At zero plus eight minutes, before the Germans had time to recover, River Trench was to be stormed. The second waves of C and D Companies were to clear and clean up Puisieux Trench, then send one platoon forward to assist in consolidating the front line. C Company's OC had to be ready to send a platoon from the second wave to assist A Company by attacking southwards along the Puisieux

Trench if necessary. The Lewis guns were to follow closely behind the last waves, moving through the battalion at Puisieux, then place themselves in shellholes to cover the consolidation of the front line.[2]

It was a fine, starlit night, with a bright moon shining and a hard frost. Visibility was good except for a slight ground mist. Leading Seaman Murray takes up the story:

> At 11 o'clock, as soon as the barrage started, it went forward and we went after it. We got to a place parallel with the Ancre. Parallel! Alongside it! We hadn't got to any trenches. I thought to myself, that's not right. The infantrymen were told to dig in.

The battalion had lost their way and moved too far to the right, at a point where the river also turns right and runs in a straight line beside the railway line before moving left again towards Baillescourt Farm. Murray continues:

> I went in front of them for about 20 to 30 yards, and placed two Lewis guns in position. I then went to reconnoitre. I came to the hillside; it was all snow and ice, not so much snow but very hard frost and very slippery. I started running like hell down this hill: I couldn't stop myself, and finished up in the marshes of the river. The ice broke and I was up to my knees in water. I climbed up the hill again, and when I got to the top I saw Petty Officer Egdell. He was technically in charge of the Lewis guns, but actually he was a quartermaster. I don't know what he was doing there. When I got to the top, having only been away 10 minutes, maybe less, I put my gun in position to keep a look-out for the men who were digging. I thought we shouldn't be digging-in in any case. We were supposed to be capturing a trench.
>
> Egdell moved forward to my gun and said, 'The digging party have all gone.' 'Where?' 'They went up that way somewhere, they haven't come this way.' So Egdell and I took the gun back to where they had been digging. Egdell then went off to find the men.
>
> I moved about 10 to 20 yards when suddenly I was challenged. Petty Officer Price said, 'What are you doing here? What's happening?' He was in a shellhole with a gun team. I said, 'I don't know. Look, we are Lewis gunners: we are supposed to be in front of the battalion, but we are behind them now apparently.' He replied, 'No, no, that's all right.' I said, 'I'm getting out of here.' All of a sudden there were about five men slinging bombs. I thought, 'Oh Christ, who are they?' I said to Petty Officer Price, 'We are getting out of this. Coming?' He agreed, and off we went straight ahead, as we should have done in the first place.

We had got about 20 yards when bang, bang, bang! A blinking shell dropped, making a hell of an explosion. I called out, 'Are you all right?' to Price. 'Yes, but I've got two fellows wounded.' He would not move on any further. Suddenly a machine gun was firing at us, so I moved another 10 or 15 yards, but he would still not move. I said, 'I'm going on,' and two of his men, thinking that Price was going to come with me, moved forward too. Only a couple of minutes after we moved off, another blinking shell dropped right where we had been. I don't know if Price was killed, but it must have been pretty close. I never saw him or his gun team from then onwards.

I kept on going, and suddenly I got to Egdell, who had found the line. I came to the Baillescourt Farm to Beaucourt roadway. It was a beautiful road, on a hill, and sloped towards the river all the time, so the road was cut out of the side of this hill. We had an embankment of five or six feet. I put one of my guns on the boundary, and said to the man, 'Look, this is the boundary. The Hawke should be on the other side of the roadway.' I also put a gun on top of the hill, telling the man to be careful as the Hawke can't know he was there. So I had guns across the road and down towards the river.

It was so hard that you couldn't make the least impression on the road. Try as you like you could not dig, so I moved forward about 10 to 15 yards and found a nice shellhole. I sent my runner, young Smithy, saying, 'Get back as quick as you can to the line and tell them I've gone over the brow; I can't dig in, and I've also got a gun on the Hawke side.' He went back and came across a Lieutenant Holland, who came back to see where we were. Jacobs was my officer, but anyway Holland came up. I pointed out Baillescourt Farm, as I thought we were going to move again; but no, we were going to stay. Holland went back to see Company Commander Bennett, then returned later agreeing that the position we had taken up was all right. We were in front of the line and didn't want anybody firing on us.

All of a sudden the Jerries began counter-attacking; not a lot, but we beat them off. I was in charge of the Lewis guns, so I kept moving about to see if each one was all right. Damn it all, there was firing going off in all directions. Suddenly I saw a whole lot coming, firing like hell. I thought they must be the Drakes coming to help us. They weren't: they were Jerries. By going in the wrong direction we had missed them, and they were all the Jerries we should have captured in the first place. We began firing like hell at them. I was in a shellhole with three men, and a German officer and three men attacked us. One with a blinking bayonet had got it on my chest, saying, '*Vic, Vic.*' I didn't know what *Vic* meant, but I took it to mean 'Get back'. We were their prisoners. Then the Drakes came up to help, and I thought, thank Christ. I was his prisoner one moment, and now he was my prisoner.

There were not many Drakes, only about 20 or 30. One minute we were firing one way, then a minute later behind. When I got back to the brow there were machine-gun bullets firing over our head; you could almost feel the bullets. I said to Smithy, 'Go and see Mr Holland again, and tell him that I cannot stay here as I must go further down the slope.' I didn't know, and I was not told until the next day, that actually it was a machine-gun company who were keeping up a barrage to protect us.

During the night the Worcester pioneer battalion, who were attached to the RND, brought up some 40,000 rounds of ammunition, but they could not reach us and left it on the roadway about 30 to 40 yards behind us. I later pinched all of this, plus some picks and shovels which had also been carried to the position. With these we were able to dig a nice little trench.

The men had been firing all the time and were tired, so I took over a Lewis gun on the ridge of the shellhole. It was semi-dark, but getting light. The Lewis gun has a tripod, but you didn't have time to play about with that. When you saw them coming you didn't have time to take aim. The damn thing was so active, you just had to press the trigger and move it sideways. A crowd comes towards you, and all you can see are black figures. Brrrr, brrrr, brrrr, and there is only an occasional one left, so poot, poot, poot.[3]

At 1.30am on 4 February Lieutenant-Colonel Munro was wounded, so Lieutenant-Commander Arthur Asquith took over command, as recorded by Thomas MacMillan:

Through some misunderstanding, an awkward gap existed between the Hawke and Hood Battalions, and but for the gallantry of Lieutenant-Commander Asquith and the alertness and bravery of Major Barnett a serious situation would have developed.

No man was more surprised than Barnett when he learned that Asquith was in the thick of it. Turning sharply to me he asked, 'Where the hell did he spring from?' I had the sense not to attempt a reply, for I was as perplexed as the major.

The favoured ones in London who did not reckon my life as precious as that of Arthur Melland Asquith were far out when they thought that by transferring him to the corps they might sleep at nights without dreading his being killed.

Asquith had conspired and secured the job of observation officer to the corps heavy artillery which supported us. Being on the spot, he could see how the fight was progressing and, observing the situation getting out of hand, he assumed the role of battalion commander.[4]

Between 5 and 10am the Germans counter-attacked strongly, suffering heavy losses and leaving about 50 or 60 dead on the ground. They also attacked River Trench and were repulsed mainly by rifle fire. But they succeeded in occupying the junction of Miraumont Alley and River Trench, and the dugouts just to the south. Puisieux Trench had not been completely cleared, and there were casualties from German sniping and machine-gun fire; Sub-Lieutenants J.C.S. Bennett and Trevor Jacobs were killed by snipers.[5]

Murray continues his account:

There was a counter-attack going on, but it seemed to peter out. Having just handed the Lewis gun to my runner Smithy to have a go and give the lads some rest, I suddenly saw a huge fellow in front. I had my revolver and I fired, naturally. He fell over and busted one of my guns. He had a rifle and a brand new serrated bayonet. Now everybody says they didn't have them, but this officer had one. I took it: it was just a bit shorter than ours, a little more than a foot long. I haven't the faintest idea how that man got there. I had a man on the ridge on top of the road; he must have crawled on the road itself, I imagine. The road was too hard to dig, so we were a little way from it.

At breakfast time Lieutenant Holland came up and told me the company commander wanted me to send men out into the front to obtain identification from the Germans. Smithy wanted to come with me, so we went out in front and walked down 20 or 30 yards. There were dozens of dead, no trouble at all finding them, and we kept taking their ID discs and paybooks for 15 or 20 minutes. We were not molested in any way: I can't remember anybody firing, yet it was broad daylight, 7am in the morning. There were two or three wounded on the roadway, but somebody else dealt with them. Apparently there was another crowd further to my right, doing as I was, and they had sent out several parties.

After about an hour back in our trenches, Lieutenant Holland arrived again. Somebody said, 'Look!' So Holland and I looked: coming across the river about 800 yards away, behind Baillescourt Farm, I saw a whole column of men, about 600 to 700; a regiment, marching. It was frozen, but perhaps they had built a bridge. We lost them for a while, then picked them up again coming this way. Holland said, 'There must be some dead ground in between.'

214

I said, 'If they are coming towards us they have got to spread out. Should we wait until they get broadside on?' He thought that was a good idea. I said, 'We don't want the infantry to start firing, as they are end on.' I thought 800 yards was too far, but they were coming towards us; we could wait until it was 600 or 700 yards. Holland agreed to the plan and crawled back, saying any fire should wait until Murray gave the signal. I had eight Lewis guns with me, but only three available in this position. The Germans moved right in front of Baillescourt Farm – there must have been a road there. Then they got broadside on and I went brrrrr with the Lewis gun. The moment I started the artillery opened up, as did the infantry, so they must have followed the plan that Holland and I agreed. Anyhow, only three or four minutes was enough; there was nothing moving at all after that.[6]

The Hood war diary states that as a result of counter-attacks the SOS was sent up from the front line, and reported to battalion HQ at 9.45am At 9.47am the barrage opened most effectively and continued for an hour, breaking up the enemy formations.[7] No doubt the information was passed by signal line, as the Hood's communication order instructed the signalling officer to lay treble lines forward as soon as possible after zero. It was to go up to number one post before the attack and then forward, so runners could report there before they came on to the battalion. Routine messages, however brief, were to be sent if possible every 15 minutes.[8]

Murray continues:

Holland came out again and told me the lieutenant-commander sent many congratulations. I called out to my men, 'Do you hear that? The governor sends his congratulations on the work you have done.' I said it rather loud, as I had got my men scattered about, and I was rather pleased to say it. They replied with their thanks. Holland said, 'I join in with the commander.'

That morning Petty Officer Egdell came up and picked up one of my Lewis guns. We looked over towards the right flank and there was an officer and about 30 men surrendering, all with their hands up. I'm positive it wasn't voluntary. We had been there all night, and because of the gap we had left half the Germans behind, as we went round instead of forward. Petty Officer Egdell walked about 10 yards, and suddenly brrrr, brrrr at them! Well, in their direction. He didn't appear to hit anybody, because they still went on going until they went out of sight. I was amazed.[9]

The Hood war diary states that Sub-Lieutenant Hillam was captured and 15 ordinary ranks were missing, believed prisoners of war.[10]

215

About 11am Sub-Lieutenant Hill was sent forward to investigate an alarmist report, but returned saying all was quiet. Lieutenant-Commander Asquith returned to the Hood from brigade at about the same time, accompanied by Sub-Lieutenant Arblaster, and carried out a reconnaissance of the whole line, duly reporting to brigade. The remainder of the day was peaceful, and plans were made to capture a post between Hood and Hawke. Hugh Kingsmill was the commanding officer of Drake's B Company:

At about 8pm our company fell in on the road. The attacking battalions, the Hood and Hawke, had lost touch with each other, and B Company was to proceed to the left extremity of the Hood and from there join up with the right flank of the Hawke.

An active and imperious figure, strongly contrasted with the tired troops who had been working hard with little rest during the last 24 hours, sprang up on the road and suffered me to be readily presented to him by our adjutant, Beak (later Commander Daniel Beak, VC). We at once set off; my companion was Arthur Asquith, at that time a lieutenant-commander temporarily on the staff. He had accompanied the Hood Battalion in their attack, got them back to their correct alignment before 8am, and had now returned to bring our company up to regain touch with the Hawke.

In my short experience of the front, I never saw anyone, officer, NCO or man, except Arthur Asquith and one young Tommy, who did not look like an illustration of the refrain, 'We're here because we're here, because we're here, because we're here.' But Arthur Asquith embodied free-will. He was there because he liked being there. Our progress over the torn ground was slow. The men kept on falling in and out of shellholes, and Asquith's impatience increased. He seemed to feel as a champion sprinter would who should find himself, on turning out to lower the world's record for the hundred yards, unaccountably compelled to do the course leading a tortoise on a string.

At last we reached one of the German trenches that had been captured in the attack. A number of dead Germans had been stood up against the side, most of them with sacks thrown over their heads. But one of them was uncovered, and his face in the bright moonlight expressed intense agony and astonishment mingled. The blood had suffused in the veins below his right eye. However, he had died quickly, his last moments must have been so painful as to amaze him with a sensation he had never even imagined. A little further on, face downwards on a dark slope, with one leg drawn up, lay a German, who looked like a life-size marionette, dropped behind the scenes by a stage-hand.

216

These sights were unreal, but the sense of reality came back when we reached the left flank of the Hood. B Company halted beside a trench manned by troops who looked disconsolate and tired of the incessant noise in which they were enveloped. A brigade runner suddenly appeared and handed Asquith a message. About 50 yards to our left, the message ran, a big shellhole was held by Germans with a machine gun. This strongpoint must be taken at once. I got the company out in four lines, and asked Asquith whether, as company commander, I should lead the attack or supervise it. 'Supervise it,' he said. My spirits, which had been fairly high during the march up, were now at their lowest, and I was relieved that my private wishes should coincide with the military requirements of the situation.

Remembering a sergeant who had placed before himself the alternatives of VC or WC in the next show, I put him in charge of the first line, another sergeant of similar temper in charge of the second line, and Harold Pound and Henry Southwood with the third and fourth lines, reserving for myself a position on the flank of the second line. The sergeants protested against this arrangement. Its impropriety became clear to me, and, placing Pound and Southwood with the first two lines, I sent the sergeants to the rear. The men having drawn the pins from their Mills bombs, we advanced on the strongpoint.

Pound strode forward with his usual deliberate tread. I watched him anxiously. He seemed unnaturally tall in the moonlight, and so isolated that the garrison of the shellhole could hardly fail to bring him down. The enemy continued to reserve their ammunition and we continued to advance. When we reached the strongpoint it was untenanted. General Phillips had been misinformed.

My depression vanished. I now felt equal to anything. The company straggled out of column of route, and we went forward, Asquith and I at the head. The men, holding Mills bombs with the pins out, so if anyone tripped he was likely to blow at any rate himself to pieces, became fretful. Once the whole company had to halt while an overwrought Tommy hurled his bomb into the night. The rest, however, seemed to prefer sticking to their bombs, as a precautionary measure, should we meet any Germans. Presently we came to a dugout, outside which lay a few dead English soldiers. One of these soldiers, a young man, was lying on his back, his arms spread out and his eyes closed. The moon illumined his unmoving face, which was more beautiful than any living face could be.

For some moments I forgot myself and my surroundings. As I looked down at him, I did not think of him as a dead man, or of myself as exposed to the risks which had proved mortal to him. My next recollection is of drawing ahead of my company, with Asquith and three Tommies. We were being fired at from our left by Germans who were between us and our own lines. Presently Asquith remarked that he was wounded and must return. I sent one of the Tommies back with him. Of the other two, one vanished, I don't know when or why. The remaining Tommy was a young boy, whose eyes were gleaming with excitement. We potted alternately with his rifle, at the black figures bobbing about in the moonlight, moving on between shots. After a few minutes, I saw a group of men a hundred yards or so away. 'These may be ours,' I said to my companion. 'Let's advance with our hands up so that they won't shoot.'

As we approached in this attitude someone shouted, *'Gefangen'*. I called to my companion to run, they were Germans, and we made off. They opened fire, and killed him before we had gone 10 yards. He was just behind me and gave a short, quick gasp. If his death was, as I think, instantaneous, the last few minutes of his life were unalloyed in excitement and enjoyment. His eager face, as I first noticed it when the others had left us, has remained always clear in my memory.

The Germans chased me for two or three hundred yards, and then gave it up. When their figures were no longer visible, lurching over the churned-up earth, I stood still to regain my breath. I must now, I thought, be so near the Hawke that it would be better to find them first, and then go back to my company.

After walking for two or three minutes I saw some figures in a large crater, and called out to them. One of them shouted back: 'We are A Company.' The accent was German, and I replied: *'Es scheint, dass Sie deutsch sind.'* They laughed good-naturedly, and I paused, a few yards from them, on the edge of a shellhole. The abnormal excitement in which I had been since the advance on the reputed strongpoint vanished, leaving me in a matter-of-fact mind. But the run in field boots and Burberry had warmed me and I felt a strong reluctance to give myself up.

The fascination of active service, so keenly felt until I left England, suddenly revived. I turned the matter over in my mind. As I was an easy mark, and as they had been amused by my answering in German, I knew they would not shoot as long as I stood still. They were probably waiting for me to resume the talk. After perhaps half a minute, I muttered, 'No, I'm damned if I will,' and rushed away. Crouching figures were stalking up to the left rear of the crater. The Hawke at last, I thought, and ran towards them. A few yards from them I saw their helmets, the German *pickelhaube*. At the same moment they saw me. I ran another four or five paces, and tripped up. When I got to my feet they had surrounded me, and I handed them my revolver.[11]

Between 5.30 and 7am on 5 February the Hood's left support company cleared the enemy out of a strongpoint on their left, capturing about

12 prisoners. At about the same time a party of this company's Lewis gunners stormed and captured a hostile machine-gun position. The gun was subsequently used with great effect against the enemy.

The situation on the left was now clear, and the remainder of the day was quieter, with much less hostile shelling; the enemy had apparently accepted the position. The Hood's right company reoccupied its posts without opposition, so all the battalion's objectives were occupied and consolidated. They were relieved that night by the 1st HAC, and the relief was completed by 12.30am on 6 February. The HAC went on and took Baillecourt Farm the next day.[12]

Thomas MacMillan described the period after the battle:

On our way back, despite the need for expedition, we had to pause to look at the gruesome effects of the enemy's heavy gunfire. The ground in the rear had been churned up afresh by their shells, and the unearthed dead were lying, kneeling and standing all around us.

The general was ever so happy at the excellent results which had been achieved . . . . I was asked to read my shorthand diary of the fight, in the course of which I referred to the messages received from rear brigade headquarters. 'Rear brigade headquarters!' exclaimed the general with a frown. 'Yes, sir,' I replied, with the pertness of a tired man. 'Rear brigade headquarters,' he muttered. It was dawning on me that I had got under his skin, and I waited his further comment. To my delight he calmed down and asked me to proceed without deigning to suggest a more suitable appellation for his abode.

Congratulations were now showering in. The commander-in-chief wired his praise and thanks, and the corps commander followed with a lengthy message to all ranks extolling their bravery and devotion to duty. Lieutenant-Commander Asquith received the DSO, while Major Barnett received a bar to his Military Cross. I felt sorry for them both, believing that much more substantial recognition would have been forthcoming had there been someone on the spot to witness and appraise the valour and understanding which they had displayed . . . .

Asquith's personality and indomitable courage gave new life to all around him and, although badly wounded, he carried on until victory was assured. Looking as white as a winding sheet from loss of blood, he hobbled to the rear without assistance to give a lucid and most helpful report to the brigade before being evacuated to hospital.

The sequel to the fight was very heartening. The 188th Brigade exploited our gains and ended by capturing the important villages of Pys and Miraumont. This series of successes opened the way to Bapaume and heralded the great German retreat on the Somme.[13]

The Hood had gone into action with 21 officers and 605 other ranks.
Total casualties on 3, 4 and 5 February amounted to:

Killed	2 officers; 25 other ranks
Wounded	5 officers; 72 other ranks
Missing	1 officer; 28 other ranks
Missing, believed prisoner	1 officer; 15 other ranks
Wounded, remained on duty	3 other ranks[14]

CHAPTER TWENTY-ONE

To the Hindenburg Line

Bernard Freyberg returned from hospital in England in February, 1917, and takes up the story:

> With the exception of the Gallipoli blizzard in November, 1915, the hardest weather conditions of the war were during 1917 in the months of February and March, and these adverse times were more acutely felt upon the Somme, owing to the enemy's policy of razing to the ground, before withdrawing, all the buildings and trees our shelling had not already levelled.
>
> During this period the German army were retiring upon undamaged roads and railways, through prepared defensive positions and with what was very essential during a winter campaign, undamaged villages for their troops to rest in close to the line. We, on the other hand, having once advanced across the old trench systems, were as effectively cut off from the rest of our world as we had been by the Aegean Sea during the Gallipoli campaign.
>
> The old trench system in winter time was a morass of mud and desolation miles across, the only projections above the earth's crust being the belts of barbed wire entanglements, mostly of enemy origin, which made our isolation the more complete, and the sole remaining link with the rest of our army being a single-way, traffic-congested plank road, which had been built forward plank by plank across the mud before the hard frosts had set in.
>
> The infantrymen actually in touch with the enemy suffered dreadfully, and as the line was continually moving forward, there were no trenches as we had known them before the Somme offensive had started; at most there were hurriedly dug platoon posts, separated by large gaps. But during the heavy frosts, when the ground was too iron-like for any impression to be made upon it, even with a pick, men were forced to take cover in shellholes, or any suitable

depression. Burying our dead became an engineering feat, graves being blasted out with explosives. The petrol tins of drinking water froze hard and had to be opened with a tin-opener, pieces of ice chipped off with the bayonet and forced into the water bottle, where they remained in a solid state till mealtime. When a drink was required the ice had to be thawed by placing the water bottle inside the shirt. Washing and shaving were an impossibility.

The occupied shellholes were usually half full of ice, upon which the men had to lie or kneel during the day; at night only was it possible to move about and stretch out the creases that had been frozen into their bodies during the cramped hours of daylight. Men were often frozen to death as they lay facing the enemy, with their rifles still tightly gripped as if ready for use. Visiting rounds frequently arrested what they believed to be sleeping sentries, only to discover their melancholy error. Under these conditions of cold our wounded stood little or no chance; drowsiness followed any loss of blood, which in turn gave way to death.

Even without the harassing we received at the hands of the enemy, occupying the line was an extraordinary searching feat of endurance, and in addition to the physical difficulties we must add the goading received from our Higher Command, who never allowed us to rest for an hour without ordering us to attack, to raid, or to reconnoitre.

During these operations our right flank, which rested on the River Ancre, was imagined to be secure. The river was deep and a considerable obstacle. But during the severe frosts the river unexpectedly froze over and a German infantry company, dressed in white nightgowns to match the snow, crossed on the ice, attacking our posts from the rear, causing great havoc, until ejected by a counterattack.

During these nights in the line it was noticeable that panic played a considerable part, even when dealing with the most stout-hearted of men. It seemed harder to be brave in the cold than on a bright sunny day.

Under these conditions men were never kept in the line for more than 48 hours. They marched in with two days' rations and water, wearing leather jerkins and sheepskin gloves, and carrying blankets to wrap round their legs, and waterproof sheets and sandbags to sit upon. Greatcoats were generally left at transport lines, to ensure having at least one dry article of clothing to sleep in on returning to rest.

When not in the line, we came back to Ovillers Camp, which was a collection of tents that were shelled by the enemy field guns and bombed by hostile aeroplanes at night. During the periods out of the line, the infantry remade the road and railway between Thiepval and Grandcourt.

The speed at which the army could move forward across this Somme desert depended entirely upon the rate roads and railways could be rebuilt. Since the enemy could demolish them far quicker than we could rebuild, our troops fought with a constant shortage of artillery ammunition, and with none of the comforts which were so necessary during this class of war. As a result the men's vitality got lower and lower, and sickness became much greater.

When the Royal Naval Division was exhausted by the active operations of February and the first week of March, we came back permanently to our camp, which stood on the side of a hill, just clear of enemy observation. There was no shelter from the cutting north wind, and we were all in a debilitated state, suffering from loss of sleep owing to the cold, which was often 30° below zero. The wind took the skin from our faces and hands, while our ears were covered with frost-bite sores.

But our sufferings were nothing compared to those of the horses, which stood in the open with no shelter at all. They had been clipped to prevent 'scab' which was prevalent, and as the enemy submarine campaign tightened its grip on England, their hay and oats were cut below a working ration. It was heart-breaking to see the way these broken-spirited animals huddled together for protection. The transport drivers did all they could to alleviate their sufferings; they walked miles to steal any extra food that was stealable, but even so, horses died in large numbers, usually dropping from exhaustion, and their carcasses and skeletons littered both sides of the roads.

Men worked six hours a day and spent two hours marching between camp and work. There were no games or social side to our lives, and we never saw a civilian from one week to another; consequently our minds were always focused on the war. At night, when the cold became too great for sleep, men walked up and down to get warm. Many were suffering from chills, exposure and strain, while all had seriously deteriorated from a military point of view.

On 10 March the rumour came that a large attack to the north was imminent. The first indication of a change of policy, on any front, was the arrival or withdrawal of large quantities of artillery. Either of these contingencies was foreshadowed by the advent of caterpillar-driven tractors, to draw the heavy guns to or from the gun positions.

Our rumours had weight lent to them by the withdrawal of a greater part of our artillery, upon the plea of resting the gunners, who had not been out of the line for months. At night the Thornycroft tractors arrived at the gun positions behind our lines, and snorted back, dragging the heavy guns away down the Bapaume Road. Staff officers, when taxed about this attack, were evasive, but all the men who came off leave returned with stories of high concentrations to the north of guns and men.

18 March saw a change in our plans. We received orders cancelling working parties, and on 19 March, bound for unknown destination northwards, we marched from Ovillers Camp.

It was with definite feelings of relief that we wheeled to the left from Ovillers Camp and marched away down the Bapaume-Albert road, turning our backs once more upon the bloody battlefields of the Somme, where in 1916 the ambitions of the German army were put to rest. For it was there, during those sledge-hammer blows from July to November, that the spirit of the German fighting soldier was finally broken . . . a spirit, born of superior training, that had made their army in defence so hard to defeat.

At the commencement of the Somme battle in July, 1916, the enemy infantry fought and so often held their trenches, using the rifle, the bomb, and the bayonet. But towards the finish of the year, to prevent defeat, the German general staff were forced to resort to other expedients than the fighting powers of their infantry. They had to accept the loss of their front positions together with their garrisons. By the judicious use of their local reserves they now endeavoured to limit the success of our operations; and even if the German Higher Command at such times as March and April, 1918, were flattered by strategic successes, the battle-winning qualities of their fighting troops had already been buried, together with the bones of our men, along those two great river valleys in Picardy.

But the Somme battle had served another purpose. It was the great training ground for our newly-made divisions, for it was here we learned how to rebuild them from the salvage that marched out even from successful operations.

When we marched into the Somme six months earlier, it was with a sun-tanned, seasoned lot of men. The battalion as it marched out made a sad picture in contrast, the men footsore and almost bootless from heavy work in the mud, while their thin white faces told of the mental as well as the physical strain they had endured. Our horses, which were nearly all strangers, walked out with their hindquarters tucked up, and were in an emaciated condition. Our original animals had either been killed in action or had died from a combination of exposure, overwork and malnutrition. There were a great number of sick men marching, as our last drafts from England had been mostly boys, who were too immature to stand the cold.

At Warloy we went into billets for the night. Some men had fallen out during the march, and many were on the verge of a collapse.

During the march the strong carried the rifles and packs of the weak, and even so we had to step short and reduce our pace. In billets the men washed and painted their feet with methylated spirit and picric acid to prevent blisters. After a meal the men walked about the village or sat in the estaminets, whilst the officers were busy making out lists of the boots, socks and equipment necessary before a long march could be undertaken. Next day, 20 March, we marched to Puchevillers, where we picked up our band instruments and drums.

It never seemed quite clear during active operations such as the ones we had just taken part in, whether the physical powers of men gave way before the mental, or vice versa. But it seemed to us, from the rise in the men's general spirits as they limped along the road, stiffer and more exhausted after their first day's march, that the mental side was the quicker to recover. It was good to hear them cheer as the drums dropped back to their company, after the hour's halt, and to watch the men rediscovering their singing voices after a couple of months' silence.

On 21 March we marched to Barley, where we billeted. Every march now saw an improvement in the men's condition. The band, strict march discipline, and no work, were doing wonders, whilst mixing with the civilians in the villages, getting *vin blanc* and omelettes, and plenty of sleep, was making the cure complete.

It was now that the most wonderful of the psychological factors of the war – the exhilaration and excitement of a move to an offensive – again made itself evident. The men commenced to show keenness for the battle to which we were marching: 'More guns than had ever been,' and 'The blow that was to end the war,' were the gist of all our talk. And with each successive march the men's health improved as their spirits rose.

On 22 and 23 March we rested, whilst the remainder of the division concentrated around Ligny. Other formations besides our own were on the move, and the scent of battle was now strong in the wind.

We were marching by stages of about 16 miles a day via St Pol, Tangry, Auchez-au-Bois and Lillers, to Vendin-Lez-Béthune, where we arrived on 28 March in the best condition, with all thoughts centred upon the battle.

The weather was warmer, our billets good, while the area itself was richly agricultural. Farm produce was plentiful and cheaper than upon the Somme.

A division marching upon a road measured 15½ miles in length, and to avoid waste of time and counter-marching at the starting points, this mass of men, guns and transport required very detailed arrangements and marshalling. All movement upon the main road was controlled by time, watches were carefully synchronized, and most meticulous accuracy was demanded. All units were given starting times, and starting points away from the main route, to ensure their arriving in their correct order. So accurate was the timing that the column arrived in position only a minute or two before the march commenced. At the given second, the unit commanders all along the line gave the command 'quick march', when the whole column moved off together, marching two and a half miles an hour.

At 10 minutes to each hour the line of march halted, the men fell out on the right side of the road, and took off their packs, which they sat upon. This movement had to be completed in 30 seconds. At a minute to each hour the order, 'get dressed and fall in' was given, and at the hour exactly, the column moved off together again.

Generals and staff officers flew about in cars, taking notes upon march discipline. They tested the distances between the units, and saw that during the halts all mounted personnel dismounted from their horses, that pack animals were relieved of their boxes of ammunition, and that all weight was taken from shaft horses by using the shaft rest. At no time during the march was any man or animal allowed to impinge on to the left side of the road, which was kept clear for two-way traffic.

At the midday halt men fell out to the right of the road and sat drumming with their knives and forks on their mess-tins, waiting for the meal to arrive. They cheered the cooks as the heavy draught horses dragged the steaming kitchens forward with the midday meal. Messmen lifted the dixies from the mobile fire and each company formed up in a queue, waiting for their pint of hot stew, which was eked out with the bread ration from their haversacks. When the meal was finished, the dixies were washed, filled with clean water and put back on the fires to be ready for tea the instant the men arrived in billets.

Our division and other troops were moving on parallel roads about a mile apart. When on the march, troops stretched away in front and rear and on either flank as far as the eye could see. At odd times we saw on the crest of a hill, silhouetted against the sky in rear, engineers' pontoons or field guns as they lumbered forward noisily over the paved roads.

Viewed in miniature on the roads on either side, the column was seen in its true perspective. First a succession of battalions of infantry, each battalion separated by a gap of 50 yards, and composed of 400 yards of infantry in column of fours headed by drums or a band, then 200 yards of transport, with four kitchen chimneys sticking up in the air, each sending its own distinct thread of smoke skyward. In the rear of the infantry came the engineers,

226

with their heavy wagons and boats, then the batteries of artillery and ammunition columns, and last of all, either the Army Service Corps supply wagons, or the field ambulances.

It was a formidable display, set to the rhythm of men's feet stamping in time, the metallic sound of heavy army wagons bumping along the uneven roads, and all to the accompaniment of drums and marching bands. And the bands in the distance seemed to echo and answer the closer bands when they ceased to play.

The whole move was an expression of military efficiency, a manifestation which heartened everyone. Units started to rival one another in smartness, while the ambition of all commanders was to finish the march without having a man fall out.

On occasions men were forced to drop behind, in spite of every help their pals and company officers could exert. These men were given certificates, and leave to wait for the rear party, who followed behind the column, picking up the halt and lame. As these stragglers were passed by other battalions, they had to put up with good-natured raillery, especially should the unit to which the straggler belong possess an army name such as 'The Tigers' or 'The Fighting Fifth'.

Perhaps the most memorable incident in any concentration march was arriving into a town at dusk, in an area already packed with troops for an offensive, gunners waiting to go to their gun positions, ammunition columns, auxiliary transport companies, and battalions of divisions that had already completed concentration.

I remember particularly marching into Lillers at dusk. The rear companies had commenced to be obscured, and the lights of the town were just coming into their own, as we marched down a slight *pavé* slope between two rows of stone buildings, which flung the sound of the drums and our feet back at us as we marched. The transport wagons rattled along behind us as we swung on to a combined band and bugle march, with an air the men were singing. The troops in the estaminets rushed to the windows and doors and out into the street, joining in the song. Everyone was shouting the same two questions: 'What division?' 'What battalion?' Before giving the final welcome of one lot of attackers to another: 'You're b . . . well for it!'

It was a most inspiring scene – everybody with champagne spirits – packs seemed no weight – sore feet were forgotten – blood surged through our limbs, and in an instant the fire which drove us out to France at the commencement of the war flared up in one great flash.

After arranging billets for the night, our men mixed in the estaminets with the men of other divisions. Wonderful stories were told about the Somme, and the battle that was to come. Towards the end of the evening, bets were made between men of rival divisions as to which would be the first on to the Vimy Ridge. It was wonderful that men could still feel trusting about life, when they knew so well the changes that must happen in the next few days. But above all, it seemed difficult to believe that these were the same dull-eyed, tired men that we brought out from the Somme 10 days before. Hardships and suffering seemed to leave no immediate scar.[1]

A poem written about this time, found among Thomas MacMillan's papers, indicates the battalion's state of mind:

> When mothers with gladness
> Their children gave to England
> The stern recruiters looked at them
> And turned them all away;
> But Winston saw them ere they fled.
> And sweetly smiled and kindly said,
> Suffer the little children to join the RND.
>
> For I will receive them
> And train them all as sailors,
> As sailors who have never sailed
> And never seen the sea.
> And so we joined old Churchill's mob,
> And took the regulation bob,
> And like little children,
> We joined the RND.
>
> He sent some to Antwerp,
> And lost a few battalions.
> The rest he sent to take their chance,
> Upon Gallipoli;
> But Johnnie Turk and foul disease
> Would soon have wiped out by degrees,
> All the little children
> Who joined the RND.
>
> But salvation came by the evacuation,
> And now we're here in France,
> And to the end we here shall be;
> And though we kick up hell for leave,
> Old Winston just laughs up his sleeve,
> So all say, 'Oh bugger him,
> And all the RND.'[2]

CHAPTER TWENTY-TWO

Gavrelle

Thomas MacMillan resumes his narrative:

After the middle of March the RND proceeded on foot to join the XIIIth Corps of the First Army, which was then the army of rest.

The weather had improved, but the roads were mud-clogged and the going was unpleasant. All ranks, however, had seen all they wanted to see of the Somme. In anticipation of a spell of rest and recreation, they marched gaily from village to village until a pleasant resting place was found in the attractive countryside which lies between Busnus and Béthune. Here we were received rather formally by the villagers, but with much sympathy and affection by the numerous refugees who had found temporary asylum in a district as yet unmarred by the ravages of war. A training and recreational programme there took place.

A month's respite was promised, but on 31 March all general staff officers accompanied by battalion commanders left for a tour of inspection of the line in the vicinity of Arras.

By 8 April we were again on the move. Snow fell heavily, transforming the roads and intermediate halting places into veritable quagmires. This change in the weather had a most adverse effect on the health of the troops. Many suffered from influenza. The sun came out again on 14 April – the date that the RND moved forward to take their place in the line. The change from foul to fair weather created a state of feverishness in the ranks, with symptoms similar to those produced by trench fever.

From intelligence reports an offensive on a grand scale had been launched on the RND's left and had resulted in the capture of many points of strategical importance, including the famous Vimy Ridge. Higher Command had decided on a major operation before

Douai and Cambrai. Gavrelle was selected as the pivot on which our Third Army was to swing in their sweep forward, and the important task of taking Gavrelle was to be entrusted to the Naval Division.

The 189th Brigade HQ was established in a railway cutting on the Arras-Douai line close to the village of Gavrelle. For a week before the impending battle the HQ was all astir. The major was busy on the operation order, and to guard against distraction he selected a small corner at the bottom of the dugout. I changed my quarters to a communication dugout, which faced a larger compartment where the general held his councils of war. All three compartments were lit by candles, and mine was living with lice. Soon the vermin were all over me, and it was always well into the night before I had the opportunity of despatching the whoppers which had mustered in the course of the day.

The major's manuscript was nearing completion when, during a consultation he was having with the general, his candle overturned. Before the mishap was discovered by a passing orderly, almost all of his work had been destroyed. He was seriously perturbed but, realizing how precious time was, he applied himself to his task with great determination and completed in good time, and early next morning stencils were cut of the order.

The village of Gavrelle had to be captured, and the general wisely decided that Freyberg and his 'Hoods' were the right men for the job. It was common knowledge that where Freyberg went the Hoods would go, and that they would take some stopping.

The operational order had no sooner been delivered than instructions were received from division to despatch Freyberg to the 173rd Brigade as its brigadier. This was a bombshell! The gallant Egerton, who was acting second in command, was nursing a wound and was not available. There was therefore no other course open but to approach Commander Asquith.

Before Asquith had quite recovered from the wounds he had received in the fight for Puisieux and River Trenches, he had reported back to the Hood Battalion and had again been ordered to return to corps. Immediately on receipt of the wire requesting his services, he wired his willingness to take over the command, to the great relief of the general and the major. He arrived on the morning of 21 April, and in the late afternoon brigade HQ was in possession of a copy of his orders to the Hood Battalion.[1]

On 20 April, 1917, Freyberg left the battalion, issuing a special order as a parting message to the men:

I wish to express my great regret at terminating command of the Hood Battalion, which as you all know, I am most proud to be associated with.

I shall think of the two years and nine months spent with you as the happiest times of my life and that any success I have had as a commanding officer has been made possible by the loyalty and bravery shown by all ranks.

I am not any prouder to command you now than I was before the Ancre. I always trusted you and knew you would do well. It is, however, a fine thing to feel that we have proved to others our value as a fighting unit. I only wish that I could command you in the brigade I am going to. My thoughts will be often with you.[2]

Orders were issued that, in the forthcoming attack, some ranks were to be left behind and assembled in the unit's transport lines:

Officers
Each battalion
Second in command
Each company

> Either company commander or second in command. Not more than two company commanders will go in with their companies, and only 20 officers in all.

Each battalion
Two company sergeant-majors
One bombing instructor
Two Lewis gun instructors

Each company
One sergeant
One corporal
One lance-corporal
One signaller

Each platoon
One rifle-bomber
One scout and sniper
One Lewis gunner

A total of 69 officers, NCOs and specialist troops would thus remain behind.

The men were to go into battle without their greatcoats or packs, but haversacks were to be carried on the back, with waterproof sheets on the top, under the flap. Each had three sandbags under the braces, across the back. Box respirators were worn in the 'alert' position.

Ammunition consisted of not more than 120 rounds per man, with only 50 for bombers, signallers, scouts, runners, Lewis and machine gunners, Stokes mortar crews and carrying parties. Each bomber had 15 number 5 grenades, carried in buckets, waistcoats or sandbags. Rifle grenadiers were supplied with 15 number 23 grenades with rods and cartridges. All ranks had two number 5 grenades in each top pocket, with two aeroplane flares in the jacket side-pockets. Each company had 12 SOS rockets. The last two waves of each battalion carried picks and shovels, in the proportion of four shovels to one pick.

Prisoners of war were to be utilized in clearing the wounded from the battlefield and regimental aid posts, under a five per cent escort. Posts were established at selected spots to collect and return stragglers via the brigade dump to the line, after examination at the advanced dressing station to see if the delay was genuinely caused by injury or there was a need for subsequent disciplinary action.[3]

There was only one line of assembly trenches, so the GOC decided that successive waves should form up for the attack on tapes. Tape-pegs were laid down on the night of 21/22 April, and their alignment checked in daylight, but the tape itself was not laid until after dark on 22 April to avoid it being visible to the enemy front-line trench.

Patrols sent out on the night of 20/21 April reported that the wire in front of the point of attack was in many places intact, and still a serious obstacle. Patrols the next night came back with the same story, so divisional artillery was ordered to assist in the wire-cutting as far as their ammunition would allow.

The enemy front line was supposed to be completely obliterated for a distance of 500 yards north of the railway by artillery barrage on 22 April. This would relieve the troops holding the defensive flank from constant bombing attacks down the trench, but the guns were unsuccessful in carrying out their task.

On the afternoon of 22 April a special air reconnaissance reported that the artillery had cut several useful gaps in the wire. At 11.45pm that night, however, when the troops were forming up for the attack, a reliable patrol from the 189th Brigade returned from the wire reporting it quite undamaged and at least 20 feet thick for a distance of 250 yards in front of Drake Battalion on the right flank. The brigadier sent a message to HQ saying he considered it essential that the attack should be postponed until the wire had been cut.

A reply came back telling the brigadier that postponement was quite impossible and that the right battalion must be formed up opposite such gaps as existed and get through where they could. This was passed on to Drake's commander, who therefore decided to form up his men on a two-platoon frontage and pass them through in eight waves. He gave orders for the section of enemy trench opposite the uncut wire to be kept under Lewis gun and Stokes mortar fire as the troops were passing through the gap.

The troops were formed up for the assault without incident, and the enemy was unusually quiet. It later transpired that they were carrying out a relief at the time.

The 189th Brigade's plan of attack was that Drake on the right and Nelson on the left should lead, with Hood in support of Nelson. Hawke was in reserve, and some Hawke men would act as carrying parties. The brigade was to be the divisional reserve, with HQ situated in a railway cutting near the Bois de la Maison Blanche.

To the left of the 189th, the 190th Brigade formed up with the 4th Bedfordshire Regiment on the right and the 7th Royal Fusiliers on the left. The 1st HAC was in support, with the 10th Royal Dublin Fusiliers, and providing carrying parties.

The attack was launched at 4.45am, just before dawn on 23 April, 1917. The morning was fine, and the timing was perfect: it was just light enough for the men to see their way when they reached the wire. Thanks to the precautions taken by their commander, Drake was able to get through the wire on the right flank and take their first Blue Line objective without many casualties. Nelson and the 4th Bedfordshire were equally successful in the centre.

On the left the 7th Royal Fusiliers discovered practically uncut wire on the greater part of their front. Enemy machine guns opened up on them, plus heavy bombing from the German trenches, and within a few minutes they lost some 30 per cent of their troops, including almost all the officers. Thrown into confusion by these losses, the remainder nevertheless succeeded in entering the German line just to the left of the 4th Bedfordshire's flank, where they were immediately subjected to a bombing attack from the north. Despite this they got as far as the neighbourhood of Foxy Trench, where they were reinforced by one company of the 1st HAC. The loss of officers and subsequent confusion meant that no news was received from this left flank for about three hours, but as soon as the situation became clear a second company of HAC was sent forward to relieve the 7th Royal Fusiliers and capture the Blue Line as far north as the railway.[4]

Asquith's account of the battle is given in the Hood's war diary:

During the day I had tried to impart to company commanders (Lieutenant Asbury, A Company; Sub-Lieutenant Matcham, B Company; Lieutenant Morrison, C Company; and Lieutenant Tamplin, D Company) the details of the brigade operational order and the barrage timetable – 10 typewritten pages. I had previously gone through these orders with the OC of the Nelson in the morning. Company commanders thus had little time in which to filter details or orders through to the men.

At 11pm on 22 April the battalion moved off by companies, C and A picking up picks and shovels en route at the brigade dump. I had sent Lieutenant-Commander Ellis, my second in command, during the afternoon to see if the brigadier could see his way to altering Hood's hour of advance, as I foresaw that if we had to wait until zero plus 20 minutes the enemy barrage would be down on us. On the way up, at about 12 midnight, I called on the brigadier to ask again if this order could be altered, and that Hood be allowed to advance 200 yards in the rear of Nelson. He said no. It appeared from the latest air photos that the wire was only indifferently cut. He did not wish Hood to be on the heels of the Nelson and as a result be cut up with them if they were held up by uncut wire.

At 2.30am all companies reported that they were ready in their positions of assembly. Rum was issued. I then ordered Sub-Lieutenant Hill, the Lewis gun officer, to do liaison with the Nelsons and to come back and let me know whether they had succeeded in taking their first objective, so that I might be able to judge whether or not to wait till zero plus 20 minutes before advancing.

At 4.30am with a clear sky and with light beginning to come I took up position in the centre of our leading wave. At 4.45am, zero, our barrage opened, which was fairly light, the Nelsons and Drakes were invisible owing to smoke and dust. The enemy guns began to answer almost immediately, on and about our assembly position.

By 4.55am the enemy barrage was intense and machine-gun fire was audible. Sub-Lieutenant Hill was not back. I therefore decided it was not worth while hanging about in full blast of the enemy barrage, so I led on, and sent back word to the rear companies to follow. By 5am we reached the enemy front line, which was fairly well cut. The second line wire was, however, little cut. In neither case did this wire provide serious obstacles to slow movement. Had it been necessary to rush any particular point, it would have embarrassed rapid movement.

Our heavy guns and some 18-pounders had got behindhand and were dropping shells short. The men were inclined to bunch and to rush on too precipitately. As a result I sent a party uphill to the right to prevent crowding. The battalion halted and the remainder were reorganized on the Blue (second) enemy line, where we collected and sent back about 20 prisoners. We advanced again slowly and half right through the villages to the Yellow Line. The enemy were still sniping at our men from cottages. They were fired at by our men and rushed, and a good deal of mixed fighting at 20 yards range took place. The enemy were still sending up red rain rockets from these cottages, which some of the Nelson and our men had passed. A few of our guns were still firing short and were causing casualties among our own men.

At 5.40am at the Yellow Line we reorganized. The street was crowded with Nelsons and Hoods in addition to about 100 Bedfords of the 190th Brigade, who should have been north of the main Arras-Fresnes road, defending our left flank. I collected their three officers and asked to move north of the road, so as to defend our flank. I warned all I could that the barrage does not move forward till 6.01am This pause of 20 minutes is a great mistake, giving the enemy a breathing space just when we have them on the run. Our barrage at this range was becoming rather ragged.[5]

Joe Murray takes up his account of the battle:

The instruction went that we were not to move until the barrage had lifted off the German front line, immediately in front of Gavrelle. Well any old campaigner knows that to wait until the barrage moves and have three or four hundred yards to walk is simply murder, because as soon as the barrage opens and they realize an attack is coming they start to shell the reserves. Asquith, instead of waiting until the barrage had lifted, took us forward – I think to within about 50 yards of the barrage. His judgement was perfect, and we were on their line before Jerry knew anything about it. I honestly think that we men of the Hood who survived the battle owe it to Asquith ignoring orders – and the orders were quite definite.

Anyhow, we got mixed up: fighting in a village is different from fighting in the open. The ground in front of us and Gavrelle was not pock-marked with shellholes like the Somme; it was quite level and open. Ideal territory for tanks, but we didn't have any. We could go forward more or less in a line, whereas on the Somme you were in and out of shellholes that were all over the place. When we got into the village it was different. Jerries were in the cellars and we were in the open, and by then it was quite light, so we were perfect targets.

In the village there were bricks flying about, rifle and machine-gun fire. You couldn't keep in any formation. Sometimes you got under a half blown-down house, and other times you got over the top. The wire in front was piled up in heaps, as it usually was by an artillery bombardment. We had to keep gathering together to get past a particular place. However, you could not climb over the 10 to 15 feet of bricks that had formed.

I remember as we got to the first objective it didn't seem too bad. We seemed to be organized, but when we got to the second objective, a road that runs through the village, oh, dear me! There was no line and no sort of direction. You couldn't see any officers and you couldn't see any men. Sometimes there were three or four together, and sometimes you were on your own, wondering where everybody had got to. When I got into this trench, which was just in front of a road, about 10 to 15 yards from it, I came across an officer lying down. He was lying flat and I remember trying to undo some barbed wire on what was left of one of his legs. He was a sub-lieutenant. I also remember turning him over and there was a sort of a grin on his face, which was red because of the brick dust, as well as the blood. Because of the smoke and dust, you had to spit all the time – you just couldn't help it – and you also kept rubbing your eyes.

The next thing was to get on to the road. The mayor's house was somewhere up this road, and there was a church there. So we made for the mayor's house, at which time there were four of us or maybe five; some to the front and some to the left, but no sign of any organized advance. Just before I got to the mayor's house I was fooling around trying to get over an old door of a house. As I stood on the damned thing I slipped forward. As I went forward I saw a rifle from a cellar, but I could only see the barrel. I saw it move. Instinctively I turned quickly to the left and fired. I had a revolver (as an NCO Lewis gunner I was entitled to one), but I always carried my rifle. I didn't need to see the smoke from his rifle to know that I had been hit. My hand was in my pocket and the bullet went through my wrist. I couldn't get my hand out of my pocket – paralysed! I couldn't get it out.

I crawled forward to where the rifle was, not more than three or four feet. There was old Jerry in a cellar, and I had blown half his head away. I happened to be quickest on the draw, but I hadn't taken any aim. I got into the cellar, having him for company. There was then a shell burst, very close. There were doors and window-frames flying about across the entrance. I thought to myself, I am going to be buried here. I crawled to make an entrance; I couldn't at first, but eventually I did. Blood was running down my trouser-leg with excruciating pain. I have often heard it said that sometimes people are wounded and they don't know that they have been. That may be all right if it's a flesh wound, but when it hits the bone and the exit is three or four times bigger than the entrance hole it's different. I tried to get my rifle off, but I still couldn't get my hand out of my pocket; I thought to myself, I have got to get out of this, somehow![6]

Asquith's account continues:

At 6.01am the forward barrage is said to be moving at the rate of 100 yards in each four minutes, ahead of us, but it is difficult to distinguish where exactly the ragged line of shell-bursts, among roofs and cottages, has reached. On emerging from the east side of the village we were held up by machine-gun and sniping fire from a trench about 150 yards due east of the mayor's house; also by two or three machine guns in the open country 600–800 yards due east of the cemetery; and from an enemy strongpoint on commanding ground north of the main road. These positions had not been silenced by our guns. Our heavy guns were still dropping a number of shells amongst us.

Drakes, about 200 yards south of the cemetery, had found and occupied a freshly-dug trench, running north-north-east. The buildings of the mayor's house, and the strip of strongly-fenced ornamental garden south of it, presented an insuperable obstacle to frontal attack on the enemy trench due east of the mayor's house. Some of us pushed up a ditch in hopes of outflanking this enemy trench. This ditch is very shallow and at one point it is necessary to jump out over a metre gauge railway, under strong sniping at close range. The helmets of 20 to 30 Germans could be seen in this trench. Four of us went up the ditch. Lieutenant Charles Asbury and one of the two men were shot dead. It became evident that the heads of enemy occupants of this trench must be kept down if the trench were to be attacked by a flanking rush.

I therefore went up the street towards the mayor's house. I found we had a Lewis gun just in the rear of it and another north of the road, 20 to 30 yards further east. I led some men into the mayor's house and occupied it, taking 10 German prisoners, some of them NCOs sleeping or shamming sleep in the two cellars. I established snipers in the upper storey, from which an excellent view could be obtained of the helmets of the enemy manning the trench due east of the house. These we sniped with good effect. I placed a Lewis gun and snipers in other parts of the house and handed its defence over to Sub-Lieutenant Cooke of the Hood, acting brigade intelligence officer, with orders to harass the enemy as much as possible. Later in the morning he led a Lewis gun team out into the open, to try to get at the enemy occupants of the trench from closer quarters. He and all his team, except

237

Charlton, became casualties. Charlton maintained himself alone for five hours, causing the enemy considerable casualties. Then, his ammunition running out, he withdrew.

It had become clear to me by now that we could not push out into the open country to the east before dark. I found about 200 Nelsons and Hoods crowding about behind the buildings of the street that leads to the cemetery. I therefore sent 50 Hoods back to the Blue Line under Sub-Lieutenant Matcham and set all remaining vagrant Hoods and Nelsons to dig themselves in north and south, connecting up the ditches in an empty piece of sandy ground with many convenient shellholes in it, and not too much bricks and mortar at hand. Before this I had set Hoods to dig in along the east side of the cemetery road. I also placed a Lewis gun and some rifles at the east end of the cemetery.

I then went by the much-sniped cemetery road to see Lieutenant-Commander Bennett, OC of the Drake; but I saw that his trench was so congested that it would take me too long to reach him, so I returned, past two blazing enemy dug-outs.

At 10am I found Colonel Lewis, OC Nelson, at the west end of a ditch. Lines and driblets of enemy began to make their appearance, advancing over the plain from the east, north-east and south-east. About 10.30am our barrage reopened, rather short of the oncoming enemy lines. Some ran back but most of them came on, and disappeared into a trench or hollow about 800 yards to our east front. Those north of the main Arras road could and did get to the high ground within about 200 yards of the north-east corner of the village.[7]

Murray takes up his story again:

I thought to myself, I have got to get out, and the pain did seem to ease up a bit. I was hopping about from one pile of bricks to another. I got to the original German line, but I couldn't recognize it at all! Off I went, and further along I jumped into a shellhole, and there was a German youngster there. Oh, dear me! I can see him now; he couldn't have been 18. He was looking at me with a kind of a stare, just hopeless. Of course I had my revolver in my hand, and I put it to his head. Honestly, why I didn't fire I haven't the faintest idea. I actually touched his forehead. I thought to myself, no, no. The bloke never moved: he was frozen stiff. I kept him covered all the time. I don't know how long we were there – some time, because they started shelling again, getting pretty close.

He looked at me and I said something to him, making signs. He was frightened, but I wanted him to get my rifle off. All of a sudden a blinking shell landed, very close. I went forward and I was lying on his lap, with my rifle across it, all mixed up. I didn't laugh, dear me, no. He helped me up. I said, 'Come on, lift it'. So he lifted up the rifle. He looked at me as if scared stiff to move, but then beckoned that he had something in his pocket. I went to his pocket and found that he had a dirty old rag, like a big handkerchief. I said, 'Come on, come on, that's fine.' But as blood was on my trousers he thought that I had been wounded in the thigh. I said, 'No, no, no, not there,' and I showed him where the wound was.

All of a sudden it dawned on him, and he put his hand on my trousers and tore the pocket off. I got my hand out; the pocket was saturated with blood. That was fine, and I put my rifle to one side. He started bandaging me up. He wanted to put my hand into a sling, because I still couldn't move my arm. So he got the handkerchief and undid my tunic. It was funny – I let him! He undid the top button and threaded the handkerchief through this first buttonhole, tied a knot in it, and he was able to put my hand upwards into this short sling. As soon as he did that I felt much better, but it was still painful. It had seemed to be burning, but now at least I had lost this burning feeling.

Now we had to get back. We had to hop from one shellhole to another. We had to get at least 600 yards before we came to the division's front line and our original trench; but it had been so badly shelled you couldn't tell where it was. That's why I say Asquith saved us by getting us out of that place. I honestly believe that had he not been the Prime Minister's son he would have been awarded the VC. Really and truly he was a great man; he knew all about it.

Anyhow, we kept going. It must have been half an hour later when we got into a shellhole and I felt myself dozing off. I was exhausted, what with loss of blood and tiredness. When I did get a move on, I was very groggy and kept falling down. The German lifted me up and arm in arm we went on – me and the bloke I had intended to kill a little while ago. We came to a railway cutting and I remember sliding down, both arm in arm. I thought, now we are all right. Apart from shells there are no rifle bullets, nothing. I must have gone to sleep, and when I got up I remember seeing trees, thinking that's the Arras-Gavrelle road and that's where I want to be. I was far enough out of the line now to chance walking towards Arras.

We went towards the roadway and there was a great big dug-out, a smashing place, originally Jerry's. An old sergeant came along: 'Hallo mate, you're beat, aren't you, mate?' They brought me out a cup of tea. I drank part of it, giving the rest to my mate the Jerry. I remember sitting down with four or five men, who I think were artillery. They wanted to ask me questions, but didn't do so as they knew that I was half dopey. We just sat there for some time and the cup of tea seemed to give me new life.

I wanted to get away from the front. Shells were coming, just a few. There was traffic on the road: if they could chance it, so could I. So eventually we got on to the road and began walking along, looking for the dressing station. In about five to six minutes a sergeant came dashing out, with his buttons brightly polished, and a good crease in his trousers, and his artillery boots up to his knee. He got hold of the Jerry fellow, saying, 'I'll see this bastard off.' I said, 'Whoa, whoa, whoa.' He said, 'No, that's all right mate, that's all right.' I said to him, 'Leave him alone, leave him alone!' 'No, no, I'll see to this bastard.' That's all he could say. I said, 'Now look, he has helped me quite a lot. Without him I wouldn't have got here.' However, he would keep on getting hold of the German. So I got my revolver out of my holster and I acted as if to see that it was loaded, pointing it at the sergeant. As soon as he saw this off he went and I saw no more of him. I have never seen anybody skidaddle as he did. Honestly, I felt like shooting him, as without my prisoner I would not have got half of the distance.

Eventually we got to the casualty clearing station. As we went in there was a sergeant at the door. I said, 'Wait a minute, sergeant. I nearly shot one of your clan down the road because he messed about with my fellow here; this chappy has helped me.' He said, 'Never mind that; sit down.' I sat down on a box with my prisoner next to me and was given a lovely cup of tea, hot, sweet tea. They also brought one for my prisoner. After about 10 minutes the sergeant said, 'You have got to hand your prisoner over.' I replied, 'Of course I will hand him over.' He said, 'I want your rifle and your revolver.' I said, 'Sergeant, look, how about the prisoner?' He replied, 'I have got to hand him over to the officer, and I give my word that he will not be harmed here. We will look after him.' I then shook hands with my prisoner and said, 'Best of luck, old boy.' He said something to me, and with that we parted.[8]

Asquith continues his account:

At 10.53am Colonel Lewis of the Nelsons received a signal, timed about 9am, from brigade ordering him and the Hoods to advance at 10.30am for about 300 yards. The 10.30am barrage which was to cease at 11.15am was to help us make this advance, not, as we had supposed, to impede the massing of the enemy opposite us. We decided that it was too late to attempt to do anything with this barrage. It was out of the question to organize any further attack in the remaining 22 minutes of barrage, even if the barrage had succeeded in quietening the snipers and machine guns on our front and north-east of us, which it had not. We sent back word to this effect.

OC Drake sent me a note about this time saying enemy were advancing in large numbers, could I send him a company. I sent Sub-Lieutenant Sennitt to tell him that they were also advancing on our front, and I did not wish to send a company by my only road to him, the exposed cemetery road. But I was close, and standing by to help him at any time. At this time we thought the enemy intended an immediate counter-attack. It was hot and cloudless. The troops were drowsy, tired and apathetic, it was difficult to stimulate them into any sort of energy or interest. The enemy had been shelling the western half of the village very heavily and were throwing some shells into our eastern part of it. Our own heavies dropped shell after shell into the buildings of the mayor's house which he held, forcing Sub-Lieutenant Grant Dalton, now commanding there in place of Sub-Lieutenant Cooke, to send away some of his garrison, and to put the rest in the cellars. I was anxious for our north and north-east flank, so I went north of the main Arras road to reconnoitre.

Here I met OC Bedfords, who had one platoon in the sunken road, who were outsniped from a cottage. He had another platoon near the church and placed these facing north. He did not know where the rest of his battalion was. All day I saw no other signs of 190th Brigade, who were supposed to be guarding our north flank. The ground rises perhaps 30 feet in 100 yards north of the Arras road, all along the north flank of the village. The enemy sniping from superior positions was vigorous all along this flank, and left us blind here. I returned to OC Nelson to find that two of my best company commanders, Lieutenants James Morrison and Gerald Tamplin, had been killed by one shell on the road at the west end of ditch A. Enemy shelling hereabouts was heavy: they were still massing by feeding their men over the plain by driblets on our east front.

During the forenoon one of our contact aeroplanes flew over. We lit flares to show our positions. Lieutenant Wainwright brought his Stokes mortars to bear on the extreme north-east cottage, from which we had been given trouble. He drove out the occupants, but soon ran short of ammunition. An enemy car drove up to within 150 yards of the mayor's house; it was Lewis-gunned by us, turned round revealing a red cross, picked up an officer from the trench east of the mayor's house, and drove back to Fresnes.

Our MO, Surgeon McCracken, left his stretcher-bearers and those of the Drake to clean up the Blue Line. He pushed forward with his orderly into the village and impressed the services of a German MO, two NCOs and 12 German Red Cross men who he found being led to the rear under escort. He established himself and them in a good cellar which had been the German RAP, and before 1am on 24 April had brought in and dealt with about 150 of our wounded, who would otherwise have been left out all day where they lay, and would probably have been blown to pieces or buried by falling houses.

All messages to and from the front line, from Hood, Nelson and Drake, passed through my advanced battalion HQ, where Lieutenant Hilton, adjutant of this battalion, was established and where he provided Hood runners.

Lieutenant James Hilton was later mentioned in despatches for his services. There were so many acts of bravery during the battalion's advance that not all can be told; as just one example, Asquith included the tale of Sub-Lieutenant George Mitchelmore in his list of recommendations for gallantry awards:

> While consolidation and the enemy counter-attacks were in progress T/Sub-Lieutenant Lionel George Mitchelmore, RNVR, as the transport officer, succeeded in bringing up in broad daylight by the Arras-Gavrelle road, under heavy enemy barrage, a convoy of pack animals with water for those on the firing line. He lost four men and four animals en route, and was himself wounded in the hand, but pushed forward with admirable determination and as a result delivered his loads in the village within 300 yards of the enemy's advanced elements.

Asquith's war diary continues:

> After noon the Germans continued to advance, sometimes still in driblets, sometimes in long lines at wide extension coming over the plain from north-east, east and south-east. I was very anxious about our blind north flank, protected only by two weak platoons of Bedfords. I suggested to OC Nelson that he should send two platoons to help them, which he did. Sub-Lieutenant Lawrence Matcham returned and was useful in helping Sub-Lieutenant Grant Dalton to organize the defence from Arras road to ditch A. Sub-Lieutenant Lamb was trying to link up shell-holes south of a point in ditch A about on a line with the forward fence of the mayor's house garden. Sub-Lieutenant Gibson was helping Sub-Lieutenant Matcham. Twelve Hood officers had become casualties. The four above were the only ones I had left forward of the Blue Line (except Sub-Lieutenant Hill, who had been with the Drakes since the attack; he rejoined me after dark).
>
> At 4.30pm orders reached OC Nelson, OC Drake and me to name our own time for a barrage to enable us to push out 300-400 yards

east and north-east. This order had taken about three hours to reach us. We all agreed that the situation did not admit to any further offensive action. After dark we could dig in to make our line conform to that of the Drakes. There was an enemy observer plane at very low altitude observing our positions for much of the afternoon, but no sign of our planes since morning. There were no signs of our machine gunners either.

At sunset we had expected the enemy to attack at dusk. Shortly before dusk some of his advancing lines were caught by our artillery. A good many scuttled for cover. We got into some with Lewis guns from the cemetery and down the main Arras road. Between 10pm until midnight the Howe Battalion relieved the Hood who withdrew under heavy shellfire to the trenches near to Point du Jour.[9]

The Hood had suffered considerable casualties:

Killed	Officers 7	Other ranks 27
Wounded	Officers 5	Other ranks 134
Missing	Officers –	Other ranks 8

The officers involved were:

Killed	T/Lieutenant Gerald Tamplin
	T/Lieutenant James Morrison
	T/Lieutenant Charles Asbury
	T/Sub-Lieutenant Arthur Stanley Cooke
	T/Sub-Lieutenant R. V. Cleves
	T/Sub-Lieutenant Claude Sennitt (died of wounds)
	T/Sub-Lieutenant Thomas Cross (died of wounds)
Wounded	T/Sub-Lieutenant Frederick Willy
	T/Sub-Lieutenant Arthur Wyrill
	T/Sub-Lieutenant Percy Pyman
	T/Sub-Lieutenant Oscar Allston
	T/Sub-Lieutenant Lionel Mitchelmore
	T/Sub-Lieutenant Donald Bailey[10]

Thomas MacMillan, the 189th Brigade clerk, continues his account:

The enemy had been completely cleared from the village, but fresh troops could be seen mustering in all directions for a counter attack, which our battalion commanders prepared to meet.

Almost all telegraph lines between advanced brigade HQ and battalions had been cut by the German artillery fire, while astute

Boches had blocked our wireless sets and rendered them useless. Visual signalling was an impossibility on account of gun smoke, so that all communication to and from the scene of the fighting had to pass over the few artillery lines which remained intact, or be conveyed by runners. As the intervening ground was swept by fire, the brave runners who managed to worm their way through were often delayed so long as to render their orders useless.

From zero hour the brigade major had done everything in his power to ensure smooth working, but the destruction of the signal lines had upset his plans considerably. By 6.30pm it was impossible to determine the exact positions of the battalions, whereupon he ordered a contact aeroplane to fly over the ground and report. The plane flew low, and in response to its klaxon horn seven flares were lit. These were plotted with wonderful precision by the observer, and the plane made off at top speed to its station. Within an hour of the plane setting off, the exact location of the flares had been wired to advance brigade HQ.

The major plotted the particulars on three copies of a Gavrelle village map and sent them by special runners to battalion commanders for identification. Commander Bennett identified the three flares on the right, Commander Asquith the two centre flares, and Colonel Lewis the two on the left. By connecting the plotting Major Barnett determined the approximate line held by the brigade and wired the information to divisional HQ, whence it was transmitted to the HQ of First Army. Following on this came news of the failure of the 111th Brigade on our right, and a wire was received direct from First Army HQ ordering us to hold on to Gavrelle, the key to Arras, at all costs.

The right flank of the Drake Battalion was now in the air through the failure of the 111th Brigade, and we were in danger of being forced to yield the ground we had so gallantly fought for and won. All reserve machine guns were therefore rushed forward and a defensive flank was formed in time to meet the German counter-attacking troops.

A hostile aeroplane flew over the front and signalled to the German artillery, who concentrated on the village with all the venom they possessed. When the fire cleared, the counter-attacking troops came on, but were caught in the open and decimated by our artillery and machine-gun fire.

The hard fighting began to tell on the Hoods, and in response to an appeal for relief the Howe Battalion of the 188th Brigade was brought forward to replace them.

At dawn on 24 April our positions were bombarded relentlessly, whilst throughout the day the bombardments were repeated with such frequency that it seemed as if the enemy intended to blast us out of the village. When the fire lifted to our back areas, however, wave after wave of German infantry pressed forward, and counter-attack succeeded counter-attack. Our artillery were now functioning as never before. No sooner was each attack launched than they placed a heavy barrage behind the advancing columns, which crept towards our lines and met a protective barrage placed in front of our own positions. Through this inferno our men poured rifle and machine-gun fire.

In all, seven organized attacks were met in this manner. When at last the guns were stilled and the air was clear again, out in the open fields lay the mangled remains of thousands of our adversaries, while here and there a solitary figure was seen to stagger, and fall to rise no more. Gavrelle was ours.[11]

CHAPTER TWENTY-THREE

Passchendaele

After the battle of Gavrelle, MacMillan continues the story:

The army commander was impatient for particulars to be sent to London, and a special message was sent to battalions for information regarding war material captured.

The first report to arrive was from Commander Asquith, who sent a slip of paper on which these words were written: 'The half of Gavrelle village'. This was construed as contempt, and the general was so upset that he sent for Asquith.

The commander duly arrived, but as the brigade office did not offer sufficient privacy he was taken outside for his telling-off. I dropped my work and observed both men closely. The general was laying down the law as he paced backwards and forwards, whilst Asquith followed at his heels looking pale but unrepentant. How the matter ended I cannot say, but neither seemed at all pleased on parting . . . .

All battalions were therefore returned fit for offensive action and on 4 May, 1917, we 'embussed' and were hurried to the village of Roclincourt – or to all that remained of it, for scarcely a stone was left standing. The Germans had so far taken leave of themselves as to dig a maze of trenches in the civilian cemetery, thus exposing the dead to wind and weather.

Fortunately for our lads, the enemy ceased to threaten, and all hands were employed in the preparation of a new defensive trench system which was calculated to make Arras impregnable. Our peaceful occupation of the line continued from week to week. [The Hood Battalion garrisoned a windmill position during this time.]

Asquith was given special instructions on the precautions to be taken for the defence of this position; but, being on the spot, and being much better informed than his advisers, he had not complied with the orders to the letter. This was considered a grievous fault and correction was conveyed by private communication. I only became aware of the friction when the entire correspondence was handed to me with instructions to guard it carefully and allow no curious eye to look upon it. There was a covert hint that the matter need not concern me overmuch.

As I folded the correspondence before stowing it away on my person, my eye caught the last communication, which was from Asquith. It was characteristically brief and bold, the purport being that he was prepared to defend his action before any court the general cared to convene. This troubled me, and the opinion I previously held that there was a 'set' against Asquith grew stronger.

Not many days afterwards, Winston Churchill arrived at divisional headquarters. Asquith sent a polite note asking to be relieved for two days in order that he might proceed to division to meet him. This was agreed to without demur; but before he returned to his battalion I was instructed to hand back the correspondence entrusted to me, as the matter was now considered closed . . . .

Too often the success in life of a man is due to the fact that he is the son of his father. This could not be said of Commander Asquith. Here was one who was master of life's rough and tumble and one who seemed fated to bear more crosses than his own.

Commander Asquith, as he appeared to me, could not by nature do anything underhand, and although I was unable to point the finger at any man or men who were exploiting their brief authority over him, inwardly I now felt convinced that he had enemies behind our lines who gave him more concern than those who wore the dull grey and sought to close with him in battle. Yet, despite the fact of his father's eminence, he seemed to scorn the idea of seeking help from that quarter against the people who were getting at him from behind. Perhaps he felt his father's cross was already enough for an ageing man to bear.[1]

Patrick Shaw-Stewart, of those distant days of Gallipoli and the *Grantully Castle*, had meanwhile been making attempts to leave his staff position at Salonica and rejoin his old companions in the Hood. On leave in England he had found that his health was poor, due to the climate in Macedonia. On 24 February, 1917, he wrote from London:

After I got the Salonica answer from the War Office, refusing to release me, I thought it was finished. But after talking to the RND people, I thought I might play my inside. I really don't know whether I was right, but I did feel a strong impulse to do everything to avoid going back to the absurd Salonica. So I got . . . to put my troubles (quite real ones) on paper, and applied to the War Office for a medical board. This has now been granted, but they haven't named a day, only ordered me to wait here in the meantime. So everything depends on the board. If they say there's not much the matter with me I shall go to Salonica after all; if they say I'm not fit for the east they will (I suppose) pass me fit for general service barring that, and then I shall be able to get back to the RND. I hope you don't think it's silly or perverse of me; you know I've wanted to go back for some time.

On 3 March, 1917, Shaw-Stewart wrote from Oxford:

I have had my board yesterday morning, and they passed me for general service with the recommendation that I should not be sent back east. That was my own suggestion: they would quite certainly have passed me for anything I jolly well liked. That being so, I shall in a day or two probably be informed of it officially by the War Office, whereupon I will communicate with Freyberg, who will apply for me.

Matters proceeded to Shaw-Stewart's satisfaction, and by 24 April he was part of a course at Le Touquet:

I can't honestly say I think it's teaching me very much I haven't known by heart these three years back, except perhaps a little about gas and bomb-throwing; but there is a terrible lot of indifferent lecturing out of books and old-fashioned sloping of arms, which I really thought I had undergone once and for all at the Crystal Palace. No doubt it is extremely good for the soul of a veteran like me to be marched about in fours and told to be in by 9pm, but occasionally one is tempted to forget how comic it all is, and also how tolerable.

Ronald Knox's book on Patrick Shaw-Stewart gives a good comment of the times:

It was generally agreed that 1917 was the most dispiriting period of the war; we had lost most of our old illusions, and the time had not yet come when we were to draw our breath and then sigh it out again in relief at the tidings of victory. We all tended to live more for the moment, to clutch at the creature comforts that were vanishing from our tables. In France itself, hopes were less buoyant among the troops, and doggedness had to replace the will to victory.

Shaw-Stewart rejoined the Hood at last, and wrote on 18 May, 1917:

Having now actually inhabited the same place for a fortnight, the battalion is beginning to make itself reasonably comfortable. We most of us inhabit old Boche dugouts of the real picture-paper kind, incredibly deep and really wonderfully spacious dugouts in which the gentle German obviously intended to pass the remainder of his days, while missiles from Britain and suchlike fell harmlessly over his head. Personally, I get claustrophobia in these dungeons, and so inhabit a bivouac with my second in command. Though the last few nights I have slightly doubted my wisdom, since the weather has broken. However, I haven't actually been flooded yet: and am triumphantly sticking to my bed, the wise OC having ordained that each 'company headquarters' may possess a bed and a bath. It just shows how prudent it is to travel as heavy as possible till you are gradually stripped, and then buy a new lot.[2]

MacMillan continues his story:

For weeks we figured in inter-brigade reliefs in a line which was now comparatively quite. Any trouble that arose was mainly of our own seeking, for we dominated no-man's-land and gave the enemy very little peace. All work of repair which he attempted was invariably spotted by our observers, and the artillery, Lewis and machine guns made all such work difficult and dangerous of execution. In addition the artillery carried out intensive destruction shoots on the enemy trench system and back areas. Dumps were set on fire at regular intervals, and the German garrison lost much of their rest in repairing the damage done to their communications and fire trenches.

It looked as if we were having it all our own way when one quiet, sunny afternoon a stray German shell found its way into a large pit filled to the brim with trench mortar bombs of the largest calibre. We were in the line at the time, and although the pit was a long way behind, so great and prolonged was the din created that I thought it betokened the end of all things.

Our divisional HQ was situated not very far from the dump. I heard that the roofs of their huts had been blown off, and that some of their tents had disappeared into thin air. Yet, despite this havoc, the bright ones at division had the sauce to broadcast that there had not been any casualties; and, in order to set our minds at ease on their account, they moved miles to the rear and advised all concerned that their new headquarters would be known as 'Victory Camp'.

On 18 September, 1917, the division was withdrawn from the Arras sector and, after a short rest, entrained for the Ypres salient.

The salient was no great distance from Arras. As usual, open horse boxes accommodated the other ranks and, as all vehicles were filled to capacity, both doors were kept open in order to prevent our being asphyxiated.

Herzeele is one of the northernmost towns of France, and during the war was a point of assembly for troops about to take part in the struggle before Ypres. I was impressed by the tidiness of the place, and by the solemn demeanour of the inhabitants. At length the call came to leave Herzeele and we hurried by bus to the Ypres Salient. On route I was impressed by the feverish activity.

The usual information about battalion strengths was forwarded to division, but more concern than usual was shown regarding the reserve officers. The battalions had been instructed to render a statement giving names of the officers who would participate in the next fight, and as the lists arrived I took them to the major. His eagle eye observed that the officer who had acted as Prisoner's Friend to the young man who was 'shot at dawn' was on the reserve list. At this his monkey rose, and in his most unbearing manner he told me to instruct the battalion commander concerned to send the 'hard-faced bastard' forward. But the young gent thus referred to knew all the tricks of his trade. On being informed of brigade's intentions concerning him, he promptly developed a raging temperature and as promptly was evacuated to England.

The weather was of the vilest description when we moved forward to the Ypres Salient and fixed our 189th Brigade HQ at Dirty Bucket Corner. A more appropriate name could not have been found for the place. There was mud to the right of us, mud to the left of us, with mud and slush as far as the eye could see. The whole countryside was marred in an abominable way by our own shells and by the enemy, who delighted in frightfulness. The captured documents sent to us for perusal were so seldom without the word 'annihilate' that one might have imagined the Germans considered the term synonymous with 'damnation', and the hellish salient, the Valley of the Shadow, which they had prepared for us.

Monster Gothas circled overhead and straddled the ground with heavy bombs. On the nights when sleep was not overpowering I lay awake listening to the confusion which their bombing created. I could hear the tooting of motor horns, the sounds of drivers of limber wagons, and the patter of their horses' hoofs in their wild scamper to clear the Menin Road, which was the principal objective of the air attacks. What between bombs and shells and gas, this road must have been the most perilous highway in any of the theatres of the war.

When all was ready for action we moved forward to the banks of Yser Canal, where the new general found us. After wallowing on the mud banks of the Yser for some days we received a movement order, and the battalion moved into battle position. The 189th Brigade HQ to be a captured pill-box called Hubner Farm.

The afternoon was well advanced when we arrived at the point on the Menin Road where a runner was posted, whose duty it was to conduct us to the pill-box. The intervening ground, from the point where we left the road to Hubner Farm, presented the most Godforsaken spectacle I had seen so far or perhaps ever shall see. We had to proceed cautiously over the greasy duck-board track, on each side of which the day's casualties lay half-buried in the mud. Occasionally we halted in order to negotiate some awkward bend on the track; to have lost a footing might have meant slow and certain death from drowning in a waterlogged shell-hole.

The clayey soil had been pulped by the enemy's artillery, while continuous rain had transformed every shellhole into a muddy pool. Succeeding salvoes had enlarged the shellholes, and in one of the largest of them I discovered all that remained of a battery of our field artillery. Men and horses, half-submerged, eyed us with a glassy stare, and the brown water ran red with their blood.[3]

The report of the 63rd (RN) Division east of Ypres during the period 24 October to 5 November, 1917, outlines the situation:

On the understanding that the division would be required to fight three battles, each on a one brigade front, it was decided to employ the 188th Infantry Brigade first, then the 189th, and lastly the 190th, which, owing to the presence of two inexperienced battalions, was most in need of training. The troops were accordingly disposed in the new area in this order, the 188th Infantry Brigade being located in the camp (Dirty Bucket Camp) nearest to the front, the 189th at Herzeele, and the 190th at Zermazeele.

On 4 October information was received that the division would probably be given 14 days training, but that one infantry brigade was requested immediately for work in the forward area for about a week. The 189th Infantry Brigade was selected for this duty, as it was not due to go into action until after the 188th Infantry Brigade and was less in need of training than the 190th. The 188th and 189th Infantry Brigades accordingly exchanged camps on 6 October, the 189th moving forward to Dirty Bucket, and the 188th being withdrawn to the Herzeele area. The following day the 190th Brigade was moved from the Zermazeele to the Houtkerque area.

From this date until they moved to the forward area on 23 and 24 October respectively the 188th and 190th Brigades carried out intensive training. Special attention was paid to attack formations suitable for local conditions in Flanders, and to the policy of allotting definite units for the capture of every known or suspected strongpoint, this point to be the final objective of the troops detailed to capture it. Unfortunately the training areas available for battalions were very inadequate, and were so scattered as to make supervision by the brigadiers a matter of great difficulty; nevertheless much useful experience was gained, and all ranks profited greatly by their 14 days' work.

Owing to the fluctuations of the battle the objectives allotted to the division had frequently to be changed, but on 18 October definite instructions were received for the attack by the 188th Brigade.

From this date this brigade was able to train for the capture of definite objectives, and each battalion commander marked out his allotted areas on such ground as was available, and definitely detailed each unit of his command for the particular duty it would be required to carry out in the attack. Each battalion also made for itself a large-scale model of the area to be attacked. Much ingenuity was shown in the construction of these models, and they were visited daily by large numbers of NCOs and men in their spare time, all ranks showing great keenness in discussing their various tasks.

Similar training was also undergone by the 190th Brigade, which was to carry on the attack from the final objective of the 188th. But it was to be found that owing to this brigade not securing all its objectives the eventual tasks of the 190th were to be different from those practised, but in spite of this unavoidable chance at the last moment, it was found that this special training was of a great value to all ranks.

The 190th Brigade had meanwhile continued to be employed on the construction of roads, railways, and duckboard tracks in the forward area. The majority of their work was carried out under shellfire, and the Hood and Hawke Battalions in particular sustained considerable casualties in the neighbourhood of St Julien and the Triangle, where the enemy's artillery was extremely active during the period 14 to 20 October. The Hood Battalion was eventually relieved from this duty on 20 October, the Hawke and Nelson Battalions on 23 October, and the Drake on 28 October.

Throughout this period the divisional staff made frequent reconnaissances of the area in which the division was to be engaged, and, with a view to selecting the most favourable positions of assembly, a careful record was kept of the barrage put down by the enemy in the forward area.

On 19 October it was decided that the first day on which the division would be required to fight was 25 October and the XVIII

Corps left to the division the choice as to which day it should take over the line. Application was therefore made to be allowed to relieve the 9th Division on the night of 24/25 October, thus giving the assaulting troops the maximum amount of training, while assuring for them a complete day in the front line in which to pick up their bearings and recognize their various objectives. Arrangements were also made for company commanders and representatives of each attacking platoon to be sent into the line on the night of 22/23 October, to be attached for 24 hours to their opposite numbers in the division to be relieved.

The 188th Brigade moved by bus route to the forward area on 23 October, and was followed by the 190th on 24 October.

The first objective allocated to the relieving troops was a line running roughly parallel to the Paddebeek stream and 100 yards to the west of it. This objective was some 1,000 yards from the kicking-off line. The second objective, a line parallel to the first objective, was 500 yards further forward. The RND report continues:

On 24 October the 188th Brigade took over the line from the 27th Infantry Brigade without incident, the Anson Battalion being on the right and the 1st Royal Marines on the left. The 2nd Royal Marines were in support and the Howe Battalion in reserve.

Two battalions of the 189th Brigade were attached to the 188th for the operation, the Hood Battalion as a counter-attacking battalion, and the Hawke as a brigade reserve, not to be used without the sanction of divisional headquarters. The counter-attacking battalion was to be our line. The time for moving it forward and the time for launching it in a counter-attack were to be left to the discretion of the battalion commander.

The frontages allotted to each attacking battalion were in accordance with the comparative difficulty of their tasks. On the right, where the ground was slightly higher, and most opposition was expected, the Anson Battalion was given a frontage of 550 yards, while on the left, where the ground was boggy, and only lightly held by the enemy, the 1st Royal Marines were allotted a frontage of 1,000 yards. These battalions were to be closely followed by the Howe and the 2nd Royal Marines respectively, which would pass through them on the line or the first objective and attack and consolidate the second.

The night of 25/26 October was brilliantly fine, but at 3.30am on 26 October the weather suddenly broke and rain was continuous throughout the day. The already heavy going was thereby made considerably worse, and the difficulties of the attack proportionately increased.

Thanks to the careful preparations which had been made, the assaulting troops were formed up without a hitch and practically without casualties.

The attack was launched at 5.40am. Two minutes later the enemy put down his barrage exactly on the line expected. As the troops had been assembled in front of this line, little damage was done by this enemy fire, and the advance was not checked.

At 7.20am it was reported at divisional HQ that the Ansons (under Lieutenant-Colonel H.F. Kirkpatrick) had captured Varlet Farm and 50 prisoners after a stiff fight. The building shown on the map as at Varlet Farm proved to be a concrete pill-box some 200 yards further east and at the southern end of Source Trench. This mistake caused a great deal of confusion at the time but was a very natural one. The concrete building shown at Varlet Farm did not exist in reality and, except for a few scattered bricks, all of the farm buildings had completely disappeared. Source Trench was also indistinguishable and, owing to the flooded shellholes in the neighbourhood, the farm moat could scarcely be recognized.

At 8am a pigeon message (despatched at 6.40am) was received from Lieutenant Careless of the 1st Royal Marines, saying that he had captured Banff House and was consolidating a position 150 yards in front of it.

In the centre, progress had not been so marked, and the attack appeared to be held up, on the road between Bray Farm and Wallemolen.

About midday it was known that the Anson Battalion was consolidating in the neighbourhood of Source Trench and an unconfirmed report stated that portions of the Howe Battalion had been seen pushing forward towards Source Farm, and all were going well. The situation of the marine battalions at that time was not clear, but it appeared to HQ that the 1st Royal Marines had gained their objectives on the left but were still held up in the centre, just east of the Wallemolen and Bray Farm Road. There was practically no news of the 2nd Royal Marines, but they had apparently been held up on the same line.

At 2pm it was clear that the 3rd Canadian Division had been forced back and that they now held the line of the first objective and wished to form an SOS line just in front of that area. It was at that time impossible for the 189th Brigade to agree to this plan so far as the inter-divisional boundary was concerned, as the Howe detachment had been seen going forward and matters were still uncertain. However, at about 3.30pm it became obvious that the RND had no troops east of Source Trench, and therefore the Canadian Division was in-formed accordingly and artillery covering the right of the 63rd's front was given an SOS line 400 yards in front of the first objective.

Later in the day the sole survivors (15 men) of the detachment which had succeeded in reaching the neighbourhood of Source Farm rejoined their battalion through the Canadian lines. They reported that they had suffered heavy casualties from rifle and machine-gun fire during their advance and that their officers had been killed. The survivors had endeavoured to consolidate their position and had gained touch with the Canadians on their right, but the heavy German counter-attack had eventually compelled all the troops in this neighbourhood to withdraw.

The remainder of the Howe Battalion were now reported to be intermixed with the Anson Battalion in the neighbourhood of Varlet Farm and Source Trench, having found it impossible, owing to heavy rifle and machine-gun fire, to make any further advance.

Towards nightfall a message was received at brigade headquarters from OC 1st Royal Marines that his troops in Banff House had been forced to withdraw and that he now held Berks House as his most advanced post, whence his line turned back westward to the Shaft. Orders were at once issued for the line to be re-established by the reserve company, but this operation was only partially successful and the most advanced post on the left flank, during the night of 26/27 October, was just west of Bray Farm.

Later information was to show that, early in the morning of 26 October, elements of the 2nd Royal Marines, supported by con-solidating machine guns, had succeeded in crossing the Paddebeek east of Banff House in the face of considerable opposition and had established themselves about 200 yards beyond the stream. Here they were subjected to considerable rifle fire and sniping from both flanks, and especially from the north. About midday a strong party of the enemy attempted to work round their flank from this position. The marines' rifles were so choked with mud that practically none of them could be fired, but the attack was beaten off by machine-gun fire; when these guns also became clogged the rifles of the machine gunners were used, as up until that moment their rifles had been in their covers and in consequence were not so badly choked. Towards evening, after they had suffered heavy casualties and lost all of their officers, this detachment, finding both its flanks in the air, unfortunately decided to fall back across the Paddebeek, and there can be little doubt that it was the sight of these men retiring which accounted for the withdrawal from Banff House.

About 6pm on 26 October information reached the GOC, 188th Infantry Brigade, that the Anson and Howe Battalions had been

suffering heavy casualties from enemy fire and were much dis-
organized. He accordingly decided to relieve them by his counter-
attacking battalion, the Hood. It was in a position of readiness near
to Inch Houses and had not been employed during the day. This
relief was carried out, with the Ansons withdrawing to Irish Farm
whilst the Howe was kept near to Albatross Farm as a reserve.[4]

The story of the Hood's role is outlined in the battalion's war diary and
other sources. The officers taking part were:

Headquarters

Co	Commander A.M. Asquith
Adjutant	Lieutenant J.C. Hilton
Information Officer	Lieutenant W. Barclay
Signals Officer	Sub-Lieutenant L.R. Sandford
Medical Officer	Surgeon W. McCracken
Chaplain	Reverend E.E. Raven

A Company
Sub-Lieutenant R. Barclay-Brown
Sub-Lieutenant I. Lloyd-Evans
Sub-Lieutenant J.B. Ramwell

B Company
Sub-Lieutenant J. Clark
Sub-Lieutenant W.R. Gibson
Sub-Lieutenant J.P. Jenkins

C Company
Lieutenant W. Arblaster
Sub-Lieutenant W.E. Bach
Sub-Lieutenant E. Bolton

D Company
Sub-Lieutenant B. Oldridge
Sub-Lieutenant N. Roberts
Sub-Lieutenant E.S. Young

At Camp
Lieutenant S.H. Fish
Lieutenant F.C. Hill
Sub-Lieutenant H.W. Bishop
Sub-Lieutenant R. Wyard
Sub-Lieutenant S.G. Luxton
Sub-Lieutenant G.A.H. Phillips

At 8pm on 25 October the battalion moved by road to the junction of Admiral's Road with Mousetrap Track. Here they took their Lewis guns from limbers, and proceeded up duckboard tracks in the trenches to the first assembly position. They lined up on tapes and dug in on a 240 yard front, 60 yards deep, under intermittent shellfire. The night was cloudless, with a bright moon. Battalion HQ was a concrete pill-box shared with Anson and Howe Battalions; a single room just large enough to allow eight officers to sit down at a squeeze.

It rained heavily between 5 and 5.30am on 26 October, then the barrage opened at zero hour, 5.40. As far as the Hood could see from their position, the enemy response was almost immediate. At about 6.30, when the shelling was rather less heavy, but still considerable, it was thought advisable to move the Hood's front companies up to the second assembly position before full daylight. They moved up in artillery formation; A Company took up a position in the old front line (cemetery to Wallemolen), with its left on Inch House Road; C Company was also on the old front line, with its left on Inch House itself. On the way up to these new positions, Sub-Lieutenant Ivor Lloyd-Evans of A Company was wounded in the chest, and Sub-Lieutenant Joseph Clark of B Company was wounded at about the same time in the first assembly position.

Lieutenant Barclay, the battalion intelligence officer, went forward with two scouts at 5.40 to pick out 'kicking off' lines in case the Hood was called on to counter-attack from the direction of Veal and Vat Cottages or Middle Copse. He pushed forward under heavy shell-fire and taped out assembly lines, then reconnoitred his way forward under considerable rifle fire to gain information on the progress of the attacking troops. One of his scouts was wounded by a sniper, so Barclay sent him back with his other man to help him. Barclay himself was already deeply wounded above the eye by a splinter of his shrapnel helmet, which had been broken away by a shell. Pushing forward nevertheless, he established liaison between two parties of attacking troops, and showed them how, by their combined action, the enemy trench which had been holding them up might be dealt with. He sent back a valuable report on the situation, remaining on duty for a further 36 hours.

257

At 8.30 D Company was ordered up; Sub-Lieutenant Bernard Oldridge, the officer in charge, was wounded by a shell just after receiving orders to move. D Company was placed in the old front line, with three of their platoons on A's left, to the south of Inch Houses Road, and one platoon on C's right, to the north of Inch Houses Road.

During the morning it became clear that British troops were holding Bellevue and three pill-boxes between Bellevue and Varlet Farm. It was not clear (but seemed probable) that the RND also held Varlet Farm; wounded and others were returning from the direction of this farm to Wallemolen. At either side of the road running into the south-west corner of the farm, men were hit, with hardly any exceptions, by machine-gun fire from the north and north-west.

There were now rumours that the enemy were massing for a counter-attack, but very little could be seen from the cemetery as to what was taking place beyond Varlet Farm – a better view could be obtained from the farm itself. A reconnaissance was therefore made by Lieutenant Gammon (commander of a six-inch battery) plus an officer and man of the Hood, who all succeeded in reaching the plantation surrounding the pill-box and ruins from the south-east.

A duel was in progress between the garrison of this pill-box and two enemy groups to the north-east and north-west. The pill-box, knee-deep in water, was being held by Sub-Lieutenant Stevenson of Anson Battalion and just 11 survivors of his platoon, with one Lewis gun. They were putting up a good fight and keeping at bay a large number of the enemy, some of whom occupied another pill-box about 100 yards away. Other Germans moved from place to place, sniping from ranges of between 30 and 100 yards. The Ansons were embarrassed by the presence of several wounded, including Lieutenant Gough of the Royal Field Artillery, and four Germans. They were running short of small arms ammunition, and it seemed probable that they must have lost some direction when attacking.

All that day (26 October) a considerable pocket of Germans was at large between Bray and Varlet Farms. Throughout the day the enemy shelled forward roads and the duckboard tracks; they also put heavy barrages, lasting from 10 to 15 minutes, on to the old British front line. The cemetery and Inch Houses came in for the worst of these, but the Stroombeek valley in the neighbourhood of Albatross Farm was shelled heavily at intervals throughout the day. Sub-Lieutenant Robert Barclay-Brown of A Company was buried on three occasions, on the last of which he was wounded and sent back. This left Sub-Lieutenant Ramwell as the only remaining officer in the company; but he was also buried, badly shaken, and had to be sent down as well. Sub-Lieutenant William Bach of C Company was therefore transferred to take charge of A Company.

About dusk a body of about 120 British troops was seen approaching the line from the north-east, at first mistaken for enemy by Hood's C Company, who were only just stopped in time from opening fire on them. Sub-Lieutenant William Arblaster of the Hood checked this retirement with great promptitude and decision, making them dig in to the left of Inch Houses, on the general path of the old front line. It appeared that these men were retiring not from any panic, but from want of leadership, ignorance of what was expected of them, and in some cases because of a rumoured order for withdrawal.

At about 7pm the Hood was ordered to take over the positions occupied by Anson and Howe. Varlet Farm was the most forward position believed to be occupied by these battalions, and it was thought some difficulty might be experienced in relieving the farm: scouts reported that enemy machine guns made it unapproachable, and there were no signs that it was still occupied by the Ansons; indeed, it was now reported to be in the hands of the enemy.

Asquith went forward himself, in bright moonlight, to explore the ground in the vicinity of Varlet Farm. He was observed by the enemy, but, in spite of heavy rifle and machine-gun fire directed at him and the awful state of the ground (which made the going very slow), he approached the farm. Alone, he entered a concrete building and found it occupied by a small British garrison, who were exhausted, mostly wounded, and almost without ammunition. After investigating the ground thoroughly, he returned to the Hood lines and led up three platoons to relieve the garrison, putting one platoon in the building itself and the other two on each flank. A very important position was thus kept in British hands, thanks to the gallant garrison of D Company troops under Sub-Lieutenant Norman Roberts.

Two platoons of B Company were now brought up from the battalion reserve to strengthen the old front line. Another two platoons of B Company worked at clearing the wounded in front of this line and carrying up rations from camp during the course of the night. The ration party came in for heavy shelling; Sub-Lieutenant Gerald Phillips was wounded and about half the rations were lost.

Stretcher parties from both sides worked at clearing up the forward areas of their wounded throughout the night and the next morning. The Hood party, under the direction of Surgeon William McCracken, had been informed that many wounded were still lying in the mud and water of shellholes, but came under heavy shellfire as they were led up. McCracken had already been working without intermission in the open at the regimental aid post near Albatross Farm. Now he ordered his men to take cover and himself advanced through the shelling and machine-gun fire, bearing a Red Cross flag on his walking stick. Eventually the enemy recognized and respected this, and the surgeon was able to bring forward his stretcher squads and work with them throughout that morning. The zone that he worked would normally have been under short-range enemy rifle fire, but his determination undoubtedly saved many valuable lives. He was helped in his work by a Canadian, Lieutenant Shipley, with his bearers.

During the morning, enemy aeroplanes dropping lights were mistaken by one of the Hood officers for British planes signalling 'Enemy massing for counter-attack'. An SOS barrage was put down, and two casualties resulted from short shooting by the garrison at Varlet Farm. At 11pm the Hood was relieved by Nelson during considerable shelling; 19 men were wounded by gas shells as they made their way back.

Hood casualties were lighter than usual, in that no officers had been killed, but were still plentiful:

Officers

Wounded Intelligence Officer	Lieutenant Barclay
A Company	Sub-Lieutenant Barclay-Brown
	Sub-Lieutenant Lloyd-Evans
	Sub-Lieutenant Ramwell
B Company	Sub-Lieutenant Clark
D Company	Sub-Lieutenant Oldridge
At Camp	Sub-Lieutenant Phillips
	(wounded on carrying party)

Other ranks

Killed	24
Died of wounds	5
Wounded	77
Wounded by shell gas	19
Wounded at duty	16
Wounded and missing	1
Missing	6
Sick	3

After the attack Arthur Asquith made a number of comments and recommendations. He believed that, had they tried only for the first objective, the RND and the 9th Division would have advanced as far as they actually did with the expenditure of only half the troops lost. The ground was simply too bad to allow an advance to objectives as far as 1,200 yards away. With the difficulties of communication in the forward areas, the duckboard tracks should have been pushed further forward and duplicated. He was of the opinion that well-trained, fresh, and lightly-equipped troops, with good knowledge of the ground, sent up for just 36 hours once a week, could take the enemy strongpoints piecemeal. Some strongpoints might also need a concentrated preliminary barrage, but others, if surrounded at night, would cave in once they found themselves in this position.

As the counter-attack battalion, he felt the Hood had lost heavily and was doing little good, and that such a force – without barrage and floundering across country by daylight under direct observation from enemy gunners on the ridge – would have had little success against a few determined, stationary enemy machine gunners.[5]

CHAPTER TWENTY-FOUR

Welsh Ridge

On 6 December the Royal Naval Division was about to return to the Passchendaele front when they were ordered instead to move and help defend the hard-pressed line in the Third Army area. Douglas Jerrold writes about the area:

> The gains remaining to us, after the German counter-attacks from the Cambrai offensive were represented by the Flesquières salient. Our offensive had opened with the capture of the Hindenburg front and support lines on a front of six and a half miles, south-east of Cambrai; this gain had been exploited with a considerable measure of success on the left. After the German counter-attacks, we still held four miles of the Hindenburg front and support lines running east from a point half a mile north of Demicourt, in front of Flesquières. In advance of this position we held a discontinuous line of posts. On our right, however, the Germans had achieved a breakthrough, and had penetrated in part beyond our old front line. We had been saved from a general withdrawal only by improvising a defensive flank running south-west along Welsh Ridge, at right angles to those sectors of the Hindenburg lines which we still held. The result was that the residue of our gains formed a very sharp salient which, in the event of a serious attack, could hardly have been held. As, however, the position was one of great natural strength, and as it commanded the approaches to Masnières and Marcoing, two important enemy centres, it had been decided to maintain and fortify it. This was the new task of the Naval Division, who between 15 and 20 December took over the front of the 31st and 62nd Divisions.
>
> The sector taken over included the apex of the salient, where the line was on the northern slopes of Welsh Ridge, and the whole length of the eastern face of the ridge. On the right of the division, the southern slopes of Welsh Ridge ran down into a valley across which

our front line, continuing on the line of Welsh Ridge, fell behind our old front line. Approximately at this point was the right divisional boundary, which was also the corps and army boundary. The division on the left of the RND, who had captured sectors of the Hindenburg line forming the northern arm of the salient, was the 19th Division. On the right, holding the re-entrant formed by the German incursion behind our original front, was the 9th Division of the Fifth Army. The new front, representing as it did a position hurriedly improvised in the stress of battle, was almost lacking in material defences.[1]

After the action at Passchendaele Arthur Asquith was promoted to brigadier-general and left the Hood to take up the post of commanding officer of the 189th Brigade on 18 December. His tenure in office was very short-lived, though, as he was severely wounded just two days later:

About my leg, I was wounded on 20 December. For about a month I had a good deal of pain while they thought they could patch it up. Then they realized that the ankle was smashed as well as the two other bones, and they took it off below the knee about three weeks ago. My temperature has been normal and I've had practically no pain for the last fortnight. Healing is retarded by the fact that the leg was septic at the time of the amputation, but it is going on well now.[2]

Patrick Shaw-Stewart took over temporary command of the Hood, having just returned from leave. He wrote home:

I sailed on Wednesday morning, or rather, afternoon. By virtue of being a major (by Jove!) I went on the staff train at 12.50, comfortable-like, instead of having to push off at 7am. I had a lovely crossing, followed by a considerable surprise; expecting to find the battalion roughly where I had left them, I found that they had gone almost as far from there as they could – and for the last 48 hours I have been trying to catch them up, so far with very little success. I have been in about a dozen trains, all smelly, and subsisted largely on chocolate and apples. I hope I fetch up soon.[3]

Meanwhile, in its new location, on 29 December the division was holding a frontage of 6,800 yards, and the length of this front made it necessary to have three brigades in the front line:

On the right
188th Infantry Brigade – Brigadier-General J.F.S.D. Coleridge
Right   1st Royal Marines

263

Left	Howe
Brigade reserve	Anson
Divisional reserve	2nd Royal Marines

In the centre

189th Infantry Brigade – Lieutenant-Colonel H.F. Kirkpatrick	
Right	Drake
Left	Hood
Brigade reserve	Nelson
Divisional reserve	Hawke

On the left

190th Infantry Brigade – Brigadier-General A.R.H. Hutchison	
Right	7th Royal Fusiliers
Left	5th Kings Shropshire Light Infantry
Brigade reserve	1st Artists' Rifles
Divisional reserve	4th Bedfordshire Regiment

There was no reason to expect an attack, as ground observers and patrols reported that the enemy were digging hard and wiring in front of their trenches. British aircraft reported no signs of any concentrations or hostile movements in the enemy lines. Enemy aircraft have been very active since 27 December, however, and there had been considerable hostile artillery activity.

At 6.30am on 30 December, 1917, the Germans subjected the entire length of the division's front, support and reserve lines to a most intense bombardment, in which hostile trench mortars, both light and heavy, co-operated. Approaches, tracks and back areas were also very heavily shelled. This bombardment was followed by an attack in force, through the thick morning mist, along the division's front line.[4] The Hood Battalion war diary describes the action:

The night of 29/30 December passed quietly. Hood patrols were pushed out actively and at 7.30pm a patrol of A Company reported enemy were digging in a section of dead ground, out of fire of the Lewis guns. The trench mortar battery was asked to deal with this matter, but the NCO in charge informed the Hood's company commander that he could not fire without orders from his own officers. These were not obtained and as a result these guns were not ready to fire until 8.40pm.

The remainder of the night was very quiet, even suspiciously so. Because of this uncertainty D Company's commander stayed on watch all night. At 6.30am on 30 December the enemy opened fire and placed a heavy barrage of 5.4 and 4.2 shells, together with heavy trench mortar, on the front line, supports and reserve. When this had opened all men were 'standing to' and the CO of the battalion, Lieutenant-Commander Patrick Shaw-Stewart, was at D Company HQ. As he moved to go out to the line he was hit and wounded but continued to proceed, but was again hit and killed a few minutes later.[5]

So the last member of the 'Latin Table' on the *Grantully Castle* back in 1915 went; the reaper had taken his toll. Rupert Brooke died before the Gallipoli dawn; Denis Browne and Charles Lister died during the campaign; Cleg Kelly and now Patrick Shaw-Stewart met their maker in France. Asquith was maimed; only Freyberg was still active, despite receiving numerous wounds. The flower of the generation had gone: the time had come for new young officers, leaving only a lingering memory of that confident, self-assured era.

Shaw-Stewart had written to Lady Desborough on 10 November:

> Being killed in France, after a nice leave in London, and in the Hood with my old friends and my old status, is one thing: being killed chillily on the Struma after being pitch-forked into God knows what Welsh Fusiliers or East Lancashire Regiment is quite another. But of course technically it's illogical of me.[6]

Lord Alexander Thynne discovered the detailed circumstances of Patrick Shaw-Stewart's death:

> By a curious coincidence, two days ago, I had as artillery liaison officer the man who was actually with Patrick Shaw-Stewart when he was killed, in the next sector. It was an exceptionally gallant death. It was in the early morning, about dawn; he was going round his line; the Germans put up a barrage. The gunner prayed him to send up the SOS rocket, but Patrick refused and maintained that it was only a minor raid on another part of the line, and that if he sent up the SOS signal the people would think he was 'windy'. They did make a big attack about an hour later, and his battalion was the only one that did not give ground.
>
> He was hit by shrapnel, the lobe of his ear was cut off and his face spattered so that the blood ran down from his forehead and blinded him for a bit. The gunner tried to make him go back to battalion HQ to be dressed, but he refused, and insisted on completing his round. Very soon afterwards a shell burst on the parapet and a fragment hit him upwards through the mouth and killed him instantaneously. This gunner, who was in the ranks of the RFA [Royal Field Artillery] before the war, and as liaison officer

with the infantry can speak with sure experience, says that he has never seen a battalion better organized. He was intensely struck with Patrick's capacity; there was no detail to do with the men's comfort to which he did not give the most close attention.[7]

After the death of the CO the barrage continued intensely for 40 minutes, but over on the Hood's left it slackened, and Sub-Lieutenant Herbert Donaldson observed the enemy attacking the Fusiliers on his left. At 7am a German entered the Hood's section of the line, but was soon taken prisoner by Sub-Lieutenant Norman Roberts (who was himself later to die of wounds). This prisoner informed Donaldson that the 185th Division was attacking at three points, the centre of which was about his position. He did not appear to be very conversant with the plan of attack, however, as his details of the barrage times did not coincide with actual events. He also said that the enemy were coming over in white overalls, but by the time this information was circulated the troops could be seen approaching, and D Company reported seeing parties of British being taken prisoner on their left. These white-clad attacking German soldiers were called 'storm troops' by the British. It appeared that their tactic was to advance into and lie down in no man's land before their bombardment commenced, so when the British barrage came down they were well inside it.

At 6.45am the barrage became so intense on a sap in the Hood's front that the men were temporarily withdrawn and placed in Ostrich Trench by Sub-Lieutenant Weir. Three enemy parties, each of about 12 men, entered the sap head, which had been demolished by shellfire, and the Hood was gradually bombed back to the support line. This incident was observed by Lieutenant G. Maudsley, second in command of the support company, who immediately sent up a platoon under Sub-Lieutenant Munds to counter-attack. The platoon was met by Weir, who at once organized C Company, plus a large bombing squad led by Petty Officer Brown of E Company, to bomb up the sap until their bombs ran out. The Germans had a large supply of stick and egg bombs, plus the advantage that their stick bombs had a superior range, and temporarily forced the Hood to give ground again. At one point two German officers got as far as battalion HQ, where they were met at the head of the dugout by the officers' cook, AB Price of B Company. Price promptly threw a Mills bomb at the invaders, killing one and wounding the other.

A fresh supply of bombs was organized from the Hood's support company, and they renewed the attack. Sub-Lieutenant Price of B Company and Sub-Lieutenant Sanford, OC of A Company, were both wounded; but the Hood succeeded in clearing Ostrich Trench and bombing up to the sap head.

Lieutenant-Commander Sidney Fish had now taken over command of the battalion; accompanying Lieutenant Bardy, the intelligence officer, Fish went up to the Apex and found the enemy had been bombed back. They proceeded to Nelson support, and made their way along this to D Company on the left. Orders were received to reinforce the 7th Royal Fusiliers and supply bombs and small arms ammunition. Sub-Lieutenant Bassett arranged this, ordering one platoon of B Company in support. The Hood was next informed of a proposed counter-attack to be made by the Artists at 10.45am, so D Company extended its flank along Eagle Trench and made contact with a fusilier barricade manned by one officer and 16 men. Movement could be seen in a part of Central Trench which had been occupied by the Fusiliers but was now in enemy hands: the artillery was called into action, but proved to be of little use.

At about 3.20pm the Hood's front was attacked on both right and left flanks, but the enemy were driven off with machine-gun fire and bombs. Sub-Lieutenant Herbert Donaldson reported that his position was becoming a death-trap, exposed on all sides to the enemy, and fought a gallant withdrawal. About 4pm a very intense barrage was put down on one whole area, but the Germans did not attack: the British barrage came down and was believed to have dispersed them. At 5.25pm D Company was forced to retire and evacuate a section of their line after continued shelling; but by 9.20pm all companies had established communication and were in touch with each other. The night of 30/31 December was very quiet.

Communications had proved to be a problem. No telephones could be used after the initial barrage, as the lines had not been buried well enough. The Hood could not use wireless, as they had no power buzzer for working the amplifier at the brigade forward station to pass a wireless message to division. One available wireless station was in any case put out of action between 10 and 10.50am, when the aerial masts were wrecked by shellfire and had to be re-erected. Pigeons had been found to be unreliable in the severe weather; only about 50 per cent turned up, mainly after a long delay which rendered the information of little use. It was left to men such as Able Seaman John Campbell, a company runner, to bring messages through to battalion HQ regardless of personal safety.

At 4.20am on 31 December the enemy shelled the Hood reserves and support lines with gas, but without casualties. This was followed at 6.40 by an intense barrage of the whole Hood area, but again an attack did not follow. German aeroplanes flew low over the British lines, but no English planes were seen. Then at 8.30 the Germans attacked Cable Trench with flame, forcing a company of Hawke to give ground. Hood's D Company counter-attacked, pushing the enemy back until the shallowness of the trench made their position untenable and 30 men of D Company were killed or taken prisoner.

The rest of the day was taken up with counter-barrage, and no other attack materialized. The Hood was eventually relieved at 3.10am on 1 January, 1918.

Among the many brave acts performed by men of the Hood Battalion during this action, one in particular was recorded by Sub-Lieutenant Walter Parry of D Company:

During our tour in the trenches from 28 to 31 December, 1917, I can personally testify to the great courage, resource and invaluable work of Sub-Lieutenant Donaldson of D Company, Hood Battalion.

During the whole time Mr Donaldson was constantly going round his whole company, and by his personal example and cheerfulness in keeping up the spirits and hopes of the men, who were holding an almost hopeless position.

The German barrage was the worst I have ever seen, but Mr Donaldson passed through it time after time, seemingly without fear. The communications trench which had to be passed was only three feet deep at first, but was literally bashed to pieces later.

When Mr Donaldson had to go forward to assist in the command of the Royal Fusiliers, he did not hesitate but went on, rallied the remaining men of the RFs, and organized a successful retreat when beaten back by superior numbers with bombs, rifle grenades, trench mortars and machine guns. He made six or seven bombing blocks in the trench and defended each to the last.

When the Germans attacked with flame next morning he was in front of the counter-attack which dislodged them from part of the position. He then organized the whole defence of our position and also that of the Bedfords in the Sunken Road.

During the whole time he did not spare himself, but kept going night and day, although utterly worn out for lack of sleep.

Sub-Lieutenant Herbert Donaldson was subsequently commended and put forward for the Distinguished Service Order by Lieutenant Commander William Egerton, who took over as commanding officer of the Hood. Overall, the battalion sustained a number of casualties in the action of 30 and 31 December 17:

	Officers	Other ranks
Killed	4	24
Wounded	3	124
Missing	2	102[9]

CHAPTER TWENTY-FIVE

Towards the End

The death of Patrick Shaw-Stewart marked not only the passing of the last of a unique group of gifted young officers; it also marks a change in the composition of this book. All the 'literary' figures have gone – not only the 'Latin Table', but also the ordinary men – weeded out by death, disease and wounds. The new generation of officers and men was concerned only with slogging through to get the war won, and had neither the time nor the inclination to write the letters and accounts which so enlivened the earlier history of the Hood. The battalion still had a vital role to play, but it becomes now a matter of official record rather than personal recollection.

The time had come for Germany to produce the knock-out blow which would win them the war. Russia had collapsed, releasing large numbers of divisions from the Eastern Front, and a last desperate thrust must be made in the early spring of 1918 before the Allies were strengthened by the Americans.

The 63rd (RN) Division had been aware for some time that a major attack would soon be launched against the Third Army front, of which they formed part, and prepared their defences accordingly. On the morning of 21 March the division's sector of defence looked strong:

Right Sector – 190th Infantry Brigade
Front line	7th Royal Fusiliers
Intermediate line	4th Bedfordshires
(brigade support)	
Divisional reserve	1st Artists' Rifles
(Eastwood camp)	

Centre sector – 189th Infantry Brigade
Front line	Hawke
Intermediate line	Drake

(brigade support)
Divisional reserve   Hood
(Eastwood Camp)

Left sector – 189th Infantry Brigade
Front line   1st Royal Marines
Intermediate line   2nd Royal Marines
(brigade support)
Divisional reserve   Anson
(Eastwood camp)

The defence principles were that though the corps' main point of resistance was to be the second system, there was no intention of giving up the front line unless they were actually compelled to do so. Provision was made for a methodical retirement on to the intermediate line, and if necessary the second line, but each successive trench was to be fought for. The divisional reserve, one battalion with eight machine guns, was to man the second system, and was not to move in front of that line without specific authority from corps.

Of each of the three counter-attack battalions, located in the intermediate line, one company was earmarked as a nucleus garrison and could not be moved without the authority of division. Each brigade commander therefore had one battalion less one company at his disposal for counter-attack.

Warning of the intended attack took the form of a series of gas bombardments. On the night of 12/13 March the enemy put down a heavy concentration of gas shells, mainly around Ribécourt and Trescault. This bombardment was repeated on the next three nights, reaching its greatest intensity on 15/16 March, when the area involved included battery positions and valleys within the divisional boundary as well as the two villages. It was estimated that 15,000 shells were fired that night, and casualties were heavy: 102 officers and 2,748 other ranks. 189th Brigade's HQ had to be evacuated. Many officers and men showed slight symptoms of having been gassed, chiefly complete loss of voice, which affected their physical fitness to varying degrees.

In the early hours of the morning of 21 March several warning messages were received from V Corps reporting that VII Corps had noticed considerable movement on their front, particularly in the vicinity of Gonnelieu and Villers Guislain. On the RND's right the 2nd Division, which was being relieved, reported signs of an enemy relief on their front at 12.35am. An enemy aeroplane flew low over their front trenches. But the RND itself saw nothing to indicate an impending attack.

At 4.45am an extremely heavy bombardment of high explosive and gas shells opened up, perhaps most severe on the flanking divisions, but nevertheless falling heavily on the 189th Brigade in the centre. Orders were given to stand to, and four machine guns earmarked for the second system were moved up. At 7am a curious fog passed over the divisional front: mostly smoke, but mixed with some chlorine and phosgene gas. It reached divisional HQ at about 7.30am.

The right and centre brigades were attacked by infantry at 7am, and the enemy succeeded in driving in posts in both fronts. Divisional reserve battalions were moved up to the second system of defence; the Hood, after suffering two clouds of phosgene gas, moved forward on wooden roads.

By now all communication with the forward battalions had been lost and the situation of the 189th Brigade in the centre was obscure. It was not until 11.10am that divisional HQ received the first authentic message that the Germans were in the front lines. But by the end of the first day's fighting the divisional front remained intact, except a small portion lost by 189th Brigade and two posts on the left of 190th Brigade.

The forenoon of 22 March passed without incident, but orders were received for a withdrawal. This was the first of a series of tactical defensive retreats which continued until 28 March: trench warfare was replaced by open combat. It was difficult to get commanders and staffs to appreciate the new situation in which they found themselves. Rations and ammunition were frequently dumped, instead of being kept on wheels until they could be delivered, and in consequence were almost invariably lost. Subordinate commanders, long used to trench warfare, could only fight with their men in line; few disposed their troops in depth, which would be more suited to open fighting. Nevertheless, divisional HQ wrote that, considering the lack of training in this new style of warfare, the results achieved by all ranks exceeded expectation.

The enemy now attacked in three lines; the men in each line were about two paces apart, while the distance between the lines themselves was some 50 paces. The advance was made in slow time, with the infantry not using their rifles. Machine guns were posted on both flanks of each defending company, firing continually at ranges of up to 2,500 yards, but they did not appear to be particularly accurate. When fired upon, the German infantry invariably halted and tried to outflank the RND rearguard.

The enemy sent in frequent strong patrols of between 20 and 40 men, armed with light machine guns, to reconnoitre the RND lines for any gaps. Whenever one was found they pushed forward to exploit it, signalling their advance with Very lights to call up more infantry.

The RND flanks were rapidly turned; the only defence was found to be an energetic advance against any enemy party seen sending up lights to close the gap before reinforcements arrived. The Germans also used Very lights to indicate positions they had occupied and to call up artillery fire. But their lights indicated their positions to the British, too, to the latter's advantage; and the RND was not slow to realize that the Germans could be confused by British Very lights. Another German technique, using frequent small smoke-screens to hide movement, was equally unsuccessful. The screens were generally very weak, and served only to draw attention to their actions.

At 5.45pm on 25 March a message was received from corps:

> If you are forced back over the Ancre you must secure the crossings in front of Authuille and Beaucourt if you possibly can. Send parties back if possible to make secure all these crossings behind. I do not know your situation. The 2nd Division has been forced back on Beaumont Hamel and is practically non-existent. 2nd Division has been ordered to hold the crossings between Hamel and Beaucourt. The GOC does not think this would be possible and it is very important that your left should not be withdrawn. Am sending Cyclists to hold crossings between Aveluy and Beaucourt, but these will not arrive for some time. Retain hold on the Pozières-Thiepval Ridge if you can.

But at 6pm V Corps telephoned with another message:

> It is probable that a general retirement across the Ancre will take place tonight. The Third Army are working out details and you should send a representative to corps HQ if called upon.

Orders came back from the Third Army conference that the corps was to continue its withdrawal across the River Ancre and take up a position on the west bank, extending from Albert to Auchonvillers. The 47th Division was to be on the right of the line, with the 63rd (RN) Division in the centre and the 2nd Division on the left. The RND sector ran from the southern outskirts of Aveluy Wood to the Hamel-Thiepval bridge. All crossings were to be destroyed after the last troops had withdrawn across the river by 4.45am the next day. The plan worked well and was completed without incident by 7am on 26 March; the RND succeeded in keeping in touch with their flanking divisions throughout, although owing to shortage of time and lack of explosives it was not possible to destroy all the crossings completely.

Later that day the RND brigades were relieved, and the Hood counted the cost of the defensive action:

	Officers	Other ranks
Killed	2	8
Wounded	3	454
Missing	13	209[1 & 2]

A raid was planned for the night of 24/25 May, 1918: the 63rd (RN) Division, co-operating with the 12th Division on its left, was to take prisoners and obtain identification, papers and maps. As a secondary task, as much damage as possible should be done to any enemy dugouts and shelters discovered.[3] Three raids would be carried out simultaneously by RND battalions; and the Hood was to cover the area from the railway line and all points west of the River Ancre.

The Hood's A Company enjoyed almost complete success on their mission, but D Company came across some stiff opposition and suffered casualties. B Company, coming to the aid of D, met with similar difficulties. The enemy posts found during the raid were most ingeniously concealed, and were sited only on the reverse slopes. Each post was covered by an overhanging tree and surrounded by rusty old wire entangled in the grass, with a camouflaged path leading to a shelter dug into the bank. One was covered by two-inch iron girders in a cone shape. But despite this information the raid was not a complete success, and there were a number of casualties: Sub-Lieutenant Egbert Hulbert was killed; Second Lieutenant D.J. Jones and Sub-Lieutenants Percy Weeks and J.W. Ellis were wounded; Sub-Lieutenants Phillip Dann and Reginald Stephenson went missing, and there were 75 casualties in other ranks.[4]

By 11 June, 1918, the RND was in reserve, but under instruction that they must be prepared to move at one hour's notice from 6am to 10pm daily or three hours' notice during the night. Training took place only in the mornings, with football matches, sports days and other activities to entertain the troops the rest of the time.[5]

Back on the front the pendulum had swung in favour of the Allies: the Germans were exhausted and almost spent, and now was the time for a British advance. The growing optimism was reflected in the front covers of RND reports and orders, which were now covered with drawings of flowers and sunny farmland scenes. The Hood played an important part in the decisive Allied advance in the summer of 1918, capturing several villages in desperate fighting, but their role tended to be one of support rather than acting as a key lead battalion. Douglas Jerrold's excellent history of the Royal Naval Division gives full details of the actions; but this is more a history of personalities than of military detail, so I have merely outlined those last few months.

The division moved northwards on 15 June, marching by night, and by 19 June were at Souastre, to the rear of a line running through the western outskirts of Bucquoy held by the 37th Division. The RND was now part of IV Corps, and was ordered into the attack on 21 August. Their objectives were the enemy front line positions in Bucquoy, Ablainzevelle and its spur, after which they were to take the Irles-Bihucourt line, then turn northwards along the Achiet-Arras railway.

At 4.55am, in thick mist, the 37th Division advanced with the two naval brigades in its rear. The Germans had suddenly retreated and there was very little open resistance. A tank accompanying the Hood lost its way, followed by one company of the battalion; after some desperate fighting, they took the village of Achiet-le-Petit. Two other tanks reached the target of the Achiet-Arras railway successfully, where two Hood companies and one of the Drake established a temporary lodgement. By 6pm the battle was at a standstill. The Germans counter-attacked several times on 22 August, but were driven back on each occasion, and the Hood was withdrawn that night.

At noon on 24 August the RND was instructed to advance in the evening on the right of the New Zealand Division. The attack was very badly organized, however, and was cancelled at the last minute. The Hood war diary and all brigade and divisional operational orders for this period are missing, almost as if some form of censorship has been imposed on the records. It is known that the Hood faced the south-west corner of Loupart Wood, where the Germans put up a great deal of resistance, and Lieutenant-Commander Sidney Fish, commanding officer of the Hood, was killed.[6]

On 30 August, 1918, the RND was encamped along the Miraumont-Grandcourt road when they received telephone orders from IV Corps transferring them back to XVII Corps immediately. Major-General C.A. Blacklock arrived at divisional HQ at 9pm, taking over command the following morning from Major-General C.E. Lawrie.

Then, at 2pm on 1 September, the RND was set its next task: in support of the 57th Division they were to capture the village of Inchy and crossings over the vital Canal du Nord. The attack started early in the morning of 2 September, and by the evening the battalion had reached the outskirts of Inchy, but heavy artillery and machine-gun fire impeded their progress. Lieutenant-Commander David Galloway and Sub-Lieutenant John Moncur were both wounded during the fighting; Lieutenant-Commander Maudsley took over command of the Hood.

At 10.30am on 3 September the Hood advanced on Inchy; by 12.30pm they had established a post on a bridge over the Canal du Nord and captured the village. Enemy opposition and machine-gun fire increased, however, and they were unable to secure the canal crossings. German resistance stiffened all afternoon, and RND units became intermingled: getting a foothold on the eastern bank of the Canal du Nord would be more difficult than expected, so at 10.30pm the 190th Brigade was moved up to the village.

On 4 September Commander Egerton resumed command of the battalion. At 4am machine-gun fire from the eastern bank was still holding up the troops, and the area to the west of the canal was being heavily shelled. The Germans counter-attacked with some 500 troops at 6.40am and entered the north-eastern quarter of Inchy, then put down a heavy barrage on the Hood at 7.30pm, but were eventually driven out by 8.25pm. Shortly afterwards the Hood was relieved by the Bedfords and returned to the rear.[7]

It was clear that the Germans were determined to hold the ground east of the Canal du Nord, and that it would be extremely difficult to dislodge them. An alternative plan was put into action on 27 September, when the Anson, Drake and Hawke Battalions distinguished themselves in taking the town of Graincourt, to the south of Inchy. The Hood took little part in this action, but suffered a number of casualties from shellfire after crossing the canal.

The next day, 28 September, the battalion moved into La Folie Wood, near the village of Anneux, as part of an attack to cross the Canal de l'Escaut and advance on the major town of Cambrai. Little progress was made until 29 September, when the Hood was able to enlarge a Drake bridgehead on the west of the canal and spearhead the advance in their sector. Fighting continued, but the battalion was allowed to withdraw on 1 October. The German 3rd Marine Division had been involved in the operation, so the RND's commander had sent a message to his troops:

Well done. Reported that German Naval Division is waiting for you on Canal de l'Escaut. When Greek meets Greek. A division has seldom been set a harder task than you were today. After 10 hours' hard fighting you completely accomplished it. A real soldierly performance.[8]

At 4.30am on 8 October the battalion advanced on the village of Niergnies, as part of a larger attack south of Cambrai. The enemy was strong in numbers but offered little resistance, and by 8.30am the Hood and Anson were working their way through the village and taking prisoners. An SOS from RND troops forced back by enemy infantry south-west of Niergnies caused problems for a while, especially since the Germans were equipped with seven captured British tanks, but they were eventually either destroyed (one by the Hood's Commander Pollock, using a captured German gun) or made off towards the town of Wambaix. By 9.55am the village was back in RND hands, and the division was relieved at 9.20 that evening. Sub-Lieutenant Arthur Loutit was killed in action that day; Commander Pollock was awarded a bar to his DSO for his successful leadership and gallant example.[9]

On 4 November the division was transferred from VIII Corps to XXII Corps, and on 5 November they moved to Aylnoy on the Mons front. The 189th brigade successfully relieved the 168th Brigade by 5am on 7 November, and lined up for an attack at 9am. The Hood led the attack, advancing on the Bois d'Audregnies and capturing the main part of it by 11am. Enemy counter-attacks were repelled as the Drake leap-frogged the Hood to a second objective, and the advance continued: the main limiting factors were the state of the roads and the difficulty of getting rations up to the troops in the forward areas.

On 8 November the Allies pushed forward towards the Aulnois-Mons railway: the Hood spent part of the day in a railway cutting whilst the Drake advanced, and later moved on into the town of Witheries. The local inhabitants produced valuable information on 9 November: the Germans had evacuated a number of villages, and appeared to be in general retreat in a bad state of demoralization. The Hood moved to Havay on 10 November, going into billets at 6pm with the news that they were to attack again the next day. They duly advanced, taking two objectives, and were advancing on the village of Givry, near Mons, when the Armistice took effect at 11am.[10]

The Hood war diary states:

Hostilities ceased as between the German Empire and Allied Powers at 11am (English time), when the battalion moved forward to billets at Estinnes-au-Mont.[11]

CHAPTER TWENTY-SIX

Disband and Remember

Little did the Royal Naval Division know that its very existence was in doubt once more – and had been since 26 June, 1918. The Select Committee on Naval Expenditure in its Fourth Report of 1918 had recommended that it be merged into the army. The War Office, as before, agreed with this plan. The Secretary of State for War prepared a memorandum on 27 July for consideration by the War Cabinet; but time passed by, and in September the War Cabinet had still not seen the report. With the ending of the war, however, the ending of the RND became inevitable, and the last entry in their file reads: 'The late S[ecretary] of S[tate] kept the file by him.'[1]

The battalions commemorating such heroes as Drake, Hawke and Hood had fought from Antwerp to Gallipoli, then through the fields of France. They were considered, even by the War Office, to have fought very well. But they were no longer needed.

The division returned to London and was billeted in South Kensington. On 6 June, 1919, they attended their final parade on Horse Guards, to be inspected and addressed by the Prince of Wales:

It is a great pleasure to me to see you all here today, and it is a privilege to inspect you on parade. More than four years have passed since the King at Blandford Camp inspected the Royal Naval Division on the occasion of your departure for the Dardanelles. Since then the story of the war has unfolded itself, and after many vicissitudes and disappointments, strange turns and changes of fortune, the complete victory of our arms, and of our cause, has in every quarter of the world been attained. In all this you have borne a part which bears comparison with the record of any division in the armies of the British Empire. In every theatre of war, your military conduct has been exemplary. Whether on the slopes of Achi Baba, or on the Somme, or in the valley of the Ancre, or down to the very end, at the storming of the Hindenburg Line, your achievements have been worthy of the best traditions both of the Royal Navy and the British Army.

There are few here today of those to whom the King bade farewell in February, 1915. Some who were lieutenants have risen to be generals, and have gained the highest honours for valour and skill. The memories of those who have fallen will be enduringly preserved by the record of the Royal Naval Division and the Royal Marines. They did not die in vain. I am proud to have been deputed by the King to welcome you back, after many perils at last to your native land, for which you have fought so well.[2]

The division dispersed to its respective battalions and, after nearly five years of brave fighting, ceased to exist. In those years the total casualties sustained by the Royal Naval Division were staggering:

	Officers	Other ranks
Killed	445	7,102
Died of Wounds	118	2,466
Died (disease, etc.)	19	647
Wounded	1,364	29,528
Prisoner/interned	119	5,084
Total	1,965	44,829[3]

Some years later plans were made for a Royal Naval Division War Memorial, to be situated at the south-west corner of the Admiralty Buildings, adjoining Horse Guards Parade and opposite St James's Park. It was designed by Sir Edwin Lutyens and consists of two superimposed basins, the upper forming a pedestal for an obelisk from which water issues on all four sides, standing on a massive square base adorned with the badges of the units which formed the division. One side bears the inscription:

1914–1918
In memory of the officers and other ranks of the Royal Naval Division who gave their lives for their country.

Another side carries Rupert Brooke's famous quotation:

Blow out, you bugles, over the rich Dead!
   There's none of these so lonely and poor of old,
   But, dying, has made us rarer gifts than gold.
These laid the world away: poured out the red
Sweet wine of youth; gave up the years to be

Of work and joy, and that unhoped serene
That men call age: and those who would have been
Their sons, they gave their immortality.

On the corners are inscribed the battle honours: Antwerp 1914, Gallipoli
1915-1916, Salonica 1916, France and Belgium 1916-1919. The memorial commemorates the death of officers and other ranks of the RND.[4]
It was unveiled on 25 April, 1925, and dedicated by Bevill Close, then
vicar of St James, Gunnersbury.[5]

Winston Churchill made a speech at the dedication ceremony:

Everyone, I think, must admire the grace and simplicity of this
fountain, which the genius of Lutyens has designed. The site is also
well chosen. Here, under the shadow of the Admiralty building,
where, 11 years ago, the Royal Naval Division was called into
martial life, this monument now records their fame and preserves
their memory. Their memory is thus linked for ever with the Royal
Navy, whose child they were, of whose traditions they were so
proud, and whose long annals, rich with romantic and splendid
feats of arms, contain no brighter page than theirs. But if the place
is well chosen, so also is the day. This is 25 April, and 10 years
ago the astonishing exploit of landing on the Gallipoli peninsula
was in full battle. And we here, who have so many memories in
common, almost seem to hear the long reverberations of the distant
cannonade, and certainly we feel again in our souls the awful hopes
and awful fears of those tragic hours.

A mellow light seems to the mind's eye to surround this monument. The passers-by who in other days pause to drink of its
water or to examine its design will be held by something else.
The famous lines of Rupert Brooke inscribed upon its panel will
make their own appeal and tell their own story to anyone who loves
this island or speaks the English tongue.

These verses, and others given in the order of service, have
brought comfort to so many who sought it long and wearily, and
whose spirit seemed broken, but who nevertheless found relief in
reading and repeating their noble utterance. Their high, calm peace
rises confidently above the tumult and the carnage, and beyond all
error and confusion; it reigns by right divine over men and over
centuries. We meet his verses everywhere. They are quoted again
and again. They are printed in newspapers, written in books, blotted
by tears, or carved in stone. But they belong to us, the Royal Naval
Division, to the memory of Rupert Brooke and his comrades and

companions. They were the inheritance he bequeathed to them, and through them to us all. They are inscribed on this memorial because it is their proper home and from here, while the stones endure, they will carry to the ears of generations differently attuned from ours the chant of valiant youth entering willing and undaunted into the valley of the Shadow of Death.

The years and more have gone since this parade ground used to be thronged by bands of volunteers marching off to join the Army amid the blare of music and at their country's call. Nearly seven years have gone since victory was won; since all the kings and emperors against whom we warred were driven into exile, and all their mighty armies shattered and dispersed. Those years have not been years of joy or triumph. They have been years of exhaustion, despondency, and bickerings all over the world, and we are often tempted to ask ourselves what have we gained by the enormous sacrifices made by those to whom this memorial is erected. But this was never the issue with those who marched away. No question of advantage presented itself to their minds. They only saw the light shining clear on the path of duty. They only saw their duty to resist opposition, to protect the weak, to vindicate the profound but unwritten law of nations, to testify to truth and justice and mercy amongst men. They never asked the question, 'What shall we gain?' They asked only the question, 'Where lies the right?' It was thus that they marched away for ever, and yet from their uncalculating exaltation and devotion, detached from all consideration of material gain, we may be sure that good will come to their countrymen and to this island they guarded in its reputation and safety so faithfully and well. Bold indeed will be the tyrant who seeks again to overthrow by military force the freedom which they established. After the confusion has passed away and the long period of reconstruction has been closed, it will be perceived by all the freedom, not only of individuals, but also of states, has been established upon a broader and stronger foundation.

Humanity, for all its sufferings and disappointments, has yet moved forward through the Great War at least one long stage towards the realization of its ideals. And this country and Empire, saved by its sons from the worst perils which have confronted it during its long history, remains still able to guide, to encourage and in large measure to inspire the peoples of the world. Doubts and disillusions may be answered by the sure assertion that the sacrifice which these men made was not made in vain. And this fountain to the memory of the Royal Naval Division will give forth not only the waters of honour but the waters of healing and the waters of hope.

Early in the Second World War the memorial was removed from Horse

Guards and replaced by a fortress-style structure used by Churchill for his direction of the war. It went into store, forgotten by most, until the Ministry of Defence instructed the architect F.L. Rotherell to produce plans for its erection at the Royal Naval College, Greenwich. Two trees were removed to accommodate it alongside Park Row.It was rededicated on 26 May, 1951, in a service conducted by the Venerable Archdeacon L. Coulshaw, chaplain of the fleet, and unveiled by the Second Sea Lord, Vice-Admiral A.C.G. Madden.[6]

An annual service of commemoration was held by the memorial, but as the years passed the number of veterans taking part gradually dwindled. Eventually it was decided that the service on 31 May, 1981, would be the last. Since then it has rested unseen and generally unknown at the far end of the college, away from the main gate. The seasons come and go, snow and frost lie, leaves fall, and the sun of summer heats the stones. No band plays, no salute is taken. The division fell between the two stalls of navy and army, and was an experiment never to be repeated. It was to rest in peace.

Today the Hood battalion flag still hangs proudly in the north aisle of the parish church of St Peter and St Paul at Blandford Forum, Dorset, where it was laid up in 1952.[7] There is a memorial to the ill-fated Collingwood Battalion at Three Mile Point, near the grounds of Blandford Camp, where the King inspected the division on that sparkling winter's day in 1915. It is still honoured at an annual service on 4 June, to commemorate the terrible battle in 1915 in which most of the battalion lost their lives, and on Remembrance Day each November. Roy Adam, who founded the Blandford Branch of the Royal Naval Association in 1953 and is the son of an RND member, works tirelessly to organize these well-attended events.[8]

The King's Colour presented to the Hood in 1919 hangs in Newcastle Cathedral. In the beautiful little church of St Mary the Virgin, Betteshanger, Kent, nestling in idyllic countryside, is a plaque in memory of the days when the RND's 2nd Brigade camped and trained there, and Canon Bliss and his two nieces were so kind to the troops:

To the glory of God and sacred to the memory of the officers, petty officers and men of the Howe, Hood, Anson and Nelson Battalions of the 2nd Brigade, Royal Naval Division, who after being encamped in this parish in the autumn of 1914 proceeded to Antwerp and subsequently to the Gallipoli peninsula, where many in action, others from wounds and others from sickness died in the service of their sovereign and their country.

Who are the happy warriors, England's heroes? They
Who from the path of duty swerved not e'er away.

A large obelisk was erected at the crossroads near Beaucourt, on which appears an iron plaque in memory of the Royal Naval Division's involvement at the battle of the River Ancre.

More recently, RND remembrance was renewed when, under the driving force of the project co-ordinator Trevor Tasker, treasurer/secretary Andrew Vollens, the Mayor of Gavrelle, M Joseph Fouache, and patron the Dowager Countess Nelson, the RND Gavrelle Memorial Fund was set up to honour the men who captured the French village of Gavrelle in April, 1917. An anchor memorial was constructed in a Park of Peace and Remembrance: a four metres square foundation crowned with a three ton anchor. One can walk around inside the monument. The brickwork, which looks like a bombed-out building, represents the destroyed village; the anchor commemorates the sailors, soldiers and marines.[9]

Over the years the Royal Naval Division Association, and such gatherings as the Hood Battalion Officer's Association, held functions and dinners to remember and renew friendships. There was an annual memorial service at St Paul's Church, Covent Garden, London. Relatives and members of the RND made a pilgrimage in April, 1934, when the liner *Duchess of Richmond* sailed from Liverpool with more than 700 passengers (257 of whom had taken part in the Gallipoli campaign) for a visit to the peninsula. On 27 April General Sir Archibald Paris joined the ship at Naples. This was a moving experience for many of the division, and the story of the pilgrimage is well told in the booklet *After Nineteen Years*, written by Lieutenant F. H. Mann, a former RND engineer. Journeys of memory have also been made to Antwerp and France.[10]

And what of the individuals whose personal histories we have followed through this book? The fates of some have been told in the narrative, but a complete summary may be helpful.

Arthur Asquith left the Hood as a brigadier-general on 18 December, 1917, and was wounded in the leg on 20 December, 1917. (He had previously received a serious gun-shot wound at Gallipoli on 6 May, 1915.) His leg was amputated three weeks later. After the war he became a director of several companies, including what is now the National Westminster Bank. He died in August, 1939, and is buried in the churchyard at Clovelly, in Devon, near to his home at Clovelly Court.

John Bentham transferred from the RND to the Royal Naval Air Station on 21 April, 1917. He later wrote an unpublished diary of his experience in war.

Oliver Backhouse transferred out of the RND to naval artillery while the division was at Gallipoli.

Rupert Brooke died aboard the French hospital ship *Duquay Trouin* on 23 April, 1915, aged 27. He is buried in a small olive grove on the Greek island of Skyros.

Denis Browne was killed in action at Gallipoli on 4 June, 1915, and has no known grave.

Johnny Dodge had his RND commission terminated on 4 April, 1916, and went into the army. He survived the war, and later stood for Parliament as an MP, but was not elected.

William Egerton was wounded in the right thigh on 21 January, 1917, but survived the war and was demobilized on 10 January, 1919.

The Reverend Henry Foster survived the war and became the vicar at Stocksbridge, near Sheffield in Yorkshire.

Bernard Freyberg, who was eventually awarded the VC, was wounded nine times during the course of the First World War. He stayed in the army, but was invalided out of the service in the 1930s. In the Second World War he joined up again, becoming commander of the 2nd New Zealand Division and seeing action in Greece, North Africa, Italy and Crete. After the war he became Governor-General of New Zealand and Deputy Governor of Windsor Castle. He died on 4 July, 1963, and is buried in St Martha's Church, St Martha's Hill.

Ivan Heald transferred to 25 Squadron of the Royal Flying Corps, and was killed when his plane was shot down on 4 December, 1916.

Hugh Hedderwick received a gun-shot wound in the left arm at Gallipoli on 4 June, 1915, and terminated his commission in the RND on 12 August, 1915. Nothing more is known of him.

Frederick 'Cleg' Kelly was wounded at Gallipoli by shrapnel in his right heel; the wound was slight, so he was sent to hospital in Alexandria on 9 June, 1915. He received a second slight head wound on 29 June, 1915. He was eventually killed in action at the Ancre on 13 November, 1916, and is buried at Mesnil-Martin-Sart.

The Hon Charles Lister died of wounds on board the hospital ship *Gasson* on 28 August, 1915, and is buried in East Mudros military cemetery on Lemnos (plot 2, row J, grave 179).

Surgeon William McCracken was awarded the DSO and Military Cross for his gallantry. He received a head wound in August, 1918, for which he was eventually given a 60 per cent disability pension. After the war he worked as a GP in Haworth in Yorkshire for 40 years, before retiring at the age of 70 to live in Bradford. He died on 10 August, 1974, one day before his 86th birthday, and is buried in the Nab Wood cemetery, Shipley.

Lionel 'Cardy' Montagu, a racehorse breeder and trainer, fulfilled his promise to name a horse Beaucourt in 1917. It ran five times, but did not win.

Joseph Murray survived the war and lived until the age of 97, latterly in a nursing home in Surrey, cared for by his daughter-in-law Vera. He died on 29 January, 1994.

Edward Nelson survived the war, but died at the age of 40 when working as scientific superintendent of the Marine Laboratory at the bay of Nigg in Scotland.

Sir Archibald Paris, who relinquished command of the RND after being injured by shellfire on 16 October, 1916, survived the war. He died on 30 October, 1937.

John Quilter was killed in action at Gallipoli on 6 May, 1915, and is buried in Skew Bridge cemetery on Cape Helles. He was 40 years old when he died.

Patrick Shaw-Stewart was killed in action on 30 December, 1917, and is buried at Metz-en-Couture cemetery (number Fr. 662).

And so we come to the end of this history of the Hood Battalion. The spirit of this unique group of men is best summed up by an RND poem written in September, 1918, with apologies to Rudyard Kipling:

YOU'RE RND
If you can keep your head when all about you
Is shot and shell and bomb and poison gas;
If you can keep your watch though dugout tempts you,
As round your post death's missiles fiercely pass,
If you with calm can face the hellish war-tune,
If you can fight, though fighting's not your aim;
If you can meet with vict'ry or misfortune,
And treat them both as part of the great game,
If you can bear the risks and daily terrors
Of front-line trench or billets nightly shelled,
And serve the staff as though they've made no errors,
Though often, perhaps, quite different views you've held;
If you can speculate upon your chances
Of winning through, and count them ten to one,
And take the lot on counting Death's last dances,
Where duty calls or honour to be won;
If you serene can face the shell-made curtain,
And through it merge, with courage undismayed,
Nor turn to right nor left to make more certain
You're not alone – alone, being unafraid;
If though you wish for peace, you've yet decided
You will not sheath the sword you wear today;
Even though in arms you may have long abided,

You'll carry on till foes shall own your sway;
If you can kill the Huns and keep on killing,
Until at length they cry aloud, 'You've won!'
Yours is the corps whose glories send hearts thrilling,
You're justly proud – You're RND, my son.[11]

The Hood Battalion Muster Roll

The muster roll of the Hood taken on board the transport en route to Antwerp. There was a total of 18 officers and 788 men.

As can be seen, each company had its own methods of taking this muster roll: some worked by platoon, others by section. On occasions Christian names are given, other companies just use the surname. These lists are as full as can be obtained. The papers in the Public Record Office at Kew (reference ADM116/1438) are in parts faded and unclear, but every effort has been made to give as complete a list as is possible.

Officers
Lieutenant-Colonel J.A.C. Quilter (Grenadier Guards)
Adjutant Viscount Bury (Scots Guards)
Naval Adjutant A.M. Willoughby
Lieutenant-Commander J. Furguson
Lieutenant-Commander G.G. Dalgleish
Lieutenant-Commander B. Freyberg
Lieutenant-Commander W. Maples
Lieutenant Hughes
Lieutenant J.S. Aspin
Sub-Lieutenant H.C. Hedderwick
Sub-Lieutenant J.E.L. Rae
Sub-Lieutenant J.B. Dodge
Sub-Lieutenant W.C. Craven
Sub-Lieutenant Hyrke-Smith
Sub-Lieutenant George Graves
Sub-Lieutenant A. Graham
Sub-Lieutenant W.F. Keay
Sub-Lieutenant Rettie
Chaplain the Reverend Robert Primrose

Band – The Dundee RNVR

Robert Christie	PO
David Carnie	Leading Seaman
Alexander Young	AB
Albert Ferguson	AB
Robert McLaner	
Arthur Farquharson	
Walter Morrison	
John Mitchell	
Robert McLeary	
James Town	
Thomas Dand	
James McLean	
Peter Brown	
John Clark	
James Hunter	
Charles Mill	
Alexander McDougall	
Murray McDougall	
James Bennet	
William Mill	
Victor Ferrar	
James McIntosh	

St Johns Ambulance Corps

William H. Hall	ASBS 638 Chatham Depot
Horace Proctor	ASBS 611
John R. Gill	ASBS 609

A Company 1st Platoon

10888	H.J. Wilson	PO K6403
7Z547	A. Callaghan	PO
71535	W. Palmer	PO, RN
9241	J. Rainly	Stoker
6526	W. Arnold	
9708	W. Bunting	SS 107140
3849	Dunsmore	SS 105483
7395	G. Goodman	
7851	R. Berryman	
925	W. Collins	275332
4135	E. Cox	295124
5707	J. Wilson	284545
7235	H. Murphy	295291
7908	O. McFarland	

7719	C. Pearl	
1239	H. Miles	
593	W. Bruce	Leading Stoker
7832	J. Finch	SS 103288
7359	W. Tamber	
3074	W. Reid	
499	J. Down	SS 102640
7496	Gilmore	SS 102815
7108	G. Grey	
102	E. Readding	SS 103945
894	W. Howson	SS 105667
0558	G. Williams	SS 109500
3933	J. Thompson	SS 105672
550	J. Connell	SS 103482
7325	J. Keatley	
2031	W. Hooker	290100
4472	A.S. Scott	296752

A Company 2nd Platoon

5612	H. Tonge	Leading Seaman 284827
7027	S. Swan	Stoker SS 101586
10	J. Neville	103651
13	J. Peters	6781
7031	W.H. Stevens	5547
269	Johnson	286074
6662	C. Sell	302432
9583	J.J. Turner	297107
	J.H. Robinson	
1463	E. Chapman	282295
1208	A.H. Denton	SS 101189
6175	J. Bird	SS 101055
7155	Forrest	308094
4642		239552
5749	Wells	SS 100702
6127	Elden	285914
6164	Fennel	306502
4699	Walton	280225
7295	G.W. Boughen	29116
10818		SS
2315	J. Smith	287472
1832	Thompson	285928
10853	J. Wallace	SS 106941
10858	C. Smith	SS
3712	W. Riddler	290457

10858	Smith	
4070	Wrigglesworth	301074
6306	W. Gilmour	286654
7213	M. Hassell	SS 1016
4187	J. Elliot	104009
43	McSxxxx	254036
10574	J. Leay	
4187	Sutton	12888
7		
8	Seymour	
	Walton	
99		
9817	Hammond	

A Company 3rd Platoon

7861	E. Uvery	PO 292507
7572	J. Wells	PO 251943
738Z	A. Cummings	Stoker 287037
7871	F. Warn	SS 103343
2029	B. Taylor	286635
8586	J. Clark	295104
2840	J. Carr	
8617	S. Park	SS 104752
9108	J. Quin	SS 106176
9029	A. Hopper	276773
1236	E. Collins	157034
3125	J. Coster	
706	A. Smelt	SS 101579
76	C. Kyland	Leading Stoker 285494
5769	Thainer	Stoker 100720
265	S. Litley	
3350	A. Russel	170185
695	E. Warner	162698
0053	F. Wilby	298457
9316	R. Wilby	SS 106550
9Z08	R. Bandon	96299
3425	P. McDonald	
207	L. Smisson	175930
902	A. Framps	296411
8828	J. Snellgrove	SS 108860
8556	J. Anderson	SS 104929
5546	J. McQuilter	SS 100594
14	J. Martindale	
28	L. Russell	

283	S.A. Todd	176397
1918	C. Smith	Leading Stoker 286320
5327	A.W. Whitehead	Stoker 285534
8460	C. Hazell	Stoker 284225
9032	J. Reims	SS 105840
94S2	J. Sanidell	

A Company 4th Division

6945	Saunders	PO
3022	T. Broughton	
6573	J. Hanson	SS 101219
4713	J.J. Turner	299867
30	J.A. Adams	
9204	J. Reid	SS 106265
5257	A. Marshal	29539
1897	W. Farrier	285925
7678	A. Jackfield	292067
4680	J. Batterham	174408
20	E. Mason	
6271	H.W. Gowing	SS 10119
8219	F. McCann	293810
9486	H. Perry	SS 106791
6020	A.H. Wild	Leading Seaman 28557
9178	W. Hyde	SS 106193
7668	G. Gamble	SS 103012
2939	G.M. Walters	172259
10557	E. Cattley	300388
6360	G. Payne	286319
9159	G. Walters	SS 106180
8708	W. Hart	SS 105232
9212	H. West	SS 106273
6885	E. Rankin	289985
7612	A. Sand	SS 105915
21	W. Frosdick	
22	Cain	
7937	H. Jeff	292910
10114	J. W. Roberts	SS 107775
3414	J. Crone	Leading Stoker 176601
9277	T.J. Carter	SS 106
7692	R. Gooch	SS 103065
24	J. Ormston	
4405	W. Stanger	
25	J. Bryson	
151	Atkins	

321	H. Healing
9180	W. McNish

B Company 1st Section

J. Adams	Leading Seaman 1/114
Birchall	AB 1/150
F. Lynes	7/187
H. Maddison	R51
G. Dickson	R52
C. Tapp	1/255
S. Grimshaw	1/185
S. Allsop	1/168
G. Suddis	R50
F. Hindle	R49
J. Farr	7/209
S.N. Waistell	R36
R. Phillips	787

B Company 2nd Section

D. Jones	Leading Seaman 1/213
A. Brown	AB 7/249
T. Burnip	R31
A. Stevenson	R38
Smith	R32
A. Baynes	7/209
A. Lever	R56
J. Lee	/309
C. Shaw	/171
R. Marshall	1/149

B Company 3rd Section

A. Dodd	Leading Seaman 7/114
T. Moody	AB 7/126
H. Dutton	1/211
T. Doherty	1/134
H. Dodd	7/258
C. Over	R39
W. Brazenall	R40
A. Atkinson	R43
Humis	R42
J. Osborn	R44
A Byers	R46
F. Frodden	R59
R. Turner	1/82

B Company 4th Section

A. Anderson	Leading Seaman 7/218
F. Graig	AB 7/250
H. Bradley	1/117
H. Neilson	1/214
R. Reevis	R48
G. Routledge	R47
R. Tatterwall	R53
D. McGowan	R34
N. Bridges	R3
J. Hill	R55
R. Andrews	R45
P. Johnson	R58
F. Wilson	
G. Kirkbride	PO 1/90
H. Bowden	Bugler 1/193

B Company 5th Section

F. Bakin	PO 1/136
Jas Muirhead	AB 1/102
Albert Williams	7/221
Sam Westhead	1/131
Stuart McKnight	7/196
George Gween	1/162
W. Barlow	1/212
Jas Daly	R61
Wallace Spowart	R63
Edward Chapman	R65
Peter Tait	R67
Adam Wilson	R66
George Spowart	R54
Jos Coulter	R62

B Company 6th Section

J. Pan	Leading Seaman 1/71
J. McGullen	1/27
Herbert Winian	1/219
Harry Simmonite	1/205
Ernest Shaw	1/200
Thomas Miller	1/190
William McLane	R70
Jas Williams	R60
Jas Purcell	R69
Jos Bradley	R72

Jas Dodds	R71	
Thomas Henderson	R74	

B Company 7th Section

Thomas Williams	Leading Seaman 1/180	
William A. Aitchison	AB 1/173	
George Hupfield	1/175	
William Smith	6/166	
Sidney Jones	1/222	
John Dearnard	R73	
Walter Day	R75	
Frank Carr	R77	
Thomas Richardson	R84	
Harold Todd	R81	
George Church	R78	
Chas Robson	R82	

B Company 8th Section

William Mahoney	Leading Seaman 1399	
Chas H. Alford	AB 1/29	
Albert A. Taylor	AB 3/249	
Frank Hughes	AB 1/181	
Jas Creswell	AB 1/143	
Sam Mason	R87	
Fred Flood	AB 7/229	
William Lavery	R86	
Jas Lavery	R85	
Andrew Gilmour	R79	
E. Jackson	R88	
Jas White	R83	
Frank Snow	R80	
J.G. Dixon	AB, Writer 1/169	
G. Dick	Signaller 6/169	
Herbert Forrest	Bugler 2200	

B Company 3rd Platoon

1/174	G. Carrington	PO
7/174	R. Tobin	PO
1/177	A. Gibson	AB
167981	C.F. Wright	CPO
		(commissioned Sub-Lieutenant)
1/197	F. Horrocks	AB
1/199	A. Moore	
89	J. Campbell	

90	J. Howie	
91	A. Lowery	
93	C. Lane	
94	J. Lowery	
95	W. Walton	
71	H. Mount	AB
7/239	E. Waters	Leading Seaman
1/120	H. Coldwell	AB
1/221	W. Elliot	
1/171	J. Sullivan	
97	D.B. Murray	
99	J. Montgomery	
101	H. Davis	
102	R. Robson	
100	J. Dickson	
98	G. Murray	
96	C. Rice	
1/119	H. McGregor	AB
1/160	F. Martin	Leading Seaman
1/215	R. Cumpotey	AB
1/198	C. Perks	
1/155	W. Dutton	
1/195	J. Hawkhead	
103	J. Newton	
105	J. Askwith	
106	J. Longstaff	
107	W. Allman	
8	C. Bell	
104	R. Morrison	
1562	A. Cater	Leading Seaman
1315	A. Roberts	AB
1/158	W. Hume	
110	J. Stephenson	
112	D. Rolpe	
115	F. Wilkinson	
116	J. Delison	
114	R. Blades	
113	J.J. Robinson	
111	J.L. Mawson	
3/193	E.V. Radcliff	
1/165	C.A. Lewis	
135224	E. Hair	PO
180688	G. Gealer	PO (now Sub-Lieutenant)

B Company 4th Platoon

2/61	R.Walker	PO
7/59	E. Suckling	PO
2087	S. McDougall	
1/182	E. Luce	
1/163	Hughes	
117	F.H. Carter	
118	J.H. Copeland	
119	W. Summerbell	
123	A. Weatherall	
122	J.S. Taylor	
121	L. Fierney	
120	W. Draper	
1/206	A. Jarvis	
1/178	H. O'Toole	
1586	P. Hayes	
1576	B. Hart	Leading Seaman
1/216	J. Pagendain	AB
636	R. Grumlay	
180	E.O. Williams	
125	O. Thomson	
127	H. Richmond	
129	D. Lynch	
1/190	H. Terry	
1/203	H. Wilkinson	
132	S. Clarkson	
28	J. Raymont	
126	H. Connage	
124	M. Codling	
88	J. Oldfield	Leading Seaman
1/167	J. Slade	
1/25	J. Thomas	
130	E. Palmer	
131	J. Perry	
135	G. Dodds	
39	J. Devon	
138	A. Franks	
34	J. Boyes	
133	J. Mouzer	
36	W. Lines	
1/233	A. Kerr	
31	G. Payne	PO
1/167	T.A. Tweede	
1/117	W. Davenport	

137	J. Harply	
142	J.H. Smith	
44	L. Jackson	
145	A. Johnson	
143	W. Smith	
141	A. Hancock	
189	J. Ditchfield	
49	W. Johnson	10535
	J. Campbell	Cook
2/10	Allan	CPO

C Company 1st Section

163358	Milton	CPO (now Sub-Lieutenant)
1230	T. Brownlee	PO
1/135	W. Inglis	
1/142	Richmond	
156	J. Brown	
1/174	D. Thompson	
153	G. Harrison	
1/161	J. Murray	
2/199	J. Scott	
2/205	W. Bruce	
165	W. Evington	
160	J. Peddie	
2/190	H. Morgan	
1/207	J. Clegg	
2/214	W. McLaren	

C Company 2nd Section

2114	R. Chamber	Leading Seaman
149	Edgell	
2155	W. Green	
146	J. Bulman	
2098	P. McLeish	
154	W. Croft	
150	T. Bland	
155	C. Govman	
148	J. Wilkinson	
1220	J. Burnett	
157	A.J. Douglas	
2206	J. Knox	
2005	T. Pincock	

C Company 3rd Section

1579	J. Kilpatrick	Leading Seaman
1/290	C. Cummings	
2/218	W. Stevenson	
2/195	D. McDonald	
2/196	A. Cameron	
2/164	B. Nicol	
1/209	W. Thomson	
2/166	E. Anlon	
2/193	G. Cantley	
162	J. Ludford	
267	J. Mowat	
27	C. Osbourne	
169	R. Hacy	
2/189	W. Nical	
1/776	J. Luscombe	
2/221	H. Marshall	

C Company 4th Section

1/150	A. Clark	Leading Seaman
2/92	A. Simson	
1/184	W. Cargill	
2/176	P. Russel	
1/113	J. Sherpard	
2/182	J. Batchlor	
2/323	A. Dallas	
R/151	J. Richard	
R/152	J. Scott	
R/159	R. McKay	
R/195	C. Aneran	
R/167	J. Stevenson	
R/164	A. Mather	

C Company 5th Section

1/14	D. Clark	PO
2/108	G. Nicoll	PO
184	H. Mollison	AB
2/80	G. Gall	
1984	G. McHicknie	
2/211	A. Dow	
2/224	G. Robertson	
2/137	D. Avilh	
2/226	G. Milton	
2/212	A. Knight	

R/171	R. Winship	
R/174	G. Gilfillan	
R/170	T. Branby	
R/202	J. Evington	

C Company 6th Section

1/96	A. Soutar	Leading Seaman
2/163	C. White	
1/215	F. Saunders	
/200	W. Morrison	
1/172	G. Berry	
2/207	F. McLean	
2/198	D. Small	
2/220	J. Turnbull	
R/173	E. Stacy	
R/209	C. Eaton	
R/213	F. Wright	
R/179	F. Simpson	
R/176	J. Laburn	
2104	A. Smith	Leading Seaman
/222	W. Taylor	

C Company 7th Section

1334	J. Gilchrist	Leading Seaman
2332	R. McKeown	AB
2417	W. Seqwright	
2286	J. Arthur	
2324	W. Mathie	
2161	R. Walker	
2438	W. Dalgleish	
2473	D. Stewart	
181	R. Monteith	
182	G. Sinton	
180	G. Chambers	

C Company 8th Section

1749	A. Smith	Leading Seaman
2333	S. Suthons	
2277	A. Smillie	
2199	R. Warnock	
2411	J. Noble	
175	G.H. Simpson	
184	G.W. Armstrong	
172	H. Kane	

299

2384	A. Anderson
2123	R. Crum
2413	T. Landels
1839	D. Douglas
168	R. Deyner
1/151	C. Lee
2092	W. Cray

C Company 9th Section

2293	Harry Russell	PO
1/179	David Smith	
2/222	James Blyth	
1/159	Charles Speed	
2073	Thomas Church	
1/105	John Donachie	
2/219	Robert Robertson	
373	James McAinsh	
2/225	Alex Duncan	
2/153	Edward Hayter	
/86	Joseph Wren	
/85	Ernest Oxley	
/89	John Straugham	
/88	James Thompson	

C Company 10th Section

787	Joseph Hughes	Leading Seaman
113	James Duncan	
2217	Fred Buck	
2139	David Low	
1214	Fenwick Yeomen	
01	Charles Grey	
1182	Archie Brown	
1202	Douglas Francis	
212	David Mill	
187	Arthur Thompson	
192	George Cook	
190	William Manson	
161	William Ancrum	
2/80	William Craig	

C Company 11th Section

1155	George Kennedy	Leading Seaman
1196	David Knight	
2050	John Fisher	

2216	Ernest Pemberton	
1185	Andrew Smith	
193	James McCutcheon	
194	James Whitfield	
197	Robert Ward	
191	John Lister	
203	Norman Keir	

C Company 12th Section

2410	Thomas Dick	Leading Seaman
1192	John Rodger	
2130	Alex Bain	
2158	Donald Morrison	
2068	Thomas Thomson	
2194	James Carr	
2181	William Walker	
2051	Robert Walker	
1131	James Ross	
1197	James Carnegie	
196	John Graham	
199	Edward Rutherford	
3166	RFR Charles Sime	PO

C Company 13th Section

Andrew Ireland	PO 1/80
80 H. Walsh	Leading Seaman
A. Cooper	2/209
W. Robins	1/195
D. Lindsay	2/201
W. McArthur	1/193
S. Ross	1/210
R. Berry	1/208
C. Anderson	2/177
J. Miller	R201
J. Stokes	R211
J. Pinkney	R212
J. Graham	R198

C Company 14th Section

W. Hoskin	Leading Seaman 1452
P. Coull	1/217
D. Duggins	1/218
G. Walker	1/425
F. Stewart	1/140

301

W. Pender	1897
W. Sime	1/216
J. Ransom	R207
W. Beat	R200
J. Simpson	R208
A. Napier	1/137

C Company 15th Section

J. Kidd	Leading Seaman 1/146
D. Johnston	1/134
W. Ferguson	2378
W. Stewert	2/215
J. Eddington	2249
A. Mitchell	R203
R. Fawcett	R210
T. Neeman	2/168

C Company 16th Section

J.M. Cabe	1/143
J. McDonald	2217
J. Scullin	1/199
G. Brookes	1/194
J. Forbes	1/145
A. Brown	1/117
R. Leighton	2/188
Harrison	2/157
J. Cruchton	1/181
R. Wallers	R204
F. Adamson	1/198

D Company 1st Section

8621	C. Beale	Leading Stoker 307403
5639	W. Smith	Stoker 1 SS 10537
6109	G. Dyke	SS 101047
7551	Jackson	291824
7177	Molyneux	290740
9288	Head	296510
9357	Langley	SS 106563
392	W. Hubberet	287422
1554	J. Hubberet	287443
6040	G. Sharpe	304295
8598	P. Price	SS 104936
7624	G. Rawson	292071
9332	Whitworth	SS 106507

| 9098 | T. Price | SS 105592 |
| 8865 | B. Heyter | SS 103455 |

D Company 2nd Section

5645	J. McGacken	Leading Seaman 28894
7543	W. McIntosh	Stoker 1 SS 102875
7454	W. Davis	SS 102661
0633	W. Hopkins	SS 101640
643	J. Page	SS 103294
289	A. Taylor	296506
314	J. Martin	SS 104258
7846	F. Sams	SS 103301
1983	G. Dale	294309
9242	W. Redioah	SS 106434
818	W. Burnhill	2318
2863	W. Sanson	294425
558	R. Ellis	291862

D Company 3rd Section

6116	Jennings	Leading Stoker 307908
1945	Stuart	Stoker 1 286331
5009	Lamb	282097
2183	Lawes	289161
5054	Arstall	293065
4977	Beight	303871
4825	Betts	299553
10662	Davis	SS 108660
2655	Evans	670252
4922	Bailey	303894
7149	Twensley	SS 107890
4965	Riches	279371
7126	Mulcock	SS 101857
6250	C. Carter	175286

D Company 4th Section

3323	H. Fairweather	Leading Stoker 287092
1240	F. Marshall	
5651	Hoptier	SS 100609
5008	S. Smith	290471
808	McColeave	143175
10637	Barnes	SS 108682
10733	Gales	
10780	Bothroyed	
6373	Warr	285490

5360	Carter	276477
2720	King	204872
9446	Reynolds	296584
6847	Collie	289626
	Thomas	Groom

D Company 5th Section

0324	S.W. Clark	Leading Stoker 299356
5489	V.G. Frost	Stoker SS 180407
8712	A. Godfrey	SS 105262
0266	C. Tyler	299077
5487	C. Sargent	SS 100406
7917	E. Sargent	SS 103602
10561	J. Fitzgerald	SS 108496
7016	J. Hurle	SS 101585
9179	J. W. Andrews	SS 106191
4635	P. Gill	277639
7360	L. Walcott	SS 102494
5957	H. Ridgion	285508
7822	A. Slater	SS 103284
6599	G. Osborne	208405
0374	A. Blater	299883
2357	E. Oliver	288376
10569	J.W. Littler	SS 108510

D Company 6th Section

5670	J.J. Andrews	Leading Stoker SS 100617
10537	W. Filston	Stoker SS 108306
9879	P. Byrne	SS 106861
10860	W. Lucas	SS 108705
6051	A.W. Mitchell	SS 100968
4575	E. East	294301
8916	A. Pilkington	SS 105655
7860	J. McBride	SS 106997
7031	G. Rutt	151218
1629	A. Ling	305895
782	W.A. Henderson	K55951
0678	G. Cooper	SS 108672

D Company 7th Section

5217	J.B. Thurber	Leading Stoker 100018
6713	H.G. Harris	Stoker 289168
6609	W. Yeomans	288593
3953	C. Bailey	281680

7380	G. Beasley	SS 102390
5442	J. McNeil	29140
654	G. Cope	153784
5835	A.E. Gillett	285244
7081	C. Moran	SS 101755
6793	H. Hornsey	289672
6925	W. Pink	SS 101449
2724	G. Greengrass	28547
3901	J. McCarty	276349
5530	H.G. Hart	SS 10049

D Company 8th Section

5171	J. Neal	Leading Stoker 282807
8335	Mallin	Stoker 294265
4151	Whitefield	277067
7059	Morgan	SS 101634
9209	Goddard	296301
3709	Challis	174273
2193	Stitson	284601
5087	Kidd	299970
5397	Walls	SS 100111
8122	Fragnor	293422
8104	Hangelion	SS 103939
9279	Sellers	SS 106487
6123	Buesdon	27801

D Company 9th Section

8031	J. Dewhurst	Leading Seaman
7978	E. Kelsey	Stoker
8310	A. Dell	
9101	H. Blades	
7833	S. Twelftree	
9602	E. Grey	
10539	W. Allanson	
6935	W. Shimmon	
7092	D. Turner	
9345	H. Rawlinson	
10455	H. Ward	
5585	T. Goodcorn	
7183	H. Strong	
6688	W. Lawrence	

D Company 10th Section

5382	W.S. Cole	PO (now Sub-Lieutenant)

4883	R. Entwistle	PO
7123	R. Webber	Stoker
8594	E. Tomsett	
7122	G. Callingford	
7881	G. Cooper	
318	J. McGuire	
5985	A. Boveman	
10223	W. Drake	
10373	W. Watson	
3803	J. Whitingham	
3286	E. Field	
5409	A. Moss	
1591	R. Day	

D Company 11th Section

8490	W. Small	Leading Stoker
6380	R. Redman	Stoker 1
9877	E. Conley	
8894	J. Richardson	
8801	J. Hindley	
0366	W. Bolton	
9709	D. Watson	
4543	H. Harding	
8891	J. Halliday	
5978	J. Mason	
7145	H. Liddiard	
1066	H. Walker	
3986	J. Hatcher	

D Company 12th Section

6926	S. Galasham
7091	F. Fenner
7117	H. Parnell
7870	Robinson
4052	A. Bright
7317	R. Warren
9119	B. Turnidge
7391	B. Baldwin
7128	A. Ridgewite
1773	R. Jenkins
9159	W. Smee
8940	W. Smith
9407	A. Moore
5531	Beckinsale
938	A. Pointing

D Company 13th Section

4919	E. Garrard	Leading Seaman
7938	L. Milne	Stoker
8512	F. Hodge	
9450	H. Blackman	
8364	H. Goodwin	
7455	J. Acott	
8292	W. Thompson	
8138	J. Wall	
7235	E. Hawthorne	
9197	C.B. Churcher	
0899	G. Rennison	
6537	F.H. Buck	
5450	T. Heath	
5214	L. Sanderson	

D Company 14th Section

4282	F. Robinson	Leading Seaman
10300	H. Ross	Stoker 1
4884	W. Bonosuski	
7955	T. Balcombe	
5842	T.L. Goll	Groom
4822	A.E. Hughisman	
1815	J. Gallagher	
992	A. Gtingara	
1287	S. Hedge	
4952	T. McGregor	
10671	A. Hunter	
7632	H. Winbourne	
8892	L. Hounsley	
1783	J. Huston	
2210	A.E. Parr	

D Company 15th Section

6489	G. Galloway	PO
7394	W. Hutchison	Stoker
4818	W. Manger	
5341	C.J. Lincoln	
3469	A. Ansile	
9511	E. Hefferman	
1632	W. Walton	
9350	C. Lloyd	
9758	G. Hill	
9760	W. Wistwood	

5253	J. Blair	
4093	J. Winchester	
4487	E. Monck	
7245	C. Rogers	
9560	J. Briennan	

D Company 16th Section

4501	J. Walker	Leading Stoker
7189	E. Coldup	Stoker
7064	H. Robinson	
7679	J. McLeod	
7134	W. Freeman	
7050	A. Lyons	
4245	R. Jackman	
7943	J. Digby	
8221	F. Haggerty	
10640	A. McBride	
6663	W. Finney	
9222	W. Byg	
7294	G. Wooley	
9364	D. Ward	
4031	F. West	

References

PAGES 1-12

INTRODUCTION

1 Walls family bible.
2 Ministry of Defence letter to L. G. Sellers of 28 September, 1989. Ref RCH/3017/89/RC
3 Bonham-Carter, Violet: *Winston Churchill As I Knew Him*, published by Eyre & Spottiswoode/Collins, 1965, page 333.
4 Keynes, Sir Geoffrey: *The Letters of Rupert Brooke*, Letter to Russell Loines, December, 1914, pages 644/5.
5 *Eton College Chronicle* of Thursday, 7 December, 1916, page 132. In Memoriam to Lieut F. S. Kelly.

CHAPTER 1

1 Jerrold, Douglas: *The Royal Naval Division*, published by Hutchinson 1928, page 2.
2 *Hansard*: Vol XVII, p738, 17 September, 1914.
3 Jerrold Douglas: Appendix A, p. 333–335 & p6.
4 Public Record Office, Kew: ADM 116/1438.
5 Benthem, John: From his diary in the Liddle Collection, Edward Boyle Library, Leeds University.
6 Suffolk Public Record Office, Ipswich. *The Suffolk Country Handbook*, 1916, p485, ref S058.
7 Freyberg, Lord: *Bernard Freyberg VC, Soldier of Two Nations*, published by Hodder & Stoughton, 1991, chs 2–4.
8 Foster, the Rev Henry: *At Antwerp and the Dardanelles*. Published by Mills & Boon, 1918. Pages 10/11.
9 Public Record Office, Kew: WO32/5084.

CHAPTER 2

1 Bonham-Carter, Violet: *Winston Churchill As I Knew Him*, ch 12, p333.
2 Imperial War Museum, Department of Documents: Special Miscellaneous Document N6.
3 Public Record Office, Kew, ADM137/1010: Report by Major-General Paris of 31 October, 1914.
4 *The Great War – I Was There*; ch 40, pp 184–5. Magazine published by The Amalgamated Press, 1939.
5 Imperial War Museum, Department of Documents: Backhouse Papers, Army Book 152 & Correspondence Book Field Service.
6 Foster, the Rev Henry: *Antwerp Adventure: Shells and Burning Oil*, from *The Great War – I Was There*, ch 40, p185.
7 Jeffries, J. M. N.: *Doom Over Antwerp*, from *The Great War – I Was There*, ch 39, p 179.
8 Public Record Office, Kew, ADM137/1010: Report on Operations, p 246 *et seq.*
9 Bonham-Carter, Violet, pp 334–7.
10 Backhouse Papers.
11 Foster, the Rev Henry, pp 186–7.
12 Backhouse Papers.
13 Public Record Office, Kew, ADM137/3065: Ist Brigade War Diary, report of 26 October, 1914.
14 Backhouse Papers.
15 Public Record Office, Kew, ADM137/3065: Report by Commodore Henderson of the 1st RN Brigade on 26 October, 1914.
16 Public Record Office Kew. ADM137/1010 Report on Operations.
17 Backhouse Papers.
18 Freyberg, Lord Paul, p41.
19 Backhouse Papers.
20 Foster, the Rev Henry: *At Antwerp and the Dardanelles*.
21 Public Record Office, Kew, ADM137/1010: Report on Operations.
22 Backhouse Papers.
23 Foster, the Rev Henry: *Antwerp Adventure: Shells and Burning Oil*, from *The Great War – I Was There*, pp 188–9.
24 Public Record Office, Kew, ADM137/1010.
25 Backhouse Papers.
26 Public Record Office, Kew, ADM137/1010.

CHAPTER 3

1 Public Record Office, Kew, ADM116/1337: Report of 22 August, 1915, memorandum A.
2 Public Record Office, Kew, ADM116/1338.

3 *The War Budget*: On Board HMS Crystal Palace, 29 July, 1915, p 329.

4 Public Record Office, Kew, ADM116/1337: Report of 3 December, 1914.

5 *The War Budget*.

6 *My Weekly*, 30 June, 1984. Article entitled *Roll Out the Carpet*.

7 *The War Budget*.

8 *With the RND On Board HMS Crystal Palace – A Souvenir*, 1915, pp 73–8. Published by W. H. Smith in 1915.

9 Murray, Joseph, in conversation with L. G. Sellers.

10 Clark, H. V.: *Observations on the Life at Crystal Palace*.

CHAPTER 4

1 Murray, Joseph, in conversation with L. G. Sellers.

2 Harfield, Major Alan, *Fighting Forces*, vol 2, no 2, November/December, 1988; and Blandford and the Military, published 1982.

3 Murray, Joseph, in conversation with L. G. Sellers.

4 Knox, Ronald: *Patrick Shaw-Stewart*, published in 1920 by Collins, p109.

5 Murray, Joseph, in conversation with L. G. Sellers.

6 RND papers in the Royal Signals Museum, Blandford, Dorset.

7 Jerrold, Douglas: *The Royal Naval Division*, published in 1928 by Hutchinson, p10.

8 Knox, Ronald, p110.

9 Mitchell-Fox, Thomas: Imperial War Museum, Department of Sound Record. Acc Number. 00315/03.

10 Hassall, Christopher: *Rupert Brooke – A Biography*, published in 1972 by Faber & Faber.

11 Keyes, Sir Geoffrey: *The Letters of Rupert Brooke*, published in 1968 by Faber & Faber. p 640, letter to Mrs Brooke of 20 December 1914.

12 Ibid, p642. Letter to Katherine Cox in December, 1914.

13 Ibid, p642. Letter to Cathleen Nesbit dated 25 December, 1914.

14 Ibid, p650. Letter to the Rev Alan Brooke dated 1 Jan, 1915.

15 Hassall, Christopher, p497.

16 Sellers Marcel, interview by L. G. Sellers.

17 Hassall, Christopher, p480.

18 Knox, Ronald, p110.

19 Keyes, Sir Geoffrey, p663. Letter to Violet Asquith dated 18 February, 1915.

20 Ibid, p660. Letter to Dudley Ward, dated 20 February, 1915.

21 Ibid, Letter to Violet Asquith in February 1915.

22 Hassall, Christopher, p488.

23 Bonham-Carter, Violet: *Winston Churchill As I Knew Him*, published in 1965 by Collins, p362.

24 Backhouse, Commander: Imperial War Museum, department of Documents. Ref 86/31/1.

25 Bonham-Carter, Violet, p362.

26 Foster, The Rev Henry: *At Antwerp and the Dardanelles*, published by Mills & Boon in 1918, p52.

27 Harfield, Major Alan. Letter to L. G. Sellers dated 24 May 1990.

28 Foster, The Rev Henry, p54

CHAPTER 5

1 Masefield, John: *Gallipoli*, p19.

2 Churchill, Winston Spencer: *The World Crisis*, 1915, p157.

3 *The British Dominion, War Facts and Figures*, p154.

4 Sparrow and McBean Ross: *On Four Fronts with the Royal Naval Division*, p36. Reproduced by permission of, for and on behalf of Edward Arnold (Publishers) Ltd.

5 Churchill, Winston Spencer, p240.

6 Sanders, Liman von: *Five Years in Turkey*, pp 57–61.

CHAPTER 6

1 Haws, Duncan: *Merchant Fleets, Union Castle Line*, published in 1990 by Travel Creatours Ltd. No 39.

2 Hurd, Archibald: *The Merchant Navy*, vol II, published in 1924 by John Murray.

3 Public Record Office, Kew, ref W095/4290 36(c)

4 Murray, Joseph: *Gallipoli As I Saw It*, published in 1965 by William Kimber & Co., pp46–7.

5 Bonham-Carter, Violet, pp364–5.

6 Murray, Joseph, pp 46–7.

7 Murray, Joseph, in conversation with L. G. Sellers.

8 Freyberg, Lord pp45–6.

9 Murray, Joseph, in conversation with L. G. Sellers.

10 Knox, Ronald, p122.

11 Murray, Joseph: Imperial War Museum, Department of Sound Record, ref 82 01/45/3–4.

12 Hassall, Christopher, p460.

13 Backhouse Papers, ref 86/31/1.

14 Foster, the Rev Henry, pp56–7.

15 Knox, Ronald, p123.

16 Hassall, Christopher, p493.

17 Murray, Joseph, in conversation with L. G. Sellers.

18 Murray, Joseph: Imperial War Museum, Department of Sound Record, ref 82 01/45/3–4.

19 Keyes, Sir Geoffrey, p674. Letter to Katherine Cox date 19–24 March, 1915, postmarked 6 April, 1915.

20 Murray, Joseph, in conversation with L. G. Sellers.
21 Ribblesdale, Lord: *Charles Lister – Letters and Recollections*, published in 1917 by T. Fisher Unwin, p152.
22 Murray, Joseph: Tape interview in the Liddle Collection, Edward Boyle Library, Leeds University.
23 Ribblesdale, Lord, pp152–3.
24 Browne, W. Denis: Ms copy in an unidentified hand of a letter to Mrs Brooke dated 24 April, 1915. King's College, Cambridge, ref XC 8.
25 Marsh, Sir Edward: Transcript in his hand of a letter from Arthur Asquith to his sister, Violet, dated 23 April, 1915. King's College, Cambridge, ref XC 15.
26 Browne, W. Denis: King's College, Cambridge, ref XC 8. See also Foster, the Rev Henry, pp 73–5.
27 Sparrow and McBean Ross: *On Four Fronts with the Royal Naval Division*, published in 1918 by Hodder & Stoughton. (Reproduced by permission of Edward Arnold (publishers) Ltd.) p 44–5.
28 Browne, W. Denis: King's College, Cambridge, ref XC 8.
29 Ribblesdale, Lord, pp 152–3.
30 Murray, Joseph, in conversation with L. G. Sellers.
31 Marsh, Sir Edward: King's College, Cambridge, ref XC 15.
32 Keyes, Sir Geoffrey, p678. Letter to Violet Asquith dated 9 April, 1915.
33 Browne, W. Denis: King's College, Cambridge, ref XC 8.
34 Foster, the Rev Henry, p72.
35 Hassall, Christopher, pp 497–8. See also Foster, the Rev Henry, p75.
36 Browne, W. Denis: King's College, Cambridge, ref XC 8.
37 Keyes, Sir Geoffrey, p 677. Letter to Lascelles Abercrombie dated 6 April, 1915.
38 Brooke, Rupert: *Complete Poems of Rupert Brooke*, p151.
39 Paris, Major-General Sir Archibald: Letter dated 10 April, 1915. Imperial War Museum, Department of Documents, ref DS/Misc/57.
40 Ribblesdale, Lord, p154.
41 Browne, W. Denis: King's College, Cambridge, ref XC 8.
42 Murray, Joseph: *Call to Arms*, published in 1980 by William Kimber & Co., p29.
43 Murray, Joseph: Tape interview in the Liddle Collection, Edward Boyle Library, Leeds University.
44 Ribblesdale, Lord, p156.
45 Public Record Office, Kew, ref W095/4290.
46 Browne, W. Denis: Carbon copy of typed transcript of letter to Sir Edward Marsh dated 25 April, 1915. King's College, Cambridge, ref XC 10.
47 Hassall, Christopher, p 504.
48 Brooke, Rupert, *Complete Poems of Rupert Brooke*, p150.
49 Browne, W. Denis: King's College, Cambridge, ref XC 8.
50 Murray, Joseph: *Gallipoli As I Saw It*, p 61.
51 Browne, W. Denis: King's College, Cambridge, ref XC 8.

52 Medical reports written by Fleet Surgeon Arthur Gaskell and Surgeon Schlesinger. King's College, Cambridge, ref XC7.

53 McCracken, Lieutenant-Commander William: ALS to Mrs Brooke dated 25 April, 1915. King's College, Cambridge, ref XC 14.

54 Browne, W. Denis: Carbon copy of a typed transcript of a letter to Sir Edward Marsh. King's College, Cambridge, ref XC10.

55 Browne, W. Denis: King's College, Cambridge, ref XC 8.

56 Hamilton, Sir Ian: Copy in the hand of Mrs Brooke of a letter to Sir Edward Marsh dated 23 April, 1915. King's College, Cambridge, ref XC 3.

57 Churchill, Major John: Telegram to Winston Churchill dated 23 April, 1915. King's College, Cambridge, ref XC 1(I).

58 Browne, W. Denis: King's College, Cambridge, ref XC 8.

59 Brooke, Rupert: Death certificate. King's College, Cambridge, ref XC 4.

60 Browne, W. Denis: King's College, Cambridge, ref XC 10.

61 Browne, W. Denis: King's College, Cambridge, ref XC 8.

62 Hassall, Christopher, p 511.

63 Browne, W. Denis: King's College, Cambridge, ref XC 10.

64 Failes, Bernard: King's College, Cambridge, ref XC 11.

65 Browne, W. Denis: King's College, Cambridge, ref XC 8. See also Foster, the Rev Henry, p 75.

66 Kelly, 'Cleg'. Letter to Sir George Herschel dated 24 September, 1916. King's College, Cambridge, ref XC 13.

67 Churchill, Winston: telegram to Major John Churchill. King's College, Cambridge, ref XC 1(IV).

68 Brooke, Rupert: *Complete Poems of Rupert Brooke*, published in 1939 by Sidgewick & Jackson. p. 148.

69 Letter to Mrs Brooke postmarked 8 May, 1915. King's College, Cambridge, ref XC 36.

70 Hamilton, Sir Ian. Diary extracts. King's College, Cambridge, ref XC 12.

71 Churchill, Winston. Letter to *The Times* date 26 April, 1915. Permission of *The Times*.

72 Browne, W. Denis: King's College, Cambridge, ref XC 8.

CHAPTER 7

1 Knox, Ronald, p126.

2 Sellers, Marcel: Tape interview with L. G. Sellers.

3 Hamilton, Sir Ian. Hamilton: Papers in the Liddell Hart Centre for Military Archives, King's College, London, ref 34.

4 McCracken, Lieutenant-Commander William: Imperial War Museum, Department of Documents.

5 Aspinall, Oglander. *Roger Keyes*, published in 1951 by The Hogarth Press, p157–159.
6 *The British Dominion, War Facts and Figures*, published 1915, p 155.
7 Aspinall Oglander, *Roger Keyes*, p157–159.
8 Burton, Claude Edward (CEB, pseudonym Touchstone). From Catherine W Reilly, *English Poetry of the First World War – A Bibliography*. Cutting of Poem found in Essex Regimental Museum, Chelmsford.

CHAPTER 8

1 Sparrow and McBean Ross, p46.
2 *The British Dominion, War Facts and Figures*, pp 68–71.
3 Public Record Office, Kew, ref W095/4290.
4 Murray, Joseph: *Gallipoli As I Saw It*, p 54 *et seq.*
5 Murray, Joseph, in conversation with L. G. Sellers.
6 Browne, W. Denis: King's College, Cambridge, ref XC 10.
7 Public Record Office, Kew, ref W095/4290.
8 Murray, Joseph: Tape interview in the Liddle Collection, Edward Boyle Library, Leeds University.
9 Public Record Office, Kew, ref W095/4290.
10 Jerrold, Douglas: *Georgian Adventure*, p158.
11 Sanders, Liman von, pp 63–4.

CHAPTER 9

1 Ribblesdale, Lord, p166.
2 Murray, Joseph, in conversation with L. G. Sellers.
3 Murray, Joseph: Tape interview in the Liddle Collection, Edward Boyle Library, Leeds University.
4 Ribblesdale, Lord, p167.
5 Murray, Joseph, in conversation with L. G. Sellers.
6 Hassall, Christopher: *Edward Marsh – A Biography*, published in 1972 by Faber & Faber, p332.
7 Quilter, Lieutenant-Colonel John: Letter to Edward Marsh, in the Rupert Brooke papers, King's College, Cambridge, ref XC 39.
8 Hamilton, Sir Ian: Hamilton Papers in the Liddell Hart Centre for Military Archives, King's College, London, ref 44.
9 Jerrold, Douglas. *Royal Naval Division*, p100.
10 Murray, Joseph, in conversation with L. G. Sellers.
11 Murray, Joseph: Tape interview in the Imperial War Museum, Department of Sound Record, ref 8201/Reel/5.
12 Ribblesdale, Lord, p167.

13 Murray, Joseph, in conversation with L. G. Sellers.
14 Jerrold, Douglas: *Royal Naval Division*, p101.
15 Murray, Joseph, in conversation with L. G. Sellers.
16 Ribblesdale, Lord, p168.
17 Murray, Joseph: *Gallipoli As I Saw It*, p.57.
18 Murray, Joseph, in conversation with L. G. Sellers.
19 Ribblesdale, Lord, p168.
20 Murray, Joseph: *Gallipoli As I Saw It*, p.58.
21 Murray, Joseph, in conversation with L. G. Sellers.
22 Murray, Joseph: *Gallipoli As I Saw It*, p.58.
23 Paris, Major-General Sir Archibald. Imperial War Museum, Department of Documents, ref DS/Misc/57.

CHAPTER 10

1 Murray, Joseph, in conversation with L. G. Sellers.
2 Murray, Joseph: *Gallipoli As I Saw It*, pp 59–63.
3 Hassall, Christopher: *Edward Marsh – A Biography*, p 332.
4 Backhouse Papers, ref 86/31/1.
5 Jerrold, Douglas: *Royal Naval Division*, p105.
6 Ministry of Defence: Letter to L. G. Sellers dated 28 September, 1989, ref ROH 3017/89/RO.
7 Backhouse Papers.
8 Backhouse Papers.
9 Foster, the Rev Henry, p107.
10 Murray, Joseph: The Joseph Murray Papers.
11 Jerrold, Douglas: *Royal Naval Division*, p106.
12 Knox, Ronald, pp 130–1.
13 Woodward, Brigadier-General E.M.: The Hamilton Papers, Liddell Hart Centre for Military Archives, King's College, London, ref 54.
14 Jerrold, Douglas: *Royal Naval Division*, p.107.
15 Backhouse Papers.
16 Jerrold, Douglas: *Royal Naval Division*, p109.
17 Braithwaite, Major-General W.P.: The Hamilton Papers, Liddell Hart Centre for Military Archives, King's College, London, ref 68.
18 Foster, the Rev Henry, pp 132–3.
19 McCracken, Lieutenant-Commander William: Imperial War Museum, Department of Documents.

CHAPTER 11

1 Geary, Lieutenant Stanley: *The Collingwood Battalion*, published by Hastings F. J. Parsons Ltd in 1917 approx, pp10–11.

2 Public Record Office, Kew W095/4290.
3 Murray, Joseph, in conversation with L. G. Sellers.
4 Hassall, Christopher: *Edward Marsh a Biography*, p364.
5 Mackenzie, Compton: *Gallipoli Memories*, published in 1929 by Cassell & Co., p123. Permission of the Society of Authors as literary representatives of the Estate of Compton Mackenzie.
6 Public Record Office, Kew.W095/4290.
7 Geary, Lieutenant Stanley, p12.
8 Ribblesdale, Lord, p194.
9 Murray, Joseph, in conversation with L. G. Sellers.
10 Mackenzie, Compton, p122.
11 Murray, Joseph, in conversation with L. G. Sellers.
12 Backhouse, Commodore Oliver: Imperial War Museum, Department of Documents. Ref 86/31/1.
13 Paris, Major-General Sir Archibald: Imperial War Museum, Department of Documents. Ref DS[misc]57.
14 Murray, Joseph, in conversation with L. G. Sellers.
15 Mackenzie, Compton, p151/152.
16 Paris, Major-General Sir Archibald, op cit.
17 Knox, Ronald, p159.

CHAPTER 12

1 Ribblesdale, Lord, pp201–3.
2 Murray, Joseph, in conversation with L. G. Sellers.
3 Mitchell-Fox, Thomas: Imperial War Museum, Department of Sound Record, Reference Acc 00315/03.
4 Murray, Joseph, in conversation with L. G. Sellers.
5 Mackenzie Compton, p68.
6 Wilson-Smith, Colonel J. L. Letter from the Regimental HQ of the Royal Scots to L. G. Sellers, dated 17 October, 1990, ref RHQ/RS/166.
7 Ribblesdale, Lord, p205.
8 Jerrold, Douglas: *Royal Naval Division*, p141.
9 Murray, Joseph, in conversation with L. G. Sellers.
10 Rhodes James, Robert: *Gallipoli*, p232.
11 Jerrold, Douglas: *Royal Naval Division*, p.145.
12 Paris, Major-General Sir Archibald: Imperial War Museum, Department of Documents, ref DS/Misc/57.
13 Jerrold, Douglas: *Royal Naval Division*, p147.
14 Public Record Office, Kew, ref W095/4291.
15 Backhouse Papers, ref 86/31/1.
16 Ribblesdale, Lord, p209.
17 Brooke, Rupert: *Complete Poems*, p209.
18 Backhouse Papers.

19 Geary, Lieutenant Stanley, p24 *et seq.*
20 Jerrold, Douglas: *Royal Naval Division*, p148–9.
21 Jerrold, Douglas: *Royal Naval Division*, p149.

CHAPTER 13

1 Forster, John C.: The Liddle Collection, Edward Boyle Library, Leeds University.
2 Mitchell–Fox, Thomas: Imperial War Museum, Department of Sound Record, ref Acc 00315/03.
3 Forster, John C.
4 Mayne, C. F. Surgeon, 2nd Field Ambulance: The Liddle Collection, Edward Boyle Library, Leeds University.
5 Public Record Office, Kew, Wo153/1199.
6 Public Record Office, Kew, ref Wo95/4290.
7 Boothway, A: The Liddle Collection, Edward Boyle Library, Leeds University.
8 Hamilton, Sir Ian Hamilton papers in the Liddell Hart Centre for Military Archives, King's College, London, ref 110.
9 Jerrold, Douglas: *Royal Naval Division*, p154.
10 Paris, Major-General Sir Archibald: Imperial War Museum, Department of Documents, ref DS/Misc/57.
11 Ribblesdale, Lord, p226–7
12 Knox, Ronald, p148.
13 Paris, Major-General Sir Archibald: Imperial War Museum.
14 Public Record Office, Kew, ref Wo95/4290.
15 Paris, Major-General Sir Archibald.
16 Public Record Office, Kew, ref Wo95/4290.
17 Paris, Major-General Sir Archibald.
18 Forster, John C.
19 Murray, Joseph, in conversation with L. G. Sellers.
20 Forster, John C.

CHAPTER 14

1 Churchill, Sir Winston, p.488.
2 Public Record Office, Kew, ref Wo95/4290.
3 Knox, Ronald, pp157–9.
4 Murray, Joseph, in conversation with L. G. Sellers.
5 Heald, Ivan: *Ivan Heald, Hero and Humorist*, pages 175/179 & 191.
6 Wettern, E. F.: Notes for the RND Evacuation Reunion on 8th January, 1963, from the Joseph Murray Papers.
7 Jerrold, Douglas: *Royal Naval Division*, Appendix C p338.
8 Murray, Joseph, in conversation with L. G. Sellers.

318

9 Wettern, E. F.

10 Streets, Sergeant John Williams, 12th Yorkshire and Lancashire Regiment, mortally wounded on the Somme on 1 July, 1916. Details from Catherine W. Reilly, *English Poetry of the First World War – A Bibliography*. The poem was found in a small cutting at Essex Regimental Museum, Chelmsford.

CHAPTER 15

1 Sellers, Marcel Albert John: Letter of the 15/3/90.

2 Commonwealth War Graves Commission Letter to L. G. Sellers, 18/4/89.

3 Public Record Office, Kew ref ADM116/1411.

4 Public Record Office, Kew ref ADM8391/278.

5 Public Record Office, Kew ref ADM137/3088A.

6 MacMillan, Thomas: Imperial War Museum, Department of Documents.

7 Heald, Ivan: *Ivan Heald, Hero and Humorist*, pp 175.

8 Public Record Office, Kew, ref ADM137/3088A.

9 Murray, Joseph, in conversation with L. G. Sellers.

10 MacMillan, Thomas.

11 Murray, Joseph: *Call To Arms*, p49.

12 Paris, Major-General Sir Archibald: Imperial War Museum, Department of Documents, ref DS/Misc/57.

13 Benthem, John: *A Young Officer's Diary*, Liddle Collection, Edward Boyle Library, Leeds University.

14 Paris, Major-General Sir Archibald.

15 Murray, Joseph: *Call To Arms*, p51.

16 Public Record Office, Kew, ref ADM116/1411.

17 Paris, Major-General Sir Archibald.

18 Murray, Joseph: *Call To Arms*, p52.

19 Public Record Office, Kew, ref ADM137/3084.

20 Public Record Office, Kew, ref W032/5075.

21 Paris, Major-General Sir Archibald.

22 Public Record Office, Kew, ref ADM137/3084.

23 Public Record Office, Kew, ref ADM137/3088A.

CHAPTER 16

1 Murray, Joseph: *Call To Arms*, p55.

2 Murray, Joseph: Imperial War Museum, Department of Sound Record, ref 8209/45 reel 31.

3 MacMillan, Thomas: Imperial War Museum, Department of Documents.

4 Murray, Joseph: *Call To Arms*, p59.

5 Public Record Office, Kew, ref W032/5075.

6 Paris, Major-General Sir Archibald: Imperial War Museum, Department of Documents, ref DS/Misc/57.

7 Public Record Office, Kew, ref ADM116/1411.
8 Murray, Joseph: Imperial War Museum, Department of Sound Record, ref 8209/45 reel 31.
9 Murray, Joseph: *Call To Arms*, p64.
10 Murray, Joseph: Imperial War Museum, Department of Sound Record, ref 8209/45 reel 31.
11 Bentham, John: *A Young Officer's Diary*, Liddle Collection, Edward Boyle Library, Leeds University.
12 Murray, Joseph: Imperial War Museum, Department of Sound Record, ref 8209/45 reel 31.
13 Clark, H. V.: *Observations on the Life at Crystal Palace*.
14 Freyberg, Bernard: *A Linesman in Picardy*, pp 5–10. Chapter 1. Unpublished Book.
15 Benthem, John, pp 27–9.
16 Murray, Joseph: Imperial War Museum, Department of Sound Record, ref 8209/45 reel 31.
17 *Eton College Chronicle*, no 1593 dated 7 December, 1916, p 132.
18 Murray, Joseph: *Call To Arms*, p105.
19 *The History of the Great European War*, vol XI, p31.
20 Heald, Ivan, pp 9–11.
21 Murray, Joseph: *Call To Arms*, p.108.
22 Jerrold, Douglas: *Royal Naval Division*, pp xiv–v. Reproduced by permission of Curtis Brown Group Ltd, on behalf of the estate of Sir Winston Churchill. Copyright the estate of Sir Winston Churchill.
23 *Who Was Who*, 1927–40, p1233.
24 Benthem, John: *A Young Officer's Diary*.
25 Herbert, A. P.: Poem by permission of A. P. Watt Ltd, Literary Agents, on behalf of Crystal Hale and Jocelyn Herbert. Found among the Benthem papers in the Liddle Collection, Edward Boyle Library, Leeds University.
26 Murray, Joseph: *Call To Arms*, p 108.
27 Benthem, John.
28 Murray, Joseph: *Call To Arms*, p 122–3.
29 Murray, Joseph: Imperial War Museum, Department of Sound Record, ref 8209/45 reel 35.
30 Murray, Joseph: *Call To Arms*, p 122–3.

CHAPTER 17

1 *The Great War – I Was There*, pt 51, p.2040.
2 Public Record Office, Kew, ref ADM137/3929.
3 Freyberg, Bernard, pp 2–5.
4 Singleton-Gates: *General Lord Freyberg, VC*, p 64. Published by Michael Joseph, 1963.
5 McCracken, Lieutenant-Commander William: Imperial War Museum, Department of Documents.

6 Public Record Office, Kew, ref ADM137/3064.

7 Freyberg, Bernard, p.9.

8 Public Record Office, Kew, ref WO32/3115.

9 Public Record Office, Kew, ref ADM137/3929.

10 Public Record Office, Kew, ref ADMWO32/3115.

11 Public Record Office, Kew, ref ADM137/3064.

12 McCracken, Lieutenant-Commander William.

13 Public Record Office, Kew, ref WO32/3115.

14 Jerrold, Douglas: *The Great War – I Was There*, pt 22, p.887.

15 McCracken, Lieutenant–Commander William.

16 Montagu, Captain the Hon Lionel: Letter dated 20 November, 1916. Public Record Office, Kew, ref WO32/3115.

17 MacMillan, Thomas: Imperial War Museum, Department of Documents.

18 Montagu, Captain the Hon Lionel.

19 Murray, Joseph: *Call To Arms*, pp 129–31.

20 Freyberg, Bernard, pp 11–15.

21 Benthem, John.

22 Public Record Office, Kew, ref ADM137/3064.

23 Montagu, Captain the Hon Lionel.

24 Public Record Office, Kew, ref ADM137/3929.

25 Public Record Office, Kew, ref ADM137/3075.

CHAPTER 18

1 Montagu, Captain the Hon Lionel: Letter dated 20 November, 1916, Public Record Office, Kew, ref WO32/3115.

2 Jacobs, Sub-Lieutenant Trevor: Letter dated 19 November, 1916. Imperial War Museum, Department of Documents, ref 88/27/1.

3 Public Record Office, Kew, ref ADM137/3929.

4 Public Record Office, Kew, ref ADM137/3075.

5 Public Record Office, Kew, ref ADM137/3929.

6 Public Record Office, Kew, ref ADM137/3075.

7 Montagu, Captain the Hon Lionel.

8 Jacobs, Sub-Lieutenant Trevor.

9 Benthem, John.

10 Montagu, Captain the Hon Lionel.

11 Benthem, John.

CHAPTER 19

1 Public Record Office, Kew, ref ADM1/8477/309.

CHAPTER 20

1 Murray, Joseph: Imperial War Museum, Department of Sound Record, reel 38.
2 Public Record Office, Kew, ref ADM137/3064.
3 Murray, Joseph: Imperial War Museum, Department of Sound Record, reels 38–9.
4 MacMillan, Thomas: Imperial War Museum, Department of Documents.
5 Public Record Office, Kew, ref ADM137/3064.
6 Murray, Joseph: Imperial War Museum, Department of Sound Record, reel 39.
7 Public Record Office, Kew, ref ADM137/3064.
8 Public Record Office, Kew, ref ADM137/3064. Operational order, p 119.
9 Murray, Joseph: Imperial War Museum, Department of Sound Record, reels 30 and 40.
11 Public Record Office, Kew, ref ADM137/3064.
11 Kingsmill, Hugh: *I Was Captured At Beaucourt*, from *The Great War – I Was There*, pp 1009–10.
12 Public Record Office, Kew, ref ADM137/3064.
13 MacMillan, Thomas. Imperial War Museum, Department of Documents, pp 179–81.
14 Public Record Office, Kew, ref ADM137/3064.

CHAPTER 21

1 Freyberg, Bernard, ch 3.
2 MacMillan, Thomas: Imperial War Museum, Department of Documents, (found in his papers).

CHAPTER 22

1 MacMillan, Thomas: Imperial War Museum, Department of Documents, pp 187–91.
2 Public Record Office, Kew, ref ADM137/3064. Special order.
3 Public Record Office, Kew, ref ADM137/3064. 189th Brigade order no 88, appendix IV.
4 Public Record Office, Kew, ref ADM137/3064. Report on operations.
5 Public Record Office, Kew, ref ADM137/3064. Hood Battalion war diary.
6 Murray, Joseph: Imperial War Museum, Department of Sound Record, reel 42.
7 Public Record Office, Kew, ref ADM137/3064. Hood Battalion war diary.

8 Murray, Joseph: Imperial War Museum, Department of Sound Record, reel 42.
9 Public Record Office, Kew, ref ADM137/3064. Hood Battalion war diary.
10 Public Record Office, Kew, ref ADM137/3085.
11 MacMillan, Thomas: Imperial War Museum, Department of Documents, pp 194–6.

CHAPTER 23

1 MacMillan, Thomas: Imperial War Museum, Department of Documents, pp 199, 201, 205 and 215.
2 Knox, Ronald, pp 192–6.
3 MacMillan, Thomas: Imperial War Museum, Department of Documents, pp 220, 225, 227–30.
4 Public Record Office, Kew, ref ADM137/3931.
5 Public Record Office, Kew, ref ADM137/3064.

CHAPTER 24

1 Jerrold, Douglas: *Royal Naval Division*, pp 265–6.
2 McCracken, Lieutenant-Commander William: Imperial War Museum, Department of Documents.
3 Knox, Ronald, pp 203–4.
4 Public Record Office, Kew, ref ADM137/3932. Report on operations of 63rd (RN) Division.
5 Public Record Office, Kew, ref ADM137/3064. Hood Battalion war diary.
6 Knox, Ronald, pp 180–1.
7 Thynne, Lord Alexander. Letter in *Patrick Shaw-Stewart*, by Ronald Knox, pp 204–5.
8 Public Record Office, Kew, ref ADM137/3064.
9 Public Record Office, Kew, ref ADM137/3085.

CHAPTER 25

1 Public Record Office, Kew, ref ADM137/3933. Report on operations.
2 Public Record Office, Kew, ref ADM137/3933. Comments in Appendix XVIII.
3 Public Record Office, Imperial War Museum, ref ADM137/3935. Hood operation order no 22.
4 Public Record Office, Imperial War Museum, ref ADM137/3935. Report on account of raid, section 111.

5 Public Record Office, Kew, ref ADM137/3064. Hood Battalion war diary.

6 Jerrold, Douglas: *Royal Naval Division*, pp 302–8.

7 Public Record Office, Kew, ref ADM137/3939. Report on operations from 30 August, 1918, to 8 September, 1918.

8 Public Record Office, Kew, ref ADM137/3940. Report on operations from 27 September, 1918, to 2 October, 1918.

9 Public Record Office, Kew, ref ADM137/3941. Report on operations from 6 October, 1918, to 8th October 1918.

10 Public Record Office, Kew, ref ADM137/3942. Report on operations from 1 to 11 November, 1918.

11 Public Record Office, Kew, ref ADM137/3064. Hood Battalion war diary.

CHAPTER 26

1 Public Record Office, Kew, ref W032/5076; Fourth Report of the Select Committee on Naval Expenditure.

2 Royal Signals Museum, Archives: Royal Naval Division papers.

3 Jerrold, Douglas: *The Royal Naval Division*; appendix C.

4 Cooper, C. S: *The Outdoor Monuments of London*, p69.

5 Taylor, Gordon: *The Sea Chaplains*, p350.

6 Royal Naval College, Greenwich: Archives, pack no ED/23. Reproduced with permission of Curtis Brown Group Ltd, London, on behalf of the estate of Sir Winston Churchill. Copyright the estate of Sir Winston Churchill.

7 St Peter and St Paul, Blandford Forum: *A Guide to Visitors*.

8 Adam, Roy. Collingwood Memorial Service, service sheet dated 4 June, 1992.

9 Tasker, Trevor: Article on RND memorial in *The Globe and the Laurel*, September/October, 1990, p.320.

10 Mann, Lieutenant F. H: *After Nineteen Years*, pp 2–4.

11 McCracken, Lieutenant-Commander William: Imperial War Museum, Department of Documents. Booklet *The Incubator*, issue 1, dated September, 1918, pp 18–19.

Acknowledgements II

Roy Adam, Royal Naval Association
Jim Alves
Captain Richard Annand, VC, DL
Batsford Publishers
J. Backhouse
John Bailey, Western Front Association
Dr S. P. Barrett
Mark Bonham-Carter
Curtis Brown
Gwen Broyd
T. Burton
Cambridge University Press
Peregrine Churchill
Winston Churchill, MP
Commonwealth War Graves Commission
Jacqueline Cox, Modern Archive Centre, King's College, Cambridge
Chatto & Windus
Daily Mail
Ivor Dallinger
Dardanelles Straits Commander, Canakkle, Turkey
Elizabeth Davidson
Dorset Publishing Company
Faber & Faber
Lord Freyberg
Tony Froom
Clive Gardner
Mr & Mrs M. Graves

Mrs L. Garrett
Lieutenant-Commander J. G. Glover
Governor of Canakkle, Turkey
Brigadier Robin Greenwood
Crystal Hale
Ian Crum Hamilton
Major A. G. Harfield, Military History Society
Harper Collins Publishers
M. Harrison, Crystal Palace Museum
Elaine Hart
Peter Hart, Imperial War Museum, Department of Sound Records
Duncan Haws, Travel Creatours Ltd
Jocelyn Herbert
David Higham Associates
Hodder & Stoughton
Viscount Hood
Ian Hook, Essex Regimental Museum
J. G. Hutton
Victoria Hyde
HMSO
International Thomson Publishing Services Ltd
Lieutenant Jachnik, RNR
A. A. Jamson
John Murray Publishers
Ann Kelly, House of Lords Library
Kent Elms Library staff
Derek King
Lieutenant S. King, RN
Roy Knott
Derek Law, King's College, London
Peter Liddle, BA, MLitt,
Macmillan Publishing Co, New York
Alan P. McGowan, MA, PhD, Royal Naval College, Greenwich
Jeffrey Mish, Commonwealth War Graves Commission, Canakkle, Turkey
Joseph Murray
Vera Murray
Mills & Boon Ltd
Mrs Nicholson, Royal Signals Museum, Blandford
Lord Northbourne
S. & D. Noyce Studios, Prittlewell
Kate O'Brien, King's College, London

Dr M. E. Occleshaw
Lieutenant-Commander F. W. G. O'Shaughnessy, RN
The Earl of Oxford and Asquith
Christopher Page
Esme Paris
Major Roger Pickard, Royal Signals Museum
Ewan Godfrey Phillips
Poetry Library, Royal Festival Hall
Eric Price, Crystal Palace Foundation
Public Record Office, Kew
Paul Quarie, Eton College
Sir Anthony Quilter
Random Century Group
Sir Robert Rhodes James, MP
The Honourable Mrs Rous
The Royal Archives
David Saunders, Gallipoli Association
Ivy Sellers
Marcel Albert John Sellers
Sir H. Shaw-Stewart
Sidwick & Jackson
Lieutenant-Colonel William Smith
Society of Authors
Bridget Spiers
Professor Jon Stallworthy
Canon Peter Strange
Nigel Steel, Imperial War Museum, Department of Documents
Volkan Susluoglu, Commonwealth War Graves Commission, Canakkle, Turkey
Trevor Tasker, RND Gavrelle Memorial Fund
Richard Taylor, King's College, London
Dr Peter Thwites, Royal Signals Museum, Blandford
Times Newspapers Ltd
Marion P. Townsend
Rosemary Tudge, Imperial War Museum, Department of Sound Records
United States Naval Institute
Andrew Vollens, RND Gavrelle Memorial Fund
R. W. Walker Publishing
Arthur J. Walls
John H. Wettern
Mrs A. White

Mary P. Wilkinson, Imperial War Museum, Department of Printed Books
M Willis, Imperial War Museum, Department of Photographs
N. J. Wookey, Royal Signals Museum
Sarah L. Wright, POWTR, RNR
Captain Yalgin Diker

Index

333